MODERNITY AND ITS FUTURES

Understanding Modern Societies Course Team

Stuart Hall	Professor of Sociology and Course Team Chair
Maureen Adams	Secretary
John Allen	Senior Lecturer in Economic Geography
Margaret Allott	Discipline Secretary, Sociology
Robert Bocock	Senior Lecturer in Sociology
David Boswell	Senior Lecturer in Sociology
Peter Braham	Lecturer in Sociology
Vivienne Brown	Lecturer in Economics
Dianne Cook	Secretary
Robert Cookson	Senior Editor, Social Sciences
Helen Crowley	Lecturer in Women's Studies, North London Polytechnic
James Donald	Senior Lecturer in Cultural and Community Studies, University of Sussex
Paul du Gay	Post-graduate student, Sociology
Molly Freeman	Discipline Secretary, Sociology
Bram Gieben	Staff Tutor, Social Sciences
Peter Hamilton	Lecturer in Sociology
David Held	Professor in Politics and Sociology
Paul Lewis	Senior Lecturer in Politics
Vic Lockwood	Senior Producer, BBC
Anthony McGrew	Senior Lecturer in Politics
Gregor McLennan	Professor of Sociology, Massey University, NZ
David Scott-Macnab	Editor, Social Sciences
Graeme Salaman	Senior Lecturer in Sociology
Jane Sheppard	Graphic Designer
Paul Smith	Media Librarian
Keith Stribley	Course Manager
Kenneth Thompson	Professor in Sociology
Alison Tucker	Producer, BBC
Pauline Turner	Secretary
Diane Watson	Staff Tutor, Social Sciences
David Wilson	Editor, Book Trade
Chris Wooldridge	Editor, Social Sciences

Consultants

Harriet Bradley	Senior Lecturer, Sunderland Polytechnic
Tom Burden	Tutor Panel
Tony Darkes	Tutor Panel
Celia Lury	Lecturer in Sociology, University of Lancaster
Denise Riley	Researcher in political philosophy
Alan Scott	Lecturer in Politics, University of East Anglia
Jeffrey Weeks	Professor in Social Relations, Bristol Polytechnic
Geoffrey Whitty	Professor of Sociology of Education, Institute of Education, University of London
Steven Yearley	Professor of Sociology, University of Ulster

External Assessor

Bryan Turner	Professor of Sociology, University of Essex

MODERNITY AND ITS FUTURES

EDITED BY STUART HALL
DAVID HELD AND TONY McGREW

POLITY PRESS IN ASSOCIATION WITH THE OPEN UNIVERSITY

Copyright © The Open University 1992

First published 1992 by Polity Press in association with Blackwell Publishers Ltd
and The Open University.
Reprinted 1993, 1994, 1996

Editorial office:
Polity Press
65 Bridge Street
Cambridge CB2 1UR, UK

Marketing and production:
Blackwell Publishers Ltd
108 Cowley Road
Oxford OX4 1JF, UK

ISBN 0–7456–0965–1

ISBN 0–7456–0966–X (pbk)

A CIP catalogue record for this book is available from the British Library.

Edited, designed and typeset by The Open University

Printed in Great Britain by Redwood Books, Trowbridge

CONTENTS

UNDERSTANDING MODERN SOCIETIES:
AN INTRODUCTION

Series editor: Stuart Hall

Book 1   *Formations of Modernity*
edited by Stuart Hall and Bram Gieben

Book 2   *Political and Economic Forms of Modernity*
edited by John Allen, Peter Braham and Paul Lewis

Book 3   *Social and Cultural Forms of Modernity*
edited by Robert Bocock and Kenneth Thompson

Book 4   *Modernity and its Futures*
edited by Stuart Hall, David Held and Anthony McGrew

For general availability of all the books in the series, please contact your regular supplier or, in case of difficulty, Polity Press.

This book forms part of the Open University course D213 *Understanding Modern Societies*. Details of this and other Open University courses can be obtained from the Central Enquiry Service, PO Box 200, The Open University, Walton Hall, Milton Keynes, MK7 6YZ.

Cover illustration: John Tandy *Abstract composition* (*c.* 1930) Private Collection, London. Reproduced by courtesy of the Redfern Gallery, London, and by kind permission of Mrs Suzanne Tandy.
Photo: A.C. Cooper.

PREFACE

Modernity and its Futures is the final book in a new series of sociology textbooks which aims to provide a comprehensive, innovative and stimulating introduction to sociology. The four books in the series, which is entitled *Understanding Modern Societies: An Introduction*, are listed on page ii. They have been written to suit students and readers who have no prior knowledge of sociology and are designed to be used on a variety of social science courses in universities and colleges. Although part of a series, each book is self-contained to facilitate use with students studying different aspects of the history, sociology and ideas of modern society and its international context.

The four books form the central part of an Open University course, also called *Understanding Modern Societies*. Open University courses are produced by an extensive course team consisting of academic authors and consultants, a panel of experienced tutors, an external academic assessor, editors and designers, BBC producers, academic administrators and secretaries. (The full course team responsible for this course is listed on the opposite page.) Every chapter has been subjected to wide-ranging discussion and improvement at each of several draft stages. The result is a unique series of textbooks which draw on the cumulative academic research and teaching experience of the Open University and the wider academic community.

All four books have three distinctive features. First, each chapter provides not only a descriptive, historical account of the key social processes which shaped modern industrial societies, and which are now, once again, rapidly transforming them, but also analysis of the key concepts, issues and current debates in the related academic literature. Secondly, each chapter includes a number of extracts from classic and contemporary books and articles, all of them pertinent to the chapter. These are printed conveniently at the end of the chapter in which they are discussed. They can be distinguished from the main text (and can thus be found easily) by the continuous line down the left-hand margin. The third important feature of the text is that it is *interactive*: every chapter contains specially designed exercises, questions and activities to help readers understand, reflect upon and retain the main teaching points at issue. From the long experience of Open University course writing, we have found that all readers will benefit from such a package of materials carefully designed for students working with a fair degree of independence.

While each book is free-standing, there are some cross-references to the other books in the series to aid readers using all the books. These take the following form: 'see Book 1 (Hall and Gieben, 1992), Chapter 4'. For further information on a writer or concept, the reader is sometimes referred to the *Penguin Dictionary of Sociology*. Full bibliographic details of this dictionary are provided where relevant at the end of each chapter, together with other references which suggest further reading which can be undertaken in each area.

In the long collaborative process by which Open University materials are made, the editors of such a volume are only the most obvious of those who have helped to shape its chapters. There are many others with responsibilities for the detailed and painstaking work of bringing a book with so many parts to completion. Our external assessor, Professor Bryan Turner, provided invaluable intellectual guidance, comment, advice, stimulus and encouragement at every stage of the production of these books. Our course manager, Keith Stribley, has done an excellent job of helping us all to keep to schedules, maintaining high standards of editorial consistency, and liaising between course team academics, editors and production. We owe special thanks to Molly Freeman, Maureen Adams, Pauline Turner, Dianne Cook and Margaret Allott for really marvellous secretarial support. Rarely in the history of word-processing can so many drafts have been produced so swiftly by so few. Our Open University editors, Chris Wooldridge, David Scott-Macnab, David Wilson and Robert Cookson, have improved each chapter with their insight and professionalism, usually under quite unreasonable pressures of time, and with unfailing good nature. Thanks also to Paul Smith, our media librarian, for his creative work in finding so many of the illustrations. Debbie Seymour, of Polity Press, has been a constant source of encouragement and good sense.

Finally, the chapter authors have borne stoically our innumerable criticisms and suggestions, and have managed to preserve the essence of their original creations through successive rounds of amendments and cuts. Their scholarship and commitment have made this book what it is.

Stuart Hall, David Held and Anthony McGrew

INTRODUCTION

Stuart Hall, David Held and Gregor McLennan

Modernity and Its Futures is the fourth and last book in the Open University series, *Understanding Modern Societies*, which seeks to examine the emergence and characteristic institutional forms of modernity. Through interpretive analysis and guided readings, the series as a whole adopts a dual focus which aims, on the one hand, to explore the central, substantive features of social reproduction and transformation in the modern epoch and, on the other, strives to highlight the nature of the theories and categories that social scientists draw upon in order to make sense of those processes. The series is concerned to examine both the concept of 'modernity' as well as modernity — the institutional nexus.

In many respects, the present volume continues the storyline set in train by its companion volumes. Substantively, it follows the fourfold analytical division of modern society into its political, economic, social and cultural dimensions. Whereas the first book, *Formations of Modernity*, investigated how modern political and economic forms first emerged, and the second and third volumes explored their consolidation in some detail, this book asks about their durability and prospects. As we approach the twenty-first century, the volume tries to assess, among other things, the meaning and implications of the collapse of communism in Russia and Eastern Europe; shifts in the dynamics and organization of the global capitalist economic order; the changing forms of contemporary culture and identity formation; the growing interconnectedness between states and societies; and challenges to that quintessentially modern political institution, the nation-state. At the same time, *Modernity and Its Futures* is concerned with the changing role of social science and the nature of modern 'knowledge', which we have depended on in the past to make sense of these changes and which, if these shifts are taken far enough, could undercut some of the underlying intellectual assumptions of leading forms of human enquiry. These latter issues will be elaborated later in this Introduction.

For the moment, it should be emphasized that in none of the chapters which follow is it simply asserted that we have left modernity behind and are moving rapidly into a new 'post-modern' world. A great deal of careful conceptual work, argument and evidence is needed before this scenario can be affirmed or denied with any confidence. The signs of contemporary change point in different, often contradictory, directions and it is difficult to make sense of them while we are still living with them. Also, much depends on the specific features of the particular institutional dimension being examined. Accordingly, each chapter in this volume attempts to lay some common basis for discussion about the direction and extent of recent social and intellectual change before addressing the question of modernity's future. For this reason, one of the main tasks of the chapters is to introduce *debates*: debates about the likely directions, central dimensions and proper naming of these changes; debates about whether the future of modernity will sustain the Enlightenment promise of greater understanding and mastery of nature, the progress of reason in human affairs, and a steady, sustainable development in the standard and quality of life for the world's populations; debates about whether there is any meaningful future for specific classical social theories (such as liberalism or Marxism); and debates about the very role and possibility of social science today.

A RÉSUMÉ OF SOME EARLIER REFLECTIONS

In the previous volumes of this series, a number of elements of modernity have been explored and questioned. These have formed a set of orientation points or recurrent themes to which our examination of modern societies has frequently returned. It may be useful briefly to summarize the main elements here, before addressing the issue of how far the shape and character of 'modernity' remain intact as we approach the end of the twentieth century. We have examined the following propositions:

1 'Modernity' is that distinct and unique form of social life which characterizes modern societies. Modern societies began to emerge in Europe from about the fifteenth century, but modernity in the sense used here could hardly be said to exist in any developed form until the idea of 'the modern' was given a decisive formulation in the discourses of the Enlightenment in the eighteenth century. In the nineteenth century, modernity became identified with industrialism and the sweeping social, economic and cultural changes associated with it. In the twentieth century, several non-European societies — for example, Australasia and Japan — joined the company of advanced industrial societies. Modernity became a progressively global phenomenon.

2 Modernity has had a long and complex historical evolution. It was constituted by the articulation of a number of different historical processes, working together in unique historical circumstances. These processes were the political (the rise of the secular state and polity), the economic (the global capitalist economy), the social (formation of classes and an advanced sexual and social division of labour), and the cultural (the transition from a religious to a secular culture). Modernity, one might say, is the sum of these different forces and processes; no single 'master process' was sufficient to produce it.

3 Modernity developed at the intersection of national and international conditions and processes. It was shaped by both 'internal' and 'external' forces. The West forged its identity and interests in relation to endogenous developments in Europe and America, and through relations of unequal exchange (material and cultural) with 'the Rest' — the frequently excluded, conquered, colonized and exploited 'other'.

4   Modernity can be characterized by a cluster of institutions, each with its own pattern of change and development. Among these we would include: the nation-state and an international system of states; a dynamic and expansionist capitalist economic order based on private property; industrialism; the growth of large-scale administrative and bureaucratic systems of social organization and regulation; the dominance of secular, materialist, rationalist and individualist cultural values; and the formal separation of the 'private' from the 'public'.

5   Although modern capitalism was from the beginning an international affair, capitalist market relations have been organized on an increasingly global scale. Capitalist relations continue to provide modernity with its economic dynamic for growth and expansion, though forms of mass production and consumption are changing. Industrial capitalism has characteristically involved striking patterns of social inequality: in particular, distinctive class relations, based on those who own and control the means of production and those who only have their labouring power to sell. These social divisions have persisted over time, while becoming more complicated as a result of the emergence of new social strata and occupational groupings. Modernity also produced distinctive social patterns of gender and racial division, as well as other social divisions which intersect with, but are not reducible to, class. This has given rise to complex patterns of asymmetrical life-chances, both within nation-states and between them.

6   Modern societies are increasingly characterized by their complexity: by the proliferation of consumer products and by a variety of lifestyles. The hold of tradition has weakened in favour of individual choice and creating one's own life project; the individual is increasingly aware of the possibility of constructing new identities. Emphasis on personal life and on the spheres of intimacy has weakened the boundaries between the public and private. Nevertheless, this greater cultural pluralism and individuation has been accompanied by a growth of organizations (from hospitals to schools) seeking greater regulation and surveillance of social life.

7   Power is a constitutive dimension of all modern social relations; and social struggles — between classes, social movements and other groups — are 'inscribed' into the organization of society as well as the structures and policies of the state. Modern states are large, interventionist, administratively bureaucratic and complex systems of power *sui generis,* which intervene to organize large areas of social life. Liberal democracy in its contemporary form is the prevailing type of political regime in the industrial societies. It is partly the result of the struggles between different social groupings and interests, and partly the result of opportunities and constraints created by 'power politics' and economic competition in national and international arenas. Socialism, an alternative to the predominantly capitalist path to modernity, developed historically into a number of different forms. State socialism, the comprehensive attempt to substitute central planning for the market and the state for the autonomous associations of civil society, is nearly everywhere on the retreat. Social democracy, the attempt to regulate the

market and social organizations in the name of greater social justice and welfare, continues to enjoy widespread support, especially in parts of Europe. Yet, it is also an intensively contested project which has had both its aims and strategies questioned.

8   Globalization, a process reaching back to the earliest stages of modernity, continues to shape and reshape politics, economics and culture, at an accelerated pace and scale. The extension of globalizing processes, operating through a variety of institutional dimensions (technological, organizational, administrative, cultural and legal), and their increased intensification within these spheres, creates new forms and limits within 'modernity' as a distinctive form of life.

This volume seeks to explore these propositions further while also asking whether developments are leading toward an intensification and acceleration of the pace and scope of modernity, broadly along the lines sketched above, or whether they are producing an altogether altered or new constellation of political, economic, social and cultural life. In pursuing these issues, we are primarily concerned, it should be stressed, to pose *questions* about modernity and its possible futures, rather than to deliver (or encourage) snap judgements, as some versions of each pole in the debates tend to do. At the same time, we are convinced that the very idea of what lies at the edge of, and beyond, modernity changes the experience of living in the modern world and sets an exciting and powerful agenda for social theory and research. We also feel that, complicated as the exchanges about the shape of the future often become, they should not be the exclusive property of established academics. Part of the great attraction of the issues confronted here is that they are not only of cerebral interest: they touch fundamentally on the changing identities of a great many people today, and affect in key ways their everyday experience of 'being-in-the-world'.

It is, therefore, important that the question of post-modernity be accessibly presented and engaged at a number of different levels of familiarity and scholarship. The topics we handle certainly have the sharp tang of the contemporary about them, but they are not going to be definitively resolved for some time to come, and this is another reason for ensuring that the driving concepts and evidential support for generalizations about modernity's future are addressed in an open and critical manner. Let us now begin to address these issues by putting aside for the moment the business of the precise label that we may wish to stick on the 'new times' that we confront, and asking the question: what is going on in the social world of the 1990s?

THE STRUCTURE OF THE VOLUME

In the political sphere, a number of earthquakes have shaken both social reality and social thinking in recent years. Most obviously, the collapse of communism in the USSR and Eastern Europe, from the late 1980s, has constituted a remarkable set of changes which few, if any, fully anticipated. These changes have set in motion, not only wide-ranging transformations in Europe and the global order, but also intensive discussion about the significance of these world historical events. Do these events herald the victory of liberal democracy as an ideological tradition and as an institutional form? Do they herald the end of socialism and the final consolidation of capitalism on a world scale? Or, are the terms of these questions too simple and the underlying reality more complex?

David Held, in Chapter 1, explores these issues and explains why the revolutions of 1989–90 constitute a profound shaking up of our very ideas of democracy and the state. Contrary to many recent claims, he explains why the future of democracy 'as we know it' is not at all secure, partly because of the high levels of uncertainty and risk that accompany many of the sweeping changes across the globe today, partly because of contradictions and tensions among different dimensions of change, and partly because an adequate blend of the positive elements in both liberal and socialist democracy has not yet been achieved either in theory or in practice. The debate about 1989–90 turns out to be a debate about, as Held puts it, 'the character and form of modernity itself: the constitutive processes and structures of the contemporary world'.

This debate is carried through into Chapter 2 by Anthony McGrew, who focuses on the prospects for the nation-state faced with the extension and deepening of regional and global interconnectedness. The consolidation of the modern states system was the result of the expansion of Europe across the globe. Key features of the European states system — the centralization of political power, the expansion of administrative rule, the legitimation of power through claims to representation, the emergence of massed armies — became prevalent features of the entire global system. Today, in the context of globalization, as McGrew explains, the viability of a sovereign, territorially-bounded, culturally and ethnically delineated state appears to be in question.

Economic processes (multinational companies, international debt, world trade, global financial institutions), ecological imperatives and global or transnational political movements are putting sustained pressure on national economies and the nation-state. The 'national' form of organization for political, economic and cultural life, once a central feature of modernity, appears to have been weakened or badly damaged, although the difficulty of establishing a stable political form 'beyond' the nation-state leads to an intricate spectrum of possible directions.

Globalization has resulted in a very *contradictory* social experience for many. On one hand, the universal spread of electronic media has rendered communications between different cultures astonishingly rapid. Along with economic pressures, the political and cultural reference points for the peoples of the world are more uniform than ever before. Our very experience of *space and time*, indeed, has been condensed and made uniform in an unprecedented fashion. Distances have been drastically compressed and people almost everywhere are more 'aware' of the existence of others than ever before.

And yet — possibly as a direct result of increasing globalization — another very significant cultural phenomenon of recent times has been a growing sense of how particular people and their social interests *differ* radically from one another, or at least a sense of the *variety* of values and customs which abound. In addition, in a globalizing world system, people become more aware of, and more attached to, their *locality* as the appropriate forum for self-assertion and democratic expression. This desire to preserve something meaningful and tangible in the existing local culture in the context of profound universalizing tendencies is arguably what lies behind many of today's most intense political phenomena, from ethnic revivalism, to political separatism, to movements for local democracy.

The impact of globalization and the tension between the 'global' and the 'local' runs through a number of chapters in the volume. It lies at the heart of the environmental movement and the astonishing growth of 'green' consciousness around the world, which have linked an awareness of the fragile character of human ecology with a concern for local environments and forms of life. In his contribution to this volume, Steven Yearley in Chapter 3 addresses a number of immensely important issues concerning the sustainability of any society today, whether it be traditional or high-tech. The problems of coping with social waste and the need rapidly to prevent further erosion of the world's forests and ozone layer are so urgent that any remotely similar ecological agenda would have been simply unimaginable only thirty years ago. Here, as elsewhere, the modernist ideas of progress and infinite growth are questioned.

Yearley carefully analyses the ecological threats to contemporary society, and some of the strengths and weaknesses of the burgeoning green ideology. No matter how potentially severe ecological problems are, he reminds us, the momentum of economic growth continues and the basic values and institutions of western society have not yet been fundamentally eroded by green thought. Moreover, he soberly concludes, 'the lack of international accord over global warming and non-renewable resources indicates that a prosperous green future is not currently on offer to everyone on this planet'.

It would be wrong to conclude from the above that the entrenched institutions orientated towards economic growth, and the economic structures geared to ever-increasing production, have not themselves undergone significant transformation in recent times. In the economic sphere, a number of central changes are apparent. For example, there appears to be a significant move 'beyond' the typical industrial structure of the modern economy. In Chapter 4, John Allen sets out these changes in detail, focusing on a move from mass production to 'flexible specialization', and from mass consumption patterns to lifestyle niches in the marketplace. In terms of the techniques of production and economic calculation, the role of computerized information and designer modelling is critical in a way it never could have been before. Some would even say that we should now speak of 'modes of information' rather than, in the old Marxist usage, 'modes of production'. And along with the change of emphasis from material production to the knowledge-based economy, we need to note the universal growth of 'knowledge' workers (programmers, financiers, marketeers, designers, administrators) within an increasingly *service*-oriented labour force (where 'servicing' includes a great variety of casual and menial work tasks as well as well-paid ones — the former often being undertaken by women). John Allen stages a debate about these issues between protagonists who, though differing in emphasis amongst themselves, tend to fall into the position of arguing, either that the fundamental dynamic which shaped the modern growth-oriented industrial economy is still operating, or that the changes taking place add up to the emergence of some new, post-industrial form of capitalist economic organization.

The economic dimension, of course, has significant implications for modern social structures — for social class and other social divisions, as well as for cultural and personal identities. In the era of mass production and manufacturing industry, social classes were tangibly related to basic patterns of *ownership* of wealth and resources, and rested upon common cultural experiences centred around the workplace and the community. Class was always hard to define precisely in sociological theory, but it was seldom disputed that the predominant forms of work, ownership and local lifestyle were all important and related. It thus provided a major category of social and political analysis. Nowadays, the touchstone of 'class' in both social *analysis* and social *experience* seems much less solid. Patterns of economic ownership have continued to move away from the image of individual persons or families being the *owning class*, while the dramatic decline of manufacture and extraction, and the changing nature of work, have turned the imposing image of the mass working class into that of a dwindling minority grouping — in the so-called 'advanced' countries at any rate. The extensive fragmentation of the broad working class into a series of highly differentiated income groups and labour market 'segments' has further prompted the thought that the end of class (in its customary image, anyway) is nigh. The extent to which the recomposition of the labouring class in western societies affects our understanding of the class structure of society as a whole is thus a major area for investigation. At the same time, other social processes, like the spread of mass consumption, and other social divisions, like those associated with gender, race and ethnicity, have assumed greater salience, producing a greater complexity of social life, and a plurality of social groupings and communities of identification.

A final point to make on the economic–social interface is that the perceived significance of work itself has shifted. There has been a marked decline in the work 'ethic', and a sharp rise in popular awareness of the possible uses of *non-work* time in people's lives. Moreover, the association of work with the physical transformation of natural materials for basic human needs is far less powerful in modern societies than it once was. We live in an epoch where the manipulation of financial symbols on a screen is arguably truer to the spirit, and perhaps more crucial to the overall well-being, of a global capitalist economy than the wrenching of coal from the earth or trading goods for banknotes. Or so it seems. And the social composition of those who work, as well as the nature of the work itself, is now highly differentiated, by class, race and gender, and by position in the international division of labour. How significant these developments actually are is itself intensely debated. Assessments vary, from those who think the broad march of modernity has only been marginally knocked off its stride, to those who believe that multifaceted processes of change have transformed the modern social landscape beyond recall or regret.

'Modernity' has always served to identify a distinctive form of experience and culture, as well as patterns of social, economic and political organization, and the shifts which characterize late twentieth-century life are as dramatic in the cultural as in other spheres. The growing social pluralism and cultural complexity of modern societies, the global impact of the electronic media of communication spreading the images and messages of 'modernity' worldwide, the permeation of daily life by the mediation of symbolic forms, the aesthetic revolution in the design of physical environments as well as in contemporary art forms — these have accelerated the pace of cultural innovation, the production of new languages, and the pursuit of novelty and experiment as cultural values. The early aesthetic movements of the twentieth century, known as modernism, ushered in a new, experimental period in aesthetic form and expression, breaking with earlier, more realist forms of representation. Now, as this cultural revolution transforms everyday life, popular culture and the social environment (and not only in 'the West'), people are questioning whether, just as a new post-industrial economy may be replacing the old industrial economy, modernism is being displaced by a new post-modern epoch.

It comes as little surprise, therefore, that some social scientists claim that our political and social values, our cultural identities, and even our very sense of *self* are in considerable flux and disarray. What is sometimes called 'late-modernity' 'unfreezes' traditional values, political alignments and emotional allegiances, which, in turn, renders the whole picture of social existence in the late modern world still more fluid.

In the advanced heartlands of the West, we might imagine — just for the sake of argument — how individuals may have lost a strong sense of class-determined identity, and how their political reference points are now criss-crossed with a variety of conflicting points of identification, thus transforming notions about who they are and what they should be thinking and doing. Ethnic, gender, local, party, family, consumer-produced, media-inspired, self-contrived passions and aspirations now blend and clash in this unstable amalgam of the self. In the 'marginal' countries, identities evolved from once-stable rural or traditional cultures compete with those borrowed from or disseminated by 'the West'; and religious allegiances for their part either get modified and modernized in order to adjust to, or mobilized in order belatedly to challenge, western-led globalization. At the 'micro-level', in the fine mesh of interpersonal relations, the fresh instability and pluralism of social and political identities bring a different range of subjective expectations, and more complex notions of intimacy, trust and dependency (see Giddens, 1991).

In Chapter 5, Kenneth Thompson explores the debate about the characteristics of this new 'post-modern' culture and whether it can be said to constitute a new cultural and social epoch. He describes its aesthetic features and introduces some major protagonists in the debate about how far these 'new times' are characterized by a new level of social pluralism and fragmentation. In Chapter 6, Stuart Hall outlines and appraises the implications of 'new times' for our sense of self, our identities and cultural 'belongingness'. Hall presents the argument that a more unified conception of the modern self is being 'de-centered' and that some of the social identities which stabilized the modern world and gave individuals firm locations in the cultural landscape of modernity are being dislocated. He explores the unsettling impact of globalization on national identities, but also discusses its contradictory outcome — the tendency towards both a 'global post-modern' culture *and* simultaneously the resurgence of nationalism, ethnicity and fundamentalism.

In this apparently shifting, novel context, what purchase can traditional social science have? Can the modern world undergo such rapid and extensive transformation while our analytic and explanatory models remain untouched? If our cultural understandings form as 'real' a part of social change as do economic and technological processes, then the same might be said about our cognitive models and intellectual allegiances. Social scientists have frequently assumed that their theories and categories offer a 'window on the world', and indeed that their concepts actually 'pick out' bits of society and reveal their inner workings. Thus, even to conceive of society — as books earlier in this series have done — as divided into four distinct dimensions or sectors, having labels such as 'the economic', 'the political', etc., is to exemplify that classical social science assumption whereby theories and categories somehow 'represent' social reality.

But let us pause for a moment to see what this aspiration to 'represent' reality involves. For one thing, in the four volumes of *Understanding Modern Societies* we have been keen to portray society, not as one unified thing 'out there', but rather as a process of overlapping institutional dimensions, each with its own patterns of change and development. The capitalist economic order, the nation-state system, military and industrial organization, administrative and bureaucratic power: none of these institutional 'clusters' is wholly separate from the others, yet each retains its special emphasis. And within any given social formation, these processes have resulted historically in very different social configurations. There are always likely to be a number of relevant causal influences to account for the evolution of distinctive patterns of inequality and structuration: class, gender, ethnicity, age, and so on. Now it could reasonably be argued that much social theory, up to the late 1970s, aspired at least in principle to an overarching or meta-theoretical perspective, which could somehow finally bring together and *rank* all these dimensions, in order to give a coherent overall picture of society. Social theory, in other words, aspired in principle to a 'total theory' which would map society as a whole.

Today, this aspiration has been severely questioned, and the Enlightenment project from which it ultimately stems seems to some commentators to lie in tatters, as Gregor McLennan shows in Chapter 7. What is interesting for our purposes here is to see how much the transformations of late-modernity challenge, even if they do not wholly undermine, the explanatory models of modern social sciences — showing as they do, for example, how hard it is to 'hold the line' at a small number of 'priority' societal factors in the explanation of social phenomena. In effect, there are always a great number of social factors to consider in any 'total picture', and the outcomes are likely to be variable, and to show the effects of contingency in historical development rather than leading to one predictable historical result.

Against this background, the role of social theory as a 'picturing' enterprise, that is, as a representational form, is put under strain. Rather than somehow representing reality, theories can instead be seen to produce variable *insights* into the complex and multiple existence that we happen to call 'society'. Similarly, it could be maintained that phrases such as 'the economic dimension' do not in effect 'pick out' bits of reality called 'the economy'. Rather, they are analytical devices which we use to say, not 'this is how things really are', but rather, 'look at it this way for a moment'. Social theory thus becomes a much more suggestive business than anticipated by the positivist strands of the Enlightenment vision of an all-encompassing science of society. And social theorists, for their part, become more aware of the ways in which they produce different social descriptions, and consequently are more hesitant and provisional in their assertions than their more ambitious predecessors.

It follows that even the attempt in this series of books to highlight certain processes, developments and dimensions in analysing modernity could be regarded as a more or less useful way of *organizing enquiry*, rather than an attempt to *partition and wrap up* reality in any definitive sense. This is part of what was referred to in the Introduction to *Formations of Modernity* as the remarkable growth of 'reflexivity', both in common experience and in social science thinking. To regard social enquiry as a hesitant process of self-understanding in a rapidly changing world is a far cry from the view that social scientists must strive to reflect reality as it is in itself, formulating the inner essence of society in abstract scientific terms.

In conclusion, it is important to note that this dialogue and sometime antagonism between two powerful images of social understanding is not new; it may even be a kind of 'eternal' oscillation in western thinking. Basically — and leaving aside for a moment our specific theoretical allegiances — there are those who habitually feel the 'pull' of strong overarching concepts and applaud the ambition of 'grand theory'. Here the primary impulse is to perceive and articulate a sense of coherence and shape in the social world and thus to pinpoint our own place within that world. Ironically, the very concept of post-modernity as a general condition of society which follows the rise and fall of another stage called modernity itself embodies the idea that social theory can provide large-scale models of order and sequence.

On the other side are those who are suspicious of enforced order and grandiose ambition, whether in society at large or in social scientific reflection. Here the main impulse is to debunk big concepts and easy generalizations. The emphasis is not on progress, totality and necessity, but on the very opposite of these intellectual emphases, namely discontinuity, plurality and contingency (see Rorty, 1989). Post-modernism in this vein is more a 'deconstructive' style of reasoning and enquiry, offering itself as a stimulant to dialogue and to conversation among human beings without the universalizing pretensions of Enlightenment philosophies. People, it is hoped, will be able to talk to one another and, in the process of playing vocabularies and cultures off against each other, produce new and better ways of acting on problems in the world.

The authors of this book have their own views on the nature of modernity and its future. They also have views on the very possibility of 'rational' social science. In one sense, we all believe that social scientific enquiry can proceed quite a long way and 'deliver' a substantial amount before profound philosophical decisions have to be made about whether social science is a necessarily 'totalizing' operation, or whether it can perfectly well survive instead by conducting 'local' forms of investigation and by promulgating a probing, critical style. However, we are also sure that at some point we do face the overall issues of whether social science can provide an adequate ordering framework, or whether it would be more enlightening and liberating to throw to the winds our overweening intellectual ambitions. It should immediately be said that amongst the contributors there is a typical range of responses to that question, as the reader will discover in the pages which follow.

References

Giddens, A. (1991) *Modernity and Self-Identity*, Cambridge, Polity Press.

Rorty, R. (1989) *Contingency, Irony, Solidarity*, Cambridge, Cambridge University Press.

CHAPTER 1 LIBERALISM, MARXISM AND DEMOCRACY

David Held

CONTENTS

1   INTRODUCTION

At the end of the Second World War Europe lay devastated and divided. The emergence of Nazism and fascism had shattered any complacent views of Europe as the cradle of progress in the world. The Holocaust appeared to negate Europe's claim — a claim made with particular force since the Enlightenment — to represent the pinnacle of civilization. Some philosophers even began to think of the Enlightenment as the origin of domination and totalitarianism in the West (see Horkheimer and Adorno, 1972). The war itself, moreover, had destroyed millions of lives, wrecked Europe's infrastructure, and left the world increasingly polarized between the democratic, capitalist West and the communist East.

Yet, scarcely more than forty years later, some were proclaiming (by means of a phrase borrowed most notably from Hegel) the 'end of history' — the triumph of the West over all political and economic alternatives. The revolutions which swept across Central and Eastern Europe at the end of 1989 and the beginning of 1990 stimulated an atmosphere of celebration. Liberal democracy was proclaimed as the agent of progress, and capitalism as the only viable economic system; ideological conflict, it was said, was being steadily displaced by universal democratic reason and market-oriented thinking (Fukuyama, 1989).

The subtitle of this chapter could be '1989 and all that', for its objective is to explore and tentatively assess the debate about the meaning of the changes and transformations which swept through Europe during 1989 and 1990, and which were accelerated further by the popular counter movement to the coup attempt in the Soviet Union during 18–21 August 1991. Has the West won? Has liberal democracy finally displaced the legitimacy of all other forms of government? Is ideological conflict at an end? These and related questions will be explored below.

It will become apparent in the course of the chapter that the debate about 1989 is much more than a debate about the events of that year and subsequent occurrences, important as these are. For it is also a debate about the character and form of modernity itself: the constitutive processes and structures of the contemporary world. The chapter presents in microcosm some of the key issues, problems and discussions about modernity, its past, present and possible futures. In other words, '1989 and all that' is a stimulus to a variety of fundamental questions about the world unfolding before us. Is the distinctively modern world a world shaped and reshaped according to liberal political and economic principles? Was 1989 important because it represented a crucial formative movement in the development and consolidation of the liberal polity and the free market economy in the global order? Or, is it significant because it was the moment at which capitalism scored a decisive victory over socialism and communism and, accordingly, finally captured modernity for itself. Is socialism dead in the face of the apparent collapse of Marxism? Or will socialism be reborn when capitalism finally establishes itself on a world scale? In short, did 1989 represent a moment at which modernity was decisively shaped by one particular set of forces and relations? Or does it represent something more complex and uncertain?

The debate about 1989, and about the form and character of modernity, is a debate about the world as it is and might be. That the debate spans *analytical* and *normative* considerations should come as no surprise. For as I have pointed out elsewhere, while this distinction may be useful as an initial point of orientation, it is hard to use as a precise classificatory device for political and social theories (see Book 1 (Hall and Gieben, 1992), Chapter 2). Events, processes and political dramas do not simply 'speak for themselves'; they are, and they have to be, interpreted; and the framework we bring to the process of interpretation determines what we 'see': what we notice and register as important. All theoretical and analytical endeavour, whether it be that of lay people or professional social scientists, involves interpretation — interpretation which embodies a particular framework of concepts, beliefs and standards. Such a framework should not be thought of as a barrier to understanding; for it is rather integral to understanding (Gadamer, 1975). It shapes our attempts to understand and assess political action, events and processes, and provides points of orientation. However, such a framework does mean that particular positions in political and social theory — relating, for example, to modernity and its consequences — ought not to be treated as offering *the* correct or final understanding of a phenomenon; for the meaning of a phenomenon is always open to future interpretations from new perspectives, each with its own practical stance or interest in political life. (For further discussion of these themes, see the Introduction to Book 1 (Hall and Gieben, 1992), and Chapter 7 of this volume.)

This chapter, accordingly, considers a range of analytical and normative questions which thread through the debate about 1989, and it highlights, especially toward the end, some of the competing conceptions of the 'political good' (the virtuous, desirable and preferred form of human association) — particularly those offered by liberalism, Marxism and, for want of a better label, a 'multi-dimensional' approach to modernity. These positions proffer quite different conceptions of the political good and some of their strengths and limitations will be explored in subsequent discussion. Consideration of the political good readily becomes, it will be seen, an analysis of, and debate about, the nature and meaning of democracy, an issue so forcefully put on the agenda by the events of and since 1989. And a sustained reflection on democracy, it will be suggested, offers clues to a more coherent and cogent account of the political good than can be found in the other positions considered here.

1.1 THE STRUCTURE OF THE CHAPTER

This chapter has a number of sections. After a brief examination of the historical background to 1989 (Section 1.2), Sections 2–4 will examine the debate about 1989 through readings which offer sharply contrasting views. Each reading is prefaced by an account of the author's general position and is followed by a critical commentary. It is hoped that the sequence of readings and commentaries will provide a cumulative discussion of the chapter's key concerns.

Section 2 focuses on an essay by Francis Fukuyama which became *a* if not *the locus classicus* in discussions — particularly in the Anglo-American world — of the political transformations sweeping the East. Fukuyama's main thesis amounts to the claim that socialism is dead and that liberalism is the sole remaining legitimate political philosophy.

Section 3 addresses writings by Alex Callinicos who takes an entirely different view. He interprets the East European revolutions as a victory for capitalism — but a victory which makes Marxism *more* relevant today, not less.

Section 4 then presents a text by Anthony Giddens about modernity and its consequences. Taking modernity to represent four institutional dimensions — capitalism, industrialism, administrative power and military might — Giddens argues that the future of modernity, like its past, is more complicated than either liberalism or Marxism can grasp.

The readings by Fukuyama, Callinicos and Giddens have been selected, in particular, because they exemplify central voices or perspectives (albeit while making original contributions) in the attempt to think through and assess the revolutions and their impact. If Fukuyama is primarily concerned with examining the significance of liberalism in the contemporary era, Callinicos is preoccupied with showing how Marxism retains its integrity and critical edge despite the weakening appeal of communism throughout the world. Giddens, by contrast, rejects the premises of both these types of position and argues that a theory of the transformations of modernity must go beyond them. Together, these three readings set up a striking debate.

Section 5 offers a brief summary of the text to that point, drawing together the threads of how the different positions conceive the political good and the role and nature of democracy. The debate among these conceptions is further explored in Section 6 through an analysis of democracy itself. It is argued here that it is possible to develop a conception of the political good *as the democratic good*, and that this offers a more promising approach to questions about the proper form of 'government' and 'politics' than is offered by the positions set out earlier.

Section 7 briefly concludes the chapter and raises questions about the proper form and limits of political community today. In this way it provides a link with the following chapter (Chapter 2) by Anthony McGrew.

1.2   THE HISTORICAL BACKDROP

The changes of political regime which swept through Central and
Eastern Europe in 1989–90 — in Poland, Hungary, East Germany,
Bulgaria, Czechoslovakia, and Romania — were world-shaking events
by any standard. An extraordinary sense of exhilaration was created
within and beyond Europe. As Callinicos aptly put it:

> Far beyond the countries directly affected, people shared a sense of
> suddenly widened possibilities. Parts of the furniture of the
> postwar world that had seemed irremovable suddenly disappeared
> — literally in the case of the Berlin wall. Previously unalterable
> assumptions — for example, that Europe would be permanently
> divided between the superpowers — abruptly collapsed.
> (Callinicos, 1991, p.8)

The sharp division between the democratic capitalist and state socialist
worlds, created in the aftermath of the Second World War, began to
disappear. The pattern of intense rivalry between the superpowers,
perhaps the single most significant feature of world politics in the
second half of the twentieth century, was almost at a stroke transformed
(see Lewis, 1990a). If this were not considered a revolution (or series of
revolutions) within the affairs of the erstwhile communist bloc, and
within the international order more generally, it is hard to see what
would qualify as revolutionary change.

But things are rarely as straightforward as they seem. While the term
'revolution' may seem to describe accurately the sweeping, dramatic

The fall of the Berlin Wall

and unexpected transformations of the state socialist system, and the extraordinary movements of people who ushered in these changes on the streets of Warsaw, Budapest, Prague, Berlin and other cities, it detracts attention from the momentum of changes and processes already under way by November 1989. Although I shall continue to refer to the 'revolutions' of 1989–90, it is as well to bear in mind that these had roots stretching back in time.

To begin with, significant political changes had begun to get under way in Poland in the early 1980s, and in Hungary a little later: the Communists had been defeated in elections in Poland and the principle of one-party rule had been renounced in Hungary before the 'dramatic' events of 1989–90 took place. There was also the massive student uprising in Tiananmen Square, Beijing, so brutally put down on 3–4 June 1989, which provided the reminder, if one was at all needed, that change in state socialist regimes might, at the very best, be tolerated only at a slow and managed pace.

Underpinning the slow but significant changes in Central and Eastern Europe in the late 1980s was, of course, the reform process initiated in the USSR by Mikhail Gorbachev — the so-called process of *perestroika* ('restructuring'). Shifts in strategic thinking in the Kremlin were probably the proximate cause of the East European revolutions, alongside the gradual erosion of communist power in the civil societies and economies of the Soviet bloc (see Lewis, 1990a and 1990b). In particular, the Soviet decision to replace the 'Brezhnev Doctrine' (i.e. the policy of protecting the 'achievements of socialism' in Eastern Europe, by force if necessary) with the 'Sinatra Doctrine' (i.e. the policy of tolerating nationally chosen paths to progress and prosperity: 'do it your way') had decisive consequences, intended and otherwise, for the capacity of state socialist regimes to survive. By removing the threat of Red Army or Warsaw Pact intervention, and by refusing to sanction the use of force to crush mass demonstrations, the Sinatra Doctrine effectively pulled the carpet from under East European communism. The developments in East Germany were a notable case in point. When Hungary opened its border with Austria, and triggered the massive emigration of East Germans to the West, pressures within East Germany rapidly intensified and demonstrations, held in Leipzig and near-by cities, escalated. Without the routine recourse to force, the East German authorities sought to placate their rebellious citizenry by sanctioning access to the West *via* new openings in the Berlin Wall. The result is well known: the authorities lost control of an already demanding situation, and within a short time both their legitimacy and effectiveness were wholly undermined.

The roots of the events of 1989–90 can be traced back further. Three particular sets of pressures can usefully be mentioned, for they shed some light, not only on why a shift in strategic thinking occurred in the Kremlin, but also on why the changes took the direction they did. First, the Soviet economy's lack of integration into the world economic system protected it in the *short-term* from the pressures and instabilities attendant on achieving the levels of competitive productivity necessary for a sustained role in the international division of labour; in the *long-run*, however, the same lack of integration left it weak and uncompetitive, particularly in relation to technology and innovation. Ever more dependent on imported technology and foreign sources of funding and investment, the centrally administered economy, rigid and relatively inflexible at the best of times, found few avenues through which to deliver better economic performance.

In the second place, this situation was compounded by renewed geopolitical pressures which followed from the intensification of the Cold War in the late 1970s and 1980s. A new arms race, in which 'smart' weapons and ever more sophisticated weapon-systems played an increasing role, put a greater and greater burden on the financial, technical and managerial resources of the Soviet Union. The costs of the Cold War became profoundly difficult to contain on both sides, but were particularly draining to the crumbling organizations and infrastructure of the Soviet economy.

Thirdly, significant conflicts and schisms had emerged in the Soviet bloc during the previous few decades, leading to massive acts of repression to contain dissent in Hungary (1956), Czechoslovakia (1968) and Poland (1981). While these acts may have effectively contained protest in the short term, they were not a permanent obstacle to the spawning of dissent, social movements and autonomous organizations in civil society. The developments in Poland in the 1980s, particularly the formation of the trade union Solidarity, were by no means typical of what was happening in Eastern Europe as a whole. For the events in Poland were shaped by a remarkable ethnic and national unity, the power of the Catholic Church and a strong sense of a foreign enemy on Polish soil corrupting its growth and identity. Nevertheless, they were indicative of a certain growing democratic pressure to 'roll back the state' and to create an independent civil society in which citizens could pursue their chosen activities free from immediate political pressure. Solidarity sought to foster such a society throughout the 1980s by creating independent networks of information, cultural interchange and social relations. In so doing, it recast and expanded the meaning of what it was to be a democratic social movement while drastically weakening the appeal of state-dominated political change.

The above account is by no means intended to be a thorough analysis of the remarkable events and developments of 1989 and subsequent years. Rather, it is intended as an historical sketch which provides a context for the main focus of the chapter — namely, the consideration of what the revolutions mean, how they should be interpreted, and what light they shed on the development of modernity and its futures.

2   THE TRIUMPH OF LIBERALISM?

Following the United States' defeat in the Vietnam war and the rise of
the Japanese economic challenge to American economic interests, a
detectable gloom settled over Washington policy-makers in the late
1970s. This gloom was reinforced by a spate of major academic
publications in the 1980s, including Robert Keohane's *After Hegemony*
(1984) and Paul Kennedy's *The Rise and Fall of the Great Powers*
(1988), which charted the (relative) decline of US power and considered
the implications of this for world politics and the world political
economy. Focusing on the growing costs of maintaining the US's
military strength, and the erosion of its productive and revenue-raising
capacities by economic rivals, these authors raised alarms about the
US's future and about the consequences of decline for the defence and
stability of the West. Few foresaw, however, how thoroughly these
considerations, important as they were, would have to be reassessed in
the light of the dramatic decline of the West's main adversary at the end
of the 1980s: the Soviet Union.

A major effort of reassessment was made by Francis Fukuyama in his
1989 essay, 'The end of history?'; this not only provided a reassuring
counterpoint to the earlier preoccupation with the US's loss of
hegemony, but, in its confident and assertive tone, went some way
toward restoring faith in the supremacy of Western values. Fukuyama,
formerly deputy director of, and currently consultant to, the US State
Department Policy Planning Staff, celebrated not only the 'triumph of
the West' but also, as he put it, 'the end of history as such; that is, the
end point of mankind's ideological evolution and the universalization of
Western liberal democracy as the final form of human government'
(1989, p.3). Fukuyama's message became widely reported in the press
and the electronic media more generally. While subjecting him to
considerable criticism, most of Fukuyama's detractors seemed to
concede that his 'main point — the current lack of competitors against
political and economic liberalism in the world ideological market place
— is surely hard to refute' (Mortimer, 1989, p.29).

Fukuyama's message recalls earlier debates in the 1950s and 1960s on
'the end of ideology' (see Held, 1989, Ch.4). But whereas these debates
focused on the significance in the West of a decline in support by
intellectuals, trade unions and left-wing political parties for Marxism,
and on a reduction in the differences among political parties towards
government intervention and welfare expenditure, Fukuyama's thesis
goes much further, philosophically and politically. His thesis comprises
four main components. First, there is a broad emphasis on conflict
among *ideologies* as the motor of history. Drawing some inspiration
from Hegel, Fukuyama argues that history can be understood as a
sequence of stages of consciousness or ideology; that is, as a sequence of
systems of political belief which embody distinctive views about the
basic principles underlying social order (Fukuyama, 1989/90, pp.22–3).
The sequence represents a progressive and purposive path in human

development from partial and particularistic ideologies to those with more universal appeal. In the modern period we have reached, in Fukuyama's judgement, the final stage of this development.

Secondly, the end of history has been reached because ideological conflict is virtually at an end. Liberalism is the last victorious ideology. At the heart of this argument, Fukuyama notes, 'lies the observation that a remarkable consensus has developed in the world concerning the legitimacy and viability of liberal democracy' (1989/90, p.22). The chief rivals to liberalism in the twentieth century, fascism and communism, have either failed or are failing. And contemporary challengers — religious movements such as Islam, or nationalist movements such as those found in Eastern Europe today — articulate only partial or incomplete ideologies; that is to say, they champion beliefs which cannot be sustained without the support of other ideologies. Neither religious nor nationalist belief systems provide coherent alternatives to liberalism in the long term and, therefore, have no 'universal significance'. Only liberal democracy, along with market principles of economic organization, constitute developments of 'truly world historical significance' (Fukuyama, 1989/90, p.23).

The end of an era? The removal of the statue of Felix Edmundovitch Dzerzhinsky, founder of the KGB, from Moscow on 22 August 1991.

The third distinctive element of Fukuyama's thesis is that the end of history should not be taken to mean the end of all conflict. Conflict can arise — indeed, is likely to arise — from diverse sources, including advocates of various (dated) ideologies, nationalist and religious groups, and peoples or collectivities locked into history or pre-history: i.e. those who remain 'outside' the liberal world (certain Third World countries) or who remain 'outsiders inside' (individuals and groups within the liberal world who have not yet fully absorbed its inescapability). Moreover, there is a danger of a progressive 'bifurcation' or splitting of the world into those who belong to the 'post-historical' liberal societies and the rest — the traditional unmodernized world. Bifurcation could certainly generate intense and violent struggles, but none of these will lead, Fukuyama maintains, to new systematic ideas of political and social justice which could displace or supersede liberalism.

Finally, Fukuyama is not wholly unambivalent about the 'end of history'. It will, he suggests, be 'a very sad time' (1989, p.18). There will no longer be daring leaps of human imagination and valiant struggles of great principle; politics will become an extension of the regulative processes of markets. Idealism will be replaced by economic management and the solving of technical problems in the pursuit of consumer satisfaction. In short, recalling one of the central themes of post-modernism, Fukuyama proclaims the exhaustion of the bold, even heroic, 'grand narratives' of human emancipation which once struggled with one another for dominance in the world. (See the Introduction to this volume and Chapter 7 for a discussion of the key ideas of post-modernism.) But while there is a detectable note of regret in his tone, it barely qualifies his generally optimistic affirmation of liberalism. Ideological consensus today may be neither 'fully universal nor automatic', but it exists to a 'higher degree than at any time in the past century' (1989/90, p.22). The 'liberal democratic revolution' and the 'capitalist revolution' form the final stage of a clear-cut pattern of historical evolution.

ACTIVITY 1   Turn now to **Reading A, 'The end of history?'**, by Francis Fukuyama, which you will find at the end of this chapter. As you read, note how Fukuyama characterizes:

• the success of liberalism and the exhaustion of its 'great alternatives';

• the prospects of conflict at 'the end of history'.

2.1   CRITICAL RESPONSE

Fukuyama's essay was widely acclaimed as one of the 'key texts for our age' (*The Guardian*, Sept. 7, 1990). In a sense, it provided a sophisticated justification for many of the commonplace pronouncements made by the leading governments of the West in the

1980s, especially those of Margaret Thatcher and Ronald Reagan (Hirst, 1989, p.14). It reinforced the message of the neo-liberal New Right, which throughout the 1980s had proclaimed the imminent death of socialism, and praised the market and minimal state as the only legitimate and viable forms for the future (see, for example, Friedman, 1989). But it would be wrong to suggest that Fukuyama's arguments were supported only by the Right. A broad spectrum of political opinion found the general political message of Fukuyama's article hard to brush aside, even if there was intense disagreement about most of its details.

There are, however, also serious questions to be raised about Fukuyama's essential argument. In the first instance, liberalism cannot be treated simply as a unity. There are distinctive liberal traditions set down by such figures as Adam Smith, John Locke and John Stuart Mill which embody quite different conceptions concerning the individual agent, autonomy, the rights and duties of subjects, and the proper nature and form of community (see, for example, Dunn, 1979). Fukuyama does not analyse the different forms of liberalism, nor does he provide any arguments about how one might choose among them. This is a striking lacuna, since liberalism itself is an ideologically contested terrain.

In addition, Fukuyama does not explore whether there are any tensions, or even perhaps contradictions, between the 'liberal' and 'democratic' components of liberal democracy; that is, between the liberal preoccupation with individual rights or 'frontiers of freedom' which 'nobody should be permitted to cross' (Berlin, 1969, pp.164ff.), and the democratic concern with the regulation of individual and collective action, i.e. with public accountability. Those who have written at length on this question have frequently resolved it in quite different ways (see Held, 1987). Where Fukuyama stands on the balance between 'liberalism' and 'democracy' is unclear. Furthermore, there is not simply one institutional form of liberal democracy. Contemporary democracies have crystallized into a number of different types — the Westminster, federal and consensual models, for example — which make any appeal to a liberal position vague at best (see Lijphart, 1984; Dahl, 1989). Fukuyama essentially leaves unanalysed the whole issue of the meaning of democracy and its possible variants.

Fukuyama's affirmation of the principles of economic liberalism, and the mechanisms of the market, also raises questions. Following a central assumption of *laissez-faire* liberalism — that markets are basically self-equilibriating and 'clear' if various 'imperfections' are eliminated (wage and price 'stickiness', for instance) — Fukuyama interprets markets as essentially 'powerless' mechanisms of coordination. He thus neglects to inquire into the extent to which market relations are themselves power relations which can constrain and limit the democratic process. He fails to consider whether persistent asymmetries in income, wealth and opportunity may not be the outcome of the existing form of market relations: capitalist market relations. For, one particular liberty — the liberty to accumulate wealth and to organize productive activity into hierarchically ordered enterprises — poses a challenge to the extent to which political liberty can be enjoyed by all citizens: i.e. the extent to which citizens can act as equals in the political process (see Dahl, 1985). Not to examine this challenge is to risk ignoring one of the main threats to liberty in the contemporary world: a threat deriving not, as thinkers like de Tocqueville and J.S. Mill thought, from demands for equality, but from inequality — inequality so great as to create violations of political liberty and democratic politics (Dahl, 1985, p.60).

Moreover, despite his remarks on the dangers of a bifurcated world, Fukuyama barely considers the degree to which inequalities of ownership and control, and determinate asymmetries of life chances, can create differences of interest which may spark clashes of value, principle, belief — i.e. ideology — within the West, and between the West and 'Third World' countries. He underestimates the potential for struggles between different ideological accounts of the nature of the economic order, and of desirable alternative forms of economic organization at national and international levels. It is by no means self-evident, for example, that the existing economic system can generate the minimum life conditions for the millions of people — 27 million at the current estimate — who currently face death by starvation in Africa and elsewhere; or, for that matter, the minimum life conditions for all the planet's population faced with possible global warming, ozone depletion and the continued destruction of life-sustaining natural resources. It is far from self-evident that the existing economic system is compatible with the central liberal concern to treat all persons as 'free and equal' (see Miller, 1989). In the absence of such compatibility, one can surmise that liberalism is likely to face renewed criticism as the search for a 'fairer' and 'safer' economic order continues.

Fukuyama's own account of the potential sources of ideological conflict is, in addition, weak. Leaving aside his characterization of ideology, which is itself problematic (see the discussion in Book 3 (Bocock and Thompson, 1992), Chapter 7; and Thompson, 1990), Fukuyama's attempt to explain away the persistence of nationalism and religious movements, especially religious fundamentalism, is unconvincing. For example, he dismisses Islam as a political ideology on the grounds that it is highly unlikely to generate a universal appeal: its appeal is restricted to the Muslim world. But this is a poor argument. For the same reasoning must surely lead one to conclude that liberalism itself should be dismissed as a political ideology because it, too, cannot generate a universal appeal; it has, after all, had limited impact on the Muslim world, on China, and so on. Furthermore, Fukuyama fails to examine some of the most vigorous sources of political debate to have emanated in the West recently, for example, from social movements like feminism and the Greens.

Finally, Fukuyama's claims about 'the end of history' are implausible, in my view. For he ignores the continued contestability of liberalism and of the liberal conception of the political good both within and beyond the borders of the Western nation-state. His claims also ignore the fact

that we cannot fully know what all the major sources of conflict and
ideological struggle will be in a world shaped as much by the
contingent, the unanticipated and the imponderable as by determinate
causal forces and bounded patterns of institutional change (Himmelfarb,
1989). What we know is largely based on what has happened — on
what was, and not on what will be. We cannot, therefore, rule out the
possibility that new doctrinal orthodoxies with mass-mobilising
potential, and capable of legitimating new kinds of regime, benevolent
or authoritarian, will arise (see Beetham, 1991). After all, who could
have predicted the fall of the Berlin wall, the peaceful reunification of
Germany, the collapse of communism in Eastern Europe and the end of
the Cold War?

3   THE NECESSITY OF MARXISM?

Liberal theory in both its classical and contemporary guises generally
assumes something that should, in fact, be carefully examined: namely,
whether existing relationships between men and women, the working,
middle and upper classes, blacks and whites, and between various
ethnic groups allow formally recognized liberties to be actually realized.
The formal existence of certain liberties in liberal *theory* is, while not
unimportant, of restricted value if these liberties cannot be exercised in
practice. An assessment of freedom must be made on the basis of
liberties that are tangible; liberty that is merely theoretical can scarcely
be said to have profound consequences for everyday life. If liberals like
Fukuyama were to take these issues seriously, they might have to come
to terms more directly with the massive number of people who, for
want of a complex mix of resources and opportunities, are
systematically restricted from participating actively in political and civil
affairs.

Pursuing ideas such as these, Alex Callinicos, one of the most vigorous
defenders of classical Marxism today, argues that liberal democracy has
broken its promises. Following the Italian political theorist Norberto
Bobbio, Callinicos conceives these promises as: (1) participation, (2)
control from below, and (3) freedom to protest and reform (Callinicos,
1991, pp.108–9; cf. Bobbio, 1987, pp.42–4). 'Really existing liberal
democracy' fails, he contends, on all three counts. For it is
distinguished by: the existence of a largely passive citizenry (less than
fifty per cent of eligible citizens in the US vote in presidential elections,
for example); the erosion and displacement of parliamentary institutions
by unelected centres of power (typified by the expansion of the role of
bureaucratic authority, of functional representatives and of the security
services); and substantial structural constraints on state action and, in
particular, on the possibility of the piecemeal reform of capitalism (the
flight of capital, for example, is a habitual threat to elected governments
with strong programmes of social reform) (Callinicos, 1991, p.109).

Against this background Callinicos seeks to defend the classical Marxist tradition by arguing that democracy, and a feasible socialist programme, can only come from 'below', from the self-organizing activity of the working class. A democratic alternative to liberal democracy can be found, Callinicos avers, in the 'rich twentieth century tradition of soviet democracy, of workers' councils ...' (1991, p.110). From this point of view, Stalinism, which dominated the Soviet Union's history until recently, can be seen as the negation of socialism. Callinicos interprets Stalinism as a counter-revolutionary force which, at the close of the 1920s, created a state capitalist regime; that is, a regime in which the state bureaucracy collectively extracts surplus value and regulates capital accumulation, fulfilling the role once performed by the bourgeoisie. For Callinicos, Stalinism destroyed the possibility of a radical workers' democracy of the sort briefly installed in the Soviet Union in October 1917 under Lenin's leadership. The collapse of Stalinism in 1989, therefore, cannot be understood (in Fukuyama's terms) as the defeat of classical Marxism; for what was defeated, Callinicos insists, was an authoritarian distortion of Marxism. And what won in 1989 was not 'democracy', but capitalism. Therefore, what the East European revolutions achieved was a political reorganization of the ruling classes — one that allowed the technical, bureaucratic elites of

Dona Martha shanty town, with the city of Rio behind

Eastern Europe to integrate their economies fully into the world market, and aided the transition from state to globally integrated capitalism (Callinicos, 1991, p.58).

Callinicos attacks the equation Marxism = Leninism = Stalinism. A 'qualitative break', he argues, separates Stalinism from Marx and Lenin (1991, p.16). Neither Marx's theory nor Lenin's practice sanctioned a system characterized, not simply by one person's rule, but by 'the hierarchically organised control of all aspects of social life, political, economic, and cultural, by a narrow oligarchy seated at the apex of the party apparatuses' (ibid., p.15). In addition, there are resources in the classical Marxist tradition, particularly in the Trotskyist tradition and the Leftist opposition to Stalinism, which provide a basis for making sense of the demise of the Stalinist regimes. Three themes are, according to Callinicos, of special relevance (ibid., pp.16–20). First, Marx's work, subsequently enriched and refined by later Marxist scholars, provides an account of epochal transformations, resulting from the essential conflict that develops between the relations and forces of production, and from class struggle which both mediates and intensifies such conflict. This account offers an indispensable framework for understanding the progressive collapse of the Stalinist order.

Secondly, in the work of the Trotskyist tradition, particularly as elaborated by Tony Cliff, a basis exists for understanding the specific nature and evolution of Stalinism (see Cliff, 1948; cf. Cliff, 1974). Cliff's account of 'state-capitalism' identifies, Callinicos maintains, the contradictions that exist in Stalinist regimes — between an exploiting dominant class which runs the bureaucracy and state factories, and the working classes, excluded from any effective control of the productive forces. It was this contradiction which brought the Stalinist regimes to an 'immense crisis'. While the crisis has been resolved temporarily by the integration of the East European economies into the world capitalist order, the contradictions of this latter order are likely to result in still greater economic and political instability in the future.

Finally, in defining a project of human emancipation, classical Marxists provide an alternative to existing class-ridden regimes in both West and East. In championing a conception of socialism as 'the self-emancipation of the working class', classical Marxism upholds a vision of a 'self-conscious independent movement of the immense majority, in the interest of the immense majority', as Marx once wrote (quoted in Callinicos, 1991, p.18). This is a vision of 'socialism from below', wholly at odds both with the form of governance which used to prevail in the USSR and the Eastern bloc and with the emasculated democracies of the West (Callinicos, 1991, p.18).

The contemporary era is constituted by a single unified economic system (Callinicos, 1991, p.134). However, it is a system marked by exploitation and inequality. 'Really existing capitalism', unlike the myth of self-equilibriating markets, is characterized by: the concentration and centralization of economic power; the growth of multinational

Street-child asleep
in the doorway of
the Bank of Brazil

corporations beyond the control of individual nation-states; cyclical
crises involving over-production, anarchy and waste; poverty in the
heartlands of the West and massive disparities in life chances between
the West and the Rest; and the creation of life-threatening side-effects of
uncontrolled capitalist accumulation in the form, for example, of global
warming (Callinicos, 1991, pp.98–106). In Callinicos's judgement,
'capitalism stands condemned'; it is time to resume the classical Marxist
project (ibid., pp.106, 134–6).

ACTIVITY 2   You should now read **Reading B, 'The end of socialism?'**, by Alex
Callinicos. Note especially his remarks on:

- the differences between Marxism and Stalinism;
- the 'capital importance' of classical Marxism and the resources it
  provides for understanding and criticizing Stalinism;
- the 'basic choices' faced in the late twentieth century, and the
  grounds for thinking that classical Marxism offers the best alternative
  to 'the anarchy and injustice of capitalism'.

3.1 CRITICAL RESPONSE

In the liberal tradition of the nineteenth and twentieth centuries, the political has often been equated with the world of government and the citizen's relation to it. Where this equation is made, and where politics is regarded as a sphere apart from the economy or culture, a vast domain of what is central to politics in other traditions of thought tends to be excluded from view. Marxism has been at the forefront of the criticism of this position, maintaining that it proceeds as if classes did not exist, as if the relationship between classes were not exploitative, as if classes did not have fundamental differences of interest, and as if these differences of interest did not largely define economic and political life. The key source of contemporary power — private ownership of the means of production — is, Marxism holds, ostensibly depoliticized by liberalism; that is, it is arbitrarily treated as if it were not a proper subject of politics.

The Marxist critique of liberalism, as Callinicos rightly stresses, raises important questions — above all, about whether productive relations and market economies can be characterized as non-political and, thus, about whether the interconnections between economic power and the state can be anything but a central matter in politics. But it also raises difficulties by postulating (even in its subtler versions) a direct connection between the political and the economic spheres. By seeking to understand the political by reference to economic and class power, and by rejecting the notion of politics as a form of activity *sui generis*, Marxism itself tends to marginalize or exclude from politics certain types of issues: essentially, all those issues which cannot be reduced to class-related matters. Important examples are ecological questions, or issues raised by the domination of women by men or of certain racial and ethnic groups by others. Other central matters neglected include the power of public administrators or bureaucrats over their clients, the use and role of resources which build up in most social organizations to sustain authority, and the form and nature of electoral institutions.

One of the chief problems with a position such as Callinicos's, therefore, concerns the questions which arise when the capitalist order is presented as an all embracing totality within which all aspects of social, political and cultural life are, in principle, located. Some mechanisms of institutional ordering (the states-system, the military order, for instance) and some types of social relationship (gender inequality and ethnic discrimination, for example) pre-existed the advent of modern capitalism, and have retained a distinctive role in the formation and structuring of modernity (see the discussions in Book 1 (Hall and Gieben, 1992), Chapter 2; Book 2 (Allen *et al.*, 1992), Chapters 1 and 2; Book 3 (Bocock and Thompson, 1992), Chapter 1). Among the implications of this are that the concepts of mode of production and class analysis are too limiting. The thesis of the primacy of production and class relations has to be discarded, though this should not be taken to mean that the analysis of class and class conflict becomes insignificant (see Book 3 (Bocock and Thompson, 1992), Chapter 1, and the Introduction to this volume).

There are additional questions to raise, especially about the relationship of classical Marxism to democracy. If not all differences of interest can be reduced to class, and if differences of opinion — for example, about the allocation of resources — can stem from a variety of positions, it is important to create the institutional space for the generation of, and debate about, alternative political strategies and programmes, as many of the social movements in Central and Eastern Europe sought to do from 1989 onward. Indeed, without such a space it is hard to see how citizens could be active participants in the determination of the conditions of their own association. Politics involves discussion and negotiation about public policy — discussion and negotiation which cannot take place according to wholly impartial or objective criteria, for there are none. (Even the philosophy of science is well known for continuous controversy about what criteria are suitable for the resolution of disputes among competing theoretical positions (see Chapter 7 of this volume).) A series of institutional procedures and mechanisms for debating and taking decisions about public affairs is, accordingly, essential. Marx defended the role of elections to choose those who might represent local views and interests: delegates who would be mandated to articulate particular positions and who would be subject to recall if they failed in this respect (see Book 1 (Hall and Gieben, 1992), Chapter 2). He was aware of the practical importance of being able to remove delegates from office. Callinicos shares this view. But such a position is, in my judgement, by no means sufficient (see Held, 1987, pp.135–9).

The fundamental problem with Marx's view of politics, and 'the end of politics' in a post-capitalist order (for politics will end when class is abolished in this account), is that it cannot accept as legitimate in and of itself any description of political difference; that is, it does not accept the notion that an individual or group has a right to hold, and negotiate about, a politically different opinion as an equal member of a polity (Polan, 1984, p.77). Marx's conception of politics in fact radically delegitimizes politics within the body of the citizenry. He saw systematic differences of political view as reflecting, above all, class interests in capitalist societies. Consequently, after the revolution, there is the strong likelihood that there can be only one genuine form of 'politics'; for there will no longer be any justified grounds for fundamental disagreement. The end of class means the end of any legitimate basis for dispute: only classes have irreconcilable interests.

It is hard to resist the view that implicit in this position is a propensity to an authoritarian form of politics (Held, 1987, pp. 135–9). There appears to be no scope for systematically encouraging and tolerating disagreement and debate about public matters. Marx, it seems, underestimated the significance of the liberal preoccupation with how to secure freedom of criticism and action — i.e. choice and diversity —

in the face of political power (although this is by no means to say that
the traditional liberal formulation of the problem is fully satisfactory;
see Section 6).

The upshot of this argument is that Stalinism is not simply an
aberration of the Marxist project — a wholly separate and distinct
political phenomenon. Rather, it is an outcome — though by no means
the only possible one — of the 'deep structure' of Marxist categories,
with their emphasis on the centrality of class, the universal standpoint
of the proletariat, and a conception of politics which roots it squarely in
production. The contributions to politics of other forms of social
structure, collectivity, agency, identity, interest and knowledge are
severely underestimated. This argument does not imply that Stalinism
was the inevitable result of the revolution of 1917; there were many
complex conditions which determined the fate of the revolution. But it
does imply that Marxism has misunderstood the liberal and liberal-
democratic preoccupation with the form and limits of state power, and
that this misunderstanding is an inextricable part of classical Marxist
political theory. Moreover, it is a misunderstanding rich in implications
for how one conceives politics, democracy and the nature of political
agency. (For an alternative view, one which, however, I find ultimately
unconvincing, see Callinicos's reply to this criticism in Chapter 4 of *The
Revenge of History* (Callinicos, 1991).)

The argument that what failed in the Soviet Union is simply Stalinism,
or the state-capitalist regime, is problematic. For it was not a form of
capitalism which failed but, rather, a form of what I call 'state-
administered socialism'. There are several different variants of state-
administered socialism, from the state socialist societies of the former
Eastern bloc to the traditional social democratic regimes of the West.
While there are major differences between these types, which I by no
means wish to underestimate, they also have certain elements in
common: all can be associated with centrally controlled bureaucratic
institutions. The programme of state-administered socialism lost its
radical appeal precisely because it failed to recognize the desirable form
and limits of state action.

State-administered socialism assumed that state power could become
the caretaker of existence. Intervening in social life by securing capital
investment, managing employment and expanding welfare
opportunities, the state tended to assume omniscience over questions of
needs and wants. In retrospect, it is hardly surprising that among its
unforeseen effects were the generation of a marked distrust of those in
charge of the apparatus of government, a deep scepticism about
expertise, and a general decline in the legitimacy of 'socialism' (see
Held, 1989, Chapters 5–6). Many citizens came to assume that socialism
meant bureaucracy, surveillance, red tape, and state control — views
prevalent not only in the New Right (and in the mass media's images of
the Soviet Union), but also among those in daily contact with, for
example, certain branches of the Western welfare state, e.g. social
security offices, social services, housing authorities and city planners.

Some of the difficulties created by state-administered socialism, in both its state socialist and social democratic variants, are explored in Reading C by David Miller.

ACTIVITY 3   You should now read **Reading C, 'Varieties of socialism'**, by David Miller. Note particularly his remarks about the relation between state planning and democracy.

To summarize, the 'crisis of socialism', in theory and in practice, goes much further than the 'crisis of Stalinism'. The relationship between socialism and democracy has to be re-thought, as does the relationship between capitalism and modernity more broadly. There are notable theoretical and practical reasons, I have suggested, for scepticism about some of the dominant elements of the traditional socialist project.

4 FROM MODERNITY TO POST-MODERNITY?

For Fukuyama, modernity can be characterized as the victory of a distinctive concept of the political — the liberal concept. Modernity is the reshaping of the world according to liberal principles. For Callinicos, modernity is *capitalist* modernity. It is the capitalist nature of modern societies and states which gives them their distinctive character. Anthony Giddens is among those who have resisted the equations of modernity with liberalism, or modernity with capitalism. While Giddens draws heavily on the thought of Marx, among others, he does so in a critical way, emphasizing the multi-dimensional nature of modernity, its complex causal patterns and institutional logics, and the inherently contingent qualities of political and social change. The fourth reading, Reading D, by Giddens, succinctly captures this difference of emphasis.

In Giddens's view, there are four main institutional aspects to modernity: (a) capitalism (the system of production of commodities for markets, in which wage labour is also a commodity); (b) industrialism (the application of inanimate sources of power through productive techniques for the transformation of nature); (c) coordinated administrative power focused through surveillance (the control of information and the monitoring of the activities of subject populations by states and other organizations); and (d) military power (the concentration of the means of violence in the hands of the state). These four institutional dimensions of modernity are irreducible to one another, for the form and logic of each one are quite different from those of the others. The development and dynamics of military power and warfare, for example, affected the shape and structure of capitalist development as well as particular patterns of class and class conflict, and helped generate an alternative power system to capital: the modern system of nation-states. The formation of the nation-state system and the dynamics of international security (and insecurity) cannot, therefore, simply be understood by reference to the logic and dynamics of capitalism (see Giddens, 1990b; and Book 1 (Hall and Gieben, 1992), Chapter 2). In Giddens's judgement, each of the four institutional dimensions consists of a distinctive set of causal processes and structures. Taken together, however, they provide a framework for understanding some of the central features, developments and tensions in modern societies.

Advertising hoardings in central Dhaka, Bangladesh. Whom are they appealing to?

Giddens holds that Marx's analysis of the mechanisms of capitalist production and exchange, and his critical deciphering of the forms of class domination and exploitation, retain their relevance today. But he argues that, however important Marx's contributions may be, there are massive lacunae in Marx's thought and in Marxism more generally, which mean that it cannot simply be updated or amended. These lacunae relate to the different dimensions of modernity and include: the absence of a satisfactory account of power, particularly military power and the use of violence by individuals, collectivities and states; an inadequate analysis of administrative power and its distinctive crystallization in nation-states; and a refusal to consider sources and forms of systematic conflict which cannot be related directly to class.

According to Giddens, each institutional complex of modernity should be understood as an area of contestation or conflict. The working-class or labour movement was always only one type of collective response to the process of change inaugurated by modern conditions. By equating capitalism with modernity, and working-class struggles with non-sectarian, progressive interests — i.e. by making the standpoint of the labour movement the general or universal standpoint — Marx failed to grasp two central matters: first, that there are forms of politics which cannot be understood from the perspective of class alone; and, secondly, that a 'critical' account of modernity must embrace a far wider perspective than labour interests if it is to claim to represent 'a humane and just social order'.

Giddens explores connections between the four central dimensions of modernity and four social movements which are both constituted by these dimensions and active agents in their re-formation. If the labour movement emerged as a product of, and critical response to, the capitalist labour contract, the environmental movement can be seen as the outcome of, and challenge to, ecological degradation which has followed in the wake of industrialism. The sites of the civil and human rights movements have been systems of unaccountable power, while the peace movement is the product of, and a key force against, the contemporary structure of military power. Linking the 'alternative visions' of these movements to an analysis of the structural possibilities of transition offered by the institutions of modernity — a perspective Giddens calls 'utopian realism' — yields a reconceptualization of what might be 'beyond modernity' . Figure 1.1 maps the institutional clusters and movements of modernity to the future projects and institutional elements of a 'post-modern' order.

Rethinking socialism after the revolutions of 1989–90, Giddens contends, means exploring alternative institutional orders to each of the key dimensions of modernity. Only such an exploration can take us

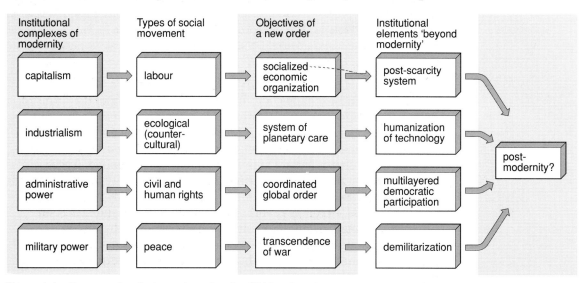

Figure 1.1   From modernity to post-modernity: Giddens's scheme

beyond modernity to envisage a post-modern order. Such an order is both far more difficult to imagine and far more complex to realize than earlier socialists or utopians had thought. Nonetheless, future-oriented social movements and an understanding of the institutional dynamics of modernity provide clues to new possibilities. While a post-modern order will be institutionally complex, it will represent a movement beyond modernity along each of the four dimensions already distinguished.

The unregulated pursuit of capitalist expansion is as unviable an option in contemporary circumstances as the survival of state socialist societies. If socialism means rigorously planned production, organized primarily within the nation-state, we know that it cannot work any longer. But nor can ceaseless capitalist accumulation, for it is not self-sustaining in terms of resources, and the massive disparities it creates between the life chances of different groups and regions bears a cost in human terms that few can accept on reflection. (The number of people who die of malnutrition each year is equivalent to dropping a Hiroshima bomb every three days, yet this is not for want of adequate food production on a global scale (see Bennett and George, 1987).) In contrast, Giddens defends the possibility of a regulated market order embedded in a post-scarcity economic system in which the developed societies make major adjustments in their economies and life-styles in order to foster greater prosperity in the less-developed world.

Such a development depends, in turn, on a more coordinated global political order, and this, Giddens believes, could emerge. Trends toward increasing globalization are forcing states to collaborate ever more with one another (albeit in a variety of different forms), just as they are increasing spaces 'below' the level of nation-states for enhanced democratic participation — by groups and movements, for example, that have gained greater autonomy as a result of the weakening of old state structures. These trends can only be effective, however, if they are linked to transformations in the sphere of military power, and these too Giddens thinks are possible. Few states today stand to gain anything durable from territorial aggrandizement faced as they are with the destructive power of military technology and the interconnectedness of peoples and territories.

Finally, Giddens argues that while certain destructive trends in the earth's eco-systems may have proceeded too far to be reversed, it is also the case that there are significant counter-trends, which might be safeguarded by the institutional complexes of a post-modern order. Although one can make no assumption that world events will move in the direction outlined by these various 'utopian considerations', 'all discussions', Giddens holds, 'which propose … possible futures, including this one, can by their very nature make some impact' (1990b, p.171). A critical account of modernity remains an indispensable project.

ACTIVITY 4   You should now read **Reading D, 'Socialism, modernity, and utopianism'**, by Anthony Giddens, and carefully consider it. Note the reasons Giddens gives for:

- characterizing modernity as a 'multi-dimensional' phenomena;
- separating out the achievements and limitations of a variety of social movements;
- asserting that socialism cannot any longer be equated with the 'overcoming of capital';
- the perspective of 'utopian realism' and his view of the 'far side of modernity'.

4.1   CRITICAL RESPONSE

Giddens's emphasis on the multi-dimensional nature of modernity, with its distinctive and complex patterns of change and development, offers advantages over theories which ignore or play down the significance of certain crucial institutions (e.g. military power) because of their single-minded focus on one set of explanatory terms (e.g. class struggle); or which fail to recognize the role of certain phenomena (e.g. forms of economic power) in relation to their categories (e.g. market relations) and, hence, conveniently disregard important questions (e.g. the links between economic and political liberty). Likewise, Giddens's view of the interconnectedness of states and societies, and of the entwinement of the national and international in shaping the modern era, offers significant advances over most of the leading nineteenth- and twentieth-century perspectives on societal change which assumed all too often that the origins of social transformation are to be found in processes internal to society — in its power structures (liberalism) or productive relations (Marxism). Moreover, his consistent attempt to think about the 'far side' of modernity — i.e. whatever lies beyond modernity — along a number of institutional axes offers important insights into both the autonomy and interrelatedness of different types of social change and, accordingly, into the weaknesses of most existing models of transformation (based, for instance, on politics or economics, on structural factors or social processes, on the local or the global).

Giddens's broad theoretical position is close to that found in a number of chapters in the volumes of this series. This is due partly to his influence on contemporary sociological debate and partly to a general rethinking of the classical sociological tradition undertaken in the last two decades; a process that has led to a convergence of viewpoints on some questions. Giddens's stress on the constitution of modernity by a cluster of institutions overlaps in particular with the standpoint of some of the authors in Book 1 (Hall and Gieben, 1992); see, for example, my chapter, Chapter 2. Yet, it is also striking that certain institutional dimensions and spheres of activity play no part in his scheme; for instance, law, culture and the separation of 'the public' and 'the private', the latter being perhaps one of the most distinctive features of modernity (see Book 1 (Hall and Gieben, 1992), Chapter 4; and Book 3 (Bocock and Thompson, 1992), Chapter 1). These lacunae raise questions about the comprehensiveness of Giddens's account and about its ability to illuminate some central shifts in social and political relations — for example, changing patterns and forms of public law, transformations in national and cultural identity, alterations in the relation between the domestic and familial spheres and those of waged work and politics; or, to put the point differently, between gender relations and citizenship, participation in politics and social welfare.

Likewise, many social movements — from religious groups to feminist activists — have no role in Giddens's scheme, suggesting again that his conceptual framework may not make adequate allowance for some of the key pressure points in contemporary culture and politics; indeed, that it mistakenly allows no place for those movements, or to the institutions to which they can be related, because they are not part of modernity and its dynamics, as he understands them. In addition, the type of connections Giddens draws between distinctive social movements and institutional clusters are themselves far from clear. Different movements, changing orientations over time (from civil concerns to perhaps wider political and social issues), and their different institutional locations at any given moment (economy, polity, local community, etc.), cannot easily be accommodated on a conceptual map which posits essentially fixed or static relations between particular institutional clusters and social groupings (see Held, 1989).

While Giddens rightly emphasizes the shifting significance and causal weight to be allocated to particular institutional dimensions over time, his account is ambiguous on certain significant questions: complexity of categories is *no guarantee* of either comprehensiveness or precision on key issues. For instance, Giddens does not adequately establish how and to what extent the modern state is enmeshed in industrial capitalism and, thus, the degree to which it can become an effective site of political transformation. Giddens's position wavers between seeing the state as a 'capitalist state' and as a 'power system' in and of itself. Or, to put the point another way, 'the relative primacies of class vs. non-class conflicts and economic vs. political power in Giddens's analysis of capitalist nation-states remains uncertain' (Jessop, 1989, p.122). The implications of this ambiguity are important, because if the non-capitalist features of the modern state are not adequately separated out, one cannot grasp many of the distinctive elements of modern politics — for instance, the centrality (in principle) of an 'impersonal' structure of public power, of constitutional forms, and of a diversity of power centres within and outside of the state. Nor can one grasp many of the central factors involved in shaping the dynamics and forms of the existing state-system itself — factors which relate directly to the interrelations of states, to the structural features of the international political system, and to the 'security dilemma' facing modern states, putting pressure on them to prepare for war in order to secure peace (see Book 1 (Hall and Gieben, 1992) Chapter 2; and Book 2 (Allen *et al.*, 1992), Chapter 2). And if these factors are not adequately understood, it is doubtful whether the 'far side' of modernity can be properly conceived.

Finally, the persuasiveness of Giddens's conception of a post-modern order is weakened by difficulties on three additional counts. First, it is not underpinned by a political theory which recasts systematically the meaning of the political good in relation to the interconnected institutions and issues we face today. Giddens's own conception of 'a humane and just social order', 'a common concern with the stewardship of the globe's resources', and a 'post-scarcity' economic system is, at best, insufficiently clear. Secondly, the institutional prescriptions he sets forth are in need of further elaboration, because the relation of the institutional clusters to one another is barely theorized and, accordingly, it is hard to know how the institutional logics might mesh together. And, thirdly, the question of which institutions and which agencies might provide a path from modernity to its 'far side' — the whole issue of transitional stages — remains largely unaddressed, though it should not be if 'utopia' is to be 'realistic'.

In short, some fundamental issues are left aside. Of course, it is easy to put difficult questions to an author; and it is unreasonable to expect them all to be fully addressed. Nonetheless, it does not seem wholly unfair to put a wide range of issues to theorists like Giddens, precisely because they offer visions of life not only as it is, but also as it might and should be. Before we accept their accounts as guiding orientations, we need to be sure of their coherence and cogency.

5   THE STORY SO FAR, AND THE QUESTION OF THE POLITICAL GOOD

The East European revolutions were, without doubt, an historical watershed. The collapse of the Soviet empire, and the retreat of communism across Europe, were not only major events of the twentieth century but probably of modern history as well. Ripples of change spread through political institutions and conventional beliefs across the globe.

The diverse interpretations of the revolutions, and of their impact upon the contemporary world, reflect at least two things: history is not at an end and ideology is not dead. Liberalism and Marxism, prominent modernist ideologies with roots stretching back into the formative moments of modernity, remain alive and kicking. While liberalism is clearly in the ascendant, Marxism is not yet exhausted. Nonetheless, both positions, I have argued, are wanting in fundamental respects.

New accounts of the complexity of modernity have been elaborated which throw further into relief some of the limitations of earlier traditions of political and social thought. But these new accounts, exemplified here by Giddens's multi-dimensional view of the modern world, also generate new questions, not all of which are answered satisfactorily.

Among these questions is a concern about the meaning of the political good, or how one should define the 'good life' in contemporary politics. This is a matter about which Fukuyama, Callinicos and Giddens all have something to say (whether directly or indirectly) and it provides, accordingly, a useful point around which to draw together some of the strands of the previous sections.

For Fukuyama, the good life follows from the progressive recasting of the modern world on liberal principles. For him, political life, like economic life, is — or ought to be — a matter of individual freedom and initiative, and the more it approximates this state of affairs, the more justifiably one might claim that the political good has been achieved. The individual is, in essence, sacrosanct, and is free and equal only to the extent that he or she can pursue and attempt to realize self-chosen ends and personal interests. Equal justice can be sustained between individuals if, above all, individuals' entitlement to certain rights or liberties is respected, and all citizens are treated as equals before the law. The preoccupation here is with the creation and defence of a world in which 'free and equal' individuals can flourish with minimum political impediment, West and East, North and South.

By contrast, Callinicos, and classical Marxists more generally, defend the desirability of certain social or collective goals and means. For them, to take equality and liberty seriously is to challenge the view that these values can be realized by individuals left, in practice, to their own devices in a 'free market' economy and a restricted or minimal state. Equality, liberty and justice — recognized by them as 'great universal ideals' — cannot be achieved in a world dominated by private ownership of property and the capitalist economy; these ideals can be realized only through struggles to ensure that the means of production are socialized, i.e. subject to collective appropriation and to procedures which ensure social control. Only such procedures can ultimately guarantee that 'the free development of each' is compatible with the 'free development of all'.

Although the revolutions of Central and Eastern Europe put democracy at the forefront of politics across the globe, the appeal and nature of democracy itself remains inadequately considered by both Fukuyama and Callinicos. In Fukuyama's writings, democracy is eclipsed by the affirmation of individualist political, economic and ethical doctrines. The question and problem of democratic accountability takes second place, at best, to the imperative of individual liberty in the face of political regulation. In Callinicos's work, the categories of class, class conflict and production displace the necessity of a thorough analysis of democracy. Giddens's conception of the political good shares some of these weaknesses. Not only is the political good undertheorized by him generally, but his position offers no account of the meaning of democracy in the contemporary era. For all its complexity, Giddens's theory of a post-modern order, with its emphasis on the necessity to create a post-scarcity economic system, humanized technology, demilitarized international relations, and increased participation, side-steps the question of how and in what particular ways it will actually be democratic.

Despite the near ubiquity of some form of democracy, its common use in political discourse and its practically universal invocation by political regimes in the late twentieth century, the concept has not been at the centre of theories of modernity or post-modernity. Democracy bestows an 'aura of legitimacy' on modern political life: policies and strategies appear justified and appropriate where they are claimed to be democratic. Yet, under what conditions they may reasonably be considered democratic, and when one can legitimately claim the mantle of democracy, remains unclear. In the final section of this chapter, I should like to turn to this issue in a preliminary way, offering some thoughts on why democracy is so central in the current period, and on what it might mean today. Addressing these issues will, hopefully, throw further light on the meaning of the 'good life' in contemporary politics.

6   DEMOCRACY: BETWEEN STATE AND CIVIL SOCIETY?

Part of the appeal of democracy lies in its denial *in principle* of any conception of the political good other than that generated by 'the people' themselves. From the pursuit of 'no taxation without representation' in seventeenth-century England, to the diverse struggles to achieve a genuinely universal franchise in the nineteenth and twentieth centuries, advocates of greater accountability in government have sought to establish satisfactory means for choosing, authorizing and controlling political decisions (see Book 1 (Hall and Gieben, 1992), Chapter 2). In the East European revolutions, the principle of self-determination and the principle of consent to government action have (once again) challenged the principle of 'single person' or, in this particular case, 'single party' rule (see Book 2 (Allen *et al.*, 1992), Chapter 2). Democracy is conceived as a way of containing the powers of the state and of mediating among competing individual and collective projects. In political circumstances constituted by a plurality of identities, cultural forms and interests, each perhaps articulating different prescriptive regimes, democracy is seen, moreover, as offering a basis for tolerating and negotiating over difference.

In this section I want to argue that democracy should be conceived as the privileged conception of the political good because it offers — in theory at least — a form of politics and life in which there are fair and just ways of negotiating values and value disputes. Democracy is, I think, the only 'grand' or 'meta-narrative' which can legitimately frame and delimit the competing 'narratives' of the contemporary age. Or, to put the point somewhat differently, democratic reason (i.e. thinking democratically) ought to be regarded as the legitimate heir of the Enlightenment project: the project of self-reflection which finds its *raison d'être* in the determination of the conditions of human association (see the Introduction to this volume, and Chapter 7). But why exactly should this be so? What is significant about democracy in an age in which some think it represents the end point of history, and others that it represents a sham in its existing form?

The *idea* of democracy is important because it does not just represent one value among many, such as liberty, equality and justice, but is the value which can link and mediate between competing prescriptive concerns. It is a guiding orientation which can help generate a basis for the specification of the relation among different normative concerns. Democracy does not presuppose agreement on diverse values. Rather, it suggests a way of relating values to each other and of leaving the resolution of value conflicts open to participants in a political dialogue, subject only to certain provisions protecting the shape and form of the dialogue itself. In this lies further elements of its appeal.

What form or conception of democracy engenders or encourages political dialogue in practice? Answers to this question, it has already been suggested, cannot simply be found in liberalism or Marxism. Liberalism's desire to create a diversity of power centres and a world marked by openness, controversy and plurality is compromised by the reality of the 'free market', by the structure and imperatives of the system of private capital accumulation. If liberalism's central failure is to see markets as 'powerless' mechanisms of coordination and, thus, to neglect the distorting nature of economic power in relation to democracy, Marxism's central failure is the reduction of political power to economic power and, thus, to neglect — as liberal democrats, among others, point out — the dangers of centralized political power and the problems of political accountability. Marxism's claim to represent the forces of progressive politics is tarnished by socialism's relation in practice, both in the East and in the West, with bureaucracy, surveillance, hierarchy and state control. Accordingly, liberalism's account of the nature of markets and economic power must be rejected, while Marxism's account of the nature of democracy must be severely questioned.

It follows that the liberal and Marxist conceptions of what it is for people to be 'free and equal' in a social order are too limited. Liberals like Fukuyama neglect a wide range of questions concerning the spheres of productive and reproductive relations. Marxists like Callinicos neglect pressing issues about the proper form and limits of the state, and underestimate the dangers of centralized political power and the problems of political accountability. While Giddens's position takes issue with the premises of both liberalism and Marxism, he also leaves out of account certain key political and cultural domains (for instance, those concerning human reproduction and the organization of the household) and, partly as a result, fails to specify some of the central conditions of involvement of women (and men) in public life. These positions generate an unnecessarily, and unacceptably, restricted view of politics and democracy — a view which obscures significant requirements for the realization of a democratic order.

The history of the clash of interpretations about democracy has given rise over time to three basic variants or models of democracy, which it is as well to bear in mind. First, there is *direct* or *participatory democracy*, a system of decision-making about public affairs in which citizens are directly involved. This was the 'original' type of democracy found in Ancient Athens, among other places. Secondly, there is *liberal* or *representative democracy*, a system of rule embracing elected 'officers' who undertake to 'represent' the interests or view of citizens within the framework of the 'rule of law'. Representative democracy means that decisions affecting a community are not taken by its members as a whole, but by a group of people whom 'the people' have elected for this purpose. In the arena of national politics, representative democracy takes the form of elections to congresses, parliaments or similar national bodies. Thirdly, there is a variant of democracy based on a *one-party* model. Until recently, the Soviet Union, many East European societies and some Third World countries have been dominated by this conception. The principle underlying one-party democracy is that a single party can be the legitimate expression of the overall will of the community. Voters choose among different candidates, putatively proposing divergent policies within an overall framework, not among different parties.

What should be made of these various models of democracy today? The participatory model cannot easily be adapted to stretch across space and time. Its emergence in the context of city-states and under conditions of 'social exclusivity' was an integral part of its successful development. (In Athens, women, an extensive slave population, and many other marginal groups were excluded from participating in the polity.) In contemporary circumstances, marked by a high degree of social, economic and political differentiation, it is very hard to envisage how a democracy of this kind could succeed on a large scale (see Held, 1987, Chapter 9). The significance of these reflections is reinforced by examining the fate of the model of democracy advocated by Marx, Engels and their followers. The suitability of their model as an institutional arrangement which allows for mediation, negotiation and compromise among struggling factions, groups or movements, is open to doubt, as I have already noted. A system of institutions to promote discussion, debate and competition among divergent views — a system encompassing the formation of movements, pressure groups and/or political parties with leaderships to help press their cases — appears both necessary and desirable. Further, the changes in Central and Eastern Europe since 1989 seem to provide remarkable confirmatory evidence of this, with their emphasis on the importance of political and civil rights, a competitive party system, and the 'rolling back of the state', i.e. the freeing of civil society from state domination.

In my judgement, one cannot escape the necessity of recognizing the importance of a number of fundamental liberal tenets: concerning the centrality, in principle, of an 'impersonal' structure of public power, of a constitution to help guarantee and protect rights, of a diversity of power centres within and outside the state, of mechanisms to promote competition and debate between alternative political platforms. What this amounts to, among other things, is confirmation of the fundamental liberal notion that the separation of state from civil society must be an essential feature of any democratic political order. Conceptions of democracy that assume that the state can replace civil society, or vice versa, must be treated with the utmost caution.

To make these points is *not*, however, to affirm any one liberal democratic model as it stands, although many advocates of democracy in Eastern Europe appear to take this view. It is one thing to accept the arguments concerning the necessary protective, conflict-mediating and redistributive functions of the democratic state; quite another to accept these as prescribed in existing accounts of liberal democracy from J.S. Mill onward (see Book 1 (Hall and Gieben, 1992), Chapter 2). Advocates of liberal democracy have tended to be concerned, above all else, with the proper principles and procedures of democratic government. But by focusing on 'government', they have attracted attention away from a thorough examination of the relations between:

(a) formal rights and actual rights;

(b) commitments to treat citizens as free and equal, and practices which do neither sufficiently;

(c) concepts of the state as, in principle, an independent authority, and involvements of the state in the reproduction of the inequalities of everyday life;

(d) notions of political parties as appropriate structures for bridging the gap between state and society, and the array of power centres which such parties and their leaders cannot reach.

To ignore these questions is to risk placing 'democracy' in the context of a sea of political, economic and social inequality. And it is to risk the creation of, at best, a very partial form of democratic politics — one in which the participation of some bears a direct relation to the limited or non-participation of others.

The implications of these points are, I believe, profound: for democracy to flourish today it has to be reconceived as a *double-sided* phenomenon; concerned, on the one hand, with the reform of state power and, on the other hand, with the restructuring of civil society.

This entails recognizing the indispensability of a process of 'double democratization': the interdependent transformation of both state and civil society. Such a process must be premised on two principles: (a) that the division between state and civil society must be a central feature of democratic life; and (b) that the power to make decisions must be free of the inequalities and constraints which (as Marx foresaw) can be imposed by an unregulated system of private capital. Of course, to recognize the importance of both these points is to recognize the necessity of recasting substantially their traditional connotations. (For texts which seek to do this, see Held, 1987, 1991; and Keane, 1988.)

If democratic life involves no more than a periodic vote, the locus of people's activities will be the 'private' realm of civil society and the scope of their actions will depend largely on the resources they can command. Few opportunities will exist for citizens to act as citizens: i.e. as participants in public life. But if democracy is understood as a double-sided process, this state of affairs might be redressed by creating opportunities for people to establish themselves 'in their capacity of being citizens' (Arendt, 1963, p.256). Of course, this model of democracy faces an array of possible objections which cannot be pursued here. Hopefully, however, the necessity to think beyond the positions of liberalism and Marxism, and beyond the lacunae in Giddens's theory of modernity and post-modernity, has — at the very least — been established.

7   CONCLUSION

One of the abiding lessons of the twentieth century must surely be that history is not closed and that human progress remains an extraordinarily fragile achievement, however one defines and approaches it. Fascism, Nazism and Stalinism came close to obliterating democracy in the West only 50 years ago. The outcomes of human action, intended and unintended, always generate surprises, some catastrophic, some offering grounds for hope. In this sense, history remains to be made; though, to adapt a saying from Marx, it cannot always be made in circumstances of one's own choosing, for it is often the result of circumstances directly given and transmitted from the past (Marx, 1963, p.15). The struggle for democracy, for a democratic conception of the political good — the 'good life' defined under 'free and equal' conditions of participation — is without guarantees, but it is a struggle for which all can find equally good grounds for commitment, or so I have argued.

Of course, groups or agencies can *refuse* to participate in a democratic dialogue, and if they do there is nothing intrinsic to the idea of democracy that can compel them to participate. If democracy is rejected as a legitimate form of governance, the politics of other forms of governance will come into play. Against this, '1989 and all that'

Militant nationalist supporters in Georgia in October 1989. Can a militant nationalism be contained?

affirmed growing support for the idea of democracy. But it also highlighted the gulf that exists today between different models of democracy, between contemporary liberal democracy and models such as those outlined above in Section 6. By ignoring such differences, Fukuyama could proclaim 'the end of history'; however, I would rather say that we remain in the flux of history with many decisive choices about the character of the contemporary order still to be made.

One area of 'decisive choices' connects the idea of democracy directly to the larger framework of international relations. If the history and practice of democracy has until now been centred on the idea of locality (the city-state, the community, the nation), it is likely that in the future it will be centred on the international or global domain. In a world of progressive global interconnectedness, mediated by modern communication systems and information technology, there are pressing questions about the very future and viability of national democracies. There are no immediate solutions to the problems posed by interconnectedness, with its complex and often profoundly uneven effects; but there is an inescapably important series of questions to be addressed, some of which are the topic of the next chapter. Certainly, one can find many good reasons for being optimistic about finding a path forward, and many good reasons for thinking that at this juncture democracy will face another critical test.

REFERENCES

Allen, J., Braham, P. and Lewis, P. (eds) (1992) *Political and Economic Forms of Modernity*, Cambridge, Polity Press.

Arendt, H. (1963) *On Revolutions*, New York, Viking Press.

Beetham, D. (1991) *The Legitimation of Power*, London, Macmillan.

Berlin, I. (1969) *Four Essays on Liberty*, Oxford, Oxford University Press.

Bennett, J. and George, S. (1987) *The Hunger Machine*, Cambridge, Polity Press.

Bobbio, N. (1987) *Which Socialism?* Cambridge, Polity Press.

Bocock, R. and Thompson, K. (eds) (1992) *Social and Cultural Forms of Modernity*, Cambridge, Polity Press.

Callinicos, A. (1991) *The Revenge of History: Marxism and the East European Revolutions,* Cambridge, Polity Press.

Cliff, T. (1948) 'The nature of Stalinist Russia', *Revolutionary Communist Party Internal Bulletin*, June.

Cliff, T. (1974) *State Capitalism in Russia*, London, Pluto.

Dahl, R.A. (1985) *A Preface to Economic Democracy*, Cambridge, Polity Press.

Dahl, R.A. (1989) *Democracy and its Critics*, New Haven, Yale University Press.

Dunn, J. (1979) *Western Political Theory in the Face of the Future*, Cambridge, Cambridge University Press.

Friedman, J. (1989) 'The new consensus. Part 1: The Fukuyama thesis', *Critical Review*, Vol. 3, Nos.3–4, pp.373–410.

Fukuyama, F. (1989) 'The end of history?' *The National Interest*, No.16, pp.3–18.

Fukuyama, F. (1989/90) 'A reply to my critics', *The National Interest*, No. 18, pp.21–8.

Gadamer, H.-G. (1975) *Truth and Method,* London, Sheed and Ward.

Giddens, A. (1990a) 'Modernity and utopia', *New Statesman,* 2 November, pp.20–2.

Giddens, A. (1990b) *The Consequences of Modernity*, Cambridge, Polity Press.

Hall, S. and Gieben, B. (eds) (1992) *Formations of Modernity*, Cambridge, Polity Press.

Held, D. (1987) *Models of Democracy*, Cambridge, Polity Press.

Held, D. (1989) *Political Theory and the Modern State*, Cambridge, Polity Press.

Held, D. (1991) 'Democracy, the nation-state and the global system', in Held, D. (ed.), *Political Theory Today*, Cambridge, Polity Press.

Himmelfarb, G. (1989) 'Response to Fukuyama', *The National Interest*, No. 16, pp.24–6.

Hirst, P.Q. (1989) 'Endism', *London Review of Books*, 23 November, p.14.

Horkheimer, M. and Adorno, T. (1972) *The Dialectic of Enlightenment*, New York, Herder and Herder.

Jessop, B. (1989) 'Capitalism, nation-states and surveillance', in Held, D. and Thompson J.B. (eds) *Social Theory of Modern Societies: Anthony Giddens and his Critics*, Cambridge, Cambridge University Press.

Keane, J. (1988) *Democracy and Civil Society*, London, Verso.

Kennedy, P. (1988) *The Rise and Fall of the Great Powers*, London, Unwin.

Keohane, R.O. (1984) *After Hegemony: Cooperation and Discord in the World Political Economy*, Princeton, Princeton University Press.

Lewis, P. (1990a) 'The long goodbye: party rule and political change in Poland since martial law', *The Journal of Communist Studies*, 6.1, pp.24–48.

Lewis, P. (1990b) 'Democratization in Eastern Europe', *Coexistence*, 27, pp.245–67.

Lijphart, A. (1984) *Democracies*, New Haven, Yale University Press.

Marx, K. (1963) *The Eighteenth Brumaire of Louis Bonaparte*, New York, International Publishers.

Miller, D. (1989) *Market, State and Community: Theoretical Foundations of Market Socialism*, Oxford, Clarendon Press.

Mortimer, E. (1989) 'The end of history?', *Marxism Today*, November, p.29.

Polan, A.J. (1984) *Lenin and the End of Politics*, London, Methuen.

Thompson, J.B. (1990) *Ideology and Modern Culture*, Cambridge, Polity Press.

READING A   THE END OF HISTORY?

Francis Fukuyama

The triumph of the West, of the Western idea, is evident first of all in the total exhaustion of viable systematic alternatives to Western liberalism. In the past decade, there have been unmistakable changes in the intellectual climate of the world's two largest communist countries, and the beginnings of significant reform movements in both. ...

What we may be witnessing is not just the end of the Cold War, or the passing of a particular period of postwar history, but the end of history as such: that is, the end point of mankind's ideological evolution and the universalization of Western liberal democracy as the final form of human government. This is not to say that there will no longer be events, ... for the victory of liberalism has occurred primarily in the realm of ideas or consciousness and is as yet incomplete in the real or material world. But there are powerful reasons for believing that it is the ideal that will govern the material world *in the long run.* ...

In the past century, there have been two major challenges to liberalism, those of fascism and of communism. ... Fascism was destroyed as a living ideology by World War II. ... The ideological challenge mounted by ... communism was far more serious. Marx, speaking Hegel's language, asserted that liberal society contained a fundamental contradiction that could not be resolved within its context, that between capital and labor, and this contradiction has constituted the chief accusation against liberalism ever since. But surely, the class issue has actually been successfully resolved in the West. ... The egalitarianism of modern America represents the essential achievement of the classless society envisioned by Marx. This is not to say that there are not rich people and poor people in the United States, or that the gap between them has not grown in recent years. But the root causes of economic inequality do not have to do with the underlying legal and social structure of our society, which remains fundamentally egalitarian and moderately redistributionist, so much as with the cultural and social characteristics of the groups that make it up, which are in turn the historical legacy of premodern conditions. ...

The power of the liberal idea would seem much less impressive if it had not infected the largest and oldest culture in Asia, China, ... [where] the past fifteen years have seen an almost total discrediting of Marxism-Leninism as an economic system. ... Economic statistics do not begin to describe the dynamism, initiative, and openness evident in China since the reform began.

China could not now be described in any way as a liberal democracy. At present, no more than 20 percent of its economy has been marketized, and most importantly it continues to be ruled by a self-appointed Communist party which has given no hint of wanting to devolve power. ... Yet the pull

Source: Fukuyama, F. (1989) 'The end of history?' *The National Interest,* No.16, pp.3–4, 8–15, 18.

of the liberal idea continues to be very strong as economic power devolves and the economy becomes more open to the outside world. ...

However, it is developments in the Soviet Union — the original "homeland of the world proletariat" — that have put the final nail in the coffin of the Marxist-Leninist alternative to liberal democracy. ... What has happened in the ... years since Gorbachev's coming to power is a revolutionary assault on the most fundamental institutions and principles of Stalinism, and their replacement by other principles which do not amount to liberalism *per se* but whose only connecting thread is liberalism. This is most evident in the economic sphere. ... There is a virtual consensus among the currently dominant school of Soviet economists now that ... if the Soviet system is ever to heal itself, it must permit free and decentralized decision-making with respect to investment, labor, and prices. ...

In the political sphere, the proposed changes to the Soviet constitution, legal system, and party rules amount to much less than the establishment of a liberal state. ... Nonetheless, the general principles underlying many of the reforms ... come from a source fundamentally alien to the USSR's Marxist-Leninist tradition, even if they are incompletely articulated and poorly implemented in practice. ...

The passing of Marxism-Leninism first from China and then from the Soviet Union will mean its death as a living ideology of world historical significance. ... And the death of this ideology means the growing "Common Marketization" of international relations, and the diminution of the likelihood of large-scale conflict between states.

This does not by any means imply the end of international conflict *per se*. For the world at that point would be divided between a part that was historical and a part that was post-historical. Conflict between states still in history, and between those states and those at the end of history, would still be possible. ... Terrorism and wars of national liberation will continue to be an important item on the international agenda. But large-scale conflict must involve large states still caught in the grip of history, and they are what appear to be passing from the scene.

READING B   THE END OF SOCIALISM?

Alex Callinicos

Left and right ... agree on the moral of the East European revolutions: capitalism has triumphed and Marxism, if not quite finished, is in what may well turn out to be a terminal crisis. ...

This line of reasoning is persuasive only if one is ready to equate Marxism and Stalinism. It is necessary here to be more precise. I say much more about Marxism below. By 'Stalinism' I mean, not one person's rule or even

Source: Callinicos, A. (1991) *The Revenge of History: Marxism and the East European Revolutions*, Cambridge, Polity Press, pp.14–20, 134–6.

a body of beliefs, but the whole system of social power that crystallized in the USSR in the 1930s, was exported to Eastern Europe in the second half of the 1940s, and survived till the late 1980s when it began to collapse, a system characterized by the hierarchically organized control of all aspects of social life, political, economic, and cultural, by a narrow oligarchy seated at the apex of the party and state apparatuses, the *nomenklatura*. The equation then involves the claim that this system of power is the practical realization of Marxism as a political tradition. This equation tends to imply another, namely: Marxism = Leninism = Stalinism. The apostolic (or diabolic) succession thus established involves tracing a direct line of political continuity between Marx's own theoretical and strategic conceptions, the Bolshevik political project which triumphed in October 1917, and the final shape assumed by the post-revolutionary regime in the 1930s. There have, of course, been many attempts to challenge these equations, to argue, for example, that Lenin betrayed Marx's own aspirations. It is, nevertheless, very striking to what extent both opponents and supporters of the USSR have since the 1930s agreed in seeing a continuity connecting Marx and Lenin to Stalinism. They have differed chiefly over whether they approved of the end result. ...

The supposed continuity underlying such praise and condemnation alike cannot be sustained. A qualitative break separates Stalinism from Marx and Lenin. This profound discontinuity can be traced in the historical record, in the process which transformed the Bolshevik Party, even in the 1920s still what Moshe Lewin calls an 'alliance of factions' rather than the monolith of liberal and Stalinist myth, into the apparatus of power, terrorized and terrorizing, that it became by the end of the 1930s. It was a transformation which evoked resistance, notably from Lenin himself during the last months of his active political life in late 1922 and early 1923. Other Bolshevik leaders contributed to the destruction of the traditions of inner-party dissent and debate through their alliances with Stalin during the faction-fights of the 1920s, till they started back in horror at the monster they had helped to create — a process vividly illustrated by the famous meeting in July 1928, when Bukharin, the defeated leader of the Right faction, told his former opponent Kamenev that Stalin was 'a Genghis Khan' who 'will cut our throats' (Trotsky, 1981, pp.379–83). One grouping alone consistently combated Stalinism from 1923 onwards, Trotsky and the Left Opposition. For this they paid a terrible price, Trotsky murdered in exile by a Russian agent, his supporters mainly perishing in the Gulag, where they were one of the few groups actively to organize resistance to the camp regime. Nevertheless, the existence of the Trotskyist tradition, though largely extirpated in the USSR and confined to the margins of the labour movement in the West, is of capital importance, since it indicates that commitment to revolutionary socialism is not equivalent to endorsement of Stalinism.

More than that, this anti-Stalinist continuation of the classical Marxist tradition provides the basis for a socialist response to the East European revolutions. Far from being disconfirmed by the collapse of the Stalinist regimes, Marxism, understood in these terms, is an indispensable means of making sense of them. Marxism is relevant here in three different dimensions. First, Marx constructed what was fundamentally a theory of social transformation. Historical materialism explains the rise and fall of social formations in terms of the underlying conflict that develops between the forces and relations of production and of the class struggle rooted in exploitative social relations which this conflict intensifies. Marx, of course, concentrated on the analysis of one specific socio-economic system, the capitalist mode of production, an analysis deepened and extended by later classical Marxists. One of the most important features of the intellectual revival of Marxism since the late 1960s has been the considerable conceptual refinement and empirical elaboration of historical materialism as a *general* theory of the development and transformation of all societies, pre-capitalist as well as capitalist. ...

But Marxism is, of course, much more than a powerful, historically oriented social theory; from Marx's time onwards, it has defined a political project of human emancipation. This is the second dimension in which Marxism is relevant to the East European revolutions. Marx developed a highly particular conception of socialism, as the self-emancipation of the working class: 'The emancipation of the working class must be achieved by the working class itself' (Marx and Engels, 1975, vol. 24, p.269). This involves, in the first instance, a specific claim about the *agency* of socialist transformation: the exploited class in capitalist society, collectivized by the very conditions of production it experiences, has the interest and capacity and will develop the organization and consciousness required to inaugurate a classless society. At the same time, however, Marx's conception of socialism implies a particular view of the *process of transformation* itself. Socialism is not something which can be achieved on behalf of the working class by some group acting in its name, whether it be a Stalinist 'vanguard' or social-democratic parliamentarians. 'The proletarian movement', Marx says, 'is the self-conscious independent movement of the immense majority, in the interest of the immense majority' (ibid., vol. 6, p.495). His is a conception, in Hal Draper's words, of 'socialism from below', springing from the self-activity of the masses themselves (Draper, 1966). This view of socialist revolution informs Marx's analysis of the Paris Commune of 1871, which concentrates on the dismantling of the bureaucratic state machine by the working people of Paris and its replacement by organs of popular self-government. It is developed by Lenin in *The State and Revolution*, one of whose main themes is the emergence during the Russian Revolutions of 1905 and 1917 of the soviets, councils of factory delegates, which he argued represented the basis of the radically democratic 'Commune-State' that would act as the political framework of the transition to a communist society without classes or a state.

It is this conception of socialism that I employ. ... The discrepancy between it and the 'really existing socialism' that used to prevail in the USSR and Eastern bloc is all too evident. By this measure, it was not socialism which went into its death agonies in the late 1980s. ...

There is, moreover, a third respect in which the classical Marxist tradition is relevant to understanding the East European revolutions. For that tradition gave birth to the first systematic attempt at a social and historical analysis of Stalinism. Trotsky's *The Revolution Betrayed* (1937) pioneered that analysis by locating the origins of the Stalin phenomenon in the conditions of material scarcity prevailing in the Civil War of 1918–21, in which the bureaucracy of party officials began to develop. He concluded that the USSR was a 'degenerated workers' state', in which the bureaucracy had succeeded in politically expropriating the proletariat but left the social and economic foundations of workers' power untouched. ... The Palestinian Trotskyist Tony Cliff refused, however, to accept this line of reasoning. Trotsky's insistence on treating the USSR as a workers' state, despite the dominance of the Stalinist bureaucracy, reflected, according to Cliff, the illicit conflation of the legal form of state ownership of the means of production with the relations of production proper, in which the working class was excluded from any effective control of the productive forces. The USSR and its replicants (*sic*) in China and Eastern Europe were, he argued, bureaucratic state-capitalist societies, in which the bureaucracy collectively fulfilled the role performed under private capitalism by the bourgeoisie of extracting surplus-value and directing the accumulation process.

This analysis, first developed by Cliff in 1947 in what became the basis of his book *State Capitalism in Russia*, provides, in my view, the best framework for understanding the nature and evolution of the Stalinist regimes. In particular, Cliff's theory allowed him to predict that these regimes would be brought down by the working class in whose name they ruled. 'The class struggle in Stalinist Russia', he wrote in 1947, '*must inevitably* express itself in gigantic spontaneous outbursts of millions', which would be 'the first chapter in the victorious proletarian revolution' (Cliff, 1948, p.142; 1974, p.276). At the end of the 1960s Chris Harman gave this perspective a more concrete form, when he analysed the dilemma posed for the Stalinist regimes by the pressures for reform represented by the Prague Spring:

> If reforms, in collaboration with foreign capital or otherwise, are not carried through ..., the chronic crisis of the Russian and East European economies can only grow worse. ... Yet it is also increasingly clear that the bureaucracy is unable to carry through reforms on anything like a successful basis without a split of the proportions that characterized Hungary in 1956 and Czechoslovakia in early 1968. Such a split could only be the prelude to an immense crisis throughout the USSR and Eastern Europe, in which the extra-bureaucratic classes would mobilize behind their own demands.
>
> (Harman, 1970, p.19)

Twenty years later that 'immense crisis' finally exploded. The East European revolutions and the turmoil in the USSR itself are thus the vindication, rather than the refutation, of the classical Marxist tradition as it has been continued by those who have sought to develop a historical materialist analysis of Stalinism itself. ...

Conclusion

In one respect the East European revolutions have simplified matters enormously. There can now be no doubt that we live in a single, unified world system. The illusion that there was a 'socialist third of the world', that a separate, post-capitalist socio-economic system was in the process of construction, has been destroyed, along with most of the regimes supposedly embodying that system. ... But the implications of the collapse of Stalinism go much further. The East European revolutions have accelerated a process already under way — the unification of world politics. Various factors have promoted this tendency: the globalization of capital, the industrialization of portions of the Third World, vast movements of people from the poor to the rich countries, the development of transcontinental telecommunications networks which mean that billions can watch *Dallas,* or the opening of the Berlin Wall, or Nelson Mandela's release. The effect is to encourage people to draw analogies between their situations and those of others, and to take inspiration from apparently remote struggles. ...

More than that, however: in São Paulo and Warsaw, Johannesburg and London, Seoul and Moscow, Cairo and New York, the same basic choices are posed. Do we let the market rip, with all the disastrous consequences that will have for the well-being of humankind and perhaps the survival of the earth? Do we seek to humanize it, as social democracy has sought ineffectually to do since the beginning of the century? Or do we struggle to replace the anarchy and injustice of capitalism with a social system based on the collective and democratic control of the world's resources by working people? It should be clear enough that I prefer the third of these alternatives and that I believe that the classical Marxist tradition represents the best way of pursuing it. ... It is time to resume unfinished business.

References

Cliff, T. (1948) 'The nature of Stalinist Russia', *Revolutionary Communist Party Internal Bulletin*, June.

Cliff, T. (1974) *State Capitalism in Russia*, London, Pluto.

Draper, H. (1966) 'The two souls of socialism', *New Politics*, 5.1.

Harman, C. (1970) 'Prospects for the seventies: the Stalinist states', *International Socialism*, 42.

Marx, K. and Engels, F. (1975–) *Collected Works* (50 vols), London, Lawrence & Wishart.

Trotsky, L.D. (1981) *The Challenge of the Left Opposition, 1928–9*, New York, Pathfinder Press.

READING C   VARIETIES OF SOCIALISM

David Miller

State socialism attempts as far as possible to substitute central planning for the working of economic markets. Its strength is that it allows the enormous resources commanded by the state to be concentrated on specific projects — hence the considerable achievements of the Soviet Union in heavy industry, armaments, space exploration and so forth. Its corresponding economic defect is that planned production is unable to respond as quickly and flexibly to consumers' preferences as a market — hence the well-documented failures of the state socialist systems in the day-to-day production of consumer goods. There are, however, other and perhaps more important criticisms to be made. One is that central planning in practice negates democracy. Given the enormous task involved in comprehensively planning a complex modern economy, there is no way to avoid the creation of a large bureaucratic machine. Even if the formalities of electoral democracy can be preserved (an issue on which the arguments seem to me inconclusive), power will inevitably gravitate to those with the specialist knowledge to oversee the planning apparatus. Thus planning of this kind is of its nature élitist. If we see socialism as involving among other things a more democratic political system, we cannot embrace the statist model.

At a much lower level, central planning severely restricts the scope for workers' self-management. If the latter idea is to have any serious meaning, it must include a substantial degree of control over decisions about which goods and services are to be produced, the technique of production to be used, the scale of the enterprise, and so forth. But a planned economy cannot function unless such decisions are transferred to the central authority, which must set production targets, pricing policy, employment policy, etc. for each unit of production. Thus the scope for workers' control will be confined to relatively minor matters, such as the number of tea-breaks in a day, which have no noticeable impact on the planners' targets. Equally serious, workers' freedom to change employment will be circumscribed. Although labour can be allocated through a market, using wage incentives, each person's choice is confined to the set of jobs that the planners decide to make available. Someone wishing to exercise a skill or try out a new idea not catered for in the plan will be frustrated.

Together with the economic defects referred to earlier, these democratic defects are fatal for state socialism, and in my view justify its poor reputation among ordinary people in the West — a reputation no doubt further sullied by capitalist propaganda, but by no means merely its creature.

The social-democratic alternative is much less obviously flawed. Social democracy can be seen essentially as an attempt to use the power of the state to humanize capitalism. The productive advantages of capitalism are to be retained, but some of its human costs eliminated. First, economic

Source: Miller, D. (1989) *Market, State and Community: Theoretical Foundations of Market Socialism*, Oxford, Clarendon Press, pp.6–9.

management techniques are to be used to smooth out business cycles and maintain full employment, which in turn will increase the bargaining power of workers *vis-à-vis* their employers. Second, the tax system is to be used to correct the excessive inequalities of income and wealth that an unreformed capitalist economy throws up. Third, a politically funded welfare state is to serve to eliminate poverty, provide for those with special needs, and contribute further to the reduction of inequality.

There is no reason to doubt either the practical success or the continuing political appeal of this programme, if compared with a full-blown policy of capitalist *laissez-faire* which not even the most libertarian of present-day governments would dare to follow. But the social-democratic strategy has increasingly evident limitations as an embodiment of socialist ideals. First, it is no longer clear that Keynesian methods can be used in the desired manner to secure full employment, particularly in a heavily unionized economy. The effect may be inflationary, in which case income redistribution is likely to occur less between employers and workers as such than between weakly organized workers and strongly organized workers occupying strategic positions in the economy. Second, there is substantial evidence that the impact of fiscal measures on the overall distribution of income and wealth has so far been quite limited; and the effectiveness of more stringent measures (a more steeply progressive income tax, say, or a wealth tax) must remain open to doubt. Such measures are liable either to be circumvented on a large scale, or else to have damaging repercussions on the economy itself — leading to under-investment, capital flight, and so forth. Finally, although the welfare state has been fairly successful as a means of tackling poverty (in an absolute sense), and of channelling resources to people with special needs, it has been far less successful as a vehicle for overall equality. The reason, in brief, is that freely provided services such as education and medical care may be used more effectively by those who are already better off to an extent which eliminates (and occasionally even reverses) the progressive element in their funding through income tax.

The danger, therefore, with the social-democratic programme is that it may lead merely to an expanded state sector, with a corresponding increase in the tax burden carried by nearly all social groups but without any very appreciable increase in social equality. The perception of this possibility may account for the recent defection of some groups — skilled workers especially — to parties with more libertarian aims.

READING D SOCIALISM, MODERNITY AND UTOPIANISM
Anthony Giddens

Has socialism a future? ... Is all we can hope for an untrammelled global capitalis[m], ... modified and humanised by laws or moral provisions which set the limits to the more cut-throat aspects of capitalist competition? To answer these questions, I shall argue, we have to consider not only the relations between capitalism and socialism, but also the broader problem of the connections between *capitalist development* and *mod-*

ernity. For many commentators, especially those on the Left, who says 'modernity' says 'capitalism': the two are the same. This view certainly has its ancestry in Marx. Although Marx sometimes spoke of 'bourgeois society', and drew a distinction between industrialism and capitalism, the whole thrust of Marx's writings treats capitalist development both as the central dynamic of the modern age and the determining framework for other institutions.

We can only begin effectively to rethink the future of socialism, I believe, if we abandon the equation of modernity and capitalism. Capitalism is undoubtedly one of the great dynamic forces of modern world history. ... Yet capitalism is not the only dynamic influence shaping the modern world, nor is it the only structuring dimension of modernity. In my view, modernity involves four institutional dimensions, which in the real world intertwine in complicated fashion, but which for analytical purposes should be kept separate.

Capitalism, of course, is one of these. Another is *industrialism*. ... If capitalism means a competitive economic system, in which commodities are bought and sold on national and international markets, and in which wage labour also becomes a commodity, it is distinguishable from industrialism. By industrialism we can understand a certain *type of production process*, linked directly to specific modes of social organisation. Industrialism presumes the applying of inanimate sources of power to production technology, and thus represents a prime medium of the interaction between human beings and the material world. ... Neither capitalism nor industrialism can be reduced to the other: they are, in some part, independent influences upon modern social and economic development.

A third, and fundamental, dimension of modernity ... is the emergence of coordinated *administrative power*. The nation-state is the prime site of such power, but it is also a distinguishing feature of modern organisations in general. Administrative power, as Foucault above all has helped us understand, is based upon control of information. Modernity has not just recently become an 'information society': it was such from its very beginnings. Indeed, the control and dissemination of information, as facilitated through the invention of printing, was one of the main conditions making possible modernity's rise. Administrative power is focused through *surveillance*: the use of information routinely to monitor the activities of subject populations, whether in the state, business organisations, schools or prisons. No less than capitalism or industrialism, surveillance is a means of levering the modern social world away from traditional modes of social activity.

The fourth dimension of modernity concerns power in a yet more direct sense, namely, *military power*. Neglect of the role of the military in, and of the impact of war on, modern society has been every bit as pronounced on the Left as has the failure to confront informational power. Once more, the

Source: Giddens, A. (1990) 'Socialism, modernity and utopianism'; a version of this essay appeared as 'Modernity and utopia' in *New Statesman and Society*, 2 November, pp.20–2.

origins of this situation can be traced back to Marx. Under the tutelage of Engels, Marx read Clausewitz, and interested himself in military tactics. Yet military power was only understood in two guises: in terms of the repressive agencies of the state, and the potentiality for revolutionary violence. War-making was not systematically analysed in relation to the nation-state or to the geo-political involvements of states in the international arena.

If we grasp the multi-dimensional character of modernity, we can see why the *labour movement* — the counter-action to capitalism — was actually only one type of collective oppositional response to modern transformations. Particularly in the current era, it has become very apparent that other types of movement, which may be at some distance from the labour movement, have a fundamental part to play in influencing modernity and its future. *Ecological movements*, for instance, can be linked to the dimension of industrialism, which has not only helped bring about environmental degradation, but has dominated human relations with nature in the modern period. Industrialism has produced a 'created environment', the result of rampant technological intervention into the natural world. Ecological movements represent a counter-response to the dynamics of the created environment.

They can in turn be distinguished from *civil and human rights movements*, which have not only been prominent in the West, but have clearly helped inspire the transitions occurring in Eastern Europe. Such movements have surveillance as their site of opposition; they are concerned to increase, in one sense or another, democratic participation within arenas of administrative power. ... We have a clear basis for seeing why such struggles are so consequential if we understand that they connect to basic institutional characteristics of modernity as a whole.

Peace movements have as their site of opposition the expansion of military power, particularly in the context of 'the industrialising of war'. Again, many on the Left have traditionally seen warfare as stemming from the expansionist ambitions of capital. No doubt capitalism, both as a real institutional force and as an ideology, has on occasion provided the motive power for war. Yet — as the advent of the Soviet Union and other socialist states made clear — the propensity to wage war is not simply an outcome of capitalist organisation. The accumulation of weaponry has its own internal logic. ... Armies become self-serving bureaucratic organisations, interested in the expansion of their resources; while technological transformations constantly increase the destructive potential of weaponry.

It was never possible for socialism to claim to be 'on the far side' of modernity along all of these dimensions. Marx was able to regard socialism as an all-embracing project because of the connections he drew between the dialectics of history and the transcendence of capitalist enterprise. The working class was the 'universal' class which, in making the revolution, would represent the interests of humanity as a whole. Today it is clear that these connections were false. In whatever guise socialism can be defended, it has nothing specifically to do with the interests of the working class, which is not a privileged historical agent. If socialism in some sense is about the overcoming of capitalism, this is not a project which can bear the weight of the totality of reconstructions needed to produce a humane and just social order.

Marx sought to distance himself from utopianism. Indeed, in Marx's hands the idea of 'utopian socialism' became a derogatory stereotype. ... In one sense Marx was surely right. ... Utopianism is at best irrelevant if it is not in some way connected to immanent possibilities of transformation. What is called for, therefore, is an interpretation of the structural possibilities of transition offered by the institutions of modernity. ... [Unlike Marx, however, I think the] utopian moment is crucial, for without it there is no transcendence. Utopianism in this sense has to go beyond the dynamism already intrinsic to modernity: it has to envisage futures whose achievement is both contingent and highly risky. I call the conjunction of these characteristics *utopian realism*.

The principle of utopian realism can be applied to each of the several dimensions of modernity. Consider, first — to reverse the previous order — the case of military power and war. We live today in a world in which there is the constant application of industrial technology to the means of waging war, and in which the arms trade is diffusing First World weaponry across the globe. Quite apart from nuclear weaponry, the destructive power of conventional armaments is now immense. Moreover, it is entirely possible that, at some point, weapons equivalent in their destructive power to nuclear arms, but cheap and easy to construct, will become available.

Given the militarisation of world society, it might appear completely utopian to envisage the world free from war. Indeed it *is* utopian: but it is not a utopia wholly without connection to immanent trends of development. For the Clausewitzian dictum — that war takes over where diplomacy ends — becomes reversed once military power has become so destructive that any gains it offers are negated. Most large-scale wars in earlier periods of modernity were fought with territorial imperatives in mind. In the present day ... when the nation-state system has become completely universal, and most states' boundaries fixed, the possibilities of territorial aggrandisement of the traditional sort become radically diminished. We can add to this the sheer impact of global interdependence: it becomes more and more apparent that, for many issues, as the German sociologist Ulrich Beck puts it, there are 'no others': all nations share certain communal interests.

Given certain trends of future development — to which organisations such as the peace movement can hope directly to contribute — it is possible to envisage a world free from the travails of large-scale war. On the other hand, such a vision clearly remains utopian: there are many divisions of interest, and many contingencies, which could provoke massive conflict, even conflict leading to the destruction of humanity as such. *High consequence risks* — risks affecting many millions of people, up to and including humanity as a whole — are an inevitable part of the globalised universe of social relations which modernity has produced. However much we verge towards utopia, such risks inevitably remain.

We find a similar admixture of hope and real possibilities for change along a second dimension of modernity: that of administrative power and surveillance. The development of information technology and the intensifying of the information systems yield possibilities of centralised control far beyond those available in pre-modern social orders. Areas of secrecy can become increased and the ordinary citizenry may be deprived of information to which only dominant groups have access. More disturbingly, information control is a medium of totalitarian power, given the capabilities of modern states and the giant transnational corporations. The overall drift of modern society, therefore, might very well be towards a renewed authoritarianism.

Yet the perspective of utopian realism would suggest that *radical democratisation,* affecting many spheres of social life, and perhaps extending right up to the global level, can be achieved. There are very few states in the world which do not call themselves 'democratic', and this is not mere rhetoric. For increasing interdependence, both within states and across their boundaries, means that underprivileged groups have many opportunities to actualise sources of countervailing power. Debates about the nature and limits of specific democratic forms will continue. But it is by no means completely utopian to suppose that thorough-going processes of democratisation can be achieved in many spheres: within the state itself, but also within the workplace, local associations, media organisations and transnational groups.

World government, in some form or another, forms part of the scenario of utopian realism in this sphere. Whether or not some form of global super-state emerges, from a utopian point of view it is essential that states and other organisations collaborate to resolve issues which in previous eras might have been approached in a more fragmented or divisive way. The possibilities of totalitarian power loom as large here as in the more restricted contexts of surveillance. A utopian engagement with immanent trends in global political integration would, however, place as central the opportunity to connect local democratic mechanisms with global involvements.

As regards the created environment, the third dimension of modernity, utopian realism suggests the possibility of radical transformations in our relations to nature. The overall trajectory of development of modernity clearly points towards the ever-increasing subjection of the natural world to industrial technology. The constant revision of technology, so characteristic of modern social life, derives in some part from pressures towards capitalist accumulation. But in substantial degree it has also become autonomous: chronic innovation is built into the relation of science and technology. No one can say with any certainty whether this trend can be reversed, or in fact whether the destruction of the earth's eco-systems has proceeded so far as to become irreversible. Yet it is plain also that there are significant counter-trends, pioneered by the green movement, and also by womens' movements, as well as reaching through to public consciousness in a very general way. From the perspective of utopian realism, such counter-trends would be mobilised as part of a radical re-thinking of how human beings should relate to the natural world (and also to each other).

We do not yet know in full what a system of ecologically sensitive 'planetary care' might actually look like, but it seems clear that it would involve a remoralising process. In other words, 'environmental ethics' would be a key element of utopian scenarios which might be developed.

Finally, we return to the question of capitalism and socialism. What can socialism possibly mean if the term can no longer be identified either with planned production or with the universalising demands of the working class? The notion of socialism, of course, is a rich and complex one, having meanings well beyond those specified by Marx. In its broader sense, socialism represents the antithesis of sectional interest. Perhaps, then, we should reformulate socialism today to express humanity's *common concern for the stewardship of its resources.* Socialism in this sense would still be 'on the far side' of capitalism, but it would no longer be regarded primarily as an alternative method of managing and distributing the fruits of industrial production. It would not be a 'third way' between unfettered capitalism and the state socialism now being dismantled in Eastern Europe and the Soviet Union. There is no 'third way'. On the level of the nation-state, one could argue that there is only '*one* way'. Unregulated capitalism, as we know from the example of the United States, produces an economic order riven with inequalities; state socialism is an experiment now explicitly being abandoned. The 'one way' of producing an economically effective, yet reasonably just, economic order within national states is social democracy, a workable mix of market and limited state economic intervention.

Utopian realism, however, would insist that history does not end at this point. 'On the far side' of capitalism and state socialism we see the possibility of a *post-scarcity economic order*, probably coordinated on a global level. From one angle, nothing could appear more blatantly utopian: for how could we seriously contemplate the construction of a post-scarcity order when large segments of the world's population still live in grinding poverty? Yet a note of realism at once interjects itself. For an immediate response is: how can we survive, as collective humanity, in our global situation unless at some point the unending accumulation process is brought to an end, or at least made subject to stringent moral limitation? A global post-scarcity order would not necessarily be one in which economic growth has been abandoned altogether; but it would be one in which radical life-style adjustments were undertaken in the developed societies as a means of fostering greater prosperity in the less-developed regions. ... We still have a world to win!

CHAPTER 2 A GLOBAL SOCIETY?

Anthony McGrew

CONTENTS

1   INTRODUCTION

One of the most significant legacies of the Enlightenment for modern social and political thought has been the belief that the universal community of humankind is in all respects '… the end or object of the highest moral endeavour' (Bull, 1977, p.27). Underlying this vision is an assumption that at root the needs and interests of all human beings are universally similar. Such a vision has shaped the emancipatory aspirations of both liberalism and Marxism, which have been committed to the eradication of those structures — the state and capitalism respectively — deemed to suppress the realization of a cosmopolitan world order based upon liberty, justice and equality for all of humanity. As the end of the twentieth century approaches, the growing recognition, reinforced by satellite images from space, that planet earth is a single 'place' has reawakened intellectual interest in Enlightenment notions of a universal community of humankind. Moreover, 'surface' events, such as the end of the Cold War, the collapse of communism and the Soviet Union, the transition from industrialism to post-industrialism, the global diffusion of democratic institutions and practices, together with the intensification of patterns of worldwide economic, financial, technological and ecological interdependence, have signalled to many observers the final clearing away of the old world order, with all its menacing features, and the inauguration of a new world order which contains the promise of an evolving world society, a single global 'community of fate'. Certainly, there can be little doubt that the world is being remade around us, that radical changes are under way which may be transforming the fundamental parameters of modern human, social and political existence. Rosenau proclaims that the world has entered the era of post-international politics, a 'historical breakpoint' in which '… present premises and understanding of history's dynamics must be treated as conceptual jails' (Rosenau, 1990, p.5).

'Spaceship Earth' as photographed by satellite

The notion of post-international politics suggests that, at the century's end, globalization — simply the intensification of global interconnectedness — is *transforming* the existing world order most conspicuously through its direct challenge to the primacy of the nation-state in its present form. One of the principal issues examined in this chapter is therefore the question of whether humanity is witnessing the unfolding of a new historical epoch (one which is distinguished by a progressive globalization of human relations and the emergence of the first truly 'global historical civilization'), or alternatively whether the present 'phase' of globalization simply conceals a renewed strengthening of the existing structures of western modernity — capitalism, industrialism and the nation-state system. Within this discursive framework, the implications of the globalization of social life, both for the viability of the modern nation-state (in its present form) and for the 'sociological imagination', will be systematically and critically explored.

1.1   THEMES AND STRUCTURE

Most traditional sociology textbooks tend to open with the claim that the sociological enterprise is primarily concerned with the study of 'modern society', understood as a cohesive, bounded totality, an integrated social system. Society, in effect, therefore becomes indistinguishable from the nation-state. This conflation of the two concepts is hardly surprising since, as a discipline, 'modern' sociology reflects its nineteenth-century origins, during an age of virulent nationalism and nation-state formation. Despite the emphasis the founding 'fathers' gave to comparative sociology, much contemporary theorizing still remains focused upon the 'national society'. As Turner notes, although it sought to be a universal science of human affairs, '... in practice sociology has been developed to explain and understand local or national destinies' (Turner, 1990, p.343). However, in a 'shrinking' world, where transnational relations, networks, activities and interconnections of all kinds transcend national boundaries, it is increasingly difficult to 'understand local or national destinies', without reference to global forces. The dynamics of the global financial system; the tremendous expansion of transnational corporate activity; the existence of global communications and media networks; the global production and dissemination of knowledge, combined with (amongst other factors) the escalating significance of transnational religious and ethnic ties; the enormous flows of peoples across national boundaries; and the emerging authority of institutions and communities above the nation-state: all these factors provide a powerful case for reassessing the traditional conception of society (and by association the nation-state) as a bounded, ordered, and unified social space — a coherent totality. If, as many would argue, globalization is reconstituting the world as 'one place', then a re-focusing of the sociological project — away from 'society' and the 'nation-state' towards the emerging 'world society' — would seem a logical prerequisite for making sense of the contemporary human condition. Bauman puts the point clearly: 'With the sovereignty of nation-states vividly displaying its limitations ... the traditional model of society loses its credence as a reliable frame of reference ...' (Bauman, 1992, p.57).

Globalization strikes at many of the orthodoxies of social science, and more particularly the sociological project. At one level, the prospect of a 'world society' resurrects the highly contentious issue, first posed and answered by the Enlightenment *philosophes*, as to the validity of universalist accounts of social phenomena. If globalization is characterized by universal socio-economic processes, does this not suggest the need for universal accounts of social affairs, and by definition the existence of some universal truths? Globalization also brings into question foundational concepts — 'society' and the 'nation-state' — which still retain a privileged position in the discourse of modern sociology and the social sciences more widely. Finally, globalization poses an interesting set of normative questions concerning the future of the nation-state and the nature of the modern political community . For, in an age in which global interconnectedness appears to be intensifying, the most pressing issue must be whether the nation-state and the national political community will remain viable and sustainable forms of political and social organization. In effect, globalization raises the prospect of the 'end of the nation-state' as the primary container of modernity. It is somewhat ironical that, as the century draws to a close, the pace of 'progress' is being indicted for dissolving one of the quintessential institutions of modernity: the nation-state. It seems equally ironical that, at the very moment sociology encounters the possibility of a 'world society', it is gripped by the discourse of post-modernity which denies the plausibility of any universal truths or knowledge through which such an emerging 'global social formation' might be comprehended (Archer, 1991).

Whilst the conclusion of the chapter will confront these apparent ironies, the main narrative will be devoted to an exegesis of the contemporary debates about globalization, with specific emphasis upon its consequences for the nation-state and the sociological imagination. The discussion will embrace:

1   an examination of the discourse of globalization;

2   a review of the dimensions of globalization;

3   the emerging debate on globalization and the formation of a global society;

4   the implications of a global society for the continued viability of the nation-state and the national political community; and

5   an assessment of why globalization invites the return of a more universal sociology, and the corresponding demise of 'society' as the basic unit of sociological analysis.

2   MODERNITY AND GLOBALIZATION

In comparison with previous historical epochs, the modern era has
supported a progressive globalization of human affairs. The primary
institutions of western modernity — industrialism, capitalism, and the
nation-state — have acquired, throughout the twentieth century, a truly
global reach. But this has not been achieved without enormous human
cost, since western globalization has been fuelled by a tremendous
'arrogance and violence' (Modelski, 1972, p.49). Whilst early phases of
globalization brought about the physical unification of the world, more
recent phases have remade the world into a single global system in
which previously distinct historical societies or civilizations have been
thrust together. This should not be taken to imply that globalization
involves global cultural homogenization or global political integration.
Rather, it defines a far more complex condition, one in which patterns
of human interaction, interconnectedness and awareness are
reconstituting the world as a single social space.

2.1   'GLOBE TALK': THE DISCOURSE OF GLOBALIZATION

During the 1980s, the concept of globalization began to permeate a
diverse body of literatures within the social sciences. This intellectual
fascination with globalization and its consequences was stimulated in
part by a concern to understand the nature of the socio-economic
changes which appeared to be enveloping all advanced capitalist
societies. In part the fascination was also associated with a perception
that the fates of individual national communities were increasingly
bound together, a perception underlined by the global economic
recession of the early 1980s, the renewed threat of nuclear armageddon
following the intensification of Soviet–American rivalry, and the
impending eco-crisis. These, and other events, became significant
reference points in a growing literature which sought to analyse the
ways in which daily existence within most countries was becoming
increasingly enmeshed in global processes and structures. This
expanded awareness of global interconnectedness was reinforced by the
electronic media, which were capable of bringing to their audience's
immediate attention distant events, so creating a sense of a globally
shared community. Today, 'globalization' has become a widely used
term within media, business, financial and intellectual circles, reflecting
a fairly widespread perception that modern communications technology
has shrunk the globe. However, popular use of the term and its many
definitions within the social sciences have imbued the concept with
multiple meanings. How then should we understand the term?

Globalization refers to the multiplicity of linkages and interconnections
that transcend the nation-states (and by implication the societies) which
make up the modern world system. It defines a process through which
events, decisions, and activities in one part of the world can come to
have significant consequences for individuals and communities in quite

distant parts of the globe. Nowadays, goods, capital, people, knowledge, images, communications, crime, culture, pollutants, drugs, fashions, and beliefs all readily flow across territorial boundaries. Transnational networks, social movements and relationships are extensive in virtually all areas of human activity from the academic to the sexual. Moreover, the existence of global systems of trade, finance and production binds together in very complicated ways the prosperity and fate of households, communities, and nations across the globe. Territorial boundaries are therefore arguably increasingly insignificant in so far as social activity and relations no longer stop — if they ever did — at the water's edge. It is thus largely irrelevant to continue to make distinctions between the internal and the external, the foreign and the domestic spheres of socio-economic activity, when globalization has resulted in a 'stretching' of social relations across national territorial boundaries (Giddens, 1990, p.14). But the concept of globalization articulates something much more profound about modern social existence than the simple fact of growing interconnectedness between nation-states.

Within the literature, two authors — Giddens and Harvey — have made a significant contribution to the theorization of globalization. Giddens considers globalization to be one of the most visible consequences of modernity. This is because globalization involves a profound reordering of time and space in social life — what Giddens refers to as 'time–space distanciation' (1990, p.14). He stresses how the development of global networks of communication and complex global systems of production and exchange diminishes the grip of local circumstances over people's lives. Thus, the jobs of Scottish miners may be more dependent upon the pricing decisions of Australian and South African coal companies in the global market than upon the immediate decisions of local management. In Giddens's view, this 'disembedding' of social relations — lifting them out 'from local contexts of interaction' and recombining them across time and space — is primarily associated with the forces of modernity. However, globalization expands the scope of such disembedding processes, with the consequence that '... larger and larger numbers of people live in circumstances in which disembedded institutions, linking local practices with globalized social relations, organize major aspects of day-to-day life' (Giddens, 1990, p.79). This certainly does not mean that 'place' or 'locale' are no longer significant in structuring social life, but rather that '... the truth of experience no longer coincides with the place in which it takes place' (Jameson quoted in Harvey, 1989, p.261). The point is that, in today's world, social relations and interaction are not dependent upon simultaneous physical 'presence' within a specific location, since the structures and institutions of modern societies, facilitated by instantaneous communication, foster intense '... relations between "absent" others, locationally distant from any given situation of face-to-face interaction' (Giddens, 1990, p.18). Globalization articulates, in a most dramatic manner, this conflation of 'presence' and 'absence' through its systemic interlocking of the 'local' and the 'global'. For Giddens, the concept of globalization therefore embraces much more than a notion of simple interconnectedness: '… the concept of globalization is best understood as expressing fundamental aspects of time–space distanciation. Globalization concerns the intersection of presence and absence, the interlacing of social events and social relations "at a distance" with local contextualities' (Giddens, 1991, p.21).

In his exploration of the 'post-modern condition', Harvey, too, conceives of globalization as an expression of our changing experience of time and space — what he labels 'time–space compression' (Harvey, 1989, p.240). By using this term, he highlights dramatically the sense in which, under the pressures of technological and economic change, space and time have been continually collapsed such that '… today we have to learn how to cope with an overwhelming sense of compression of our spatial and temporal worlds' (Harvey, 1989, p.240). What is distinctive about Harvey's analysis of globalization is the emphasis placed upon the 'speeding up' or intensity of time–space compression.

For Harvey, today's 'global village' is not the product of some smooth linear or exponential process of time–space compression, but rather results from a more discontinuous historical process, a process punctuated by discrete phases or bursts of intense time–space compression. These phases, he argues, are associated with the periodic crises and restructuring of capitalism, which involve a 'speeding up' of economic and social processes. We are all aware from our own experiences of the way in which, particularly in the current era, the quickening pace of change seems to have become a 'normal' feature of social life. Virtually as they are launched, new fashions, new products, even major historical events, seem to become redundant 'history'. One of the consequences of this speeding up of socio-economic change is an intensification of time–space compression, and with this comes an acceleration in the pace of globalization.

According to Harvey, '… we have been experiencing, these last two decades, an intense phase of time–space compression that has had a disorienting and disruptive impact upon political-economic practices, the balance of class power, as well as upon cultural and social life' (Harvey, 1989, p.284). This phase coincided with a deep crisis of capitalist accumulation, which was at its most intense in the late 1970s and early 1980s, and has been associated with a dramatic intensification of globalization. This intensification of globalization has been most pronounced in the spheres of manufacturing production and finance. In both these sectors, the speeding up of technological and organizational change has fostered an increased global mobility of capital, such that a new international division of labour appears to be emerging. Central to this has been the creation of the first truly global financial system, with twenty-four hour a day trading: 'The formation of a global stock market, of global commodity (even debt) futures markets, of currency and interest rate swaps, together with an accelerated geographical mobility of funds, meant, for the first time, the formation of a single world market for money and credit supply' (Harvey, 1989, p.161).

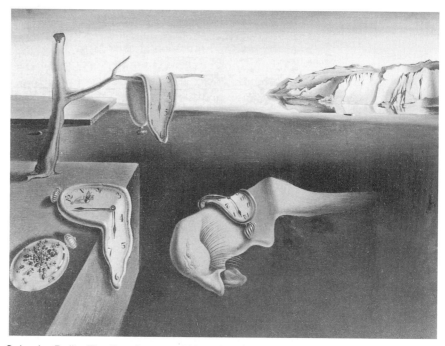

Salvador Dali's *The Persistence of Memory* (1931), or *The Soft Watches* as it was originally titled. The surrealist imagery represents the subjective (or soft) nature of our experience of time and space. As Dali noted, the 'famous limp watches are nothing but the tender, extravagant and solitary paranoiac-critical Camembert of time and space' (quoted in Maddox, 1990, p.25).

Globalization, in Harvey's analysis, is therefore intimately associated with the speeding up or intensification of time–space compression in social life.

These distinctive 'meanings' attached to the concept of globalization share much in common, even though the theoretical approaches of Giddens and Harvey are very different. How can these 'meanings' be distilled into a general conceptualization of the term? An acceptable solution is to conceive of globalization as having two interrelated dimensions: scope (or 'stretching') and intensity (or 'deepening'). On the one hand, the concept of globalization defines a universal process or set of processes which generate a multiplicity of linkages and interconnections between the states and societies which make up the modern world system: the concept therefore has a spatial connotation. Social, political and economic activities are becoming 'stretched' across the globe, such that events, decisions, and activities in one part of the world can come to have immediate significance for individuals and communities in quite distant parts of the global system. On the other hand, globalization also implies an intensification in the levels of interaction, interconnectedness, or interdependence between the states and societies which constitute the modern world community. Accordingly, alongside this 'stretching' goes a 'deepening', such that, even though '… everyone has a local life, phenomenal worlds for the most part are truly global' (Giddens, 1991, p.187). Thus, globalization involves a growing interpenetration of the global human condition with the particularities of place and individuality (Giddens, 1990, 1991).

3   MAPPING THE DIMENSIONS OF GLOBALIZATION

Clarifying the meaning of globalization invites further consideration of how it has been theorized within the literature. There is considerable debate concerning both the main driving force(s) behind globalization and how exactly it is reconstituting the world into a single social space. Section 3 will outline the theoretical debates with respect to the underlying causal logic(s) and dynamics of globalization. It will introduce the main protagonists in these debates and their respective theoretical positions on these issues.

3.1   LOGICS

A review of the literature on globalization highlights one fundamental axis of theoretical disagreement. As David Held noted in Chapter 1, accounts of modernity divide into two camps: those which stress a single causal logic, and those which emphasize a complex multi-causal logic. Similarly, in discussions of globalization, it is possible to distinguish between those accounts which give primacy to a single causal dynamic, such as technology or the economy, and others which rely upon a multi-causal logic. Obviously, this is a somewhat crude typology of theoretical approaches, and no single account fits snugly within either category. Nevertheless, despite the oversimplification, this typology has considerable utility in structuring this brief discussion of the primary theorizations of globalization.

Turning initially to those accounts which stress the primacy of one particular causal logic, the three key authors are Wallerstein, Rosenau and Gilpin. Wallerstein has introduced the concept of the world system into the social sciences and has stressed the centrality of capitalism to the process of globalization (both past and present). Rosenau and Gilpin, in comparison, are located within the discipline of international relations and have exploited some of its orthodoxies in accounting for globalization. Thus, Rosenau associates globalization with technological 'progress', whilst Gilpin considers it to be an expression of politico-military factors (power politics). Accordingly, each of these three authors locates the causal logic of globalization in a specific institutional domain: the economic, the technological, and the political, respectively.

In his pioneering studies of the emergence of 'one world', Wallerstein focuses primarily on the dynamics of historical capitalism, '... that concrete, time-bounded, space-bounded integrated locale of productive activities within which the endless accumulation of capital has been the economic objective or "law" that has governed or prevailed' (Wallerstein, 1983, p.18). For Wallerstein, the logic of historical capitalism is necessarily global in reach. From its origins in sixteenth-century Europe, capitalism has acquired a truly global reach in as much as, nowadays, '... the entire globe is operating within the framework of this singular social division of labour we are calling the capitalist world-economy' (Wallerstein, 1984, p.18). Wallerstein considers this capitalist world-economy to be historically unique, in that, whilst it has gradually created a universal economic space, humanity remains fragmented into discrete nation-states, each with its own centre of sovereign political rule. Moreover, the world-economy is conceived as having a distinctive, unequal structural arrangement with core, semi-peripheral and peripheral areas — each of which has a specific functional role in sustaining the overall integrity of the system. The material fate of states, communities and households flows from their location in this structure; a structure which maintains enormous inequalities in power and wealth. In addition, the periodic crises of capitalism mean that the world-economy is subject to discrete phases of global economic restructuring which reinforce these inequalities of power and wealth. But this restructuring also heightens the internal contradictions of the world-economy. Wallerstein argues that the universalization and deepening of capitalism provokes resistance on a global scale in the form of anti-systemic movements (e.g. environmental, socialist, and nationalist movements). The institutionalization of the world capitalist economy therefore embraces both processes of global integration and fragmentation, which produces instabilities and contradictions which Wallerstein believes will eventually lead to its collapse (Wallerstein, 1991). Embedded in this analysis is an unambiguous thesis: namely, that the driving force of globalization is to be located in the logic of the capitalist world-economy.

If Wallerstein gives primacy to capitalism as a globalizing imperative, Rosenau privileges technology and its transformative capacities. An international relations scholar, Rosenau has written extensively on the growth and significance of global 'interdependence' (Rosenau, 1980, 1989, 1990). In his attempt to make sense of the intensification of global interconnectedness he attaches enormous significance to technology:

> It is technology ... that has so greatly diminished geographic and social distances through the jet-powered airliner, the computer, the orbiting satellite, and the many other innovations that now move people, ideas and goods more rapidly and surely across space and time than ever before. It is technology that has profoundly altered the scale on which human affairs take place ... It is technology, in short, that has fostered the interdependence of local, national and international communities that is far greater than any previous experienced.
> (Rosenau, 1990, p.17)

Rosenau considers that an underlying shift from an industrial to a post-industrial order is transforming the global human condition. Accordingly, he argues that humankind has escaped the age of international politics — an age in which nation-states dominated the global scene — and is today witnessing the arrival of the era of 'post-international politics' — an era in which nation-states have to share the global stage with international organizations, transnational corporations and transnational movements. The state is therefore no longer the primary unit of global affairs. Although a novel account of globalization, Rosenau's thesis derives from a fairly extensive literature, with its origins in nineteenth-century sociology, which views industrialism (and now 'post-industrialism') as a powerful agent of global socio-economic and political transformation (Parkinson, 1977, ch.6). (This particular strand of theorizing will be explored further in Section 4.3.)

In comparison with Rosenau, Gilpin's account of globalization issues very much from within the orthodox approach to the study of international relations. Highly sceptical of any claim that globalization is transforming the world in which we live, Gilpin none the less acknowledges that nation-states are now profoundly interconnected in many different ways (Gilpin, 1987a). But, unlike Rosenau and Wallerstein, he argues that the process of globalization is a product of political factors, in particular the existence of a 'permissive' global order — a political order which generates the stability and security necessary to sustain and foster expanding linkages between nation-states. In a global states system, where sovereign nations recognize no authority above their own, the creation of such a permissive political order can only arise from the exercise of power. For Gilpin, globalization is therefore a historically contingent process; contingent in the sense that it relies upon the hegemonic (i.e. dominant, most powerful) state(s) in the international system to impose a form of world order which fosters interaction, openness, cooperation and interdependence (Gilpin, 1981, 1987a). Thus, he asserts:

> My position is that a hegemon is necessary to the existence of a liberal international economy ... historical experience suggests, that in the absence of a dominant liberal power, international economic cooperation has been extremely difficult to attain or sustain and conflict has been the norm ... The expansion and success of the market in integrating modern [global] economic life could not have occurred without the favourable environment provided by the liberal hegemonic power.
> (Gilpin, 1987a, pp.88 and 85)

Historically, globalization has been associated, particularly in the era of the European empires, largely with the expansionist drives of hegemonic powers. But, for Gilpin, the age of empires has now passed. Accordingly, more recent phases of globalization can be attributed instead to the permissive nature of the liberal world order, nurtured by the might of the hegemonic liberal state(s). Thus, in the age of Pax

Britannica, high levels of international interdependence existed, whilst during the era of Pax Americana globalizing processes intensified, underwritten by a stable security order and US military might (Gilpin, 1986). The key point, for Gilpin and those who share his analysis, is that in the modern era global interconnectedness (and its intensification) is conditional upon the existence of a stable and secure world order guaranteed by the power and military supremacy of a hegemonic (liberal) state. Globalization is shaped primarily by a political logic: the rise and decline of hegemonic powers in the inter-state system. So, in recent history, the most intense periods of globalization have been associated with the apogee of the hegemonic state's power in the global system (e.g. the US in the post-war era), whilst the decline of the hegemon (for instance, the United States today) can bring increased instability and an attenuation of global 'interdependence' (Gilpin, 1987b).

Wallerstein, Rosenau and Gilpin provide quite different accounts of globalization, although they share in common the fact that each privileges a single causal logic. However, a rather different 'school' of theorizing exists within the literature, giving weight to a multi-causal logic in accounting for globalization. Giddens and Robertson are amongst the central figures within this particular 'school'.

As part of his systematic exploration of the contours of modernity, Giddens approaches the phenomenon of globalization by distinguishing between what he understands to be its constituent dimensions (Giddens, 1990, p.70). Instead of a single causal logic, Giddens points to four discrete, but none the less intersecting, dimensions of globalization: capitalism; the inter-state system; militarism; and industrialism. Each of these dimensions embodies a distinctive globalizing imperative, nurtured by quite different institutional forces and constituencies. Thus, the logic and contradictions of the capitalist world-economy influence the pace and pattern of economic globalization whilst, within the inter-state system, it is the 'universalism of the nation-state' form which is responsible for the creation of a single world (Giddens, 1987, p.283) . Similarly, '... the globalising of military power ...' (Giddens, 1990, p.75) is tied to the logic of militarism, whilst the changing global division of labour is conditioned by the logic of industrialism. By theorizing these institutional dimensions of globalization, Giddens articulates an account of the global condition in which the '... connections between the emergence and spread of capitalism, industrialism and the nation-state system' are emphasized (Giddens, 1987, p.288). Globalization is therefore understood as something '... more than a diffusion of Western institutions across the world, in which other cultures are crushed', but rather embraces a complex, discontinuous and contingent process, which is driven by a number of distinct but intersecting logics; it is '... a process of uneven development that fragments as it coordinates' (Giddens, 1990, p.175). Within Giddens's analytical framework, globalization and '... the world system should be seen as influenced by several sets of primary processes associated with the nation-state system, coordinated through global networks of information exchange, the world capitalist economy and the world military order' (Giddens, 1987, p.288).

Whilst Robertson disagrees with important aspects of Giddens's analysis, he too is highly critical of the fact that '... in the present climate of "globality" there is a strong temptation for some to insist that the single world of our day can be accounted for in terms of one particular process or factor ...' (Robertson, 1990, p.22). Stressing that '... in the contemporary period a major task for sociological theory is to account for the trajectories of globalization in a multidimensional fashion' (Robertson and Lechner, 1985, p.113), Robertson advocates a theoretical approach which goes '... beyond simple models of "world polity" or a "world economy" by [pointing] to the independent dynamics of global culture ... to cultural aspects of globalization' (ibid., p.103). This requires a theory of globalization which involves '... the analytical separation of the factors which have facilitated the shift towards a single world — e.g. the spread of capitalism, western imperialism and the development of a global media system — from the general and global agency-structure (and/or culture) theme' (Robertson, 1990, p.22). Although he does not fully develop a systematic account of the interrelationships between the political, economic and cultural dimensions of globalization, it is abundantly evident from Robertson's work that each is understood to have a distinctive logic (Robertson, 1990; 1991a; 1991b). However, his approach is fundamentally different from that of Giddens, since he is less concerned with mapping the intersections between these dimensions, or their independent logics, than in understanding how they foster the duality of universalization and particularization — themes which will be explored in Chapter 6 in the context of culture and the formation of identity in 'one world' (Robertson, 1991a).

This brief exegesis of the two most important 'schools' of theorizing about globalization raises many difficult questions. Most obviously, it elicits a desire to establish the 'truth' or at least the validity of these accounts: are they competing or contradictory views, can they be conflated, are there criteria by which we can judge their worth as 'explanations'? As will become apparent in Chapter 7, such questions are driven by a particular view of knowledge which has come under increasing attack from post-modernist challenges to the prevailing orthodoxies within the social sciences. Rather than engage with those issues here, it is sufficient to acknowledge that a healthy debate exists between two distinctive 'traditions' of theorizing about globalization — between those theorists such as Wallerstein, Rosenau and Gilpin who privilege one causal 'logic' in their accounts of globalization, and those theorists such as Giddens and Robertson who emphasize intersecting causal 'logics'. However, my own sympathies lie with the work of Giddens and others who stress the multi-causal logic shaping the nature of contemporary globalization (McGrew, 1992). This attachment to a multi-causal account of globalization reflects the intellectual position adopted in many of the chapters of this volume. For the present, our gaze must turn away from the logics of globalization to its dynamics.

3.2   DYNAMICS

It should be apparent by this stage that the discourse of globalization — 'global babble' or 'globe talk' — is characterized by considerable complexity. This may well reflect the 'real' nature of globalization, or it may simply issue from the nature of the discourse itself. In exploring the dynamics of globalization, a more intense sense of complexity, and even ambiguity, surfaces. This arises because, within the existing literature, globalization is understood as a process which is essentially *dialectical* in nature and *unevenly* experienced across time and space.

Sophisticated accounts of globalization are not teleological in the sense that they assume the existence of an inexorable historical process leading to a universal human community. Rather, globalization is generally understood to be a *contingent* and *dialectical* process; dialectical in the simple sense of embracing contradictory dynamics. As Giddens explicitly acknowledges, globalization '... is a dialectical process because ...' it does not bring about '... a generalized set of changes acting in a uniform direction, but consists in mutually opposed tendencies' (Giddens, 1990, p.64). But what is the substantive form which these 'opposed tendencies' take? Several 'binary oppositions' or dualities are commonly identified within the discourse of globalization:

Universalization versus particularization

In the same way that globalization universalizes aspects of modern social life (e.g. the nation-state, assembly line production, consumer fashions, etc.), it simultaneously encourages particularization by relativizing both 'locale' and 'place' so that an intensification (or manufacturing) of uniqueness (or difference) is thereby fostered (e.g. the resurgence of nationalism and ethnic identities) (Robertson, 1990; Wallerstein, 1991; Harvey, 1989).

Homogenization versus differentiation

In as much as globalization brings about an essential 'sameness' to the surface appearance and institutions of modern social life across the globe (e.g. city life, religion, MacDonalds, the existence of human rights, bureaucratization, etc.), it also involves the assimilation and re-articulation of the global in relation to local circumstances (e.g. human rights are interpreted in very different ways across the globe; the practice of Islam is quite different in different countries, etc.) (Hannerz, 1991).

Integration versus fragmentation

Whilst globalization creates new forms of global, regional and transnational communities or organizations which unite people across territorial boundaries (e.g. the transnational corporation, international

MacDonalds reaches Moscow: Muscovites queuing for their first bite of a Big Mac
following the opening of the first MacDonalds in Moscow in 1990

trade unions, transnational class formations), equally, it also divides and
fragments communities, both within and across traditional nation-state
boundaries. For example, labour becomes increasingly divided along
local, national and sectoral lines; and ethnic and racial divisions
become more acute as the 'others' become more proximate (Bull, 1977;
Bozeman, 1984).

Centralization versus decentralization

Although globalization facilitates an increasing concentration of power,
knowledge, information, wealth and decision-making authority (e.g. the
European Community, transnational companies), it also generates a
powerful decentralizing dynamic as nations, communities, and
individuals attempt to take greater control over the forces which
influence their 'fate' (e.g. the activities of new social movements, such
as the peace, women's, or environmental movements) (Rosenau, 1990;
Wallerstein, 1991).

Juxtaposition versus syncretization

By compressing time and space, globalization forces the juxtaposition of
different civilizations, ways of life, and social practices. This both
reinforces social and cultural prejudices and boundaries whilst
simultaneously creating 'shared' cultural and social spaces in which
there is an evolving 'hybridization' of ideas, values, knowledge and
institutions (e.g. the mixing of cuisines, New Age lifestyles, architecture,
advertising images, etc.) (Perlmutter, 1991; Jameson, 1991).

These contradictory tendencies are inscribed in the very dynamics of globalization; a process which is by definition dialectical. For the participants in 'globe talk', the contradictory nature of globalization serves to remind us of its essential contingency and complexity. This is further reinforced by the *unevenness* with which globalization has been experienced across time and space.

In *The Principles of World Politics*, Modelski (1972) provides what must be amongst the first — if not the first — serious use and systematic discussion of the concept of globalization within the social sciences. Central to his analysis is the notion of globalization as a historical process; a process which has distinctive (if not discrete) phases during which the pace of globalization appears to 'speed up' or be attenuated. In respect of the present historical epoch, many writers, including Rosenau, Harvey and Jameson, point to an intensification of globalization which marks a profound break with the past. Whether the current epoch is defined as 'post-international politics' (Rosenau, 1990, p.6), an emerging 'postmodern global space' (Jameson, 1991, p.363), or a new world capitalist order (Harvey, 1989, ch.9), what is common to these authors is a sense of globalization as a discontinuous historical process.

This unevenness across time is also reflected in the differential reach of globalization. Not only is it considered to 'speed up' at various historical conjunctures, but similarly its consequences are not uniformly experienced across the globe. Some regions of the globe are more deeply implicated in global processes than others, and some are more deeply integrated into the global order than others. Within nation-states, some communities (e.g. financial ones) are tightly enmeshed in global networks, whilst others (e.g. the urban homeless) are totally excluded (although not entirely unaffected) by them. And, even within the same street, some households are more deeply embedded in global processes than others. This unevenness characterizes a highly asymmetrical structure of power relations. For globalization tends on the whole to reinforce (if not to increase) inequalities of power and wealth, both between nation-states and across them, so reproducing global hierarchies of privilege, control and exclusion (Walker, 1988). Yet, as noted above, there are contradictory forces at work here, since globalization generates new centres of resistance. As Modelski comments, '... globalization has ... been profoundly divisive and the effects of this divisiveness are yet to be fully experienced' (Modelski, 1972, p.55).

3.3   GLOBALIZATION: A SUMMARY STATEMENT

This section has examined both the logics and the dynamics of globalization. In respect of the causal logic of globalization, two distinct 'schools' of theorizing have been identified: the first 'school' embraces the work of Wallerstein, Rosenau and Gilpin, who consider globalization to be driven essentially by a single causal logic; and the second 'school' embraces writers such as Giddens and Robertson, who stress the multiple causal logics of globalization as a historical process.

ACTIVITY 1   At this point, you should note down what you can recall of the central ideas of each of these authors and what distinguishes them. Having done this, return to the appropriate sections to check your notes against the text.

In discussing the dynamics of globalization, considerable emphasis has been placed upon its dialectical and uneven character. Globalization is defined by historical phases of variable intensity and is by no means experienced uniformly across the globe. The central message of this section has been an articulation of the complexities and the ambiguities of globalization. This leads inevitably to a consideration of the highly intriguing question as to whether globalization is bringing into being a truly global society or whether this is simply a benign illusion.

4   A GLOBAL SOCIETY?

Both liberalism and Marxism have their roots in an 'enlightened' universalism which looked forward to the eventual emergence of a cosmopolitan world society; a global community in which transnational social bonds and universally held notions of peace, justice, equality and freedom defined the conditions of human existence. To some extent much of our present-day thinking about globalization is imprisoned within these nineteenth-century traditions. Thus, as discussed in the previous chapter, Fukuyama considers the recent 'triumph' of liberalism across the world as the beginnings of a new era of 'perpetual peace' (Fukuyama, 1989), whilst Wallerstein represents the contemporary era not as the triumph of capitalism but as an epoch of crisis which will bring in its wake emancipation on a global scale (Wallerstein, 1991). But liberalism and Marxism are increasingly inadequate guides to the complex global social architecture associated with recent phases of globalization. For globalization is transforming the basic parameters of modern social life. In doing so, it provokes the question as to how we as students (as well as subjects) of globalization should reflect upon, represent and theorize the contemporary global condition. This in turn involves tracking the potential trajectories of social change brought about by globalization. In what follows, four discrete answers are provided to the question of where globalization might be leading humanity.

4.1   A GLOBAL CIVILIZATION

In Reading A, Howard Perlmutter delivers a powerful argument for viewing globalization as the harbinger of the first truly global civilization. His account of where globalization is leading is representative of a substantial and progressive body of literature which discerns in the growing intensification of global interconnectedness the emerging infrastructure of a 'world society'. Rather than conceiving humanity as organized vertically into discrete nation-state units, this 'world society' perspective considers humanity as a single, universal 'community of fate'. As Modelski observes, today's extensive patterns of global interaction and global awareness, combined with the deepening of universal values (e.g. environmentalism, human rights, survival, etc.), point to 'the reality of world society' (1972, p.227). The complex web of transnational ties, which connects communities, households and individuals across national boundaries, undermines the image of humanity as imprisoned within bounded national societies, and instead supports a rather different image in which humanity is pictured as being organized horizontally into multiple, overlapping and permeable communities or systems of social interaction. This image of a world society suggests that the '... boundaries of states would be hidden from view' (Burton, 1972, p.43).

ACTIVITY 2   Now read **Reading A, 'On the rocky road to the first global civilization'**, by Howard V. Perlmutter, which you will find at the end of this chapter. You should take notes on the following issues:

1   How does Perlmutter conceive the term 'global civilization'?

2   In what sense is humanity reaching a profound turning point in its history?

3   What role does globalization play in his account of this global civilization?

Interestingly, Perlmutter does not equate globalization with westernization. Rather, he considers globalization to be a complex process, for he points, later in the article, to the transformation within western societies (in medicine, cuisine, lifestyles, ethnic divisions, etc.) brought about by the widespread appropriation and global diffusion of non-western values and social practices. Indeed, he believes globalization is responsible for creating a world civilization in which there is a dynamic form of global 'syncretization'. He defines syncretization as ' ... the attempted reconciliation or union of different or opposing principles, practices, or parties as in philosophy or religion' (Perlmutter, 1991, p.911). For Perlmutter, world society is a much more pluralistic and de-centred construct than our traditional 'models' of the hierarchical, ordered nature of domestic (i.e. national) society. But, for most post-modernists, even domestic (national) society can no longer be

conceived as a highly integrated, highly structured social space
(Bauman, 1992, p.350). Accordingly, Perlmutter implies that, in a post-
modern world of cultural fragmentation and the de-centring of power,
globalization is re-articulating on a global scale the pluralism,
syncretism and diversity of contemporary domestic society. Thus, the
first 'global civilization' may be a post-modern one.

4.2   A CAPITALIST WORLD SOCIETY

Neo-marxists would consider Perlmutter's account somewhat naïve,
since it fails to recognize the global power structures created by
processes of globalization. With the integration of the former command
economies of Eastern Europe and the former Soviet Union into the
world-economy, the global grip of capitalism now appears firmer than
ever. Thus, rather than representing the present epoch as the dawning of
a 'global civilization', it might be more accurate to describe it as the
final consolidation of a 'capitalist world society'. For one factor alone
has a crucial bearing on the material well-being — and thus the fate —
of the bulk of the world's population: namely, the dynamics of the
capitalist world-economy.

To argue, as Wallerstein does, that there is a single, capitalist world-
economy is to acknowledge that the prospects of the constituent parts of
that economy (the states, peoples, communities and households) are
intimately bound up with the functioning of the whole. Despite the
appearance of fragmentation, the nature of global markets and the global
mobility of capital ensure that few states or peoples can opt out of the
logic of this capitalist world political economy. According to Harvey
and Jameson, in the last thirty years capital has extended its reach and,
because of new technologies of communication and control, has become
ever more mobile (Harvey, 1989; Jameson, 1991). Furthermore, they
argue that this increasingly global form of capitalism is associated with
a profound transformation in the nature of the existing world capitalist
order. A new form of global capitalism ('late capitalism', 'disorganized
capitalism', or 'transnational capitalism') has extended and deepened its
reach across the globe. With this has come an increasing penetration
and consolidation of capitalist social relations on a global scale.
However, those excluded from or resisting this transformation have
become ever more marginalized. Thus, within this world capitalist
society there exist simultaneous processes of transnational integration
and national disintegration, as some communities are incorporated into
the system and others organized out. So, within the same state,
community, and street, there will be those whose lives are deeply
implicated in and tied to this new 'transnational capitalism', and many
others who are either its victims or exist on its margins.

Perhaps the most visible 'agent' of this new form of global capitalist
order is the transnational corporation (TNC). Production, trade and
finance are now increasingly organized on a transnational basis to reap
maximum economic advantage in a highly competitive world. To think

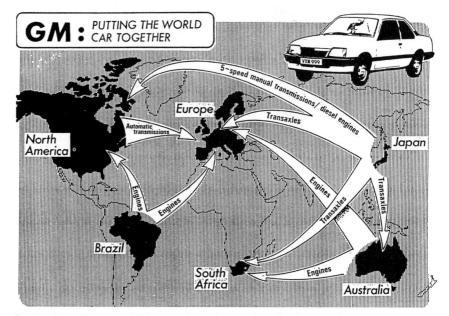

Production of motor vehicle parts is so internationally dispersed that one manufacturer launched one of its products as a 'world car' in 1981

in terms of a territorially bounded 'British' economy or an 'American' economy is to overlook the complex transnational networks of production, ownership, finance, and economic activity which make national territorial boundaries almost meaningless; as King notes, 'Germany's largest industrial city is Sao Paulo in Brazil' (King, 1990, p.69). Alongside these networks is also an expanding array of élite interactions. Indeed, a number of writers have suggested that these '... are coming together to produce a transnational capitalist class or class fraction with its own particular form of "strategic class" consciousness' (Gill and Law, 1989, p.484).

This shift to a more complex and spatially differentiated global capitalist order has also contributed to the internationalization of the state. The 'territorial non-coincidence of capital', as Murray conceives it, has forced states to cooperate more intensively at the global level (Murray, 1971). An enormous range of functional international regimes, global and regional institutions (e.g. the International Monetary Fund, the European Community (EC), etc.) is required, both to manage the problems associated with this capitalist order, and to ensure its continued reproduction. The Group of Seven leading capitalist states (the G7), for instance, operates as a powerful forum for global economic coordination (Lewis, 1991). Thus, world capitalist society is subject to extensive processes of 'governance' or regulation, even though no formal world government exists. These global regulatory structures are far from democratic, but rather sustain a geometry of power relations which is conducive to the needs of global capital. Because labour is primarily organized at the national level, it is therefore incredibly weak in the face of transnational capital. This is also the case for other anti-

poorer states. As a result, there is an
...tional collaboration and coalition-building
...by this new order. Yet these are the very
groups whose political and economic resources are minimal.

ACTIVITY 3   Now read **Reading B, 'The global capitalist system'**, by Leslie Sklair.

1   Note down the three transnational practices Sklair outlines and the institutions connected with each.

2   What is the role of the hegemonic capitalist state in this system?

3   In what sense does Sklair suggest global capitalism creates a world capitalist society?

Sklair points to the transnational organization of production and exchange as producing distinctively capitalist global social arrangements and practices. This world capitalist society is one in which the primary capitalist dynamic is located at the transnational as opposed to the national level, and in which the social relations of production are no longer imprisoned within national territorial boundaries.

4.3   A BIFURCATED WORLD

Unlike Sklair, Rosenau locates the logic of globalization in technology — specifically the shift to a post-industrial order — and arrives at correspondingly different conclusions as to the developing form of the contemporary global system.

Rosenau, whose work has been discussed in Section 3.1, shares much in common with the intellectual tradition established by Auguste Comte, one of the founding figures of modern sociology, who envisaged a world society arising from the global diffusion of techno-industrial civilization (Parkinson, 1977, p.68). Comte's faith in the universalizing imperatives of modern industrialism has been reflected since in the work of many other writers, including Rosenau, who identifies the arrival of 'post-industrialism' with yet a further transformation in the global system.

ACTIVITY 4

Now read **Reading C, 'The two worlds of world politics'**, by James Rosenau. In this reading, Rosenau develops an interesting argument with respect to the impact of 'post-industrialism' on existing global structures. Read the extract through quickly and then return for a more leisurely read, concentrating on the following issues:

1   What does Rosenau mean by the terms 'post-international politics' and 'bifurcation'?

2   What do you understand by the phrase the 'two worlds' of world politics?

3   Identify the major characteristics of each of these 'worlds'.

4   How do these 'worlds' relate to each other?

Rosenau has produced a highly original account of the contemporary global condition. He rejects not only the notion of a 'global civilization' but also that of a 'capitalist world society'. Instead, he identifies a complete fracturing of the global system, a structural bifurcation, as the full force of post-industrialism is experienced across the globe. His argument indicates that there is no longer a single global society (or system) but rather two: a society of states, in which diplomacy and national power remain the critical variables; and a world in which multifarious organizations, groups, and individuals, each pursuing its own interests, create an ever more intricate web of transnational relations, structures and interactions which are outside the control of any single nation-state and which constitute a kind of hyper-pluralist 'transnational society'.

This 'multi-centric world', as Rosenau labels it, is a world of:

- *transnational organizations,* such as Greenpeace, transnational banks, the Catholic Church, the International Sociological Association, the Red Cross, Oxfam, Cafod, IBM, Ford, drug cartels, international trade unions, social movements, etc.;

- *transnational problems,* such as pollution, drugs, aid, ethnicity, currency crises;

- *transnational events* or happenings, such as live TV broadcasts from Baghdad and Ridiyah during the Gulf War of 1991; or the publication of Salman Rushdie's novel in the UK leading to riots in Pakistan and the withdrawal of ambassadors from Iran; or US and British foundations and political parties advising politicians in Poland, Czechoslovakia, and other states on democratic process, etc.;

- *transnational communities*, based upon religion (e.g. Islam, Catholicism), knowledge (e.g. academic networks), lifestyles (e.g. environmentalists), culture (e.g. the art world), or ideology (e.g. the New Right), etc.; and

- *transnational structures*, such as those of production, finance and knowledge.

Of course, as Rosenau makes clear, these two worlds (the state-centric and the multi-centric) do interact. Thus, Greenpeace can be found lobbying the US government, the EC, the British government, and the World Bank to make lending policies to the Third World sensitive to environmental concerns. Conversely, governments and inter-governmental agencies legislate the global or regional rules (e.g. technical standards for pharmaceuticals, or for high-definition television), within which transnational corporations and other agencies operate. However, because each of these worlds has its own norms, structures and principles, they co-exist in an unstable and indeterminate relationship. As a consequence, global order appears to be breaking down as the world, given the dynamics of post-industrialism, undergoes a profound de-centring of power and action. Turbulence, rather than stability, is the defining characteristic of the present epoch. Accordingly, Rosenau argues, this is now the era of the bifurcated world — the age of post-international politics.

4.4   A GLOBAL SOCIETY OF STATES

One of the criticisms of Rosenau's 'world view' is that by concentrating upon the visible turbulence and 'disorder' in the global system he completely misreads the significance of the continuities in global life. To some observers, the continued existence (if not strengthening) of the nation-state, combined with the reassertion of nationalism across the globe, and (following the collapse of communism) the formation of a host of new states, suggests that globalization has far from transformed the global situation. In other words, there is no 'post-international politics', or capitalist world society, nor even an emerging global civilization. Rather, the primary trajectory of global development is to be tracked in the tightening hold of the nation-states system over human affairs. The nation-state and the inter-state system, it is argued, are and will continue to remain the dominant 'reality' of modern social life.

A further criticism of Rosenau's thesis (and of the other three positions elaborated in this section) concerns its ethnocentricity. It extrapolates the experience of socio-economic transformation within late capitalist societies on to the global level. Yet, as John Allen indicates in Chapter 4, there is enormous controversy concerning both the nature of that transformation (post-industrial, post-Fordist, post-capitalist) and how far it is appropriate even to think in terms of socio-economic transformations.

These criticisms provide a launching pad for the final reading by Robert Gilpin. For it is Gilpin's contention (which, by the way, has a great deal of support within the transnational community of international relations scholars) that globalization has not altered fundamentally the structure of the global system, nor does it require a reorientation of our thinking or theorizing with respect to the future trajectory of global socio-political development.

ACTIVITY 5   Now read **Reading D, 'Change and continuity in world politics'**, by Robert Gilpin, paying specific attention to the following:

1   What reasons does Gilpin give for suggesting that growing interconnectedness has not created a 'world society'?

2   What do you understand by the term 'political realism'?

3   What does he identify as being the key continuities with the past?

Gilpin's argument is a very powerful restatement of 'realism' in the context of accelerated globalization. Whilst he does not dispute that the world may be increasingly interconnected, he is adamant that this by no means prefigures the arrival of a 'world society'. On the contrary, his position is that, in a global system in which there is no authority above the sovereign nation-state, there exists the constant danger of conflict and even war. This danger is compounded by the absence of any institution to enforce the peace. The result is a condition of anarchy and insecurity which pushes the political leaders of all states to maximize national power capabilities. Realists, such as Gilpin, therefore view the global states system as a system of power politics in which conflict and insecurity are the norm. In this context, the state acquires a critical role in securing and defending the interests and safety of its peoples in a dangerous world. Despite the enormous expansion in transnational and global activity, for realists it is still the case, as it was in Greek times, that only state power can secure the peaceful milieu within which such activity is able to flourish. In contrast with Rosenau's thesis of 'two worlds', Gilpin argues unambiguously for the primacy of the nation-state system.

Moreover, realists would take issue with their 'idealist' colleagues who conceive globalization either as a permanent fixture of the modern age or as necessarily leading to a more interdependent world. Instead, Gilpin, as noted earlier (see Section 3.1), argues vehemently that the more historically recent phases of globalization have depended upon a specific configuration of global power. It is worth quoting him in full:

As I have argued, a liberal [interdependent] international economy rests on three political foundations (Gilpin, 1981, p.129). The first is a dominant liberal hegemonic power, or, I would also stress, liberal powers able and willing to manage and enforce the rules of a liberal commercial [capitalist] order. The second is a set of

common economic, political, and security interests that help bind
liberal [capitalist] states together. And the third is a shared
ideological commitment to liberal values ... Thus, since the end of
the Second World War, American global hegemony, the anti-Soviet
alliance, and a Keynesian welfare state ideology ... cemented
together economic relations among the three principal centres of
industrial power outside the Soviet block — the United States,
Japan and Western Europe.

It was on the basis of this conceptualization of the relationship
between international economics and politics that I and a number
of other 'neo-realists' were highly sceptical of the argument of the
more extreme exponents of interdependence theory. Their
projections into the indefinite future of an increasingly
interdependent world, in which nation-states and tribal loyalties
(read nationalism) would cease to exist, seemed to us to be a
misreading of history ... Such theorizing assumed the preeminence
and autonomy of economic and technological forces over all others
in effecting political and social change. Thus, it neglected the
political base on which this interdependent world economy rests
and, more importantly, the political forces that were eroding these
political foundations.
(Gilpin, 1986, pp.311–12)

To summarize: for Gilpin, globalization has been contingent historically
upon strategic and political factors, the geometry of global power
relations and the ideological predispositions of the dominant states.
This is a very timely argument, since the relative decline of the US, the
absence of a global ideological threat to unite the most powerful
capitalist states, and the resurgence everywhere of nationalist and
protectionist political forces suggest the end of 'the golden era' of
globalization. Accordingly, for 'realists', globalization does not prefigure
the emergence of a 'world society'. On the contrary, the world is still
best described (and understood) as a 'society of states'.

4.5   TRAJECTORIES OF CHANGE

Each of the authors discussed in Section 4 identifies globalization with
quite different trajectories of change. Each tells a different story about
where globalization is leading and what form of global society appears
to be emerging. Indeed, there is little common ground between these
positions, in the sense that each delivers its own distinctive response to
the critical issue of the consequences of globalization for the social
architecture of modernity. By their very nature, none of these positions
can be judged to be either wholly right or wrong, true or false, since
each is essentially attempting little more than claiming to represent the
most judicious assessment of where contemporary trends are leading.
Moreover, the intellectual debate on these great matters remains
extremely fluid whilst, as Rosenau suggests, the world of experience

remains highly turbulent. As the 'jury' is likely to remain out for some time, the issue becomes one of which account(s) appears to be more or less convincing.

ACTIVITY 6

To assist you in coming to your own judgement on this issue, you should spend some time reviewing and then comparing each of the four positions. You might want to consider in respect of each:

1   whether globalization is held responsible for transforming the social world;

2   the form which global society appears to be taking;

3   the implications for the nation-state.

Although these four readings offer quite different visions of the global predicament, they do share some common ground. In particular, whilst each posits a quite different kind of global social architecture arising from globalization, they all share a belief that modern societies can only be understood within a global setting. Additionally, each raises the question of whether the nation-state is any longer the most appropriate political unit for organizing human affairs in a more interconnected world system. Even Gilpin, a staunch champion of realism, acknowledges that the intensification of economic interdependence '... has decreased national economic autonomy', and that it is unclear what the implications of '... contemporary military and economic developments will be on the scale of political organization' (Gilpin, 1981 p.229). As the end of the century draws near, globalization is forcing us to rethink the nature of the 'political community', the basic unit of human affairs. Indeed, globalization appears to be challenging the modern orthodoxy that the nation-state defines the 'good community' (Modelski, 1972, p.56).

5   GLOBALIZATION AND THE FUTURE POLITICAL COMMUNITY

Writing in 1957, John Hertz predicted the 'demise' of the territorial state as the primary political unit in world affairs (Hertz, 1957). His prediction derived from the argument that nuclear weapons made it impossible for states to defend their citizens against attack. Once states could no longer fulfil this essential duty they became, Hertz suggested, obsolete. Slightly in excess of three decades later, Jameson, commenting on the '... prodigious expansion of capitalism in its third (or multinational) stage' (1991, p.319), observed that '... not merely the older city but even the nation-state itself has ceased to play a central functional and formal role in a process that has in a new quantum leap of capital prodigiously expanded beyond them, leaving them behind as ruined and archaic remains of earlier stages in the development of this mode of production' (ibid., p.412). However, to talk the now fashionable language of the 'end of the nation-state' may be to invite the twin dangers of completely misreading its contemporary predicament whilst simultaneously neglecting the real underlying challenges to the nature of the 'modern political community' inscribed within the processes of globalization.

5.1   DISSOLVING THE NATION-STATE

Globalization has been, and continues to be, associated with a 'crisis of the territorial nation-state'. Daniel Bell, writing about the US position in the future global order, captured this sentiment memorably in his comment that the nation-state was '... too small for the big problems of life, and too big for the small problems of life' (Bell, 1987, p.14). Whilst the unevenness of globalization and the diversity of modern state forms mean that any generalization on this issue demands careful qualification, nevertheless, in respect of the late (or advanced) capitalist states, there is a powerful argument which indicates that globalization is dissolving the essential structures of modern statehood. In effect, globalization is understood to be compromising four critical aspects of the modern nation-state: its competence; its form; its autonomy; and, ultimately, its authority or legitimacy.

In a global economic system in which productive capital, finance, and trade flow across national boundaries, the traditional distinction between the internal and external domains no longer holds. Such interconnectedness creates a situation in which decisions in one state can produce major consequences for the citizens of many other states. A recession in the United States, for instance, takes its toll in the factories of Europe, Japan, Latin America and Asia. States therefore face extensive pressures from their citizens and domestic groups to regulate those transnational activities which directly impinge upon their interests and livelihoods. Such pressures, as in the environmental or economic issue-areas, generate a significant political momentum for the expansion of international regimes and international regulatory frameworks at the regional or global levels. Accordingly, as Morse argues, in conditions of systemic 'interdependence', the inability of governments to fulfil the demands of their citizens without international cooperation is evidence of the declining competence of states (Morse, 1976). Whilst this may be particularly acute in the economic domain, a dwindling number of policy problems can now be resolved through purely domestic actions or decisions (e.g. drugs, environment, national security, immigration, etc.). Moreover, the corollary is also the case, since the resolution of international problems increasingly demands domestic action. Throughout the 1980s, for example, western governments, in response to the greater mobility of capital, were forced into extensive international coordination of '... monetary and fiscal

policies — policies that had traditionally been considered "internal" '
(Webb, 1991, p.311). Morse argues that 'interdependence' has eroded the
traditional boundaries between the internal and external domains, so
encouraging an expansion in the functions and responsibilities of the
state whilst simultaneously denying it effective national control over
policy formulation and policy outcomes (Morse, 1976). This condition
has been referred to as the 'widening and weakening' of the state, or, as
Rosenau prefers to label it, 'the widening and withering' of the state's
competence.

Strongly associated with this declining competence is an erosion of the
capacity of the state to enforce its demands on others as the traditional
instruments of policy are undermined by accelerating globalization.
Whereas military force has been fundamental to state power, it is now of
limited utility in achieving all but the most restricted of national goals
(Jervis, 1991). Military force remains a last resort, and is largely
irrelevant to the resolution of some of the key problems confronting
modern states, such as economic welfare, environmental problems,
trade matters, etc. According to Rosecrance, economic power and
economic diplomacy are central to state security in the contemporary
age because economic capabilities are extremely 'fungible' (i.e.
transferable into direct influence or power) (Rosecrance, 1986). In effect,
the suggestion is that the currency of power in the global system has
been transformed from military to economic capabilities (Nye, 1989). In
the post-Cold War era of rapid demilitarization, this shift in the primary
currency of power has doubly compounded the problems for states in
trying to protect and secure their interests in a highly complex and
dynamically interconnected world order (Shaw, 1991). The result is a
significant shift towards multilateral diplomacy and collective action,
which in the process further erodes the competence of states to control
their own destiny.

It is not only the competence of states which is diminished by
globalizing pressures; the form of the state is also subtly altered. With
the increased emphasis upon international coordination and
cooperation has come a staggering expansion in the numbers of inter-
governmental organizations and international regimes. Thus, in
whatever sector of state policy one cares to name, there exists a
corresponding set of international regulatory institutions or agencies.
For instance, there exists an international monetary regime which
embraces inter-governmental organizations (e.g. the IMF) together with a
set of international norms, rules, principles, regulations, and decision
making fora, supplemented by informal policy coordination networks
between the finance ministries of the major western states (the G7), as
well as between central banks, and the major private transnational
banks. In the post-war era, there has been an explosive growth in the
number and significance of international regimes and organizations. Cox
refers to this as the 'internationalization' of the state (Cox, 1987). Whilst
not juridically above the state, most western governments are so deeply
enmeshed in these regulatory and decision-making structures that

European Community foreign and finance ministers sign the Maastricht Treaty, a historic landmark in the deeper political and economic integration of the member states of the EC (7 February 1992)

national and international policy formulation have become inseparable. Moreover, some international organizations and regimes have acquired quasi-supranational powers. The European Community is a primary example, in that decisions (in some domains) taken by a majority can be legally imposed on other member governments, thus compromising their juridical sovereignty.

In effect, the 'internationalization' of the state has created forms of international governance in which collective policy making and coordination of policy between governments have become vital to the achievement of national and international goals. Without knowing it, many aspects of people's daily existence are now shaped by the regulatory activities of a host of international regimes. This process of the 'internationalization' of the state has fundamental implications for the coherence of the state apparatus and, ultimately, challenges democratic practices. Domestic bureaucracies become internationalized with the result that ministers and cabinets find it difficult to maintain direct control over policy formulation. Within international fora, transgovernmental coalitions of bureaucrats develop with the result that policy outcomes are no longer decided by elected politicians or by the organs of central government (Keohane and Nye, 1977). This kind of multi-bureaucratic decision making, as Kaiser calls it, dissolves the notion of the state as a monolithic creature pursuing a coherent national interest (Kaiser, 1972). Instead, the state appears on the international stage as a fragmented coalition of bureaucratic agencies each pursuing its own agenda with minimal central direction or control.

If the institutional form of the state is recast by the processes of globalization, its effects are also experienced at a deeper structural level.

Recent studies have begun to explore the relationship between globalization and the effectiveness of state strategies for managing the domestic socio-economic domain. What emerges from many of these studies is an awareness of how greater interconnectedness between states imposes intense pressures for a convergence in state socio-economic strategies. Gourevitch argues that the global economic and competitive pressures on states in the 1980s forced them '... to curtail state spending and interventions. Whatever the differences in partisan outcomes, all governments have been pressed in the same direction' (Gourevitch 1986, p.33). As a result, most governments have discarded strategies of full employment and interventionism because they might reduce their competitive edge in global markets. In a highly competitive but interconnected global economy, state strategies and the domestic socio-political coalitions which underpin them are increasingly sensitive to world economic conditions. According to Garrett and Lange, 'The new international economic environment has undercut the effectiveness of the partisan strategies of the left and right based respectively on broadly "Keynesian" and "monetarist" fiscal and monetary policies' (Garrett and Lange, 1991, p.541).

The discussion so far points to a third aspect of the consequences of globalization: the diminution of state autonomy. Clearly, states have always operated under constraints of all kinds; none has ever been free to act completely independently from external pressures. However, it is frequently argued that globalization has imposed tighter limits on the exercise of state autonomy across a range of policy domains (McGrew, 1992). State autonomy can be defined in terms of a state's capacity to act independently, within circumscribed parameters, in the articulation and pursuit of domestic and international policy objectives. State autonomy can be further differentiated with respect to both its 'scope' and the 'domains' within which it can be exercised. By 'scope' is meant the level or intensity of constraints on state action, whilst 'domains' refers to the policy spaces or issue-areas within which such constraints operate (McGrew, 1992). This conceptual definition allows an important distinction to be made between sovereignty — the *de jure* use of power through supreme legal authority or competence within a defined territory — and autonomy. It also suggests that the notion of a loss of state autonomy has to be specified and qualified quite carefully.

As implied already, one of the structural consequences of globalization is to deny the relevance or practicality of autarky — strategies of self-reliance. Thus, states operate within a set of prefigured strategic and policy options which immediately restrict the menu of policies from which state managers can choose. This is particularly evident in the economic and financial policy domains. The scale of financial transactions is such that no single state by itself can effectively control the system in which it is enmeshed. Frieden observes that, 'In April 1989, foreign exchange trading in the world's financial centres averaged about $650 billion a day, equivalent to nearly $500 million a minute and to forty times the amount of world trade a day' (Frieden, 1991, p.428). This, as Webb indicates, was twice the amount of the total foreign reserve holdings of the US, Japanese, and UK central banks combined for the entire month (Webb, 1991, p.320). A very convincing argument can thus be made that the '... implications of interdependence ... are clear: governments no longer possess the autonomy to pursue independent macroeconomic strategies effectively, even if they were to seek to do so' (Garrett and Lange, 1991, p.543). This is simply because it is exceedingly difficult to 'buck' the global markets, for '... differences in the macroeconomic policies pursued by various countries immediately trigger large flows of capital' (Webb, 1991, p.318). However, whilst shifts in state socio-economic strategies are severely constrained, this does not mean that governments are completely immobilized.

Whilst state autonomy appears most compromised in the economic and financial domains, similar intense constraints operate in other areas too. Global warming compromises state autonomy, as does the parcelling out and regulation of the world airwaves, without which effective global communications would be impossible (Starke, 1990; Vogler, 1992). While acknowledging the constraints on state autonomy, it is nevertheless important to recognize that effective diminution of state autonomy varies considerably between different kinds of nation-state, as well as across time and in different policy sectors. Thus, advanced capitalist states may have greater autonomy in the global system than peripheral states, whilst the US has greater autonomy in some domains (e.g. military) than in others (e.g. financial). Propositions suggesting the general erosion of state autonomy in the face of increasing globalization therefore demand considerable qualification.

Finally, the combined consequences of eroding competence, converging forms and diminishing autonomy have contributed to an erosion of state authority and legitimacy. Influenced by 'crisis of governability' theories of the 1970s, a number of writers have argued that globalization is contributing to a crisis of compliance and authority within the nation-state (Rosenau, 1990; Burton, 1972). This view is driven by a conception of authority and legitimacy located in a discourse of performance and effectiveness. Very succinctly, the thesis is that, because globalization undermines the competence and autonomy of the nation-state, it reduces the effectiveness of government which, in turn, undermines the legitimacy and authority of the state (Rosenau, 1990). Moreover, in a world of global communications, where citizens can readily observe the global context of 'domestic' problems and the parochial nature of domestic political debate, further strains are placed upon compliance and authority relationships. Governments too contribute enormously to the sense of immobilization and despair which this situation generates by constantly stressing the international constraints upon state action. In consequence, the dwindling efficacy of the state and its bases of authority is underlined.

In addition, the existence of global regimes and international organizations poses a further challenge to the actual authority of the state. Global and regional institutions, such as the IMF and the EC, may directly challenge the sovereignty and authority of member states when they impose decisions and policies upon them. National authorities, in some circumstances, may appear as little more than the 'local' machinery for implementing regional or international policies. In a system in which international regimes and forms of international regulatory activity are expanding rapidly, the 'threat from above' to the authority of the nation-state is arguably a real one.

But globalization also enhances the 'threats from below'. What Rosenau refers to as the proliferation of 'sub-groupism', and others the fragmentation of civil society, is fuelled by globalizing imperatives (Rosenau, 1990, p.40). As Section 3.2 discussed, transnational integration and national disintegration of communities, the rise of ethnicity, the resurgence of nationalism, and the surfacing of new loyalties (e.g. environmentalism) are all associated with the dynamics of accelerating globalization. Globalization stimulates a search for new identities, so challenging the traditional 'integrating' ideologies which have defined the boundaries of the 'national' political community. As Rosenau observes, because of the diverse ethnic make up of most states, the label '... nation-state fits only a quarter of the members of the global states system' (Rosenau, 1990, p.406). This suggests that the divisive consequences of globalization operate on an enormously fertile terrain. Globalization is therefore considered by a number of writers to be undermining compliance and contributing to the erosion of state authority 'from below'.

A powerful argument can be made that globalization is compromising the authority, the autonomy, the nature and the competence of the modern nation-state. Whilst generalizing is fraught with dangers, there is a significant community of scholars within the social sciences who would agree with Freeman that '... the nation-state has become at best immobilized and at worst obsolete' (quoted in Frieden, 1991, p.427). However, countervailing tendencies do exist.

5.2 REJUVENATING THE NATION-STATE

Convincing though the 'declinist' argument appears, it is also crucial to acknowledge the significance of powerful countervailing forces which may be strengthening the nation-state. Here we will examine briefly the four main countervailing forces which are identified in the literature: the state's monopoly of military power; the potency of nationalism; the empowerment of states through international cooperation; and finally the 'myth' of interdependence.

As Reading D by Gilpin concluded, the primary *problematique* in the global states system remains the prevention of war and the maintenance of peace. States, through their monopoly over the means of violence, and their attention to the balance of power, are therefore critical agents in maintaining global order. Whilst military power may appear of less utility in the modern context, this, as Waltz argues, is a tribute to its vital role in sustaining the peace: 'Possession of power should not be identified with the use of force, and the usefulness of force should not be confused with its usability ... Power maintains an order; the use of force signals its breakdown' (Waltz, 1979, p.185). Thus, the fact that military force is used infrequently to sustain the global order is not an indictment of the declining relevance of military power (and by implication the nation-state), but, on the contrary, can be seen as evidence of its centrality to the contemporary global order. Thus, for Bull, the state retains a 'positive role' in the modern world primarily because its monopoly of military power provides its citizens with relative security in a highly dangerous world (Bull, 1979).

Alongside security, the state also provides a focus for personal and communal identity. As Modelski comments, the 'nationalization' of the global system is a fairly recent phenomenon and it is, as daily events indicate, a largely unfinished project. Nationalism along with the newly resurgent forms of ethnic nationalism are extremely powerful evidence that, even if the state is functionally redundant, culturally and psychologically it remains of critical significance in structuring the political and social organization of humankind. As Hanreider notes: 'Nationalism ... is alive and well. Far from being secondary or obsolete, the nation-state, nationalism, and the idea of the national interest are central elements in contemporary world politics' (Hanreider, 1978, p.1277).

Whilst pursuing their national interest through cooperation and collaboration, states also empower themselves. As Keohane and Gilpin argue, the creation of international regimes and institutions of cooperation does not in any sense weaken the nation-state (Keohane, 1984; Gilpin, 1987a). On the contrary, in many cases, international cooperation, as opposed to unilateral action, allows states simultaneously to pursue their national interests and to achieve more effective control over their national destiny. Within the context of a global economy, international coordination of exchange rates (for instance, the European Exchange Rate Mechanism) can enhance state autonomy rather than diminish it because it affords, through collective action, greater security and benefits than any corresponding attempts at unilateral action. To suggest that globalization necessarily undermines state autonomy is therefore to ignore the ways in which states empower themselves against the vagaries of global forces through collective action. According to Gordon:

> ... the role of the state has grown substantially since the early 1970s; state policies have become increasingly decisive on the international front, not more futile ... And small consolation though it may be ... everyone including transnational corporations has become increasingly dependent upon coordinated state intervention for restructuring and resolution of the underlying dynamics of the [economic] crisis.
> (Gordon, 1988, p.63)

Finally, a number of writers question whether globalization is really creating a more 'interdependent' world or convergence amongst state policies. Care must be taken here to distinguish between the concepts of interconnectedness and interdependence; interdependence should not be elided with notions of interconnectedness (or globalization). Interdependence implies a condition of *mutual* vulnerability to external events, whereas dependence implies a condition of *asymmetrical* vulnerability. Whilst processes of globalization may generate interdependencies between national communities, equally they can generate relationships of dependence and reinforce existing inequalities in the world system. Moreover, globalization often involves little more than interconnectedness, which implies a *sensitivity*, as opposed to a *vulnerability*, to external events or actions. Accordingly, globalization embraces both interconnectedness and interdependence, but these are radically different outcomes to the same process. Definitions aside, what is significant is the emphasis given in the 'declinist' argument to the evidence of an increasingly *interdependent* world in which state strategies and policies are converging. Yet both Krasner and Gordon, coming from radically opposing analytical positions, conclude that, although it may be more *interconnected*, the world is less *interdependent* today than it was before the First World War (Krasner 1991; Gordon 1988). Similarly, Scharpf argues convincingly that states do matter by demonstrating that, despite global constraints, state strategies of socio-economic management in the 1980s have not converged as much as the 'declinist' view suggests (Scharpf, 1991).

It follows from these points that the 'declinist' vision of the 'end of the nation-state' seems somewhat premature. Yet there are contradictory processes at work, so that it would seem equally untenable to suggest either that the state has been left unscathed by globalization or that it has been strengthened. None of these conclusions seem entirely convincing, recognizing the dialectics of globalization and the adaptive capacities of the modern nation-state. Cerny discerns in this growing intersection of global and domestic forces the beginnings of the 'changing architecture of the modern state' (Cerny, 1990). Globalization, in other words, requires us to accept the uncomfortable conclusion that the modern nation-state is '… both indispensable and inadequate' (Deutsch, 1988, p.54). But it also invites us to rethink our understanding of the modern political community.

5.3   RETHINKING SOVEREIGNTY AND POLITICAL COMMUNITY

Sovereignty is concerned with the location of ultimate power within a territorially bounded political community. Indeed, sovereignty defines the 'good community' by manufacturing the political space which separates the 'community' from the 'others'. In the modern era the 'good community' has come to be associated with the 'national community', although this was not always the case. But today globalization may be tearing away the notion of sovereignty from its rootedness in the national community and the territorially bounded state (Beitz, 1991). As Held observes:

> The modern theory of the sovereign democratic state presupposes the idea of a 'national community of fate' — a community which rightly governs itself and determines its own future. This idea is challenged fundamentally by the nature and pattern of global interconnections ... National communities by no means exclusively 'programme' the actions, decisions and policies of their governments and the latter by no means simply determine what is right or appropriate for their citizens alone.
> (Held, 1991, p.202)

Rather than the decline or the transcendence of the modern nation-state, globalization may be bringing about a '... re-articulation of international political space' (Ruggie, 1991, p.37), introducing a much more complex architecture of sovereign political power than presently exists. Sovereignty, along with the notion of political community, has become imbued, in Bauman's language, with incredible ambiguity (Bauman, 1992). In his explanation of the consequences of globalization for national sovereignty, Held concludes that globalization reveals:

> ... a set of forces which combine to restrict the freedom of action of governments and states by blurring the boundaries of domestic politics, transforming the conditions of political decision making, changing the institutional and organizational context of national polities, altering the legal framework and administrative practices of governments and obscuring the lines of responsibility and accountability of national states themselves. These processes alone warrant the statement that the operation of states in an ever more complex international system both limits their autonomy and impinges increasingly upon their sovereignty. Any conception of sovereignty which interprets it as an illimitable and indivisible form of public power is undermined. Sovereignty itself has to be conceived today as already divided among a number of agencies, national, regional and international, and limited by the very nature of this plurality.
> (Held, 1991, p.222)

This model of overlapping and pluralistic authority structures has much in common with mediaeval political practice and organization (Cook and Hertzman, 1983, ch.8). Bull, for instance, refers to a 'new mediaevalism':

> If modern states were to come to share their authority over their citizens, and their ability to command their loyalties, on the one hand with regional and world authorities, and on the other with sub-state or sub-national authorities, to such an extent that the

concept of sovereignty ceased to be applicable, then a neo-mediaeval form of universal political order might be said to have emerged.
(Bull, 1977, pp.254–5)

This 'new mediaevalism' suggests a reconstitution of political community, such that it is no longer identified solely with the territorial nation-state but is conceived in more pluralistic terms. Thus, as in mediaeval times, we are forced to think in terms of overlapping global, regional, transnational, national, and local political communities.

A global political forum: the United Nations takes on a vital role in the 'new world order' following the end of the Cold War

It is in this sense that globalization can be said to be dissolving, rather than contributing to, the transcendence of the sovereign nation-state and the bounded national political community. Sovereignty, and with it the nature of the 'political community', is being reconstituted by the forces of globalization.

6 GLOBALIZATION AND A UNIVERSAL SOCIOLOGY

If globalization invites us to rethink our notions of the sovereign nation-state and political community, then it certainly demands a reconsideration of the foundational concept in modern sociological thought: the concept of 'society'. Bauman defines the problem in transparent terms:

> It seems that most sociologists of the era of modern orthodoxy believed that — all being said — the nation state is close enough to its own postulate of sovereignty to validate the use of its theoretical expression — the 'society' concept — as an adequate framework for sociological analysis ... In the postmodern world, this belief carries less conviction than ever before.
> (Bauman, 1992, p.57)

There is little need to rehearse again the arguments which make Bauman's proposition so convincing, since they have been discussed in previous sections. Instead, the objective here is to think through the implications of the 'globalist turn' for the contemporary sociological enterprise. For it should be evident that, if the 'society' — the ordered, bounded totality — of modern sociology turns out to be a porous, fragmented and permeable social space, then a new 'subject', or primary unit of analysis, is required. In some respects the recent writings of Mann, Giddens, Robertson and Bauman can be conceived as attempts to refocus the discipline around a conception of the social which acknowledges the significance of the 'globalist turn' and thereby distances itself from the orthodox approach in which 'society' is the central *problematique* (Mann, 1986; Giddens, 1990, 1991; Robertson, 1990; Robertson and Lechner, 1985; Bauman, 1992). Mann, for instance, states: 'I would abolish the concept of "society" altogether' (Mann, 1986, p.2). Instead, he conceives of societies not as unitary social systems or bounded totalities but as constituted by '... multiple overlapping and intersecting sociospatial networks of power' (ibid., p.1). Giddens too stresses that, 'The undue reliance which sociologists have placed upon the idea of "society", where this means a bounded system, should be replaced by a starting point that concentrates upon analysing how social life is ordered across time and space — the problem of time–space distanciation' (Giddens, 1990, p.64). Globalization thus dislodges 'society' from its focal position in the discourse of modern sociology. But what is to replace it?

Post-modernists might appear initially to have the answer, because of their attachment to diversity, difference and the plurality of communities and identities which define the post-modern condition. Proponents of post-modernism on the whole argue that the notion of 'society' is a totalizing concept which is completely redundant in the contemporary era. This is because post-modernism is associated with '... a view of the human world as irreducibly and irrevocably pluralistic, split into a multitude of sovereign units and sites of authority, with no horizontal or vertical order, either in actuality or potency' (Bauman, 1992, p.35). Understanding this world, for many post-modernist theorists, requires accepting its essentially incoherent character and avoiding the temptation to impose order on it through totalizing and universal theoretical discourses. As Jameson notes, post-modernism prosecutes a 'war on totality' (Jameson, 1991, p.400). It denies the possibility of universal reasoning and accounts of the social life which claim universal validity. Paradoxically, for post-modernists, the existence of a 'postmodern global space' (Jameson, 1991, p.363) is not considered problematic, despite the implication that it assumes the operation of universal processes which are actively unifying humankind. Thus, Robertson refers to 'the universalization of particularism' and the 'particularization of universalism' (Robertson, 1991a). Yet this seems a logical contradiction. It might therefore be argued that post-modernism too, alongside the orthodox conception of society, is a victim of globalization. Indeed, in significant respects post-modernism, like much conventional sociological thinking, fails to confront the profound implications for its own conceptual categories and theoretical discourse which flow from globalization. Rather than looking to post-modernism to redress our uncertainty about the primary focus of the contemporary sociological enterprise, Archer suggests the solution is to be found elsewhere in a 'sociology for one world' — a re-visioning of the Enlightenment project (Archer, 1991).

The Enlightenment project was premised upon a belief in the universality of reason and the universal character of scientific explanation. A science of society was thus by definition a universal enterprise. However, as Chapter 7 will indicate, few social scientists today would accept that it is possible to construct wholly objective or universal accounts of social phenomena. Within modern sociology (whose intellectual foundations are rooted in the Enlightenment project's commitment to rational enquiry and human emancipation), post-modernism and the critique of a positive science of social affairs have prosecuted a 'war on universalism'. Yet the intensity of globalization in the current epoch produces a startling irony: just as the world is being compressed into one 'place', sociology is becoming increasingly localized and relativized (Archer, 1991).

In a stinging critique of the 'post-modernizing' and 'relativizing' of sociology, Archer delivers a convincing case that globalization '... supplies us with good reasons for overhauling our theoretical assumptions and frameworks' (ibid., p.133). This involves accepting that '... the globalization of society means that societies are no longer the prime units of sociology' (ibid., p.133). What is to replace this focus on societies is a 'sociology of One World' which recognizes that 'global processes are now partly constitutive of social reality everywhere' (ibid., p.134).

In cultivating this position, Archer is delivering a radical challenge to both orthodox and post-modernist sociological thinking. For, put simply, she is arguing that globalization demands a critical rethinking of the sociological enterprise to reflect the arrival of 'One World'. Such rethinking, she proposes, has to be fired by a commitment to both reason and humanity, and so requires a re-centring of reasoning and the human being within the sociological enterprise. In some respects she invites a reconstitution of the Enlightenment project, but shorn of its pretensions to be a positive science of social affairs and its de-humanizing of the human subject. For Archer, '... reasoning and humanity constitutes the bridge to international sociology' and so to delivering a 'sociology for one world' (ibid., p.144).

This chapter began with the claim that globalization invites a reconceptualization of the social architecture of modernity. In exploring this claim it has examined the dimensions of globalization, competing visions of today's global society, and the implications of globalization for the future of the nation-state and political community. What has emerged from this discussion is the urgent need for a re-visioning of the sociological project to confront the existence of a late twentieth-century 'global social formation'. As Archer concludes, this sociology for one world must aim '... at no less than the mobilization of Humanity itself as one self-conscious social agent. What ecologists have done for the protection of the natural world, only the sociologist can attempt for the most dangerous and endangered species ... For commitment to Humanity is also an affirmation that it is ultimately one and indivisible' (ibid., p.146).

REFERENCES

Archer, M.S. (1991) 'Sociology for one world: unity and diversity', *International Sociology,* vol.6, no.2, pp.131–47.

Bauman, Z. (1992) *Intimations of Postmodernity*, London, Routledge.

Beitz, C. (1991) 'Sovereignty and morality in international affairs', in Held, D. (ed.) *Political Theory Today*, Cambridge, Polity Press.

Bell, D. (1987) 'The world and the United States in 2013', *Daedlus*, vol.116, no.3, pp.1–32.

Bozeman, A. (1984) 'The international order in a multicultural world', in Bull, H. and Watson, A. (eds) *The Expansion of International Society*, Oxford, Oxford University Press.

Bull, H. (1977) *The Anarchical Society*, London, Macmillan.

Bull, H. (1979) 'The state's positive role in world affairs', *Daedlus,* vol.108, no.3, pp.111–24.

Burton, J. (1972) *World Society*, Cambridge, Cambridge University Press.

Cerny, P. (1990) *The Changing Architecture of the State*, London, Sage.

Cook, W. and Hertzman, R. (1983) *The Medieval World View*, Oxford, Oxford University Press.

Cox, R. (1987) *Power, Production and World Order*, New York, St Martins Press.

Deutsch, K. (1988) 'Learning-state and the self-transformation of politics', in Campanella, M. (ed.) *Between Rationality and Cognition* , Torio, Italy, Albert Meynier.

Featherstone, M. (ed.) (1990) *Global Culture*, London, Sage.

Frieden, J. (1991) 'Invested interests: the politics of national economic policies in a world of global finance', *International Organization*, vol.45, no.4, pp.425–53.

Fukuyama, F. (1989) 'The end of history?', *The National Interest*, no.16, Summer, pp.3–18.

Garrett, G. and Lange, P. (1991) 'Political responses to interdependence: what's "left" for the left?', *International Organization*, vol.45, no.4, pp.539–65.

Giddens, A. (1987) *The Nation-state and Violence*, Cambridge, Polity Press.

Giddens, A. (1990) *The Consequences of Modernity*, Cambridge, Polity Press.

Giddens, A. (1991) *Modernity and Self-Identity*, Cambridge, Polity Press.

Gill, P. and Law, D. (1989) 'Global hegemony and the structural power of capital', *International Studies Quarterly*, vol.33, no.4, pp.475–500.

Gilpin, R. (1981) *War and Change in World Politics*, Cambridge, Cambridge University Press.

Gilpin, R. (1986) 'The richness of the tradition of political realism', in Keohane, R. (ed.) *Neo-Realism and its Critics*, New York, Columbia University Press.

Gilpin, R. (1987a) *The Political Economy of International Relations*, Princeton, Princeton University Press.

Gilpin, R. (1987b) 'American policy in the post-Reagan era', *Daedlus*, vol.116, no.3, pp.33–69.

Gordon, D. (1988) 'The global economy: new edifice or crumbling foundations?', *New Left Review*, no.168, pp.24–65.

Gourevitch, P. (1986) *Politics in Hard Times*, New York, Cornell University Press.

Hannerz, U. (1991) 'Scenarios for peripheral cultures', in King, A. (ed.) (1991).

Hanreider, W. (1978) 'Dissolving international politics: reflections on the nation-state', *American Political Science Review*, vol.72, no.4, pp.1276–87.

Harvey, D. (1989) *The Condition of Postmodernity*, Oxford, Basil Blackwell.

Held, D. (1991) 'Democracy, the nation-state and the global system', in *Political Theory Today*, Cambridge, Polity Press.

Hertz, J. (1957) 'The rise and demise of the territorial nation-state', *World Politics*, vol.ix, pp.473ff.

Jameson, F. (1991) *Postmodernism or the Cultural Logic of Late Capitalism*, London, Verso Press.

Jervis, R. (1991) 'The future of world politics', *International Security*, vol.16, no.3, pp.39–73.

Kaiser, K. (1972) 'Transnational relations as a threat to the democratic process', in Keohane, R. and Nye, J. (eds) *Transnational Relations and World Politics*, Boston, Harvard University Press.

Keohane, R. (1984) *After Hegemony*, Princeton, Princeton University Press.

Keohane, R. and Nye, J. (1977) *Power and Interdependence*, Boston, Little Brown.

King, A. (1990) *Urbanism, Colonialism and the World-Economy*, London, Routledge.

King, A. (ed.) (1991) *Culture, Globalization and the World System*, London, Macmillan.

Krasner, S. (1991) 'Economic interdependence and independent statehood', mimeo.

Lewis, F. (1991) 'The "G-7$\frac{1}{2}$" Directorate', *Foreign Policy*, no.85, pp.25–40.

Maddox, C. (1990) *Salvador Dali*, Köln, Benedikt Taschen.

Mann, M. (1986) *The Sources of Social Power*, Cambridge, Cambridge University Press.

McGrew, A. (1992) 'Global politics in transition', in McGrew, A. and Lewis, P. (eds) (1992).

McGrew, A. and Lewis, P. (eds) (1992) *Global Politics*, Cambridge, Polity Press.

Modelski, G. (1972) *The Principles of World Politics*, New York, Free Press.

Morse, E. (1976) *Modernization and the Transformation of International Relations*, New York, Free Press.

Murray, R. (1971) 'The internationalization of capital and the nation-state', *New Left Review*, no.67, pp.84–109.

Nye, J. (1989) *Bound to Lead*, New York, Basic Books.

Parkinson, F. (1977) *The Philosophy of International Relations*, London, Sage.

Perlmutter, H.V. (1991) 'On the rocky road to the first global civilization', *Human Relations*, vol. 44, no.9, pp.897–1010.

Robertson, R. (1990) 'Mapping the global condition', in Featherstone, M. (ed.) (1990).

Robertson, R. (1991a) 'Social theory, cultural relativity and the problem of globality', in King, A. (1991).

Robertson, R. (1991b) 'The globalization paradigm', in Bromley, D.G. (ed.) *Religion and the Social Order*, London, JAI Press.

Robertson, R. and Lechner, F. (1985) 'Modernization, globalization and the problem of culture in world systems theory', *Theory, Culture and Society*, vol.2, no.3, pp.103–19.

Rosecrance, R. (1986) *The Rise of the Trading State*, New York, Basic Books.

Rosenau, J. (1980) *The Study of Global Interdependence*, London, Frances Pinter.

Rosenau, J. (1989) *Interdependence and Conflict in World Politics*, Lexington, USA, D.C. Heath.

Rosenau, J. (1990) *Turbulence in World Politics*, Brighton, Harvester Wheatsheaf.

Ruggie, J. (1991) 'Finding our feet in territoriality: problematizing modernity in international relations', mimeo.

Scharpf, F. (1991) *Crisis and Choice in European Social Democracy*, Cornell, Cornell University Press.

Shaw, M. (1991) *Post-Military Society*, Cambridge, Polity Press.

Sklair, L. (1991) *Sociology of the Global System*, Brighton, Harvester Wheatsheaf.

Starke, L. (1990) *Signs of Hope*, Oxford, Oxford University Press.

Turner, B.S. (1990) 'The two faces of sociology: global or national?', in Featherstone, M. (ed.) (1990).

Vogler, J. (1992) 'Regimes and the global commons: space, atmosphere and the oceans', in McGrew, A. and Lewis, P. (eds) (1992).

Walker, R. (1988) *One World, Many Worlds*, New York, Lynne Rienner.

Wallerstein, I. (1983) *Historical Capitalism*, London, Verso.

Wallerstein, I. (1984) 'Patterns and prospectives of the capitalist world-economy', in *The Politics of the World-Economy*, Cambridge, Cambridge University Press.

Wallerstein, I. (1991) 'The lessons of the 1980s', in *Geopolitics and Geoculture*, Cambridge, Cambridge University Press.

Waltz, K. (1979) *Theory of International Politics*, New York, Addison-Wesley.

Webb, M.C. (1991) 'International economic structures, government interests and international co-ordination of macroeconomic adjustment policies', *International Organization*, vol.45, no.3, pp.309–43.

READING A   ON THE ROCKY ROAD TO THE FIRST GLOBAL
CIVILIZATION

Howard V. Perlmutter

By the *first global civilization* we mean a world order, with shared values, processes, and structures: (1) whereby nations and cultures become more open to influence by each other, (2) whereby there is recognition of the identities and diversities of peoples in various groups, and ethnic and religious pluralism, (3) where peoples of different ideologies and values both cooperate and compete but no ideology prevails over all the others, (4) where the global civilization becomes unique in a holistic sense while still being pluralist, and heterogeneous in its character, and (5) where increasingly these values are perceived as shared despite varying interpretations, e.g, such as we currently see for the values of openness, human rights, freedom, and democracy. ...

For the first time in human history and with the help of major political and technological changes, we have the possibility of a real time, simul-taneously-experienced global civilization with almost daily global events, where global cooperation is in a more horizontal than vertical mode. This is why we now see the possibility of the emergence of one single world civilization with great diversity in its constituent cultures and interdepen-dence among poles. In fact, it would be a civilization whose distinctive-ness comes from the attitudes toward and acceptance of diversity along with some shared values which act as a glue for the civilization. ...

So for us, the first global civilization is a vision seen at the dawn of univer-sal history, as Raymond Aron (1961) has put it, not the end of history as Fukuyama (1989) has recently proclaimed. From this historical perspec-tive, there is but one human civilization which is seamless and global in its character but with a magnificent variety of indigenous variations on the life experience. This is the meaning Teilhard de Chardin (1965) gave to the planetization of humankind.

An Explanation for Current Trends

... The first explanatory reason for postulating the emergence of a first global civilization is that we can understand the current profundity of the interpenetration of globalization trends better by examining their impacts in the major civilizational arenas. The civilizational arenas where current trends can be observed include: political-military-legal, economic-indus-trial, social-cultural-physiological (including the arts, psychological, and physiological dimensions), the spiritual-religious, science and tech-nology, and ecology.

In the *political* arena, we can understand how a civilization is emerging in which nation states seek more democratic and open models and to fit with

Source: Perlmutter, H.V. (1991) *Human Relations*, vol.44, no.9, September, pp.898, 902–6.

the globalization of the world-economy. The most dramatic at this writing is the reunification of Germany and the transformation of the Soviet Union. But all of the nations of Eastern Europe are now embarked on a national-rebuilding process under the conditions of irreversible interdependence which were not as major a concern when they were locked into the Soviet Bloc.

In the *economic* arena, we already see a civilization in which firms, called transnational corporations, by seeking to globalize in order to survive, begin to respond to and create needs for convenience and material well being which already produces about 25% of the world's GNP. This has led to the rapid growth of global competition in almost all business sectors and stock markets in both advanced and emerging industrialized countries. The social architectural changes in the Transnational Corporation (TNC) are also well underway. It would appear that there are converging visions among executives from East and West about the future properties of leading TNCs (Perlmutter, 1990).

In the *social and cultural* arenas, we are for example in some parts of the world moving beyond the earliest stages of acknowledging that globalizing university curricula will have to produce such educational innovations so that students can develop world cognitive maps which permit them to understand daily events. ...

The arts are slowly becoming seen as a common heritage of humankind, in part because Picassos are subject to global auctions, with a global market value, in part because some kind of concept of universal aesthetic value may be taking hold.

In the *psychological* arena, we can begin to see the early stages of the globalization of the self. This involves a critique of the modern world's liberal individualist theory of the person, and the introduction of recent psychological formulations to show how globalization will require a change in psychology's current theory of the person (Sampson, 1989).

In the *spiritual-religious* arena, with increasing pluralism, we may see a greater willingness to accept the various forms of religion, as in Spain for the first time since 1492, and an incipient spirit of ecumenism, based on the respect for human rights, the dignity of humans, and indeed all forms of life.

In the *scientific and technological* arenas, we see global cooperation and competition in all the leading domains, such as superconductivity and space, biogenetics, and biosensors. Scientific knowledge is already part of the global commons. When it comes to mapping the human genome or exploring space, passports don't determine who will contribute.

In the *ecological* arena, we are at the earliest stages of developing world standards and structures for monitoring environmental damage, and for environmental maintenance, for dealing with global warming trends, for dealing with the disposal of waste and with toxic pollutants, and the re-greening of the planet.

These civilizational arenas can be viewed in terms of *multi-dimensional increases in global interdependence* and the systemic interrelationships between these interdependencies. For each of these arenas, we see an increase not only in the *quality and quantity* of global interdependencies but in the widely shared perceptions of those interdependencies in different groups. Some of the aspects of the changes in these interdependencies are evident in the following:

The *geographical scope* along different directions of the global compass (north-north, east-west, north-south, etc.) of global interdependencies: New alliances are being formed daily in each of these directions.

The *density* (how many linkages and bonds there are) of global interdependencies has also increased. The density of these alliances can be measured in volumes of communication, frequency of world conferences, air travel, etc. We now speak not of isolated cities but of global networks of cities like London, Tokyo, New York, Moscow, Bonn, Paris, and most capital cities of the world, which increasingly have communication networks which join people in cities around the world.

Interdependencies have matured in *depth* as well (the growing personal and institutional commitments). Friendships, interlinked careers, and organizational purposes are examples of the kinds of forces that have led to greater depth in global alliances.

Interdependencies develop with greater *speed* (how quickly good and bad ideas travel). Global interdependencies grow faster than ever before in the political, economic, sociocultural, technological, and ecological arenas.

Interdependencies are becoming more *irreversible* (once formed, difficult to dissolve). This irreversibility is necessary for the global techno-structure that permits real time global networks to work. Considerable investments of time and money are needed to establish networks that have impact; parties to agreements are less likely, given large investments, to back away from the interdependencies they have formed.

We have also enhanced our ability to form and manage global alliances. The number and size of transnational global organizations has increased steadily since World War II; today, by some accounts, there may be over 20,000 of these organizations in existence. ...

Interdependencies have become larger in *scale and consciousness* (the public's awareness of events taking place outside of the home country). Visual images from films and videotapes, increased personal communications, or travel and a greater openness toward borders have all contributed to events becoming larger and more public. It now makes sense to stage a rally of 50,000 people, since size is a prerequisite for global media coverage; and importantly, global media coverage is more important than it has ever been, as world leaders are more concerned about how global attitudes affect local social and economic decision-making.

Thus, what happens in Bucharest and Brazilia is no longer a purely local affair. More people experience some shared values regarding, for instance, how mass protest can be expressed or how Indians in the Amazon should be treated. This means that events are now not only seen locally but are played out on a global stage (as Boulding, 1990, notes). In one evening, the images move from Johannesburg (the freeing of Nelson Mandela) to the Cartagena, Columbia meeting of the 'first anti-drug cartel', to consultants meeting with the President of Brazil concerning the environment, to the two plus four meeting on the reunification of Germany, to a debate on the deforestation process in Indonesia.

The total impact of these interdependencies has been to make it difficult conceptually and empirically to isolate different parts of the world from each other or to hold on to the notion that international boundaries are impermeable. This has an extremely important consequence. ... *National transparency* is by now a largely irreversible phenomenon.

References

Aron, R. (1961) *The Dawn of Universal History,* Praeger, New York.

Boulding, E. (1990) *The Old and the New Transnationalism: An Evolutionary Perspective,* Case Western Reserve Social Innovations Conference, Cleveland, Ohio.

de Chardin, T. (1965) *The Phenomenon of Man,* London, Fontana Books.

Fukuyama, F. (1989) 'The end of history?', *The National Interest*, no.16.

Perlmutter, H.V. (1990) 'Marketing in the twenty-first century TNC', *Marketing 2000,* American Marketing Association, to appear.

Sampson, E.E. (1989) 'The challenge of social change for psychology: globalization and psychology's theory of the person', *American Psychologist*, vol.44, no.6.

READING B   THE GLOBAL CAPITALIST SYSTEM

Leslie Sklair

This book argues that we need to take a step towards a *sociology* of the global system. ... We cannot ignore the nation-state, but this book attempts to offer in addition a conception of the global system based on *transnational practices* (TNPs).

TNPs are analytically distinguished on three levels, economic, political and cultural-ideological, what I take to constitute the sociological totality. In the concrete conditions of the world as it is, a world largely structured by global capitalism, each of these TNPs is typically, but not exclusively, characterized by a major institution. The transnational corporation (TNC) is the major locus of transnational economic practices; what I shall term the transnational capitalist class is the major locus of transnational political practices; and the major locus of transnational cultural-ideological practice is to be found in the culture-ideology of consumerism. Not all culture is ideological, even in capitalist societies. The reason why I run

Source: Sklair, L. (1991) *Sociology of the Global System*, Brighton, Harvester Wheatsheaf, pp.5–8.

culture and *ideology* together to identify the institutionalization of consumerism is that consumerism in the global system can only be fully
understood as a cultural-ideological practice. When we buy something
that has been imported we are engaged in a typical economic transnational
practice. When we are influenced to vote or support a cause by those
whose interests are transnational we are engaged in a typical political
transnational practice. When we experience the need for a global product
we are engaged in a typical cultural-ideological transnational practice.

TNPs make sense only in the context of the global system. ...

The global system is marked by a very great asymmetry. The most important economic, political and cultural-ideological goods that circulate
around the globe tend to be owned and/or controlled by small groups in a
relatively small number of countries. Until recently it was both convenient and accurate to use the term 'Western' to describe this asymmetry,
and the idea of 'Western imperialism' was widely acknowledged as a way
of analyzing the global system. However, the present global status of Japan
makes these terms obsolete. In this book I shall use the awkward but
evocative term *hegemon* to describe the asymmetry in the global system.
The hegemon is the agent of the key TNPs, it can be a representative
individual, organization, state or class, whose interests prevail in the
struggle for global resources. ... While there is only one country, the
United States, whose agents, organizations and classes are hegemonic in
all three spheres, other countries and agents, organizations and classes are
hegemonic, or realistically claim to share hegemony, within each sphere.

The nation-state, therefore, is the spatial reference point for most of the
crucial transnational practices that go to make up the structures of the
global system, in the sense that most transnational practices intersect in
particular countries and come under the jurisdiction of particular nation-
states. But it is not the only reference point. The most important is, of
course, the global capitalist system, based on a variegated global capitalist
class, which unquestionably dictates economic transnational practices,
and is the most important single force in the struggle to dominate political
and cultural-ideological transnational practices. There are several other
systems, regionally important, ethnically, culturally and/or theologically
based but none has, as yet, had the pervasive success that capitalism has
enjoyed in the twentieth century.

The success of a system is often bound up with the success of the state that
is its main proponent. Britain in the nineteenth century was, and the
United States of America in the twentieth century is, the hegemon of global capitalism, though of rather different versions of it. Through their
(respective) straightforward colonial and convoluted imperialist trajectories the transnational practices of these two countries etched the forms
of capitalism onto the global system. It was this hegemonic combination of
a mighty domestic economy, a progressive ruling class (in comparison
with most others actually existing), and at least some desirable cultural-
ideological features particularly attractive to 'modernizing' elites, that
opened the global door to them and ensured the creation, persistence and

often aggrandisement of social classes in countries all over the world willing and eager to adopt their transnational practices.

These classes are widely known by the label 'comprador' though this term has attracted a great deal of criticism. Here, I shall convert the idea into a concept of the *transnational capitalist class* (TCC). This class consists of those people who see their own interests and/or the interests of their nation, as best served by an identification with the interests of the capitalist global system, in particular the interests of the countries of the capitalist core and the transnational corporations domiciled in them. The TCC holds certain transnational practices to be more valuable than domestic practices. It is quite possible for a fraction of it to identify more with economic transnational practices than with political or cultural-ideological ones, or vice versa. Indeed, the fundamental in-built instability of the global system, and the most important contradiction with which any theory of the global system has to grapple, is that the hegemonic ideology of the system is under constant challenge, particularly outside the First World. The substantive content of the theory, how the transnational corporations harness the transnational capitalist classes to solidify their hegemonic control of consumerist culture and ideology, is the site of the many struggles for the global system. Who will win and who will lose these struggles is not a foregone conclusion.

READING C   THE TWO WORLDS OF WORLD POLITICS

James N. Rosenau

… The very notion of 'international relations' seems obsolete in the face of an apparent trend in which more and more of the interactions that sustain world politics unfold without the direct involvement of nations or states. So a new term is needed, one that denotes the presence of new structures and processes while at the same time allowing for still further structural development. A suitable label would be *postinternational politics.*

… It is a shorthand for the changes wrought by global turbulence; for an ever more dynamic interdependence in which labor is increasingly specialized and the number of collective actors thereby proliferates; for the centralizing and decentralizing tendencies that are altering the identity and number of actors on the world stage; for the shifting orientations that are transforming authority relations among the actors; and for the dynamics of structural bifurcation that are fostering new arrangements through which the diverse actors pursue their goals. Postinternational politics is that hitherto unimaginable scheme, a generic conception of how the human links that span the globe have been affected by the complexity and dynamism that are coming into view as the present millennium draws to a close. …

Source: Rosenau, J.N. (1990) *Turbulence in World Politics*, Brighton, Harvester Wheatsheaf, pp.6–7, 97–100, 102–4, 249–52.

... Four broad patterns emerge as salient outcomes of the dynamics of change that are at work in world politics. ...

1   The universe of global politics has come to consist of two interactive worlds with overlapping memberships: a multi-centric world of diverse, relatively equal actors, and a state-centric world in which national actors are still primary.

2   The norms governing the conduct of politics in the multi-centric world have evolved so as to diminish the utility of force, compelling most of its actors to confine the threat of actual use of force to those situations that arise in the state-centric world of international politics.

3   An autonomy dilemma serves as the driving force of the multi-centric world and a security dilemma constitutes a dominant concern in the state-centric world; at the same time, in the latter case, acquiring or preserving what is held to be a proper share of the world market has come to rival the acquisition or preservation of territory as a preoccupation of states.

4   Changes at the level of macro structures and processes have served as both sources and products of corresponding micro-level shifts wherein individuals are becoming more analytically skillful and cathectically competent, thus fostering the replacement of traditional criteria of legitimacy and authority with performance criteria that, in turn, serve to intensify both the centralizing and the decentralizing tendencies at work within and among macro collectivities.

Setting forth these patterns does not imply that the current scene is exclusively one of profound change. What follows does presume that powerful and transforming dynamics are unfolding on a global scale, but, ... these dynamics are conceived as existing in continuous tension with a wide array of static forces that press for continuity. ...

... The conceptualization of a multi-centric world of diverse actors that coexists with the state-centric world of national actors virtually assures consideration of the tensions between the statics of continuity and the dynamics of change. For, as will be seen, this nexus of the two worlds is a prime arena wherein clashes occur between the past and the present, between the tendencies toward decentralization and those toward centralization, between the diminished relevance of force and the growing stress on increased shares of the global market.

... These two worlds embrace the same actors, but they have distinctive structures and processes that require the actors to employ very different decision rules as they move back and forth between them. As individuals are active in both their personal and professional worlds, so do states, corporations, ethnic groups, international organizations, churches, and many other collectives with transnational aspirations and responsibilities live in two worlds. To be sure, these two worlds are interactive and overlapping, but each nevertheless retains its identity as a separate sphere of activity because of the different structures and processes through which its actors relate to each other. Thus, the organizing principle of realism — that states continuously confront a security dilemma in the form of threats from other states — is joined in competition with the driving force of the multi-centric world — that systems and subsystems at diverse macro levels continuously face an autonomy dilemma in the form of challenges to their identity and integrity. ...

Adding to the complexity and dynamism at the global level are structural changes at the national and subnational levels. ... [A]t both of these levels decentralizing tendencies are conceived to have fragmented long-established hierarchies presided over by narrowly based elites, replacing them with a multiplicity of organizations that have more pluralistic leaderships. By its very nature, such a structural arrangement means that actors are more interdependent, that they have a need for and relations with a widening array of other actors, and that consequently the patterns of interaction that mark their daily lives encompass more extensive networks than was the case in the industrial or agrarian eras. In short, the structural arrangements of postinternational politics are marked by considerably greater density and interdependence than those they replaced, and these characteristics are among the hallmarks of turbulence.

... the decentralizing tendencies of the postindustrial era have fragmented the previous sources of power and authority. Where authority relations at the global level in the state system were to a considerable extent established on the basis of military capabilities, the sources of power in the current era are much more varied, and authority links are thus that much more complex. A host of new actors at all three levels [global, national, and subnational] now have the wherewithal to lay claim to their goals and to pursue them in diverse ways. Moreover, this fragmentation of the number and diversity of relationships has altered the nature of authority, making compliance more problematical and venturesomeness more likely. ... In previous eras, citizenship skills were much more rudimentary than is presently the case. ... [T]he enlarged capacities of individuals have also led to a diffusion and reorientation in the levels at which loyalties and legitimacy sentiments are focused, with the main tendency being toward subsystems and away from national entities. ...

... That a group of concerned scientists negotiates with superpowers to monitor nuclear testing or that a church official undertakes to mediate with terrorists for the release of hostages is readily explained, for example, by the advent of a multi-centric world in which authority is so widely dispersed that governments must be ready to accept the involvement of private actors if they are to move toward their goals. This very same devolution of authority to nongovernmental subsystems also serves to account for the actions of chiefs of state and foreign ministers in taking their cases to the streets of New York and the airwaves of the Middle East, just as the greater analytic skills of citizens and the shift of their loyalties and legitimacy sentiments towards subgroups facilitated the success of Solidarity in Poland, the Tamils in Sri Lanka, the antiwar movement in the United States, and the disinvestment campaign directed at South Africa. Likewise, the fragmentation of authority and the complex interdependencies accompanying the bifurcation of the global system provide a basis for understanding such developments as the ability of an international organization, the IMF, to alter the policies of national governments, the impact of the Nobel Prize committee on a delicate diplomatic situation, and the ability of a bureaucratic agency in the White House to implement (at least for a time) policies outside the framework of its own governmental structure. ...

Although the emergence of a multi-centric world accounts well for the events and developments that are anomalous from a state-centric perspective, what accounts for the emergence itself? Why now, late in the twentieth century, has turbulence overcome world politics, weakening national states to the point where they must share the political stage with private subgroups, transnational organizations, and their own bureaucratic agencies? A brief answer is that the world has moved into the postindustrial era of interdependence. ...

The Two Worlds of World Politics

The main features of the two worlds are contrasted in Table 1. Here it can be seen that the state-centric world is much more coherent and structured than is its multi-centric counterpart. It is to some degree anarchic and decentralized, because of the lack of an overarching world government, but that anarchy is minimal compared to the chaos that results from the much greater decentralization that marks the multi-centric system. Not only are there many fewer points at which action originates in the state-centric than in the multi-centric system, but action and interaction in the former is also considerably more subject to formal procedures and hierarchical precepts than in the latter. In the multi-centric world, relations among actors are on more equal footing, are more temporary and ad hoc, and more susceptible to change, but are less symmetrical and less constrained by power differentials, formal authority, and established institutions. ...

For the sovereignty-free actors of the multi-centric world, in other words, states are external and not constitutive — obstacles, nuisances, or opportunities to be surmounted, tolerated, or seized — as long as security and territorial issues do not draw them into the sovereignty networks of the state-centric world. ... Its actors accept that states establish legal boundaries within which they must conduct their affairs, even that states can employ considerable resources to fix political limits within which they must operate, but they do not view the exercise of state prerogatives as amounting to a 'crunch' (as Waltz puts it) requiring them to set aside their own goals.

Moreover, not all the actors in the multi-centric world are caught up in the authority networks of the state-centric world. Some have managed to obfuscate, even elude, the jurisdiction of a single state. As one observer has pointed out: 'In high growth areas such as financial services, increasingly large segments of international markets are outside the legal boundaries of the major trading nations. This ... trend is disturbing because it implies increasing lack of control by national or international agencies.' (Brown, 1988, pp.96–7) ...

Table 1   Structure and process in the two worlds of world politics

	State-centric world	Multi-centric world
Number of essential actors	Fewer than 200	Hundreds of thousands
Prime dilemma of actors	Security	Autonomy
Principal goals of actors	Preservation of territorial integrity, and physical security	Increase in world market shares, maintenance of integration of subsystems
Ultimate resort for realizing goals	Armed force	Withholding of cooperation or compliance
Normative priorities	Processes, especially those that preserve sovereignty and the rule of law	Outcomes, especially those that expand human rights, justice, and wealth
Modes of collaboration	Formal alliances whenever possible	Temporary coalitions
Scope of agenda	Limited	Unlimited
Rules governing interactions among actors	Diplomatic practices	Ad hoc, situational
Distribution of power among actors	Hierarchical by amount of power	Relative equality as far as initiating action is concerned
Interaction patterns among actors	Symmetrical	Asymmetrical
Locus of leadership	Great powers	Innovative actors with extensive resources
Institutionalization	Well established	Emergent
Susceptibility to change	Relatively low	Relatively high
Control over outcomes	Concentrated	Diffused
Bases of decisional structures	Formal authority, law	Various types of authority, effective leadership

The emergence of the multi-centric world has not, of course, undermined the autonomy of the state-centric world. Sovereignty-bound actors retain the capacity to set the rules by which their systems and subsystems conduct themselves. ... For states, too, therefore, the actors in the multi-centric world, even those over whom they exercise sovereignty, are external and not constitutive — constraints and opportunities to be managed and developed through proof, persuasion, bargaining, and the exercise of authority whenever possible, or through coercive means if necessary. ...

In sum, it is in the sense that both sovereignty-bound and sovereignty-free actors have come to define themselves as the subjects of world politics, while viewing the other as its objects, that global life can be said to consist of two worlds. ...

Reference

Brown, C.J. (1988) 'The globalization of information technologies', *Washington Quarterly*, 11 (Winter), pp.96–7.

READING D CHANGE AND CONTINUITY IN WORLD
POLITICS

Robert Gilpin

The distinguished sociologist Alex Inkeles best captured the spirit of
much contemporary scholarship and its assertion that a discontinuity has
appeared in international relations:

> In the second half of the twentieth century, laymen and professional
> intellectuals alike have frequently expressed the sense that the
> relationship of all of us, all humankind, to each other and to our
> world has been undergoing a series of profound changes. We seem to
> be living in one of those rare historical eras in which a progressive
> quantitative process becomes a qualitative transformation. Even
> when, in more sober moments, we recognize that we are yet far from
> being there, we have the unmistakable sense that we are definitely
> set off on some new trajectory, and that we are not merely launched
> but are already well along toward an only vaguely identified desti-
> nation. The widespread diffusion of this sense of a new, emergent
> global interrelatedness is expressed in numerous ideas, slogans, and
> catchphrases which have wide currency, such as 'world govern-
> ment', 'the global village', 'spaceship earth', 'the biosphere', and the
> ubiquitous cartoon of a crowded globe with a lighted fuse protruding
> from one end, the whole labelled 'the world population bomb'.
> Although the pervasiveness of the response to this emergent situ-
> ation certainly tells us that *something* is happening, its diversity
> highlights our confusion as to exactly *what* it is that is happening.
> (Inkeles, 1975, p.467)

The Advent of Global Society

... Contemporary developments have suggested to many observers the
transcendence of the traditional mentality and character of international
statecraft: advances in communications and transportation have unified
the planet physically. New types of transnational and international actors
more responsive to modern science, technology, and economics have
broken the monopoly of the state in the management and governance of
the international system. Global ecological problems, as well as resource
constraints and limits to growth, have placed on the world's agenda a set
of pressing issues whose solutions are beyond the means of self-serving
nation-states. Modern science, advances in knowledge, and social technologies permit a more rational approach to the solution of international
problems than do strife and conflict. The universal commitment to modernization and a better life for all gives diverse peoples a common set of
concerns and aspirations. In short, those values and interests that unite the
human race are said to be displacing those factors that historically have

Source: Gilpin, R. (1981) *War and Change in World Politics*, Cambridge, Cambridge
University Press, pp.212, 223–26, 228–30.

divided it and have been the underlying causes of wars and violent change. Or, as Inkeles (1975, p.495) put it, 'the emergence of a uniform world culture' is a reality, and a transformation in human consciousness is occurring that will provide escape from the irrational struggle for national advantage.

This thesis that a transformation in human consciousness has taken place in concert with the advent of a global society must also be highly qualified. This position is founded on the belief that modern science and its off-spring, technology, are making the world one, both mentally and physically. Advances in scientific knowledge are believed to be leading toward a more rational approach to the solution of human problems at the same time that modern technological advances have given all mankind a common destiny and the tools necessary to solve the fundamental problems of the planet. It is argued that science and technology imply a morality of international cooperation and make possible a world order that is more nearly just. Through the use of reason and the exploitation of technology, the human race can transcend the irrational struggle over relative gains in order to pursue gains for all mankind and especially to solve the global problems of ecological degradation and resource depletion.

Unfortunately, past expressions of neo-Malthusian ideas similar to the current limits-to-growth thesis have not led to the transcendence of narrow circumscribed loyalties; on the contrary, national fears concerning overpopulation and insufficiency of raw materials have led to the most destructive and irrational of human impulses. Eras of arrested growth, diminishing returns, and market constriction have historically been associated with conflict and war. Social Darwinism, imperialism, and the struggle for *Lebensraum* were the intellectual progeny of neo-Malthusian fears in the late nineteenth century and in the 1930s, and there is little evidence to suggest that mankind has advanced much beyond this level of jungle morality. ...

Even if modern science and technology have given mankind a new consciousness of shared values and common problems, this situation is no guarantee of common interest or of a willingness to subordinate selfish concerns to the larger good. On the contrary, modern science and technology may intensify the conflict over the globe's scarce resources. But it is more important to inquire whether or not a unified humanity really exists. Unfortunately, it does not. The modern 'unified world' has been a creation of the West, which has sought to impose its values and way of life on a recalcitrant set of diverse cultures. ... Emergent power centers with cultural and diplomatic traditions vastly different from those of the once-dominant West may presage a return to the civilizational conflicts reminiscent of the premodern era. In short, one should not confuse the physical unity of the globe with moral unity; the human species remains deeply divided by race, religion, and wealth.

In actuality, the political fragmentation of the world has increased in recent decades. The world now encompasses approximately one hundred and fifty separate sovereignties; nationalism, with its roots in seventeenth-century Europe, has become the predominant religion of modern man. As has been the case in Europe, the continuing formation of nation-states and the spread of nationalism have unleashed powerful and dangerous forces of destruction. The present era is witnessing the proliferation of the nation-state, not its transcendence. ... If the history of European state formation and nationalism is any guide, a true global society and a new consciousness may be far in the future.

Embedded in most social sciences and in the study of international relations is the belief that through science and reason the human race can gain control over its destiny. ...

Political realism is, of course, the very embodiment of this faith in reason and science. An offspring of modern science and the Enlightenment, realism holds that through calculations of power and national interest statesmen can create order out of anarchy and thereby moderate the inevitable conflicts of autonomous, self-centered, and competitive states. If states would pursue only their own security interests (forsaking religious goals and ideology) and respect equally the vital interests of other states, a basis of compromise and orderly change would be possible (Morgenthau, 1973, pp.540–4). Although the content of international-relations theory has changed dramatically over the centuries, this faith that a 'science of international relations' will ultimately save mankind still lies at the heart of its studies.

The major difference between political realism and much contemporary theorizing about international relations is that realism assumes the continuity of statecraft. Realism is based on practices of states, and it seeks to understand how states have always behaved and presumably will always behave. It does not believe that the condition of anarchy can be transcended except through a universal imperium, and thus it contrasts with a powerful strain in contemporary thinking. The advance of technology may open up opportunities for mutual benefit, but it also increases the power available for political struggle. The advance of human reason and understanding will not end this power struggle, but it does make possible a more enlightened understanding and pursuit of national self-interest.

... Ultimately, international politics still can be characterized as it was by Thucydides: the interplay of impersonal forces and great leaders. Technological, economic, and demographic factors push states toward both war and peaceful cooperation. The prudent and enlightened leader can guide the ship of state in one direction or the other. Though always constrained, choices always exist. Historical experience helps teach us what these choices are and what their probable consequences are. In this sense, one can say that learning can take place and can influence the course of international relations.

... In the final decades of the twentieth century, technological, economic, and other developments have suggested to many individuals that the nation-state has finally ceased to be the most efficient unit of economic and political organization. It is argued that a larger regional or even global organization of economic and political affairs is necessary, that new types of economic and political entities would be more efficient than the nation-state. In the interest of world peace and global welfare, some have proposed that more modern forms of international and transnational organization should supplant the increasingly anachronistic nation-state. ...

Unfortunately (or, perhaps, fortunately), no contemporary political entrepreneur appears to regard forcing the transition from the nation-state to some other basis of world economic and political order as a profitable proposition. ...

It is not clear, however, what the ultimate effect of contemporary military and economic developments will be on the scale of political organization. The scope of nuclear warfare and the immense cost of a retaliatory force would appear to favor an enlargement of political entities. At the same time, however, an attempt to conquer a small state possessing even a very modest nuclear capability may be prohibitively expensive. Increasing economic interdependence certainly has decreased national economic autonomy. However, it has also meant that states can have access to large markets without the necessity of integrating politically and that states have increased their intervention in the economy in order to protect national values against potentially harmful external economic forces. Although the emergence of global ecological and related problems necessitates a comparable organization of human affairs, the hold of the nation-state concept on the minds of men grows ever more tenacious. ...

... World politics is still characterized by the struggle of political entities for power, prestige, and wealth in a condition of global anarchy. Nuclear weapons have not made the resort to force irrelevant; economic interdependence does not guarantee that cooperation will triumph over conflict; a global community of common values and outlook has yet to displace international anarchy. The fundamental problem of international relations in the contemporary world is the problem of peaceful adjustment to the consequences of the uneven growth of power among states, just as it was in the past. International society cannot and does not stand still. War and violence remain serious possibilities as the world moves from the decay of one international system toward the creation of another.

References

Inkeles, A. (1975) 'The emerging social structure of the world', *World Politics*, vol.27, no.4, pp.467–95.

Morgenthau, H. (1973) *Politics Among Nations*, New York, A. Knopf.

CHAPTER 3 ENVIRONMENTAL CHALLENGES

Steven Yearley

CONTENTS

1   INTRODUCTION

At the start of the 1990s it appears that everyone is an environmentalist of some sort, be they politicians, supermarket chains, advertisers, the media or big business. Even McDonalds, long associated with the modern American values of convenience and disposability, is now cultivating a 'green' image. The firm is careful to boast that its cattle farming does no damage to the world's rainforests and that the company has withdrawn ozone-threatening CFCs from its burger packaging. A major aim of this chapter is to understand why such concern for the environment is now so prominent. But my analysis will go further than this and develop the theme in two directions. First, I shall assess the wider consequences of this 'greening' for modern societies: for example, its impact on political parties and on people's attitudes to economic growth. Secondly, I shall examine how social scientists have themselves been affected by a growing awareness of environmental issues and how, in many cases, their interpretation of contemporary society has been influenced; in particular, how an appreciation of Western societies' environmental problems has encouraged social scientists to question in a new way the Enlightenment 'achievements' of economic growth, technological progress and scientific advance.

In the course of this analysis I shall look at two major issues: (a) the environmental threats confronting modern societies, and (b) environmentalists' challenges to modern forms of social and political organization. By the former, I refer to our leading ecological problems, such as global warming or the build-up of toxic wastes — problems which may pose a physical threat to the viability of present-day society. By the latter, I mean the claims by environmentalists or 'greens' that our current way of living is unsustainable and that the ambitions which predominate in contemporary society (particularly the wish for our society to become steadily more wealthy) are fundamentally mistaken.

While the ecological threat is a physical one, the environmentalists' challenge takes an ideological form. Naturally, these two issues are closely related. In the absence of ecological problems, environmentalists would find it hard to gain public support for their arguments. Equally, it has in many cases been members of the environmental movement who have brought ecological threats to public attention. But there is no automatic relationship between the two. Environmental consciousness does not arise just because there are ecological problems. As we shall see, social and political forces have played an important role in preparing the way for, and in shaping responses to, ecological issues.

I shall shortly present a brief account of the principal environmental problems with which our society is faced. However, before this it will be useful to set our problems in historical perspective.

One of the most significant, although often unnoticed, achievements of Western society has been radically to diminish our subordination to natural forces and constraints. For example, in practical terms, we have vastly shortened distances between our cities through innovations in transport technology. Nowadays, electronic communications permit virtually instantaneous interaction between one continent and another. Our ability to harness energy from coal, gas and petrol has lessened our dependence on the climate. In this way people can live essentially similar lives, using essentially the same products, eating more or less the same food, whether in Glasgow or Paris, in New York or Sydney. Through technology we have even tried to combat the tendency for food to perish: in many countries, food may now be irradiated to forestall natural deterioration. In other words, people (or at least *some* people) have more or less overcome the environmental constraints presented by distances, the climate, and even the limitations which stem from the nature of living organisms.

In all these and in many other ways, human dependence on the natural environment has been so reduced that an author such as McKibben (1990, pp.43–60) has recently been able to speak of the 'end of nature'. In other words, no inhabitants of the West typically have to face nature without its effects being mediated by human technologies. And even in those parts of the world where nature's force is still felt in an apparently unaltered manner, nature itself has been affected by human activity. Traditional inhabitants of the Amazonian rain forests are having their 'natural' environment altered by development policies; traditional fishing peoples of the Pacific are having their catches affected by the fish-processing ships of the developed world. Even the low-lying farm landscape of Bangladesh — which suffered the worst effects of the flooding of early 1991 — has been decisively shaped by Western-led drainage policies and by development projects which have caused erosion in the uplands. Nature isn't what it was. In McKibben's words, 'we have ended the thing that has, at least in modern times, defined nature for us — its separation from human society' (1990, p.60).

This line of thinking may lead one to assume that past societies — in touch with nature as they had to be — were also in harmony with it. They may not have dominated nature in the way that we hope to, but, by being subordinate to it, they may perhaps have lived sustainably with it. Ironically, this view of the past has been encouraged by the lenses through which we usually look at history. As modern industrial society has developed, nature has been progressively marginalized. In parallel with this development, when historians have come to reflect on the factors which have exerted the greatest influence on human history they have tended, over the years, to grant nature a smaller and smaller role. The histories that have come to be written have typically been dominated by references to political conflict, to wars, to economic trends, to intellectual innovations, or to technical inventions. Certainly, these have been the major explanatory factors put forward by sociological and political theorists such as Weber and Marx. Thus, when we look back to previous civilizations we have tended to interpret their fate, their collapse, in these political and economic terms. However, as

Reading A shows, a plausible case can be put forward for the disruption of early civilizations by essentially ecological factors.

Seymour and Girardet (1990) argue, for example, that there are significant ecological elements underlying the decline of Rome. 'Deforestation, loss of topsoil [and] the spread of swamps' led to diminishing agricultural productivity at home and spurred the pursuit of colonial territories, with first Sicily and then North Africa serving as sources for the staple food, wheat (Seymour and Girardet, 1990, p.49). But years of intensive agricultural exploitation in these conquered regions led to erosion and a loss of soil fertility. Quite apart from external military threats, the empire was unsustainable:

> The Romans were the first to test the viability of large-scale commercial agriculture. They could only make it work by gaining access to ever larger areas of land. But, clearly, in the end they recognized the limits to growth. They left much exhausted land behind them, as well as a trail of human tragedy.
> (ibid., 1990, p.54)

ACTIVITY 1   You should now read **Reading A, 'Far from paradise'**, by John Seymour and Herbert Girardet, which you will find at the end of this chapter. When you have read it, compile a brief list of the ecological factors involved in the downfall of ancient civilizations. Are any of the same factors threatening present-day societies?

In putting their case, Seymour and Girardet seem too ready to dismiss non-ecological explanations for major social change; and their remark about Marx is certainly simplistic and misleading. But they make a convincing — and, to many, surprising — argument that excessive exploitation of the Mediterranean forests, and remorseless extension of foodcrop agriculture, resulted in the collapse of an advanced civilization on Crete and in the declining viability of the Roman Empire. But these societies were not alone in precipitating environmental catastrophe. Ponting (1990) makes a related case for the downfall of the sophisticated Mayan society in the lowland rainforest of upper Central America (now parts of Mexico, Guatemala, Belize and Honduras), and for the dwindling of the ancient Mesopotamian civilization in the Middle East (see also Thomas, 1984, p.24).

These studies and their examples have two significant implications. First, they dispel any excessively romantic view of how well in touch with nature past cultures were: we are not alone in facing ecological problems. But if this realization is comforting, its corollary is most certainly not: this is that ecological problems can help bring about the downfall of whole societies. Therefore, according to these authors, we had better take ecological threats seriously.

2 ECOLOGICAL THREATS TO MODERN SOCIETY: AN OVERVIEW

By 1990, some of the ecological threats to modern Western societies had become very widely known. No comedy routine was complete without some joke about global warming, about pollution from cars or about the ozone layer. Shelves in the newly created 'green' departments of bookstores strained under the weight of rainforest picture books and environmental diaries. But there was still widespread confusion. Comedians, among others, persisted in mixing up the destruction of the ozone layer with the greenhouse effect. And in December 1990 Friends of the Earth (FoE) were able to present their 'Green Con' award to one of the newly privatized English electricity generating companies, Eastern Electricity. A senior executive of the company had written to a customer stating that people could reduce their contribution to global warming by using more electrical power, since domestic electrical heating produces fewer pollutants than gas. In his letter, this executive failed to mention the huge carbon dioxide emissions from fossil fuel-burning power stations. Under most circumstances, gas heating actually leads to the production of less 'greenhouse gas' than does electrical; better insulation, leading to more efficient use of heating, is of decisive importance whatever fuel is used. The executive's advice would thus have aggravated ecological problems while benefiting his own company through increased profits.

Given this lack of clarity about environmental problems a short overview is probably useful (for a more comprehensive account, also from a social scientific perspective, see Yearley, 1991, pp.11–46; see also FoE, 1990; and Elsworth, 1990). There is no single best way to classify these problems, though we can make a helpful initial division into problems of wastes and of declining resources. I shall deal with them in this order, picking up a few neglected themes at the end.

2.1 WASTE AND AIR POLLUTION

Some waste is produced by nearly everything we do, at home, at work, driving in the car, and so on. Most often we think of waste in terms of the solid rubbish that goes into our dustbins and the liquids which enter the sewers. But environmentalists also focus a great deal of attention on gaseous wastes. In particular, there are three kinds of gaseous effluent which give cause for the most concern: (a) the carbon dioxide which results from burning fossil fuels such as coal and petrol in furnaces, power stations and motor vehicles; (b) the acidic gases (notably sulphur dioxide) which arise mainly from the combustion of impurities in these fuels; and (c) the ozone-destroying gases which are released into the atmosphere from the use of aerosols, and from the manufacture and ultimate breakdown of insulating foams, refrigerators and air-conditioning units.

In each case, the dangers which result from these gases have not been immediately apparent. For example, carbon dioxide is odourless and colourless; it is not poisonous and is produced naturally when animals breathe out and when organic matter decays. However, the burning of fossil fuels — predominantly in the industrialized world — has led to an increase in the proportion of this gas in the atmosphere. Although it still makes up only a tiny fraction of the atmosphere (just over a thirtieth of one per cent by volume), it is steadily increasing and is believed to be far more plentiful now than at any other time since early prehistory (Leggett, 1990, pp.26–7). Carbon dioxide (as well as other, even rarer gases) tends to trap the sun's heat in the atmosphere. Acting rather like the panes of glass in a greenhouse, molecules of carbon dioxide permit the sun's rays to pass through (and thus to warm the earth), and then tend to prevent the resulting heat (in the form of infrared radiation) from passing back out through the atmosphere and being dissipated in space. Accordingly, the earth's average temperature is likely to rise, disrupting our climate, affecting vegetation and agriculture, and — most notoriously — prompting a rise in sea levels as the oceans warm and expand, and as land-based ice melts into the seas. This seemingly innocuous waste gas could have catastrophic consequences on a worldwide scale.

If fuelstuffs were chemically pure, waste gases would comprise virtually only water vapour and oxides of carbon. But they are not. The gases emitted from power stations, from cars, from domestic heating systems and from industry contain small amounts of acidic gases: sulphur dioxide and various oxides of nitrogen. As these gases spread through the atmosphere they mix with water vapour to form acidic compounds which, sooner or later, fall as 'acid rain'. Although acid emissions make up only a small part of waste gases, our overall output of such waste is so large that in Britain alone we generated over six million tonnes of acid gases in 1988 (FoE, 1990, p.3).

Acid rain gives rise to many problems (see Elsworth, 1990, pp.1–17). Rivers and lakes can become acidified, especially in areas of Scandinavia and Scotland where the make-up of the soil means that it has only a limited ability to neutralize acidity. Acidity can kill fish, and some other animals, especially birds, are susceptible to acid poisoning too. In concentrated form — for example, from vehicle exhaust fumes in congested traffic — acidic gases can be harmful to human health. Acid rain is also believed to contribute to the death of trees by lowering their tolerance to disease and other biological hazards. Lastly, it erodes buildings and monuments.

Debate about the exact effects of acid rain and about different countries' respective responsibility for causing it persisted over the last two decades. This debate dragged on for several reasons: because the alleged results were often found very far away from the presumed causes; because the precise chemistry of acid rain production was open to dispute; and because acidification can be caused in other ways too: through algal activity, for example. The countries held chiefly

London traffic officer,
August 1989

responsible — among them, Britain — were able to claim that there was
no definitive proof that it was their pollution which was to blame for
other countries' acid rain. And since the evidence was not decisive,
they could argue for a delay in taking practical action until even
stronger proof was available. Governments were highly motivated to do
this since it is expensive to clean acid out of waste gases and in the UK
the Conservative administration wanted to keep electricity generation in
an economically favourable situation prior to its privatization.

The third major problem with effluent gases concerns the accidental
destruction of ozone. Ozone is a gas very closely related to oxygen, but
is relatively unstable and is very liable to enter into reactions and to be
converted into oxygen in the process. At ground level, ozone is
therefore short-lived. But high in the atmosphere (between about 20 and
50 kilometres up), ozone is more common, although still very rare. At
these altitudes, some molecules of oxygen convert naturally into ozone
which is then able to make up a shield, absorbing a great deal of the
harmful ultraviolet radiation striking the atmosphere.

However, some gases synthesized for industrial uses this century —
notably, but not exclusively, CFCs (chlorofluorocarbons) — have
gradually drifted into the upper atmosphere, where they have broken
down under the influence of solar radiation. The reactive components

formed by their breakdown are very effective in encouraging the decomposition of ozone, and it is believed that it is these chemicals which have led to severe thinning of the ozone layer at both poles. On the eve of 1991, the *Independent on Sunday* noted that, 'This year, the hole in the ozone layer over the Antarctic reached a record size. Next spring, measurements over the Arctic will probably show that ozone loss is intensifying over northern latitudes' (30 December 1990, p.8). Such damage to the ozone layer threatens to allow more high-energy radiation into the atmosphere, which is likely to cause an increase in the incidence of skin cancer and to lead to disruption of the marine food chain through its harmful effect on planktonic plants in polar waters — the most basic source of food in the oceans.

It is important to note in this case that the CFCs causing the damage are themselves not directly harmful. Indeed, they were developed precisely to be non-toxic and incombustible so that they could be safely used in aerosols, in insulating materials, and so on. But it is this very stability that has allowed them to get as far as the stratosphere without breaking down. Now that there is wide agreement on the dangers of 'ozone-eaters', action can be taken to limit their production and release. Once their release is stopped the ozone layer will eventually heal itself. But there are still millions of tonnes of them on their way into the atmosphere, as well as vast amounts left in insulating foams and discarded refrigerators. It is also uncertain that we have identified all the potential ozone-eaters; Friends of the Earth has noted that solvents used in typing-correction fluids and for other industrial applications, as well as some of the proposed substitutes for CFCs, may also lead to ozone depletion.

Yet CFCs are harmful in another way too, for they are also a major form of greenhouse gas, and are responsible for about one quarter of the global warming effect (Leggett, 1990, p.17).

I have described these problems in some detail for two reasons: first, to show that exhaust gases, though less obvious than some other questions of waste disposal (such as the treatment of radioactive materials), do highlight the basic connection between waste and pollution. As Elsworth sharply points out, 'Pouring industrial garbage into the air is a cheap form of waste disposal [especially if] it drifts into someone else's back yard' (1990, p.15). Even waste which is apparently quite innocuous, such as carbon dioxide and CFCs, can pose a serious pollution hazard. Secondly, these gases pose major international, possibly global, threats. Even on its own, global warming might just result in the deaths of hundreds of thousands of people, and devastate the world economy. The atmosphere has been treated in a careless way; people have polluted our common environment presuming, if they thought about it at all, that the atmosphere was large enough to absorb anything we could dump into it. It looks as though the atmosphere is far more sensitive than we had assumed. These waste gases show us just how pervasively harmful modern forms of pollution can be.

Table 3.1   Gaseous wastes and air pollution

Effluent Type	Source	Impact
Carbon dioxide: the leading 'greenhouse' gas	Carbon dioxide is released when fossil fuels are burnt. It is produced in roughly equal proportions by power stations, industry and vehicle exhausts.	Carbon dioxide absorbs infrared energy and thus traps heat in the atmosphere. The more carbon dioxide we release, the hotter the atmosphere is likely to become. Such heating is expected to affect the climate, disrupt agriculture and cause flooding.
Acidic gases	Sulphur dioxide comes mostly from the burning of impurities in coal and oil. Oxides of nitrogen come partly from impurities and partly from the nitrogen already in the air which is oxidized at very high temperatures and in furnaces.	Acidic gases react with rainwater and moisture in the air to produce 'acid rain'. The gases can travel large distances causing problems hundreds of kilometres from their source. Acid rain is harmful to trees, river life, soils and even buildings. The acidic gases can also be directly harmful to human health.
Ozone-destroying gases	The most important of these are the CFCs which are produced commercially for use as solvents and cleaning fluids, and for use in refrigerators and air-conditioning equipment. They are also used to blow foams for insulating and packaging materials, and as propellants in aerosols.	CFCs are very long-lived chemicals. When they escape into the atmosphere (when solvents evaporate for example) some eventually drift upwards and come into contact with the earth's protective ozone layer. They help break down that layer, which in turn permits harmful radiation from the sun to reach the earth's surface. That radiation is dangerous to many forms of life including human beings in whom it can promote cancer. Currently, the ozone layer is most affected at the poles, so very northerly and very southerly peoples are at most risk.

2.2   EARTH-BOUND WASTES

Our other waste disposal problems can be viewed within the same general perspective. Seas and rivers have too often be seen as useful, free waste repositories, and refuse from firms, farms and houses has been dumped in fresh and salt waters. This waste disposal has led to serious pollution. For example, human and animal wastes can, under the right conditions, break down in a natural and harmless way. In principle, they could be applied as fertilizers to farmland or just allowed to decay in watercourses and in the ocean. But they have often been discharged in such concentrations that they have upset the biological balance of rivers and estuaries. These wastes have poisoned fish and so contaminated shellfish (which feed by straining nutrients out of water) that these creatures have become inedible. Growing human and livestock populations threaten to make this problem worse.

Similarly, in industrialized areas, firms have released small (and sometimes large) amounts of chemicals — for example, the metals mercury and cadmium — into watercourses. Often these chemicals have subsequently become concentrated in the fatty parts of aquatic animals' bodies to such an extent that the chemicals can become hazardous at the top of the food chain; that is, for otters, large fish or even humans. Elsewhere, small quantities of dangerous chemicals discharged into sewers mean that the sewage sludge becomes contaminated and cannot be applied as a fertilizer. It is not only big companies which are responsible for this pollution, but also ordinary citizens and small businesses who empty engine oil and other chemicals into the drains.

Additionally, there is solid waste from industry and from domestic sources. In principle, much of this could be recycled if the appropriate techniques could be devised and implemented and suitable markets developed. But at the moment, domestic waste (composed of vegetable wastes and cinders, paper, metals, glass and plastics, roughly in that descending order) is not usually sorted. It is usually dumped in holes in the ground: in former quarries, or on to the beds of drained lakes. But these sites are rapidly filling up and the price of waste disposal is no longer negligible. Worse, these dumps themselves pose a threat. Rainwater seeping through them can leach out chemicals which can then enter water supplies. Natural decay in the dumps also leads to the production of methane gas which can spontaneously ignite. Although dumping on such sites is now regulated (in theory at least), it is difficult to prevent dangerous materials from finding their way on to these tips. Indeed, in the past, dangerous wastes were disposed of by 'diluting' them with ordinary refuse; this procedure was dignified with the name 'co-disposal'. Accordingly, the threat of poisoning from long-established dumps could be much worse than we realize.

There are some wastes, both solid and liquid, which are known to be highly dangerous. Such toxic materials — typically coming from the chemical, pharmaceutical and nuclear industries, and even from hospitals — generate acute disposal problems since nobody is keen to have them incinerated, dumped or even stored close to their home or town. The difficulties posed by the management of these materials have increased recently, both because people are more aware of their potential dangers and because the old practice of incineration at sea has virtually ceased. The disposal costs of these wastes are now very high, a fact which has attracted the attention of unscrupulous, sometimes criminal operators. Some 'entrepreneurs' have spotted the opportunity to take these materials to Third-World countries (notably the poor

Europa Point dumpsite, Gibraltar, July 1989: 45 tons of rubbish were dumped into the Mediterranean every day at this site

nations of west Africa) where they can be dumped very cheaply. This dumping can be carried out either because these countries lack laws specifically prohibiting the dumping of these toxic materials — materials which, of course, they do not make themselves — or because the material has been misleadingly relabelled. Closer to home, the 'processing' of these substances has proved attractive to illegal operators who may be willing to 'lose' them at sea or to subcontract people to dump them illicitly (for an example, see Allen and Jones, 1990, pp.230–1).

The final problem I wish to mention is not strictly one of waste, but of the pollution caused by chemicals applied on farms, in parks, and on railway and road verges. Fertilizers and herbicides are not completely absorbed by the plants on to which they are sprayed. The remainder is then carried away by rainwater into underground watercourses or rivers. Either way, chemicals which are designed to have a biological impact, to kill bugs or weeds for instance, may end up in our drinking water. Such pollution can be directly harmful to human health. In a survey published by *The Observer* and FoE in 1989, European Community limits for pesticides and nitrates were found to be exceeded in many parts of England and Wales, particularly in East Anglia and the East Midlands (FoE, 1989).

In all the ways highlighted here, our problems of waste disposal — understood in the widest sense — lead to dangers for our society. For a long time economists referred to such issues as 'externalities', meaning costs which are borne neither by the consumer nor the producer but assumed by the environment. These can no longer be seen as just a side

The River Tinto, Spain, polluted by the outflow of a pulp and paper factory

issue (see Pearce *et al.*, 1989, pp.5–7). Our wastes threaten our health and that of innocent citizens of Third-World countries, they endanger wildlife and the natural environment, and may even jeopardize the global temperature-control system. Aside from these dangers, wastes and pollution pose a growing economic problem: the costs of pollution control are rising and the price of dumping can be expected to rise steeply. Waste endangers our health and our wealth.

2.3 DEPLETION OF RESOURCES

If the way of life of our civilization is imperilled by the manner in which we have polluted the globe, it is also under threat because we are using up the world's resources. Economic growth since the Second World War has been consistently large for all the First World and for parts of the Third World; even comparatively unsuccessful economies, such as that of the UK, have been doubling in size every twenty or so years. To feed this economic growth we have consumed more and more energy, minerals and agricultural products, which plainly cannot go on for ever. Stocks of minerals (whether metal ores, or nitrates for fertilizers, or whatever) are finite; thus, in Britain we are already coming to the end of new discoveries of North Sea oil. Nor are agricultural crops an infinite, replenishable resource; first, because agricultural productivity is currently only maintained by the use of agrochemicals which themselves rely on other mineral resources, and, secondly, because some agricultural exploitation is so intensive that it exhausts the land, in some cases turning it into infertile desert.

Of course, there are always likely to be more, as yet undiscovered, deposits of the natural resources, but they can be expected to be increasingly remote or difficult to work. Alternatively, new technologies may allow us to utilize existing resources more efficiently, or permit us to substitute a relatively common resource for an uncommon one. For instance, in the early years of the industrial revolution a projected catastrophic timber shortage was offset by the introduction of coal power. In the 1950s and 1960s it was hoped that nuclear power generated from uranium would replace that from fossil fuels; however, as it turned out, nuclear power was also very expensive once the costs of waste disposal and decommissioning were taken into account.

Thus, the argument about resource depletion is not cut and dried. The anticipated shortages have not yet occurred, at least if we judge by the continuing low prices of minerals. Indeed, in a ten-year public bet between an ecologist, Paul Ehrlich, and an economist, Julian Simon, made in 1980 over the future scarcity (and so the future price) of five metals, the ecologist had to pay up. He had expected that shortages would arise during the 1980s and that prices would mount accordingly. Yet, by the end of 1990, the price of each of the metals cited in the bet had actually fallen (Tierney, 1990). It is unclear when the anticipated shortages will start to be felt. Certainly, successive gloomy forecasts — that minerals will *soon* begin to be in short supply — have left their authors embarrassed. Thus, the simple, logical point that resources obviously *must be* finite is complicated by the question of when their scarcity will become felt.

Still, it cannot be denied that with economic growth consumption not only increases but increases faster and faster. Every year the number of cars on the world's roads grows, on average, by more than the amount it grew the year before. We are thus using up our steel at a faster and faster rate. Furthermore, the low price of raw materials in the 1980s has been accompanied by huge Third World debts and falling real incomes in many underdeveloped countries. In terms of resources, therefore, our way of life may be sustainable for some time to come, but probably only at the cost of Third-World poverty. Even people who are optimistic about the continued potential for growth are unclear about where the energy resources would come from if we were to try to provide everybody with the same standard of living as is currently enjoyed by an average West European or North American citizen.

ACTIVITY 2   Please list and evaluate the arguments for (a) an optimistic, and (b) a pessimistic view of the future availability of non-renewable resources. You may like to reassess this exercise at a later stage when you have read Readings E and F.

2.4   ADDITIONAL ECOLOGICAL ISSUES

Pollution and resource depletion act together as a joint threat to modern society. But there are other important issues highlighted by environmentalists; in particular, threats to animals, to plants and trees, and to natural habitats. In fact, the largest and most established environmental organizations in the UK have tended to be devoted, not to questions of resources and pollution, but to nature conservation. Thus, the Royal Society for the Protection of Birds (RSPB), now over a century old, is still the largest nature conservation/environmental group in the UK. However, it is important to note that while such groups have retained nature conservation as their central focus, they have lately broadened their objectives to include more wide-ranging environmental concerns. These groups originally tended to concentrate on threats to particular creatures or to certain endangered species, but more recently they have switched most of their attention to threats to the habitats in which wild animals live. This has meant, for example, that rather than concentrate on hunting or shooting which endangers particular birds, they have worried more about changes to agricultural practices which threaten to obliterate the hedges and small woods in which the birds live and find their food. For this reason, nature conservation groups are increasingly involved in environmental campaigns, addressing issues such as the siting of roads, agricultural policy, pollution from factories, and the treatment of the rainforests (see Yearley, 1991, pp.54–67).

There are other issues which have also been important to the growth of the green movement and have motivated people to become concerned about their environment: from the perceived threat from nuclear power and its closeness to the nuclear weapons industry, through anxieties about cruelty to animals and the use of animal testing in the developing of medical and cosmetic preparations, to worries about the loss of landscape and the destruction of our architectural heritage. In many cases, as I will show, these particular anxieties have been decisive in encouraging people's interest in the green movement. My review, therefore, cannot claim to be comprehensive, but it does serve to outline the issues which have most preoccupied the leading environmental groups. In particular, it helps us understand the twin threat, from pollution and resource depletion, which many greens would argue hangs over the contemporary world.

3   PUTTING THE ENVIRONMENT ON THE AGENDA

I have offered a view of today's environmental threats as the accumulated consequences of our technological society's neglect of its natural context. Our farming practices threaten to make our water undrinkable and to reduce the diversity of natural habitats; the industry which supplies our wealth and leisure pollutes the land and the air we would hope to enjoy; sea dumping harms the very fish to which we are turning for a 'healthier' diet. But how did these issues come to occupy such a prominent position in the public consciousness?

As I suggested earlier, we should not think that the ecological threats have themselves forced us to treat the issue seriously. The social profile and political salience of environmental issues can rise and fall quite independently of the fortune of the environment. Thus, environmental concerns were high on the public agenda in the late 1960s and early 1970s, but they faded in the face of 'a much more unfavourable political climate as the deepening recession generated a hostile and pervasive mentality of "growth at any price"' (Lowe and Flynn, 1989, p.268). Environmental problems are by no means always treated as problems for society to solve. All the same, we cannot reasonably deny that there has been a real growth in the number of people and organizations making claims about environmental problems over the last quarter century: nature conservation and environmental organizations have flourished while green parties have been established in around thirty countries (Parkin, 1989). The environmental movement is well established as a social movement.

3.1 THE ACTOR APPROACH AND THE STRUCTURAL APPROACH

As Alan Scott makes clear, sociological analyses of the growth of public concern and of social movements tend to focus on one or other of two factors (see Book 2 (Allen *et al.*, 1992), Chapter 3). Some authors concentrate on the activities of the groups and voluntary organizations — often referred to as 'social movement organizations' (SMOs) — which campaign about and publicize these issues. The SMOs' role has been to keep up the pressure to have ecological issues viewed as social problems. By contrast, other analysts focus on the socio-economic changes which bring into being social groups receptive to claims about certain kinds of problem. Scott labels the former view the 'actor' approach, and the latter the 'structural' approach.

Reasonably enough, nearly everyone agrees that both elements have some role to play; that a message about a supposed new social problem (such as acid rain or ozone depletion) needs a propagandist as well as a receptive audience. But advocates of the 'structural' approach believe that when historical developments produce a receptive audience, relevant campaign groups who can feed its beliefs will readily spring up. According to this view, the particular 'actors' (the campaign groups) play only a small part in the development of social movements, as may be observed in the diversity of environmental groups which now supply the environmental 'market'. Supporters of the 'actor' approach, on the other hand, consider that skilled campaigning and publicity are of paramount importance. They would argue that in very diverse modern societies it is possible to find some audience for more or less any beliefs (whether about UFOs, reincarnation or aromatherapy) provided they are marketed skilfully. Hence the actions of campaigners are decisive in determining which movements take off and which do not.

Both kinds of approach have been applied to interpreting the growth of the green movement. A lucid version of the structural approach is provided by Peter Berger in Reading B.

ACTIVITY 3   You should now read **Reading B 'The capitalist revolution'**, by Peter Berger.

Why, according to Berger, would members of the knowledge class be likely to respond favourably to the message of environmental groups?

What Berger calls the 'knowledge class' was born out of the productive success of advanced capitalism, yet, ironically, has a distrust of free-market capitalism. Its members tend to welcome planning and regulation, to favour the expansion of state intervention and to espouse non-material values. They constitute a receptive audience for claims about environmental problems and would be well disposed to the idea that governmental agencies should become involved in environmental regulation and protection. This general argument is supported by the research of Cotgrove and Duff who surveyed members of environmental organizations and found students and 'service, welfare and creative' occupations very strongly represented (1980, p.342).

However, this is not a simple case of explanatory success for the 'structural' approach. The chief reason for this can be seen in Berger's own account when he notes that, 'the category of the knowledge class covers quite a large number of people … certainly comprising several millions'. Given such a very large pool of recruits, how are we to explain why some people adopt one ideological cause (the plight of the arts, civil rights, or prison reform as well as environmental issues) while others pursue another? Of course, one could try to find subsets of people within the knowledge class who have additional 'structural' features in common. But such efforts do not meet with success; they are in any case confounded by the finding that over five per cent of Cotgrove and Duff's environmentalists were manual workers. The structural approach yields much less than a complete answer to our question.

Accordingly, we must turn to the 'actor' approach as well. Kitsuse and Spector are strong advocates of the actor approach, arguing that:

> The existence of social problems depends on the continued existence of groups or agencies that define some condition as a problem and attempt to do something about it. To ask what are the effective causes of social problems, or what keeps social problem activities going, is to ask what keeps these various groups going. (1981, p.201)

In other words, the work of environmental pressure groups is absolutely central to the explanation of continuing environmental concern since these groups have played the major role in keeping ecological problems in the public eye — in defining some condition (say, pollution) as a problem and attempting to do something about it.

Of course, we have to be careful to ask what benefit is to be gained from putting the argument in this way. It would be easy to adopt these authors' terms without significantly altering the way we think about social problems. It is important to accept their point that the 'problems' highlighted by pressure groups are not just a reflection of existing, objective ecological problems, but are — in a sense — socially constructed (Spector and Kitsuse, 1977). Once we adopt this view we can begin to ask interesting sociological questions about the causes of, and influences on, public concerns about the environment.

For example, we can ask why certain environmental issues have received more public attention, and have been the focus of more official action, than others. As I have already noted, the most well-established groups in Britain have tended to take a nature conservation approach, notably the RSPB and the Royal Society for Nature Conservation (RSNC). If we take the RSNC as an example, we can see that its history is very important to the way in which environmental problems are now viewed in the UK. The society began as a group committed to preserving wildlife sites which were of importance to natural history and the science of ecology (see Lowe, 1983). During its development, the RSNC acquired influence in government circles on account of its scientific expertise; it was centrally involved in setting up the official conservation body, the Nature Conservancy, and in helping formulate environmental legislation. Even today the RSNC and its constituent regional bodies, the Wildlife Trusts, retain a good deal of this natural history and scientific orientation. It is therefore hardly surprising that the most pervasive environmental designation in Great Britain is the 'Site of Special Scientific Interest' (SSSI). Clearly, the concerns of the problem-defining group have had a large influence over how the problem is conceptualized. The way the RSNC defined the problem is reflected in official perceptions of the problem. A similar case can be made with respect to the RSPB and the treatment of birds' conservation needs. Fish, for example, receive much less extensive attention than birds, even though in many cases the dangers they face may be just as severe (for an extended analysis of this kind of problem, see Yearley, 1991, pp.52–77). The groups which assert the existence of a social problem decisively shape the way that that social problem is perceived.

So far, I have argued two points from (in Scott's terms) the 'actor' approach: first, that SMOs play an active role in moulding and directing the concerns of their audience, and, secondly, that pressure groups shape environmental problems rather than simply reflecting the underlying and objective ecological issues. But these 'actors' do not have things wholly their own way: environmental groups are themselves constrained in the way they can do this shaping. For

Greenpeace ship Sirius confronting the toxic waste carrier Karin B off Livorno, Italy, in 1988

example, the media are an important resource for green pressure groups. From early in their campaigning, Greenpeace activists saw the virtues of taking filming equipment with them on their ocean protests in order both to document what took place and to ensure that their story was given maximum publicity at home since their footage made very exciting television news.

But, if the newsworthiness of their actions potentially favours environmental groups, it is also a constraint on them; they have to bear the needs of the media in mind. Issues which are perceived as 'newsworthy' are likely to receive more attention than other issues, even if the latter are regarded by environmentalists as of equal objective importance.

These external influences on environmental groups' work are also illustrated by the way in which groups have to compete with each other for sponsors and members. Generally speaking, the effectiveness of groups rises with their membership and with their income. Yet the number of firms which are keen to provide sponsorship *and* which are acceptable to environmentalists is limited. (In general, groups would be glad to receive sponsorship from the Body Shop but unwilling to accept it from British Nuclear Fuels.) Accordingly, there is once again competition to be the pressure group which makes the most successful deal.

The fortunes of environmental organizations are also affected by more specifically political events. In Reading C, Lowe and Flynn provide a good review of the situation in Britain during the 1980s.

ACTIVITY 4   You should now read **Reading C, 'Environmental politics and policy in the 1980s'**, by Philip Lowe and Andrew Flynn.

Why are good media relations especially important to environmental SMOs? Can you suggest an example which illustrates this relationship?

From Lowe and Flynn's assessment we can see that in the UK
environmental organizations have successfully managed to keep green
issues defined as a social problem despite the constraints they face.
Certain factors assist them, such as the appeal of environmental issues
to the mass media. The media tend to view such stories favourably
because they can often be perceived as being in the public interest and
as relatively neutral in relation to the leading political parties. Other
factors, such as the well-established official influence of business
interests, act as obstacles to the success of environmentalists' claims.
But the overall conclusion must be that environmental SMOs have been
successful in cultivating and developing their 'natural' audience —
Berger's knowledge class. Indeed, during the late 1980s they performed
rather better than their organizational competitors. As 'actors' they acted
well, keeping ecological issues in the public eye and shaping popular
perceptions of environmental threats.

4   DEVELOPING A GREEN POLITICAL IDEOLOGY

There are a great number of pressure groups which together have put
green arguments on the political agenda. Indeed they are rather more
diverse than one would expect from a 'structural' view of SMOs,
ranging from small nature conservation groups like the Marine
Conservation Group, or groups for bats or for dolphins, through to the
RSPB and the National Trust — a huge and wealthy organization,
committed to heritage as well as wildlife conservation. There are also
amenity and landscape groups and the well-known campaigning bodies
such as FoE and Greenpeace. Given all this variation, the groups could
probably be classified in any number of ways. But one particular divide
has been accentuated by Jonathon Porritt, former director of FoE, who
noted that, in a survey published in 1988:

> FoE is quoted as the only environmental organization 'which
> argued that green growth is logically impossible'.
>
> I can't say I'm surprised by that, but I continue to be fairly
> depressed by it. … The vast majority of UK environmental groups,
> consciously or subconsciously, have been co-opted by the
> growthist (*sic*) obsessions of our industrial culture.
> (Porritt, 1988, p.22)

The argument about limits to growth, specifically about resource
depletion, has already been mentioned and I will return to it later. The
present point (indeed, Porritt's point too) is that those groups which
have played the largest part in bringing green issues to public attention
have not (publicly at least) espoused the need for a sharp break with
current societal arrangements. They have challenged some specific

things which we do (such as using leaded petrol or buying 'biological' washing powders) but have stopped short of criticizing our basically capitalistic 'industrial culture'. This verdict matches that given by Lowe and Flynn who emphasized the 'reformist strategies' of the UK green movement. In practice, even FoE has been reformist; it has tacitly supported the replacement of ozone-eating deodorants with non-ozone-depleting ones, rather than campaigning directly for the elimination of aerosols (an expensive, energy consuming, non-recyclable form of packaging).

Yet this reformist view is not the only available approach to current environmental threats: the last two decades have also witnessed the formulation of more radical green political ideologies. In his recent analysis of this line of political thought Dobson refers to reformist environmental concerns as 'green' while the more radical, ecologist line he calls 'Green'. (This distinction can also be made using the terms 'deep green' and 'light green'.) For presentation purposes, Dobson's distinction is a useful device and one which I shall adopt from now on.

How then does 'green' differ from 'Green'? In Dobson's view, Green political ideology, or 'ecologism',

> ... questions growth and technology, and suggests that the Good Life will involve more work and fewer material objects. Fundamentally, ecologism takes seriously the universal condition of the finitude of the planet and asks what kinds of political, economic and social practices are (a) possible and (b) desirable within that framework. Environmentalism [i.e. green thinking], typically, does no such thing.
> (Dobson, 1990, p.205)

In his book *Green Political Thought,* Dobson sets out to give an objective description of ecologism and to establish that it is a coherent political ideology. This ideology contains a two-fold critique of contemporary society, arguing both that it is, in fact, unsustainable (because of resource depletion and pollution) and that it is undesirable. It is undesirable because our 'industrial culture' demands that we adopt an exploitative attitude to the natural world and that we alienate ourselves from our natural environment. In principle, therefore, Green beliefs could be persuasive even to people who did not yet feel themselves threatened by environmental disaster. But the present environmental crisis lends the Green argument an immediate credibility.

Greens take our current ecological problems very seriously, arguing that we must take immediate steps to decrease our consumption of energy and raw materials, and to reduce drastically our polluting behaviour. In their view, we must lower our expectations of material goods and learn to enjoy simpler, sustainable lives. We must begin to decentralize our societies and learn to live predominantly with the resources of our local region. They argue, however, that this will not be a deprivation for us;

both because our standard of living will be better than that which awaits us if we continue on our present course to its catastrophic end, and because the simpler life brings its own communal and spiritual dividends.

Part of the basis for these positive claims about the appeal of a Green lifestyle comes from a critical interpretation of the development of western thought, particularly scientific thought, which has been directed to taking nature apart (mentally and, often, physically) and considering its parts in isolation. By contrast, Greens value holistic thinking. The rational orientation, epitomized in the Enlightenment, is viewed by Greens as having played a large part in encouraging our exploitative attitude to the natural world. In their view, this way of thinking is partly responsible for precipitating the environmental crisis. Green political thought is thus opposed to the Enlightenment in many respects. Dobson clarifies many of these points in the extract provided as Reading D.

ACTIVITY 5	You should now read **Reading D, 'Green political thought'**, by Andrew Dobson.
	Using Dobson's account, draw up a table contrasting Green and green political views.

Dobson concludes by noting that ecologism, despite the occasional pronouncements of its advocates, is not anti-Enlightenment. By this he means that Greens are actually profoundly in debt to, and make active use of, aspects of Enlightenment thinking. Thus, Green thinking typically wishes to grant extensive rights to non-human (as well as human) forms of life, to recognize the inherent value of animal and vegetable life. And the fact that Greens talk about this process in terms of rights is indicative of ecologism's continuity with Enlightenment political thinking. Similarly, Greens tend to stress freedom of information and many kinds of equality. Yet these principles are not demanded by the need for ecological survival; they draw on other, pre-existing traditions of political analysis, particularly 'socialistic' ones (Dobson, 1990, p.183). Lastly, as Dobson mentions in Reading D, Greens even depend on science to a large extent, for example in determining the threat from ozone depletion or the dangers of acid rain. The Green case is in many respects a scientific one (Yearley, 1991, pp.113–48). At the risk of seeming sophistical, one might say that Greens put forward an enlightenment critique of the Enlightenment rather than a romantic one.

4.1 TAKING GREEN IDEAS TO THE POLLS

The connection between Green thought and existing, especially Left-leaning, political philosophies is an important one and I shall return to it in Section 5 when I consider the connection between growth, capitalism and environmental problems. But there is a prior empirical question to be addressed — namely, what has happened to Green political ideas when people have attempted to convince the public on a large scale? For those convinced of the correctness of Green ideas there is clearly an urgent need for change. But it is far from clear how that change is to be brought about. For example, Greens may feel compelled to make radical alterations in their own lifestyles: they will try to consume much less, to live sustainably, to live non-exploitatively. They may even join together in communities to pursue this way of life. But they will also know that even if they give up their cars, travel by motor vehicles only when it is necessary, radically economize on power, and so on, this will not make a great deal of difference to the burdens of pollution and resource depletion. In the UK alone, annual sales of cars are hovering a little below two million. Self denial by even several thousand Greens will not affect these figures significantly. Greens may argue that their example will become infectious, that others will be attracted by what they see. There is as yet little evidence to support this notion. Many Greens will believe that although they know the planet is heading for ecological disaster the rest of the world will not be won over in time just by the force of their example. Accordingly, the most obvious strategy is to seek to bring about change through intervention in the political process, in particular, by forming Green political parties.

Party formation offers at least two advantages. First, it provides a public platform from which to expound Green views. A party, particularly an innovative and reasonably successful one, is assured of publicity and is

Tepee Valley, Wales: a radical alternative to modern urban life

likely to gain media time at elections. Secondly, a party may become politically successful and thus win the opportunity to influence legislation. It can do this not only by entering government itself but also by becoming sufficiently popular at the polls that other parties are obliged to adopt some of its policies for fear of losing support to it. This was arguably the biggest impact of the UK Green Party after its unexpectedly successful showing in the 1989 European elections, when it won just short of 15 per cent of the vote. Sensing the rise in the importance of the environmental vote, both the leading parties quickly set about greening their own images and — to some extent — their policies.

However attractive it may be to form a Green political party, it is by no means straightforward. No doubt it is difficult to launch any new party, but there are special, internal ideological obstacles to party formation within ecologism. For one thing, Greens are uneasy about appointing leaders or introducing hierarchies. They are attracted to the notion of direct democracy and have typically resisted the delegation of power to parliamentary representatives. There is also a tendency to view existing political structures (parliaments, councils, governmental committees, and so on) as part of the old 'growthist' order. There is a corresponding fear that elected Green representatives would become seduced by the system. Worse still, since any early successes have resulted in Green parties acquiring only a few seats, there has been the problem of forming political alliances. If they hold firm to their principles, Green parties are unlikely to achieve any legislative changes, but if they compromise and form alliances with existing parties — especially larger parties — their radical Green identity is likely to be lost.

All party-based systems depend on electoral competition which in turn demands that voters are wooed. Greens face the problem that if their manifesto stresses the more austere aspects of Green beliefs, then support is likely to be reduced. If, however, the claims are moderated, support may rise but the intensity of commitment is likely to fall. This dilemma is felt very acutely in relation to economic growth, something routinely promised by all other parties. I will examine the question of Greens and growth in more detail below, but first deal with the important strategic point about the party's perceived attitude to growth. Green parties find it hard to appeal to voters on a no-growth platform; at the 1989 party conference David Spaven of the UK Greens was quoted as saying 'we are not a no-growth party. We are not an anti-technology party' (*The Independent,* 25 September, 1989, p.4). The following year the correspondent from the *Independent on Sunday* claimed that:

> The Green Party yesterday attempted to distance itself from its image as a 'no-growth' party by holding out the prospect of a booming green economy. ... Green policies would create a boom in such areas as home insulation, energy efficiency and recycling. (23 September 1990, p.2)

Clearly, it is difficult to put forward an electorally attractive package which is also true to Green sentiments.

Nonetheless, Green Parties have been successful in entering national parliaments in, for example, West Germany, Austria, Italy, Sweden and Belgium. Of these, the Green Party in pre-unification West Germany — *die Grünen* — has attracted the most attention since it was one of essentially only four parties in the parliament of Europe's strongest and most influential economy. The West German electoral system was so arranged that parties had to cross a threshold of support (effectively five per cent) before they were eligible for any representation. But once past this minimum, they gained a reasonable number of seats (for *die Grünen*, 27 in 1983 and 44 in 1987 (Urwin, 1990, p.155)). The two largest parties were close in size and a coalition with the third, small, liberal party was vital for the exercise of power. *Die Grünen* could thus be reasonably hopeful that they too might come to wield real parliamentary power before too long. This prospect obliged the West German Greens to confront difficult political choices: if the chance presented itself, should they make an arrangement with the social democrats (the SPD) in the hope of passing green (even Green) legislation, or would they lose their integrity if they cooperated with a much larger party which was committed to economic growth and increased prosperity?

With German reunification and the triumph of the Right in the all-German election of December 1990, these questions lost much of their immediacy. In what was formerly West Germany, *die Grünen* polled less than the crucial 5 per cent of the vote. But this setback for the party is itself instructive since it shows the diversity of factors involved in determining the success of Green groups. In part, success is affected by the voting system. In the first-past-the-post systems of the UK and — effectively — the USA, it is difficult for small parties to achieve any success. At the other extreme, in multi-party parliaments with proportional representation, Greens may readily win seats but still not be well placed to make a large impact on policy. Success is also affected by the timing of the election and the kinds of issues which have the highest political profile. In the case of Germany in 1990, the dominant issue was reunification and the economic management of the new Germany. This eclipsed matters on which Greens had distinctive views. Voting is also affected by the conduct of the parties themselves and by the composition of the Green movement within particular countries. These factors have produced a variety of ecology parties, as Urwin observes:

> The input into the green parties of the many disparate groups that made up the ecology movement varied from country to country. In general, the combinations produced two broad categories of party. On the one hand were those — the majority — where the dominant element was environmentalist [i.e. green] and the strategy broadly reformist within the prevailing neocapitalist system. Others, by

contrast … rejected more explicitly the prevailing modes of
participation and decision-making. No matter how vaguely, they
expressed a broader and alternative world picture that, if
implemented, would entail far-reaching reform of the social order,
and rejected any form of political cooperation except on their own
terms.
(Urwin, 1990, pp.155–6)

According to Urwin, therefore, the situation of ecology parties is very
diverse and complex. Nature conservationists and many environmental
groups may be green; though in Dobson's view only 'political ecologism'
is Green. It now seems that ecology parties may be either Green or
green. In other words, while Dobson is fundamentally correct that
ecologism provides a distinctive Green political philosophy, it is very
difficult to run a successful Green political party in modern western
societies. Such parties face considerable pressures leading them to
moderate their Greenness in much the same way that successful
parliamentary socialist parties have tempered their socialism. In both
cases the parties find themselves open to persistent ideological attack
from those in the vanguard of their respective movements.

4.2   PUBLIC AWARENESS AND CITIZENS' ACTION

Up to this point I have emphasized the role of organizations —
particularly pressure groups and political parties — in putting
environmental issues on the public agenda. But their actions have been
complemented by a public response. Membership of environmental
pressure groups remains at record levels: the RSPB has around half a
million members, Greenpeace UK over a quarter of a million supporters.
Similarly, the persistent use of boasts about 'environmental-friendliness'
in advertising copy and marketing slogans is clear testimony to
sustained public sympathy for these issues.

Earlier, we saw an attempt to interpret this public response in terms of
socio-economic class (Section 3.1). Certainly, as with virtually all
voluntary associations, environmental groups have received most of
their support from the middle classes. Cotgrove and Duff's research, you
will recall, suggested that this support is strongest among those
members of the middle classes who work in public services (1980,
pp.340–4). I argued that interpretations, such as Berger's, based on
social class are important but that they do not help us specify in detail
who will participate in the green movement. I will return to the issue of
the class basis of environmental politics in the next section; for the
moment it is important to note that people's response to green issues is
also affected by features of their own locality. As I have noted
elsewhere:

> While individuals or families may be beset by a range of
> environmentally related problems, there appear to be certain types
> of development which frequently lead to collective responses.

> Some characteristics of these developments are rather obvious. All
> other things being equal, large projects are likely to catalyse action
> since they disturb many people at once. Yet while motorways will
> disturb large numbers of people, those people are socially and
> geographically dispersed. Airports, large factories and nuclear
> power plants on the other hand are concentrated. The last of these,
> as well as some factories, are additionally associated with
> insidious dangers, even occasional catastrophies. It is not
> surprising therefore that nuclear power plants have been rallying
> points for environmental action and 'politicization' throughout
> almost the whole of the first world.
> (Yearley, 1991, p.83)

As western governments proceeded with nuclear power programmes
after the sudden oil price rise of the early 1970s, opposition mounted,
bringing together local residents or working people (though not
necessarily the working class), members of the traditional nature
conservation groups, more radical green groups, and representatives of
the new Left (see Rüdig, 1986, pp.378–80; and Lowe and Flynn, 1989,
p.273). Such alliances fused the so-called NIMBY (not in my back yard)
interests of locals, the green/Green concerns of environmentalists, and
the anti-nuclear, often anti-militarist, attitude of the Left. These
groupings — whose members initially seemed to have little in common
— encouraged some of the participants to adopt a comprehensive green/
Green political outlook and fed directly the growth of Green parties
(Scott, 1990, pp.82–5). The precise make-up of these parties, as we have
seen, varies from one country to another, but in every case support has
been driven up by a section of the population's experience of
environmental protest.

Although these protests have often been directed against the
construction of nuclear power stations — indeed such stations seem to
be the 'ideal' provocation for political action — they have not been the
sole spur to protest. Facilities for the dumping of nuclear waste (in the
UK; see Lowe and Flynn, 1989, p.275), the construction of large airports
(notably in Germany and Japan) and incinerators for toxic materials (in
Ireland; see Allen and Jones, 1990, pp.237–42), and even plans to build
over local beauty spots and wildlife sites have had similar effects.

Thus, an understanding of the reasons for particular individuals'
participation in the green movement needs to encompass the dynamics
of specific environmental protests as well as the effects of social-class
position and the campaigning work of pressure groups. Seen from the
environmentalists' perspective, however, this fact has an ironic
consequence: it is typically harder to mount a strong public campaign
about the allegedly global problems of atmospheric warming and ozone
depletion than it is to get people to take political action about a local
development.

The difficulties in getting the public involved in international issues are
compounded in the cases of global warming, ozone depletion, and acid

Protest against UK plans to dump radioactive waste in the Atlantic, 3 July 1983 (a practice which has now ended)

rain because, as I mentioned earlier, the evidence is remote from everyday experience and the scientific details are complex and contested. For two decades the authorities in Britain were able to argue that there was no conclusive proof that British pollution was responsible for acid rain and its damage on the Continent. Equally, the scientific uncertainty over the mechanism of global warming can be used by industrialists and governments as a 'reason' to wait-and-see before making policy changes. With authoritative sections of society keen to stress the uncertainty surrounding these issues, environmentalists have found it hard to make their case in an incontrovertible way. Their difficulties have been aggravated by the fact that some radical environmentalists are, in any case, sceptical of science and of our high-technology society. Accordingly, science has proved a rather slippery friend to environmental campaigners (see Yearley, 1991, pp.113–48).

Despite these difficulties, environmental groups have recognized the importance of campaigning on international issues and have devised appropriate techniques. First, the groups have themselves cooperated and organized at an international level: notably Greenpeace and FoE

International, but also more 'establishment' groups such as the RSPB, which has established relationships with conservationists in the countries to which (and over which) birds migrate.

Environmentalists have also used international comparisons to outflank national governments, arguing — for example — that if catalytic converters can be adopted in the USA without endangering its motor industry, there can be no obstacle to their use in Britain. Lastly, these organizations have quickly learnt to enlist the power of European Community legislation to circumvent national governments. In 1986, FoE began to threaten to take the British government to court over its failure to comply with European regulations on the quality of drinking water; in the end the government backed down (FoE, 1990, pp.31–2). Equally, the RSPB and the World Wide Fund for Nature (WWF) have both been quick to appreciate the power of European legislation to hasten environmental reform and to force the hand of reluctant governments. Because both these groups are large and relatively wealthy, they are well placed to dedicate staff to Europe-watching. Thus, by organizing internationally, environmental groups can sometimes gain access to more information and authority than are available to national governments; this compensates to a large extent for the difficulties inherent in campaigning on non-local issues.

5   GROWTH, CAPITALISM, AND GREEN CONSUMERISM

Although large numbers of people in the UK are now members of green groups and many are prepared, at least sometimes, to vote Green, even larger numbers of people can participate in the movement through green consumerism. They can use their purchasing power to favour products which are less polluting than average or which contain recycled components. Some commentators take this phenomenon very seriously: Richard Adams of the consumers' magazine *New Consumer* was quoted in 1989 as proclaiming to the Green Party that 'The shopping centre was the polling station and the cash till the ballot box' (*The Guardian*, 22 September 1989, p.6). Others are more hostile, seeing dangers lurking behind the attractions of green consumerism.

Critics of green consumerism tend to adopt one or other of two sorts of response. On the one hand, it is possible to feel equivocal about green consumerism because of a fear that it may get highjacked. Knowing how much effort manufacturers are prepared to put into appearing to give customers what they want, one may legitimately fear that the greening of produce may be largely cosmetic. Already we are seeing bags and cans which bear the legend 'recyclable'. This does not mean that they have been recycled; it's a reminder that, in principle, they could be recycled in the future. There is no guarantee that the consumer will find a handy facility for recycling bags (in fact it's unlikely), nor any assurance that the manufacturer will prefer to buy materials from recycled sources. In short, the label may attract and comfort the greenish consumer while barely altering the environmental impact of our lifestyles.

The second line of criticism is more Green. It regards the idea of shopping your way to the salvation of the planet as a contradiction in terms. We need to consume less, not just carry on buying, though in a more discriminating way (Dobson, 1990, p.17). This point of view leads us directly into a major debate within the environmental movement concerning the compatibility of economic growth and environmental protection. Advocates of green consumerism have to believe that we can reform our current economic system in such a way that it is sustainable *and* can still offer us new goods and growth. Others, such as Porritt, argue that we must forgo growth. This debate is represented by Readings E and F.

ACTIVITY 6   You should now read **Reading E, 'Greens and growth'**, by Jonathon Porritt, and **Reading F, 'Greens and growth — a reply'**, by John Pezzey.

Jonathon Porritt claims that 'if you're into logic, green growth and green consumerism are highly dubious notions'. What arguments can be put forward against his view?

What will strike many social scientific readers of these passages is that Porritt's attack is directed at what he calls 'industrialism' rather than at a more narrowly defined socio-economic system: capitalism or state socialism. Many Left-leaning analysts who are otherwise sensitive to Green arguments would maintain that it is crucial to recognize the special connection between capitalism, growth and environmental despoliation (see Yearley, 1991, pp.104–7; and Dobson, 1990, pp.186–90).

Essentially, their argument is as follows. The capitalist system is inherently competitive and firms have to compete by raising their productivity. As a capitalist, if you stay still you perish. Accordingly, growth is necessary to the system. Moreover, the system continually generates growth. Now, this 'growth' may not all be desirable — indeed, it may in a certain sense be self-defeating. It may include more powerful cars *and* better in-car entertainment for whiling away the long hours spent in traffic queues. It may even include new forms of junk food. 'Growth' will certainly include money spent on cleaning up environmental disasters such as oil spills. Furthermore, huge resources need to be spent on encouraging consumers to want the new products, such as DAT recorders or domestic ultra-violet lamps, for which they never knew they had a craving. Capitalist production leads to the proliferation of 'gift shops' selling wholly useless executive toys and valueless presents. For these reasons, capitalist industrialism is seen by many as the special enemy of the environment. And among some neo-Marxists it is believed that capitalism will be undermined by the environmental problem to which it inevitably gives rise. Ecology here takes on the role of capital's implacable enemy, a role which the proletariat has been so slow to fill (for an early exposition of this view, see Bosquet, 1977).

Greens have not, by and large, been too impressed with this argument, pointing out that the environmental problems of state socialist countries (in terms of air pollution, the contamination of water, health and safety at work, and so on) have been, if anything, considerably greater than in capitalist countries. Certainly, more environmental problems have been caused under state socialism per dollar of wealth created. Less radical greens have been equally unimpressed; they are, as I mentioned, reformist in their attitudes and look to the market as part of the solution to our environmental problems — through green consumerism and related initiatives.

Just like the debate over resource depletion, the argument about the supposed incompatibility of capitalism and sustainable development is impossible to assess in abstract, logical terms. It is an empirical issue. Admittedly, there is an asymmetry between capitalist and socialist systems; the former appear to need growth while the latter do not depend on it. But a great number of assumptions are needed to put any flesh on the bones of this argument and these assumptions can all be contested. Thus, advocates of capitalism will argue that, even if this asymmetry really exists, growth need not be polluting. For example, most recent economic growth has occurred in the service and information sectors. It is not certain, in principle, that growth has to entail greater depletion of scarce resources or the creation of ever more pollution. Of course, there will always be some pollution, but the planet can tolerate *some* and, anyway, capitalist societies have seen falls in certain forms of environmental contamination, for example, as a result of the phasing-out of smoky fuels.

Critics of capitalism will reply that, even if markets could respond to ecological problems (for example, by including the environmental impact of goods in their price; see Pearce *et al.*, 1989, pp.55–6), this will typically not come about soon enough. Capitalist economies develop through booms and slumps precisely because warnings feed back into the system too slowly. This will be true for ecological warnings too, as illustrated by the hunting of many species to extinction.

It appears that Greens and greens are mistaken if they do not have worries about features which are specific to the capitalist system. It seems very unlikely that a capitalist economy could function without growth and the burden of proof must lie with those advocates of the market who say that ecologically supportable economic growth is possible for the indefinite future. But this is not to say that Greens should be attracted to existing socialist models for the economy. Command economies were bad at delivering growth; there is no reason to suppose that they will be much better at delivering a steady state. Their technical inefficiencies are likely to be equally as pronounced in both cases. Moreover, under state socialist systems many individuals acted in a market-like way: hoarding scarce items, selling their services privately in the 'black' economy, and so on. They would be likely to do so again in an economy designed to be growth-less, leading to disparities in wealth and to severe strains on the system.

5.1 BRINGING GREENERY ABOUT

Greens have good reason to be sceptical about existing forms of capitalist and socialist economies. They believe that profound social change is needed and they know some of the characteristics which they would like to see in the new order (for a sympathetic but critical overview, see Dobson, 1990, pp.81–129). But, as both Scott and Dobson make clear, Greens often appear naive about how this change may come about. On their behalf, Dobson asks how change might come about, and then suggests:

> The answer to this question might just turn on initially sidestepping it and asking instead: who is best placed to bring about social change? A central characteristic of Green political theory is that it has never consistently asked that question, principally because the answer is held to be obvious: everyone. (Dobson, 1990, p.152)

In other words, if we are all threatened by global warming or by the contamination of drinking water, then it is in all our interests to bring about change. But of course the matter is not this simple. Many people may not believe the warnings about climate change; I have already described how the complexity of the scientific evidence allows plenty of room for the determined sceptic. And, even if our drinking water is badly polluted, the pollution is not the same everywhere, and the wealthy among us can buy bottled water or purification equipment. Many of us, business owners and workers alike, actually profit from polluting aspects of current society. There is therefore little prospect of us all combining to bring about profound social change.

These issues are explored in Reading G, in which Scott discusses proposals for social change put forward by Rudolf Bahro, formerly a leading socialist thinker who now espouses a radical Green (or 'fundamentalist') position. Scott sums up Bahro's views as follows:

> The only viable means of averting ecological catastrophe is the importation of small-scale models of production into industrial societies. ... [Furthermore] Bahro maintains that the working class cannot be agents of progressive change since they too have a stake

in the growth model: 'If I look at the problem from the point of view of the whole of humanity, not just that of Europe, then I must say that the metropolitan working class is the worst exploiting class in history'.
(Scott, 1990, pp.90–1)

But Scott then goes on to criticize Bahro's vision, particularly on the grounds that Bahro does not spell out how the desired changes could be brought about.

ACTIVITY 7   You should now read **Reading G, 'Ideology and the new social movements'**, by Alan Scott.

How might Bahro, or any other Green, reply to the two types of criticism offered by Scott?

As Scott observes, Bahro does not 'identify agents who could bring about' the social changes that he believes are desirable. The activists in environmental organizations, as we have seen, tend to be drawn from the middle classes. Although some of these people may adopt Green lifestyles out of personal conviction, in general, the middle classes are the people who can best cocoon themselves from ecological problems (by living in country villages, eating organic foods, and so on) and who would have most to lose from wholesale political and economic changes. Indeed, as Berger made clear, the 'knowledge class' owes its very existence to the productive success of modern industrial society; without economic surplus this class would wither away. The middle classes can hardly be expected to sweep radical Greens to power; they are much more likely to adopt reformist positions.

In Marxist thought, the working class is expected (however erroneously) to usher in socialism precisely because workers are the victims of the capitalist system. It is in their political and material interests to alter the system. Marx anticipated that conditions would become sufficiently bad that workers would risk participating in radical social change. Greens find it hard to identify any group that is in an analogous position As Bahro noted, the working class is barely a contender. Dobson views the long-term unemployed and others marginalized from Western industrial society as the only group which might fulfil this role (1990, pp.167–9). They have little to wed them to the system, share few of the benefits of growth, might not suffer materially from the introduction of a Green society, and might be attracted by the notion of a decentralized society with local economic initiatives. This idea has a certain plausibility but there is as yet little evidence of political consciousness developing in this group, nor of mass affiliation to Green organizations. Further, it is unclear how a group composed chiefly of the marginalized could hope to obtain political power. In other words, the majority of current sociological thinking suggests that, even if radical Greens are correct in their diagnosis, there is little prospect of collective action to bring about the changes they seek.

5.2   BEYOND THE GREENING OF THE WEST

It is clear that if environmentalists are at all justified in their arguments then green issues are not just pressing for the West but for all countries. Global warming is likely to be intensified as China and India begin to expand their power generation facilities and increase industrial development; and Bangladesh will be one of the nations most threatened by any associated rise in sea level. Acid rain over southern Asia from the burning oil-fields of Kuwait in 1991 is likely to be a precursor of industrial pollution in that region. Mining, mineral processing, logging and agribusiness will all add to the likely environmental burden of development. Yet, for the Third World there is no choice about the need for development, as is expressed in the report of the World Commission on Environment and Development:

> While attainable growth rates [in the third world] will vary, a certain minimum is needed to have any impact on *absolute poverty*. It seems unlikely that, taking developing countries as a whole, these objectives can be accomplished with per capita income growth of under 3 per cent. Given current population growth rates, this would require overall national income growth of around 5 per cent a year in the developing economies of Asia, 5.5 per cent in Latin America, and 6 per cent in Africa and West Asia. (1987, p.50; my emphasis)

Just to reduce absolute poverty, these economies have to grow at these rates for around twenty years, tripling (for instance) the size of the Latin American economies.

Consequently, although I have so far concentrated on the West, the Third World must not be omitted from any assessment of ecological threats to present-day society. Of course, there are good reasons for focusing on the West: the Western countries are the major polluters and the major consumers of raw materials, our current scientific understanding of environmental threats was largely worked out there, Western nations have witnessed the greatest growth in environmental politics and protest, and the Green challenge to enlightenment attitudes was initiated there (Dobson, 1990, p.10). But any proposals for addressing our (the West's) ecological problems must take into account the rest of the globe too. And I say 'must' not just because many commentators believe that we should, but because the West cannot insulate its environment from that of the rest of the world. In the long run, it could be threatened by marine pollution, by atmospheric contamination, by threats to species, or by resource depletion.

Already this interdependence has been graphically illustrated by the contamination in western Europe from the Chernobyl explosion and by Europe's own experience of 'trans-boundary' pollution through acid rain. The message that ecological threats do not respect national boundaries has been reinforced by environmental groups campaigning at a European and supranational level, as described above. Recognizing the importance of international environmental problems, and the general reluctance of national governments to engage in coordinated responses, these groups have begun to lobby governments, official aid agencies and international bodies such as the World Bank and the International Monetary Fund, bodies which largely determine the West's attitude to Third-World countries' problems (see Hayter, 1989; and Searle, 1987).

Poor nations with an urgent need for economic growth naturally find it difficult to resist Western development proposals or offers of trade even if the environmental implications are not likely to be benign. Typically, the West has not helped them to resolve this dilemma. Considerations of commercial and political self-interest still appear uppermost in the West's dealings with the Third World. But there are encouraging signs that, at least in the case of the threat posed by CFCs, the West may be willing to organize technical assistance to Third-World countries to enable them to manufacture safer alternatives. Given the dangers associated with ozone depletion, this is only enlightened self-interest, but it is a start. The next major negotiations will concern greenhouse gases and these are likely to proceed much less smoothly. In this case there is no 'technical fix', no ready substitute to allow emissions to be reduced. Just to limit pollution to present-day levels, the West will have to reduce its output of greenhouse gases while Third-World industrialization proceeds. Already, the USA and Japan — the largest polluters — have shown themselves willing to make very few concessions. It is unclear how this sharp conflict of interests can be resolved.

In this context of uncertainty, the only safe prediction is that environmental questions will figure ever more conspicuously in discussions of development, and that green groups will increasingly direct their campaigning work to international causes. Thus, in 1990, FoE ran a campaign aimed at encouraging British banks to reduce Third-World debt, hoping thereby to limit the short-term pressures which are leading to rainforest destruction and environmentally-damaging mining. Such internationalism can only grow.

6   CONCLUSION: ENVIRONMENTAL CHALLENGES AND THE ENLIGHTENMENT

In this chapter we have seen that the ecological hazards of pollution and resource depletion pose a potentially catastrophic threat to industrial society, perhaps even to the planet. Since the earth's material resources must be finite, one might think it certain that economic growth cannot long continue on its present path. But successive predictions about resource depletion have appeared alarmist. The predicted shortages have so far failed to appear. It has turned out that, to date, pollution has had a much more pronounced impact on the West, with widespread experience of acid rain, of agricultural pollutants in our foodstuffs, and the loss of species from our countryside, rivers and seas. Particularly within the last decade, environmental threats have come to be widely recognized in the West. We have explained this increased recognition partly in terms of individuals' experience of these ecological problems. But other factors have played a large role in this explanation too, notably shrewd environmental campaigning — aided by the media — and the growth of a 'knowledge class' whose members' structural position makes them receptive to the environmental message.

No matter how potentially severe these ecological problems are, the majority response has been reformist and gradualist. Campaigners have lured us on to more 'environmentally friendly' aerosols, and legislators have begun to tighten up the limits on acidic emissions from power stations. Still, economic growth is continuing and the basic values and institutions of Western society have not been challenged.

However, some environmentalists have taken this opportunity to devise a new, comprehensive Green ideology which claims to offer new social and political goals, to transcend the old divisions of Right and Left, and to displace humans from their central position in our moral philosophy. In this new view, all of nature is to command the same moral respect that used to be reserved for humans alone. We have seen that this Green ideology poses a challenge to many of the Enlightenment assumptions of our society: it questions our commitment to growth and material progress, it stresses restraint and thrift, it favours holism over individualism. But this ideology is not simply anti-Enlightenment. As Dobson showed, it retains elements of Enlightenment thought, such as a concern for rights (even animal rights) and a heavy dependence on scientific modes of thinking. Without science we could know little of the greenhouse effect or of the ozone layer.

Green thought thus offers an innovative and challenging political ideology, but, as we saw, it is not an easy ideology to introduce into contemporary Western democracies. The tenets of the Green political philosophy make life difficult for Green parties since they breed a resistance to leadership, authority and political compromise. Moreover, the audience for Green views is much smaller than that for environmentalist views. Accordingly, social support for this new ideology is growing only very slowly, a fact reflected in opinion polls which show the UK Green Party's support falling from its 1989 peak to around two per cent for much of 1990 and 1991, and in the equally poor performance of the German Greens in the 1990 election.

By contrast, the reformist, green position appears firmly established throughout the West. Welcomed on the 'soft' Left and in the liberal middle classes, it has even begun to find a home in the Conservative Party, with the Tory administration's acceptance of many of the principles of the 'Pearce report' (Pearce *et al.*, 1989).

Yet there is no proof that the reformist path is sustainable. Nobody has shown that green reforms can penetrate deeply enough to overcome the global threats of pollution, species extinction and habitat loss. In any case, companies or nations can at any time dig their heels in and resist reforms which are particularly unfavourable to them (as the British electricity supply industry did for so long over acid rain). Capitalist, market-based growth and sustainability may just not be compatible. Moreover, the lack of international accord over global warming and non-renewable resources indicates that a prosperous green future is not currently on offer to everyone on this planet.

In summary, therefore, radical Green thinking does challenge the Enlightenment project, but its challenge lacks a firm social basis; greens, on the other hand, try to accommodate to the Enlightenment, but there is no guarantee that they can pull this trick off.

REFERENCES

Allen, J., Braham, P. and Lewis, P. (1992) *Political and Economic Forms of Modernity*, Cambridge, Polity Press.

Allen, R. and Jones, T. (1990) *Guests of the Nation: People of Ireland versus the Multinationals,* London, Earthscan.

Berger, P.L. (1987) *The Capitalist Revolution,* Aldershot, Wildwood House.

Bosquet, M. (1977) *Capitalism in Crisis and Everyday Life,* Brighton, Harvester.

Cotgrove, S. and Duff, A. (1980) 'Environmentalism, middle class radicalism and politics', *Sociological Review,* Vol.28, pp.333–51.

Dobson, A. (1990) *Green Political Thought,* London, Unwin Hyman.

Elsworth, S. (1990) *A Dictionary of the Environment,* London, Paladin.

FoE, see Friends of the Earth.

Friends of the Earth (UK) (1989) 'Your tap water, pure or poisoned?', *Observer Magazine,* 6 August, pp.16–24.

Friends of the Earth (UK) (1990) *How Green is Britain?,* London, Hutchinson.

Hayter, T. (1989) *Exploited Earth: British Aid and the Environment,* London, Earthscan.

Kitsuse, J.I. and Spector, M. (1981) 'The labelling of social problems', in Rubington, E. and Weinberg, M.S. (eds), *The Study of Social Problems,* New York, Oxford University Press.

Leggett, J. (1990) 'The nature of the greenhouse threat', in Leggett, J. (ed.), *Global Warming: The Greenpeace Report,* Oxford, Oxford University Press.

Lowe, P. (1983) 'Values and institutions in the history of British nature conservation', in Warren, A. and Goldsmith, F.B. (eds), *Conservation in Perspective,* Chichester, John Wiley.

Lowe, P. and Flynn, A. (1989) 'Environmental politics and policy in the 1980s', in Moran, J. (ed.), *The Political Geography of Contemporary Britain,* London, Macmillan.

McKibben, B. (1990) *The End of Nature,* Harmondsworth, Penguin.

Parkin, S. (1989) *Green Parties: An International Guide,* London, Heretic Books.

Pearce, D., Markandya, A. and Barbier, E.B. (1989) *Blueprint for a Green Economy,* London, Earthscan.

Pezzey, J. (1989) 'Greens and growth — a reply', *UK Centre for Economic and Environmental Development Bulletin,* No. 22, pp.22–3.

Ponting, C. (1990) 'Historical perspectives on the environmental crisis', paper presented to the British Association for the Advancement of Science, Swansea.

Porritt, J. (1988) 'Greens and growth', *UK Centre for Economic and Environmental Development Bulletin,* No. 19, pp.22–3.

Rüdig, W. (1986) 'Nuclear power: an international comparison of public protest in the USA, Great Britain, France and West Germany', in Williams, R. and Mills, S. (eds), *Public Acceptance of New Technologies: An International Review,* London, Croom Helm.

Scott, A. (1990) *Ideology and the New Social Movements,* London, Unwin Hyman.

Searle, G. (1987) *Major World Bank Projects,* Camelford, Cornwall, Wadebridge Ecological Centre.

Seymour, J. and Girardet, H. (1990) *Far From Paradise: The Story of Human Impact on the Environment,* London, Green Print.

Spector, M. and Kitsuse, J.I. (1977) *Constructing Social Problems,* Menlo Park, California, Cummings.

Thomas, K. (1984) *Man and the Natural World,* Harmondsworth, Penguin.

Tierney, J. (1990), 'Betting the planet', *The Guardian,* 28 December, p.25.

Urwin, D. (1990) 'Green politics in Western Europe', *Social Studies Review,* 5.4, pp.152–7.

World Commission on Environment and Development, (1987) *Our Common Future,* Oxford, Oxford University Press.

Yearley, S. (1991) *The Green Case,* London, Harper Collins.

READING A   FAR FROM PARADISE

John Seymour and Herbert Girardet

Some time between 1700 and 1400 BC a significant change was made in the burial customs of the people of Crete. Hitherto, the dead had been buried in wooden coffins. After the change they were buried in earthenware ones. Potters will say that any inference drawn from this that the change was due to an increasing shortage of trees on the island is invalid because pottery takes wood to fire it. The answer to this is that you can fire pottery, as Cretan potters do today, with very small wood. You can only make proper coffins with large planks, which are cut out of large trees. Also, the pillars which held up many palaces of the Minoans were made from huge cedars. You would be hard put to find a cedar, or any other tree, big enough to make one such pillar on the island now.

Pollen analysis and all the archaeological evidence indicate that the lands around the Mediterranean basin were once well-wooded and fertile. You cannot say that about them now. ...

The Minoans were a people without armies or land-based weapons. They relied for their defence on their unrivalled command of the sea. Their cities needed no walls to defend them. ... In the middle of [the fifteenth century BC] a terrible disaster came upon them. Some people attribute this to the volcanic explosion on the Island of Thera, with its tidal waves and earthquakes, but there had been devastating earthquakes before on the island and the towns and palaces had been rebuilt. Certainly, whatever the disaster was, the Minoans never recovered from it. Their civilization quickly decayed and the island was overwhelmed by the far less civilized Achaeans who came over from the Greek mainland.

Karl Marx interpreted all human history as being the product of economic forces only. The Reading Room of the British Museum Library is very far removed from the soil. The human population of Crete was very large in Minoan times: Arthur Evans, who excavated Knossos in the two years following 1900, estimated that there were 80,000 people in Knossos alone and there were many other palaces, villas and towns all over the island then. Crete was an exporter of food at that time: the gold, copper, precious stones and other valuable raw materials found so copiously in the ruins were all bought by the export of food. I contend that the Minoans lost their *soil*, and that it was that which weakened and finally destroyed their civilization: the volcanic explosion was just the final *coup de grâce*.

Source: Seymour, J., and Girardet, H. (1990) *Far From Paradise: The Story of Human Impact on the Environment*, London, Green Print, pp.41–2.

READING B   THE CAPITALIST REVOLUTION

Peter L. Berger

Roughly since World War II (although the origins lie farther back) there has been a very significant change in the character of the Western middle classes. … It can be summarized by saying that, whereas before there was one horizontally stratified middle class (from upper-middle to lower-middle), there now are two vertically divided middle classes, each one stratified within itself. In other words, there now are two middle classes instead of one. There continues to be the old middle class, consisting of the business community and its professional as well as clerical affiliates. Even at some remove (as, say, with accountants or even dentists), these are people who derive their livelihood from the production and distribution of material goods or services. But then there is a new middle class (recently referred to as the 'New Class'), consisting of people whose occupations deal with the production and distribution of symbolic knowledge. Let this be called the 'knowledge class'.

The economic and technological roots of this phenomenon are not mysterious: Material production has become so efficient that a progressively smaller proportion of the labor force is required to keep it going. In consequence, more and more people are employed in the so-called quaternary, or service, sector of the economy. That covers too much ground, though; after all, services are provided by psychiatric social workers, by hair stylists, by janitors, and by call girls; only the first of these occupations is likely to produce members of the new class at issue. Then there is another category, that of the 'knowledge industry', employing large numbers of people in the production and distribution of knowledge. That category, however, is also too broad: It lumps in the psychiatric social workers with all those people in what John Kenneth Galbraith called the 'technostructure' — such as nuclear engineers, stock market analysts, brain surgeons — most of whom continue to be concerned with material production and (in the case of the brain surgeons) services of a material kind. That is why the focus here is on the purveyors of *symbolic* knowledge — knowledge that is not directly, or in most cases even indirectly, oriented toward material life. Helmut Schelsky, in his analysis of intellectuals in contemporary society, has described three areas of activity that fairly coincide with the boundaries of the new class suggested here — *Belehrung, Betreuung, Beplanung,* roughly translated as indoctrination, therapy and planning (Schelsky, 1975). (It should be added that the planning too is of the symbolic kind, as in the area of 'quality of life'; it should exclude such activities as planning for the water supply of a metropolitan area or the raw materials needed by the automobile industry.) But even with these restrictions, the category of the knowledge class covers quite a large number of people — in the United States, certainly comprising several million. These are the people employed in the educational system, the communications media, the vast counselling and guidance networks, and the

Berger, P.L. (1987) *The Capitalist Revolution,* Aldershot, Wildwood House, pp.66–9.

bureaucratic agencies planning for the putative nonmaterial needs of the society (from racial amity to geriatric recreation).

It is important to stress that this knowledge class is a much larger group than the people conventionally called 'intellectuals'. These people (presumably definable as primary producers of symbolic knowledge) are only a sort of upper crust of the knowledge class. For instance, there are professors of psychiatry or psychology at prestige universities who can reasonably be described as intellectuals. But they share their class affiliation with much larger numbers of people — ordinary practising therapists, social workers and counsellors, and even clerical employees in therapeutic organizations — who also derive their livelihood from the *Betreuung* of their fellow citizens. In other words, the new middle class, like the old one, is stratified within itself; just as there was an haute and a petite bourgeoisie (and, with changes in nomenclature, continues to be), so there is an upper- and a petty-knowledge class. There are tensions between these strata; but they also share common class interests and a common class culture.

Proposition: *Contemporary Western societies are characterized by a protracted conflict between two classes, the old middle class (occupied in the production and distribution of material goods and services), and a new middle class (occupied in the production and distribution of symbolic knowledge).*

… Class conflict is always about interests, in the hard material sense. But classes also develop a specific culture or subculture (or, if one prefers, a specific class consciousness). This has always been so, as Marx correctly perceived, and the contemporary situation is no exception. It follows that class-specific cultural traits are symbolic of the class interests in contention — *not* in the sense that they are not valued by people for their own sakes but rather in the sense that inevitably these cultural traits are drawn into the conflict. Thus, in the older conflict between aristocracy and bourgeoisie, each group was attached to forms of etiquette and of aesthetic taste ('aristocratic manners', 'bourgeois sensibilities') that by no stretch of the sociological imagination could be described as direct expressions of class interests. But once these cultural traits are established in a class (as a result of whatever historical circumstances), they serve as symbols of mutual recognition and of collective solidarity, and any disagreements over these cultural items become part and parcel of the underlying class conflict. … The above proposition hypothesizes that this is the case with many cultural divisions in Western society today, such as those over sexual morality, the role of women, the environment, patriotism. …

As one looks at the societal location of the knowledge class, two interests suggest themselves. The first is an interest in having privilege based on educational credentials, in which this class has an obvious advantage. This interest could well underlie a general antagonism against privilege based on 'raw' achievement in economic terms and thus against the capitalist market system that, in principle, is open to anyone regardless of education or other extra-economic certification. But there is also a second interest, which is due to the fact that a large proportion of this knowledge class depends for its livelihood on government payrolls or subsidies. This suggests a built-in vested interest in the expansion of the welfare state, which, of course, is that part of government in which this class finds employment and subsidization. Put differently, the knowledge class has an interest in the distributive machinery of government, as against the production system, and this naturally pushes it to the left in the context of Western politics (whatever 'left' may mean in ideological terms, politically it means an expansion of the welfare state in the Western democracies). ...

Reference

Schelsky, H. (1975) *Die Arbeit tun die anderen*, Opladen, Westdeutsche Verlag.

READING C ENVIRONMENTAL POLITICS AND POLICY IN THE 1980s

Philip Lowe and Andrew Flynn

The environmental movement

Britain has perhaps the most highly organized environmental lobby of any European country. ... Of the social causes that came to prominence during the 1960s, including feminism, consumerism, and minority rights, environmentalism has best weathered the economic tribulations of the 1970s and 1980s and the right-ward shift in national politics. Indeed the contemporary environmental lobby would appear to enjoy greater legitimacy and influence than some traditional sources of social power, such as the trade union movement.

Its resilience is due to certain fundamental strengths. First, environmental groups command mass support. They include some of the biggest voluntary organizations in Britain, with a combined membership of between three-and-a-half and four million. Membership is predominantly middle class, but evidence from opinion surveys suggests that passive environmental concern is even more widespread and socially much more broadly based. ...

Because of the strength of its popular support, environmental opinion is an important factor in government decision-making although environmental groups are less of an influence than major economic interests. Not being of central importance to the effective performance of government or the economy they do not have the close, symbiotic relationship with senior civil servants in the central departments which corporate interest groups enjoy. They are not automatically included, therefore, in the most

Lowe, P. and Flynn, A. (1989) 'Environmental politics and policy in the 1980s', in Moran, J. (ed.), *The Political Geography of Contemporary Britain*, London, Macmillan, pp.268–70.

formative stages of policy-making, though they are usually consulted but often at a later stage.

Failure to be closely involved with policy formulation in the crucial initial stages often means that national environmental groups are later faced with an uphill campaign against a course of action to which Ministers, officials and major interests have become committed. Good media and parliamentary relations can compensate to a certain extent by enabling groups to raise issues for government attention and by ensuring considerable opprobrium for any official initiatives with blatant and damaging environmental implications. Many MPs and peers are sympathetic to conservation issues, and most groups have good contacts with the mass media and can count on a ready and usually favourable treatment for their views. Environmental topics are public-interest issues of a non-partisan nature which makes them an attractive and important outlet for campaigning and investigative journalism. As a result, a combination of public censure and parliamentary pressure can prove an effective weapon, enabling environmental groups to take the offensive against recalcitrant government departments and win important concessions. ...

Environmental groups in Britain pursue reformist strategies, and incidents of militancy have been few in number and mainly in keeping with the British dissentient tradition of civil disobedience of a non-violent and often symbolic kind. ... On the whole, the environmental movement has not adopted a radical stance. Oppositional elements seeking structural rather than policy change have not emerged as a significant political force. Most other advanced industrialized countries, in contrast, have witnessed the emergence of radical green movements during the past decade. ... Having faced a similarly harsh climate for environmental concerns during this period, it is of interest to speculate why Britain has not followed suit.

First, in comparative terms, British environmental groups enjoy relatively easy access to government and the political system. However, unlike some other countries, such as the United States, Sweden, Denmark and Switzerland, where the environmental lobby is also highly integrated into established political processes, access for groups in Britain is entirely by discretion and custom. Maintaining good links with the executive, therefore, is of particular importance for pressure groups because of the absence of such alternative institutional mechanisms for pursuing dissent as are provided elsewhere by federal constitutions, popular referenda, the separation of the legislature from the executive, or judicial review of executive actions. Consultative status is gained and maintained by adhering to an unwritten code of moderate and responsible behaviour. It may be forfeited if a group is too outspoken in its criticisms or fails to show the necessary tact and discretion. Overall, the general receptivity of the British political system to group activity, pervasive cultural pressures and fear of disrupting established relationships reinforce a tradition of moderation and pragmatism and discourage militant and unorthodox approaches.

The predominant ethos of activism within the British environmental movement inclines in a quite different and apolitical direction, towards practical action, inspired by an ethos of voluntarism and a liberal ideology implicitly sceptical of state action. Most environmental groups see themselves as *voluntary* organizations; indeed, they fulfil a range of executive tasks of their own, including education and research, the provision of information and technical advice, practical conservation work, and the ownership and management of land and property. With the growth of such responsibilities, their role as pressure groups has diminished, though not necessarily their influence. Finally, most groups are charities and therefore, in principle, are debarred from overt political activities. Consequently, their lobbying is discreet and restrained, and their efforts to inform opinion are presented as public education and not propaganda.

READING D   GREEN POLITICAL THOUGHT
Andrew Dobson

My understanding of the historical significance of Green politics is that it constitutes a challenge to the late twentieth century consensus over the desirability of affluent, technological, service societies. Green politics is far more a friend of the subordinate interpretation of post-industrialism — a decentralized economy following in the wake of a failed industrialism — than of its dominant counterpart. Jonathon Porritt and [David] Winner assert that,

> the most radical [Green aim] seeks nothing less than a non-violent revolution to overthrow our whole polluting, plundering and materialistic industrial society and, in its place, to create a new economic and social order which will allow human beings to live in harmony with the planet. In those terms, the Green Movement lays claim to being the most radical and important political and cultural force since the birth of socialism.
> (1988, p.9)

It is in these terms that I see Green politics, ... first, so as to keep a fuller picture of the movement in mind than is presently the case; second, to understand better the challenge that it presents to the dominant consensus; and third, to establish ecologism as a political ideology in its own right. This last is important because I believe Barbara Goodwin (among others) to be wrong in calling ecologism a 'cross-cutting ideology' which 'falls into other existing ideological categories' (1987, p.vii).

In a sense Porritt and Winner do the movement a disfavour by likening the profundity of its challenge to that of early socialism. Much of socialism's intellectual work, at least, had already been done by the time it came on the scene. Liberal theorists had long since laid the ground for calls for liberty and equality, and socialism's job was to pick up and reconstitute the pieces created by liberalism's apparent failure to turn theory into practice (1987, p.vii).

Source: Dobson, A. (1990) *Green Political Thought*, London, Unwin Hyman, pp.7–10.

In this sense the Green movement is in a position more akin to that of the early liberals than that of the early socialists — it is self-consciously seeking to call into question an entire world view rather than tinker with one that already exists. For the sake of convenience, but at the risk of blind blundering on territory where specialists themselves quite properly fear to tread, the world view that modern political ecologists challenge is the one that grew out of the (early) Enlightenment. Norman Hampson has suggested a number of characteristics salient to the Enlightenment world view: 'a period when the culture of the educated man was thought to take in the whole of educated knowledge'; 'that man was to a great extent the master of his own destiny'; that 'God was a mathematician whose calculations, although infinite in their subtle complexity, were accessible to man's intelligence'; and that 'universal reason' was held to be preferable to 'local habit', principally because it helps to drive out superstition (Hampson, 1979, pp.11, 35, 37–8, 152).

The general tenor of these characteristics is the exaltation of human beings and their particular faculties (e.g. reason) — the placing of the human being in a pre-eminent position with respect to the rest of, not only terrestrial phenomena, but the universe at large. If Isaac Newton humbly saw himself as a boy playing on the sea shore finding only the odd shiny pebble while the 'great ocean of truth' lay before him, this was surely more because he hadn't the time to set sail than because he thought he lacked the equipment to do so. This belief in the centrality of 'man' was encapsulated in the principle of *bienfaisance,* or benevolence, according to which the world was the best of all possible worlds for human beings. Hampson quotes Pluche as writing that 'It is for him [Man] that the sun rises; it is for him that the stars shine', and goes on to observe that, 'Almost everything could be pressed into service, from the density of water, which Fenelon considered exactly calculated to facilitate navigation, to the shape of the water-melon, which makes it easy to slice' (Hampson, 1979, p.81). In these respects the Enlightenment attitude was that the world had been made for human beings and that, in principle, nothing in it could be kept secret from them.

In a tortuous way this attitude has remained dominant ever since in the cultures and societies that have most obviously incubated the modern Green movement. They inform, too, [a dominant interpretation] of what post-industrial society both is and ought to be: Baconian science has helped produce its technology and its material affluence, and the Promethean project to which the Enlightenment gave birth in its modern form is substantially intact. Now the historical significance of Green politics as I see it is that it constitutes a challenge to this project and to the norms and practices that sustain it. Green politics explicitly seeks to decentre the human being, to question mechanistic science and its technological consequences, to refuse to believe that the world was made for human beings — and it does this because it has been led to wonder whether dominant post-industrialism's project of material affluence is either desirable or sustainable. All this will be missed if we choose to restrict our understanding of Green politics to what is becoming its principal guise: an environmentalism that seeks a cleaner service economy, sustained by cleaner technology and producing cleaner affluence.

These thoughts on the Enlightenment help to identify ecologism's present historical significance, but there is danger here too. The analytic temptation is to see the ideology as a recreation of the romantic reaction that the Enlightenment and then early forms of industrialization themselves brought about. So we cast ecologism in terms of passion opposing reason, of the joys of a bucolic life and of mystery as against transparency. And of course it is true that most manifestations of the Green movement argue for a repopulation of the countryside and for the reawakening of a sense of awe in the face of natural phenomena.

At the same time, however, modern Green politics turns out to be based on a self-consciously hard-headed assessment of the unsustainability of present political and economic practices — it is remarkable, indeed, to see the extent to which the success of modern political ecology has been mediated and sustained by scientific research. This could hardly be said of the romantic reaction to the Enlightenment. Similarly, ecologism's political Utopia is (by and large) informed by interpretations of the principle of equality — a principle that was minted and put into circulation during the Enlightenment, and certainly not popular with romantics. Again, as far as romanticism is concerned, Green politics has little time for individualism or for geniuses, and one suspects (although this will be disputed by members of the movement) that the nonconformity so beloved of romantics would be a pretty scarce commodity in Green communities. Finally, if we hold the Green movement to believe that one can only recognize the value of the natural world through intuition (as we are likely to do if we see it merely as a resurgence of romanticism), than we are blind to the enormous range and influence of rationalist attempts to account for such value, and which are of great importance to the movement's intellectual archaeology.

So while (in terms of its present historical significance) Green politics ought to be characterized as a challenge to the contemporary consensus over norms and practices that has its most immediate sources in the early Enlightenment, it would be a mistake to think it pays no mind whatever to those norms and practices. And this would be an especially big mistake if we were to jump to the conclusion that modern Green politics is only a form of reincarnated romanticism. To guard against this we should say that its challenge most generally takes the form of an attempt to shift the terms of the burden of persuasion from those who would question the dominant post-industrial embodiment (an affluent, technological, service society) of politics and society, onto those who would defend it. In doing so Greens may sometimes speak, even if often *sotto voce,* in the Enlightenment idiom.

References

Goodwin, B. (1987) *Using Political Ideas*, Chichester, John Wiley.

Hampson, N. (1979) *The Enlightenment*, Harmondsworth, Penguin.

Porritt, J. and Winner, D. (1988) *The Coming of the Greens,* London, Fontana.

READING E   GREENS AND GROWTH

Jonathon Porritt

In a survey carried out by John Elkington and Julia Hailes for their book *Green Pages,* which came out earlier this year, Friends of the Earth is quoted as the only environmental organization 'which argued that green growth is logically impossible'.

I can't say I'm surprised by that, but I continue to be fairly depressed by it. What it means, at its starkest, is that the vast majority of UK environmental groups, consciously or subconsciously, have been co-opted by the grow-thist obsessions of our industrial culture.

It is an unrewarding business to end up permanently carping at those in one's sister organizations who are striving to establish better relations with industry, economists, and all those politicians who are as yet blind to the state of the planet. But carp, on occasions, one must.

I detect a disturbing element of complacency amongst contemporary environmentalists. The last five years have seen an explosion of interest in environmental issues throughout the developed world. What's more, things are at last beginning to stir in Eastern Europe, and there has been an enormous increase both in the numbers and influence of Non-Governmental Organizations in the Third World. Politicians of every ilk profess to be more concerned about the environment; no less a guru than Sir Alfred Sherman recently declared 'we're all ecologists now'.

And yet, judged against all the main parameters of environmental quality, the situation is worsening or, at best, in some kind of easy equilibrium. This deterioration is taking place despite significant improvements in legislative controls, particularly in the developed world, and despite the establishment or strengthening of several major international conventions. Recent revelations about damage to the ozone layer and the likely consequences of the Greenhouse Effect amply confirm so gloomy an overview.

How long do we have to live with that disparity (between our growing success and the environment's continuing collapse) before realising that all our efforts can only slow the juggernaut of industrialism, but never stop it? How long before we accept that even green growth is *logically* impossible if it entails infinite expansion on a finite resource base?

The difference between growth and green growth is analogous to the difference between an ordinary vehicle and a vehicle fitted with a catalytic converter. The latter is indisputably less polluting that the former, but is still a petrol-guzzling, environment-bashing vehicle. Green growth *may* turn out to be less polluting, less wasteful and more efficient in terms of energy and resources (all of which are highly desirable goals, enthusiastically to be campaigned for), but its adherents still seem to subscribe to one

Porritt, J. (1988) 'Greens and growth', *UK Centre for Economic and Environmental Development Bulletin*, No. 19, pp.22–3.

all-powerful item of economic dogma: that it is a only through a *perma-nent* process of expansion in production and consumption that it is poss-ible to meet human needs, improve standards of living, and ensure that wealth trickles down to the unfortunate *billions* who haven't yet had 'their share of the cake'.

It is indeed the lack of logic in all this which really irks me. Let us assume that all readers of this article subscribe to a vision of an equitable, just and sustainable future. That is easily said, but not so easily achieved. Though equity does not entail absolutely equal shares, it certainly implies far fairer shares for everyone. That either means that our existing material standard of living will gradually become available to all five billion souls with whom we currently share this planet (let alone the ten billion souls with whom we shall be sharing in the not so distant future), or it means that we must be prepared to reduce our own standard of living to a point where some approximation of equity may be achieved.

If you subscribe to the former view, then you cannot, *by definition,* sub-scribe to the principles of sustainability. Five billion people abusing the planet as we in the developed world do now — bearing in mind that it is only such uncompromising abuse which affords us such a high material standard of living — would precipitate irreparable ecological damage before we even get halfway through the next century. If you subscribed to the latter view, then you must also accept that an equitable, just and sus-tainable future cannot possibly derive from *any* variation of today's indus-trial materialism — not even a marginally greener one. If you're into logic, green growth and green consumerism are therefore highly dubious notions. On balance, I still believe that more good will be done by them than harm, but only if they are seen as part of a transitional strategy to a genuinely green economy, the success of which is **not** exclusively meas-ured by increases in GNP or further industrial expansion.

But the problem about any transitional strategy is its potential to lull peo-ple into the belief that the getting there is in fact the goal. Those who promulgate the benefits of green consumerism may see it as but a step in the right direction; those who subsequently avail themselves of the benefits of green consumerism may be more inclined to see it as the end of the road. They may even suppose that their consumptive conversion to the green cause will restore some kind of ecological balance.

It won't. Not in a millenium of green Sundays. At best, it may mitigate the most immediate symptoms of ecological decline, but the short-term advantages gained in the process are almost certainly outweighed by the simultaneous immunisation of such consumers against reality. And there-in, I suggest, lies a basic dilemma which most [environmentalists] remain remarkably reluctant to confront.

READING F   GREENS AND GROWTH — A REPLY

John Pezzey

Jonathon Porritt's thought-provoking article raised some important and timely questions about 'green growth'. However, I feel he has prejudged the answers because he has assumed that there is a fixed relationship between economic output and the physical resource inputs needed to produce that output. The contrary assumption is that this relationship can be flexible, up to a point. This allows the possibility of a third policy choice — green growth — in addition to his dire alternatives of either reducing our standard of living or precipitating irreparable ecological damage by 2050, or allowing gross inequalities in income to persist.

This is not to fall into the complacency that Jonathon rightly fears. I am not saying that green growth can be never-ending; nor that it will be easy to achieve, for it will probably require ever more demanding environmental policies; nor that there is no place for any moral restraint in the demands we place on the planet. But I do feel that using market forces to encourage green growth is a more workable way of moving toward sustainability than the radical social and political changes he envisages, at least in the near future, and is certainly an approach worth trying.

The crux of his 'impossibility' argument is his assumption that: '... it is only such uncompromising abuse [of the planet] which affords us such a high material standard of living'.

However, the very essence of the green growth idea is that it is possible to raise our material standard of living without increasing the flow of energy and material resources extracted from the environment, and the flow of waste energy and materials that is the inevitable end result of such extraction (call it 'planetary abuse' if you will). Contrary to Jonathon's view, this idea is not logically impossible.

The problem lies with the phrase 'material standard of living', which is inherently ambiguous. Does it measure the physical rate of resource throughput, or the lifestyle supported by such throughput? It does not seem sensible to measure 'standard of living' in physical terms. This would have no more meaning than measuring the value of a chandelier by its weight. (Apparently Russian planners did this once, and the chandelier factories simply responded by making chandeliers so thick and heavy that they could not be hung from normal ceilings.) Instead the standard of living should be, and normally is, measured in real dollars (i.e. corrected for inflation) of GNP per capita. I am not for one moment suggesting that GNP per capita is all there is to the quality of life, as the deficiencies of GNP as a measure of welfare are all too well known: that is a separate debate. The point here is that there is no iron law that a fixed physical amount of energy and materials is required to produce one real dollar's worth of GNP.

Pezzey, J. (1989) 'Greens and growth — a reply', *UK Centre for Economic and Environmental Development Bulletin*, No. 22, pp.22–3.

This is because real GNP per capita (roughly) measures the total value of services that we buy. All goods can be seen as ultimately giving us services: bodily strength and health, warmth, cleanliness, aesthetic pleasure, access to information and to places of work and entertainment, etc. Only for food and drink is it obvious that the foods must embody a more or less fixed amount of energy and materials to provide a given level of service. The striking reductions in energy/GNP ratios achieved in developed countries in the decade or so since the energy crisis of the early 1970s are sufficient to prove the point.

Investing in man-made capital (insulation, more efficient engines) allowed the same level of service (warm homes, a journey to work, etc.) to be produced with less energy input: something that Friends of the Earth always stressed in their arguments with energy planners. Modern electronics have decreased the energy required to process one unit of 'information'. Granted, the savings are often not as big as at first they seem, for one has to allow for the energy used to make fibreglass insulation or silicon chips, but the net savings are still substantial.

So, green growth is logically possible, but this is not to say that it will be easy to achieve in practice — far from it. I tend to agree that the global environment cannot sustain present levels of physical resource throughput (in say tonnes per year) into the distant future, although this is a complex empirical judgement, not a simple logical deduction. Achieving green growth, whereby the quality of life is sustained for the rich and improved for the poor, therefore requires radical changes in industrial technology over the coming decades and centuries. These changes must substitute capital for resource inputs in the world's economies: both physical capital (more resource-efficient machines) and human capital (improved education and knowledge of efficient resource use). Whether such far-reaching changes are seen as leading to a 'genuinely green economy', or merely to a 'variation of today's industrial materialism' as Jonathon dismissively suggests, seems an unimportant distinction.

The really important questions in the green growth debate do not have simple logical answers. What are the limits to the substitutability of capital for resources? There must be some limits, as the idea of producing GNP from infinitesimal resources and huge amounts of capital is simply absurd, but we are surely nowhere near the minimum resources/GNP ratio yet. How can we know what the distant future will look like when we reach those limits? By then we will have exhausted all our fossil fuels and high quality mineral ores, and instead will rely on renewable (and possibly nuclear?) sources of energy, on recycling waste materials — and on all the physical and human capital we will have accumulated by then. Who can easily say whether the drag of degraded resource stocks will outweigh the life of accumulated physical and intellectual capital, or vice versa?

One thing that does seem logically certain is that green growth will not be achieved without a growing role for environmental policy. Market forces can certainly achieve much of the required substitution of capital for resources, as easily accessible or high quality reserves become depleted and relative resource prices rise. But free market forces alone will never provide adequate protection for the environment, and I join Jonathon Porritt in failing to see how green consumerism and producerism will be sufficient to bridge the gap. Only intervention by governments, to make resource users take account of the full social cost of their activities, will be enough.

Given that the continuing flow of resources through the world's economies is still adding to the many cumulative pollution problems that have been recognised in the past few years — the continuing accumulation of carbon dioxide and CFCs in the atmosphere, of toxic and radioactive wastes in storage facilities, of nitrates in groundwater, of heavy metals and acid rain effects in the soil — I cannot but see an increasing need for environmental policy intervention in the future. The current rapid depletion of many renewable resources in the Third World merely adds to this concern at a global level.

Finally, even if an efficient combination of market forces and environmental policy can achieve a green growth path that is 'socially optimal' for the current generation, this path still might lead to a life in the distant future that is less pleasant than it is now. To me this would be a *survivable* but not *sustainable* future; and fairness to future generations would then require even tighter environmental and resources policies, implying some sacrifices by current generations in rich nations.

However, proving that green growth might lead to an unsustainable future is again not a simple matter of logical deduction. Only a continual balance of detailed empirical study, examination of our collective consciences and a willingness to take decisions in the face of the huge uncertainty that will inevitably remain, can lead to wise and fair decisions on global resource use.

READING G IDEOLOGY AND THE NEW SOCIAL MOVEMENTS
Alan Scott

Bahro is a powerful, articulate and relentless critic of industrial society. His warning is clear, and his solutions are unambiguous. But his arguments, and those of fundamentalists generally, are vulnerable to two types of criticism from the perspective of the realists. First, the fundamentalist position does not face the issue of the feasibility of their proposals for complex industrial societies even if the will to bring about such change could be secured. Fundamentalists do not tackle questions of distribution and planning within an economy of small-scale production. It is not clear, for example, whether we are speaking of individual self-sufficient communities or some form of division of labour between communities. If the latter, then questions of central co-ordination and distribution become unavoidable. But even if the communities are to be self-sufficient, how are

Scott, A. (1990) *Ideology and the New Social Movements,* London, Unwin Hyman, p.91.

political relations between them to be regulated? Whichever is the case, how are we to dismantle an international division of labour, a complex industrial system and institutionalized science and technology? Second, it fails to explain how that will could be secured, or to identify agents who could bring about such change. Were Bahro's alternative politically realizable it would have to be possible to persuade considerable sections of the population that it was in their interests to bring these changes about. But how is the German working class, or the Western working class in general, to be persuaded that their major goals and achievements — the Welfare State, increasing standards of living, etc. — were premised upon a basic error? Likewise, how are the poorer populations of the Third World to be persuaded that economic development is not a means to elevate poverty, or that if it were, the consequences would be worse than the problems they resolve? Bahro's call for constraints in the West is unlikely to persuade such people that his is not a recipe for Western ethnocentrism.

CHAPTER 4 POST-INDUSTRIALISM AND POST-FORDISM

John Allen

CONTENTS

1   INTRODUCTION: THE ECONOMY IN TRANSITION

It is perhaps one of the characteristics of modern life to claim that the changes which we witness around us represent the beginnings of something qualitatively new. That such a claim has a familiar ring and causes little surprise is due in no small way to the quickened pace and widespread scale of change in the latter half of the twentieth century. This state of affairs holds true for all aspects of modern life, especially those of work and the economy. This chapter considers the structure of the modern capitalist economy and examines the view that far-reaching changes are under way in the make-up of modern industry; changes which may signal the end of the old manufacturing economy and the emergence of a very different kind of economic order.

A sense of economic transformation within the western industrial economies has been present for quite some time, at least since the 1970s. It may not be surprising, therefore, to learn that there are a number of different views in circulation about what kind of economy we are moving away from and the type of economy that we are moving towards.

For some, it is a world of industrialism and its long-standing imagery that we are leaving behind — the modern factories in an urban setting, the heavy machinery and the ever-present noise, along with the massed ranks of overalled men. In its place, we are told that we have entered a *post-industrial* era; one that is characterized by information technologies and networked offices rather than by coal or steam power and sprawling workshops. For others, it is not the whole of industry which is disappearing from view, but rather one specific form of industry — that of large-scale, mass production or, as it is otherwise known, Fordist manufacture. (For a discussion of the concept of 'Fordism', see Book 2 (Allen *et al.*, 1992), Chapter 5.) Opening up before us, it is claimed, is an altogether different kind of economy; one which is organized around flexible forms of production, in both the technologies used and in the kinds of work expected. In contrast to mass production and mass markets, it is argued that flexible production techniques are becoming increasingly important as a means of responding to the greater diversity of consumer demand and fragmented market tastes. The name given to describe this shift from a mass to a more pluralistic kind of society is *neo-* or *post-Fordist*, depending upon which characteristics of the route out of Fordism you wish to stress. The former emphasizes the continuities with Fordism, while the latter stresses a break with the Fordist era. However, both neo- and post-Fordist accounts regard flexibility as the hallmark of the new economic era, overcoming what many take to be the rigidities of an economy organized along Fordist lines.

There is also another sense of ending which is apparent in both the post-industrial and the post-Fordist discourses. It is the sense that the ideas of progress that we associate with a modern industrial economy, especially those based upon the methods of mass production, are also losing their relevance. Among the foundations of a modern industrial economy is the notion that progress can be measured by the extent to which the natural world is transformed into tangible goods. The modern economy is, above all, a manufacturing economy; one that regards the making of things, the transformation of raw materials, as its core activity. But in their daily round of work, fewer and fewer people in the West experience work in this way.

Moreover, if the sheer volume and scale of modern mass manufacture can rightly be regarded as the height of industrial progress, then the passing of this moment must surely call into question the appropriateness of the term 'modern' to describe the economic trends that have been labelled variously 'post-industrial' or 'post-Fordist'. Thus, the perceptible shift away from bureaucratization and centralization towards more flexible, less hierarchical modes of economic organization may well signify a movement *beyond* economic modernity. Alternatively, such trends may simply represent a *continuation* of the dynamics of a modern economy: the emergence of a new form of industry, perhaps in much the same way that mass manufacture displaced the factory system in the earlier part of this century.

The transformation of the *modern* economy is one of the underlying issues discussed in this chapter. The question of economic modernity connects with the broader theme of the future shape of modern societies, but here it acts as a backdrop to the claims that we are in a *transitional* period — one that is taking us beyond industrialism, beyond Fordism. And in any period of transition, if we wish to make sense of the emergent trends, we need to identify the directions of change.

1.1   DIRECTIONS OF CHANGE

There are a number of sound reasons for stressing the importance of discerning the *direction* of economic change. In the first place, those who argue that modern industrial economies have undergone major changes in recent times are not necessarily suggesting that a total transformation of the economy has occurred. The emphasis placed upon the transitional nature of events is intended to convey something of the *incomplete* and *uneven* character of the changes under way. At best, we can distinguish the lines of direction — the direction in which an economy faces and is moving towards.

The implication here is that some kind of qualitative shift in the organization of the economy is under way; one which is greater than the sum of a number of potentially disparate changes. Of course, it is possible to misread such shifts: to confuse short-term, ephemeral changes for those of a more long-term, substantial nature. But that is a risk one has to take when attempting to make sense of the present as opposed to the past. Economies are always in a state of change, but they are less often in the midst of a period of transformation that leads to a *radical shift* in the direction of the economy.

We can minimize such misreadings by spelling out what is entailed by a radical shift in the direction of an economy.

First, it should be possible to detect changes on a number of fronts which, together, are radically altering the general direction of an economy. The stress here is upon the *interconnected* nature of such changes, so that what happens in one part of an economy will have some effect upon the rest of the economy. So, for instance, if we look at some of the recent trends in the UK economy — such as the growth of service jobs and the decline of manufacturing employment; the introduction of new technologies based upon the microchip; the shift in the structure and composition of labour markets, from a male, full-time workforce towards a female, part-time workforce; a change in consumption practices, with a greater emphasis placed upon choice and specialization; and so on — which changes, if any, are interconnected? And if they are interconnected, what kind of economy is taking shape?

Secondly, a radical economic shift implies that a different set of *dynamics* is driving an economy. So identifying such a shift is not simply a question of tracing the connections between a variety of changes; it also involves an identification of which elements are key to the direction of change. For example, in the discussion of the contours of post-industrialization which follows, the movement beyond industrialism is not marked merely by a sectoral shift in an economy from manufacturing to services; rather, it is defined by the generation of knowledge and information which act as the dynamics of change. Indeed, as we shall see, the transformation of office work by information-processing technology is regarded by some, such as Manuel Castells, to be equivalent to the radical shift in industrial society from craft-based, factory production to a system of mass manufacture.

Bearing these two points in mind, we are now in a position to look at the claims that lie behind the first of our two possible directions, that of post-industrialism.

2 FROM INDUSTRIALISM TO POST-INDUSTRIALISM AND BEYOND

Industrialism, as we have noted, has a long-standing imagery attached to it, one that conjures up heavy machinery, smoke-stacked factories, and large workforces. The dominant role of machinery in the manufacture of goods, driven first by coal and steam and then by oil and electricity, gives a more precise focus to this industrial imagery.

With the rise of post-industrialism a new kind of dynamic is said to have displaced the centrality of manufacturing technologies and the making of things. We referred to this in passing as the generation of knowledge and the control of information, a less tangible form of economic power organized around the 'clean' technologies of information and microelectronics. In common with such phenomena as rationalization and bureaucratization, post-industrialism is seen to cut across capitalist economies, radically reshaping the social structure and patterns of work. This section will explore the context in which such claims have been advanced, and the different emphases that such claims have been given by writers on post-industrialism.

2.1 POST-INDUSTRIAL POSSIBILITIES

The idea that we may be moving towards a post-industrial society first took hold in the US in the 1960s against a background of rising prosperity and increased automation at the workplace. The image of post-industrialism was given a certain currency by a popular belief that an age of economic plenty was just around the corner and a general expectation that technology would solve the problem of mind-numbing jobs. Commentators from across the political spectrum in the US spoke about the emergence of a new kind of society, although the clearest statement of what that society might look like is attributed to Daniel Bell. In *The Coming of Post-Industrial Society*, published in 1973, he outlined the nature of the transition that industrial societies had embarked upon.

Drawing upon the works of two economists writing in the 1930s, Fisher and Clark, Bell adopted a 'stages' model of development which identified three successive phases of economic progress: a pre-industrial, an industrial, and a post-industrial phase. The first phase is dominated by agriculture, the second by manufacturing, and the third, the phase that he suggests we have now entered, is dominated by services. In this scenario, historical progress involves a march through these three sectors. The movement refers to historical shifts in the bulk of the workforce, with the majority moving first from agriculture to manufacturing, and then on to the service sector. Today, for example, the US, Japan and all the major European economies have more than half of their workforce in the service sector. And behind all this, driving the movement, as it were, are rises in productivity levels; initially, in agriculture and then in manufacturing. This movement of labour, in turn, is said to have been spurred by a shift in the pattern of demand as rising affluence among consumers leads them to purchase more services relative to manufactured goods and foodstuffs.

According to Bell, the general direction of economic change within the western economies is therefore clearly towards a *service economy*. However, his account of economic change amounts to more than a series of aggregate sectoral shifts in the economy. He wants to argue that each successive economic phase is organized around what he refers to as 'axial principles'. Loosely translated, Bell is referring to the mechanisms or dynamics that give shape to an economy. The 'axial principles' are, so to speak, its driving force. In an industrial society, the driving forces are seen as those of production and profit, the rational pursuit of economic growth through the application of energy and machinery. In contrast, the dynamic forces of post-industrial society are, as we have seen, taken to be those of *knowledge and information*. On this view, it is the generation of knowledge and the processing of information that stimulate economic growth. They act as a source of innovation in the organization and management of the economy and take the form of a final product. Alongside the new technologies that are transforming and automating goods production we find a different product — reams of information. We shall look more closely at this dynamic of knowledge and information shortly, but for the moment I want to draw your attention to the wide range of changes in the social structure that Bell points to as a consequence of this new economic dynamic. There are three aspects to consider.

The first is a shift in the *kinds of work* that people do. Work is transformed, as knowledge (through its embodiment in the new technologies) leads to a fall in the number of manual, manufacturing jobs. At the same time, the growth of the service sector is represented as a source of non-manual work which involves at least some degree of creativity and sociability. Instead of working upon things, people work with other people to deliver a service, which for some provides a more rewarding and interesting form of work. The second, related, aspect is the change in the *occupational structure* as manual jobs give way to white-collar and professional occupations. On this view, old skills requiring strength and physical dexterity have given way to new forms of 'think' work. It is these two trends which lie behind the assertion that we are witnessing the transformation of the working class (see Book 3 (Bocock and Thompson, 1992), Chapter 1), although it is the rise of a professional middle class which draws Bell's attention. Finally, Bell's emphasis upon knowledge and information as the key resources of a post-industrial society alert him to the significance of those who actually control those resources, the *knowledge élites*, as he refers to them. In his view, the entrepreneurs who held sway in industrial society are giving way under a post-industrial ethos to the new technical élites in the universities, government institutions, and economic enterprises. Moreover, as intellectual work becomes more specialized, he sees the emergence of new hierarchies of technical élites alongside the increased professionalization of work and a shift towards the bureaucratization of 'think' work within the advanced western economies.

The emergence of a post-industrial society, however, was not something that was hailed only in the US. In France, in the 1960s, against the backdrop of a radical student movement, Alain Touraine in *The Post-Industrial Society* (1971) spoke about a move from one kind of society to another. Although less explicit than Bell about the economic

characteristics of the new society, he also gave central place to the
disposal of knowledge and the control of information, and stressed the
importance of technology in what he termed the 'programmed society'.
Like Bell, he too identified the agents of change with the control of
knowledge and referred to them, among other terms, as a 'technocracy'.
At this point however these two accounts of post-industrialism part
ways.

'Knowledge workers' — the new workforce?

At the base of their differences is their treatment of social conflict — or,
in Bell's case, its relative neglect. Pivotal to Touraine's analysis of post-
industrialism is the formation of a new social divide between, on the
one hand, technocrats and bureaucrats, and, on the other, a range of
social groupings, including workers as well as students and consumers.
On this account, the principal opposition between social classes does
not stem from the ownership and control of private property but from
access to information and its uses. To speak of a dominant class in this
context is thus to refer to those who have power over the livelihood and
lifestyle of social groups within and beyond the sphere of economic
production. This view represents a shift away from the more
conventional Marxist views of social conflict held at that time, which
located class tensions at the point of production, in the factory or
workplace. The lines of protest may now take a variety of forms, which
have little connection to industry or particular material needs, and thus
generate *new social movements* that are quite distinct from the older
forms of class conflict. In the 1960s, the student movement and the
women's movement were among the best known examples and, today, it
is probably the environmental movement which is taken to represent

the move beyond class politics. (See Book 2 (Allen *et al.*, 1992), Chapter 3, for a discussion of the new social movements.)

Despite the absence of popular resistance in Bell's account of social change, it would be wrong to caricature his position as one of consensual change. Writing from a conservative standpoint in *The Cultural Contradictions of Capitalism* (1976), he attempts to demonstrate how a (post-)modern culture based on an unrestrained individualism is increasingly at odds with the economic rationality of a post-industrial society in which the work ethic still holds firm. Economic progress in this instance, he argues, is rapidly being undermined by a cultural lifestyle that owes its very existence to that self-same economic progress. Whereas Touraine sees post-industrial society as a setting in which the lack of power among certain social groups provides the basis for new lines of social conflict and resistance, Bell identifies a structural dislocation between the economic and the cultural realms of post-industrialism in which the Protestant values of economic efficiency and restraint, on the one hand, are undercut by a material sufficiency, on the other. The self-same values which created the expansion of the post-war US economy and the rise of mass consumption are thus now threatened by the desire among many for a more individualistic and culturally expressive lifestyle. In short, there is a clash between the work ethic and the desire for a more hedonistic lifestyle in post-industrial society.

Aside from the differences of emphasis among post-industrial writers, however, there is considerable agreement over the *idea* of post-industrialism and the economic direction in which it faces. The general thesis attracted much criticism in the 1970s, partly from those who mistook Bell to be saying that post-industrialism heralded the demise of capitalism as a competitive economic system, but also because the advanced economies had begun to experience a more sustained downturn in the pattern of post-war economic growth. None the less, the term 'post-industrial' proved to be quite resilient and slipped into popular usage in a largely uncritical manner, until it resurfaced in the 1980s in the midst of a new, but related, set of debates.

The information society

The first debate concerned the celebrated arrival of the *information society*. Drawing extensively upon post-industrial arguments, information in all its various guises was projected as a major force in the shaping of advanced economies, affecting the nature of work as well as the occupational structure. Again, Daniel Bell was a key contributor to the debate, arguing that the information society is a recent expression of post-industrial society. In an article entitled 'The social framework of the information society' (1980), he spelt out the parameters of an information society and how it rested upon a *knowledge theory of value*. By this, he means that knowledge has replaced (productive) labour as the source of value which yields future profits. One way to think about this is to see knowledge and its applications as *the* resource, one that has the potential to transform almost any kind of activity in an economy. If we take the example of information processing activities, then virtually every sector of the economy may be subject to its influence, from education to telecommunications through to the health services and the social benefits system. In this sense, information processing has the ability radically to alter familiar ways of doing things. Moreover, behind such a capacity lies the new information technologies, which it is argued have the potential to reshape the ways in which we produce and consume, as well as where we perform these activities.

Information in Bell's projection is regarded as more than a resource, however. It is also regarded as a commodity which can be bought and sold in the marketplace. For example, the commercialization of information has opened up a whole new sector of the modern economy, which includes anything from personalized 'junk mail' and tradeable mailing lists to remote sensing systems capable of charting the planet's natural resources, or to satellite TV broadcasting. Little, it would seem, is left untouched by the new technologies, including the commodification of culture and the appearance of the 'wired' home.

Overall, then, the image of the information society is one of a qualitative change in the nature of the western economies, with an ever-increasing proportion of the social structure consisting of professional and technical workers, many of whom are concerned with the production, processing or distribution of information. Following Porat (1977), Bell argues that it is these *information occupations* which are now becoming increasingly important to the success of post-industrial economies and that the wider diffusion of information technologies will enhance this trend. Indeed, when you reach the final chapter of this volume, you will find that commentators such as Lyotard (1984) have argued that the transformation of knowledge and its effects in the current period represent the economic basis of an emergent post-modern age. The role of information, therefore, as both an economic resource and as a commodity, is central to arguments which may take us beyond the modern period. We shall return to this overarching question in Section 2.2, but for the moment I want to remain with the discussion of the rise of the information society and to take it further by considering the more recent account offered by Manuel Castells.

Before you read an extract from Castells's book *The Informational City* (1989), it may be useful to provide something of the context in which he developed his line of argument.

There are principally two points to note. The first is that Castells — although keen to draw attention to the central importance of informational activities within western economies and the US in particular — is also anxious to distance himself from the concept of post-industrialism. The intention is not to reject or dismiss the analyses put forward by Bell and Touraine. On the contrary, it is to stress that an information-based society 'is no more post-industrial than the industrial society was post-agrarian' (ibid., p.367). It is important to Castells that the information society is not simply confused with a service society in which the manufacturing sector has all but disappeared from view. Like Bell and Touraine, he identifies the dynamic of the coming society as the role of knowledge and the use of information, not the predominance of any one particular sector of an economy.

The second point to note is that Castells is responding to earlier accounts of an emergent information society which tended to adopt a rather mechanistic stance towards the social impact of the new technologies. At worst, some of the more 'futuristic' post-industrial writers spoke about changes in the nature of work and the occupational structure *as if* they were inscribed within the technologies themselves. Little sensitivity, if any, was displayed to the fact that societies mould their technologies and select their patterns of use, both within the workplace and beyond. For Castells, however, who draws his ideas from a Marxist tradition, technological change can only be understood in the context of the prevailing social relations of capitalism.

ACTIVITY 1   You should now turn to **Reading A, 'The informational mode of development'**, by Manuel Castells, which you will find at the end of this chapter.

As you read the extract, you will find the by now familiar account of the centrality of knowledge in what Castells refers to as the informational mode of development (in contrast to the industrial mode of development). What is distinctive about his contribution is the argument that the restructuring of capitalism, which occurred in the advanced economies during the 1970s and 1980s, has produced a set of economic and political circumstances which have both shaped the growth of informationalism and been shaped by it. Here, however, I would like you to focus initially upon the shift from the industrial to the informational mode of development and to identify what, according to Castells, is distinctive about the *role* of knowledge in the coming society which differs from its role in an industrial society.

All economies, past and present, would in different ways acknowledge a role for technology and knowledge in shaping the way in which they organize their processes of production. What is novel about the informational mode of development as outlined by Castells is that knowledge is used to generate new knowledge which itself acts as a catalyst for further economic development. Put another way, because information is both a raw material, a resource to be worked upon, and the outcome of the process of production, a commodity in its own right, it is regarded as a central means of improving economic performance. It intensifies the process of economic innovation. Information, as noted at the beginning of this sub-section, can be used to transform a wide range of economic activities — as a technological process or as a product embodied in a variety of manufactured goods and services. Its centrality within the contemporary economy is regarded as crucial, especially as a considerable number of recent social and economic changes rest upon this claim.

One of the more interesting changes identified by Castells is that the new technologies have enabled firms, especially the large multinationals, to operate in new ways. I noted two examples, although you may have noticed others. The first is the combined advances in communication technologies, systems of management and technologies of production which have provided firms with the potential to operate in a more 'footloose' fashion, while retaining their links with markets and production complexes. As you may recall from Chapter 2, there is a sense here in which social distances and time are being 'shrunk' or compressed. The second example is related and concerns the growth of multiple networks between corporations. These networks enable firms to develop products jointly or to serve specific markets, and thus represent a different economic strategy from the establishment of multinational 'empires'. And what both examples speak to is *power*, especially in relation to the kinds of labour employed by these large corporations. Among the changes that informationalism holds for today's workforce, Castells identifies the move towards a core–periphery model of the labour market, the concentration of 'information power' among a knowledge élite in the corporations, and the automation of low-skilled jobs, especially among the unionized workforce in manufacturing. In other words, there is a marked trend towards the polarization and segmentation of the social structure.

Overall, then, many of the trends that Castells identifies do accord with earlier post-industrial themes. The focus upon the activities of multinational corporations is different, but the priority accorded to knowledge and information as the driving forces of the coming society is there, as is the stress upon technology. What is absent from the Castells's age of information, however, is the historical optimism present in some of the early post-industrial accounts.

The divided society

A related debate around the future shape of the post-industrial society is to be found in the work of André Gorz. In *Farewell to the Working Class* (1982), Gorz develops a set of arguments concerning the changing *role of work* in post-industrial economies. The strong claim advanced by Gorz is that the new technologies are altering the structure of employment within society, and that this has led to a social division between an 'aristocracy' of secure, well-paid workers, on the one hand, and a growing mass of unemployed, on the other. In between, the majority of the population are said to belong to a post-industrial working class, for whom work no longer represents a source of identity or a meaningful activity. Automation at the workplace has created 'jobless growth' and its rapid extension will, it is argued, progressively undermine the quality and status of the remaining working-class jobs.

Work, in this scenario, thus becomes an instrumental activity for the majority, undertaken solely to earn a wage with little or no satisfaction or skill content attached.

Gorz's interpretation of the impact of the new technologies thus stresses a particular aspect of the post-industrial transition. It runs parallel to Castells's concerns about the growing segmentation of the workforce, but it is expressed in more social terms and without undue stress upon the role of information as a dynamic which is shaping the social structure. A casualized and disorganized working class is in the foreground of his account, with a privileged minority akin to Bell's knowledge élite occupying the background locations. In a later text, *Critique of Economic Reason* (1989), Gorz intensifies this vision by referring to a society polarized between an emergent 'servile' class and a securely employed, professional class.

ACTIVITY 2   Now read **Reading B, 'Work and post-industrialism'**, by André Gorz, which is a short extract from the Introduction to *Critique of Economic Reason*.

The extract comprises a response by Gorz to the ideas of Lionel Stoleru as set out in the popular French newspaper *Le Monde* (31 October, 1986). The application of technology at the workplace still appears to take a leading role in reshaping the employment structure, but there is more than this to his argument. As before, work is the central focus, with a class of workers able to monopolize the well-paid, professional jobs. Now, however, there is another group of workers who are effectively constrained to 'service' the professional class, in terms of their domestic and personal service needs. The absence of choice in this context, it appears, is only possible in an economy that is marked by a widening gulf between the 'haves' and the 'have nots'. What line of reasoning does Gorz employ to justify this view?

Gorz's reasoning is rather dense on this point, although it would appear that the advances in technology, far from enabling society as a whole to enjoy more free time, have resulted in an economic élite being able to purchase at low cost the services that they had previously been capable of doing for themselves. The commodification of domestic tasks, the incorporation of such tasks into the realm of economic rationality, has worked to the advantage of those who already have secure, well-paid employment. In the language of post-industrialism, work for the new 'servile' class lacks any dignity that may have been associated with industrial tasks at the time of, say, mining and heavy manufacture. For Gorz, it would appear that the new service jobs not only lack economic rationality from the point of view of society as a whole, they are also not considered as 'real jobs' — whatever that may mean.

This line of argument thus stresses a growing social inequality as a marked feature of post-industrialism, and this places Gorz's account closer to that of Touraine's post-industrial vision and Castells's information age rather than to Bell's information society. In his later work, Gorz puts less theoretical weight upon the concept of post-industrialism, but it is apparent that the direction of economic and social change which he outlines represents an extension of his earlier speculations. It may also be useful to note that whereas both Touraine and Gorz wrote within a broad European context, Bell's account is US-centred, as is that of Castells. In many of the western economies, however, the arguments for post-industrialism still chime with the experience of many in work and out of work. And it is this resonance that gives the discourse of post-industrialism its coherence.

2.2   THE POST-INDUSTRIAL TURN? AN OVERVIEW

Despite differences of emphasis and the range of aspects stressed among post-industrial writers, the arrival of post-industrialism can be signalled on a number of economic and social fronts. Above all, the writers seem to agree on one thing: that there has indeed been a shift away from industrialism. In broad terms, this movement can be identified with a shift in the balance of the western economies from a manufacturing to a service base, primarily in terms of employment, although it is often extended to include the output of an economy. However, not all of the writers that we have considered stress this aspect of the transition. Touraine and Gorz, for example, are less concerned than Bell to emphasize the changes that have taken place in the sectoral division of labour.

On the occupational and class fronts, it becomes harder to identify common post-industrial themes. At best, it could be said that Bell and Gorz focus upon different aspects of the same transition. Where Bell sees the growth of white-collar occupations and the formation of knowledge élites, Gorz emphasizes the irrelevance of work to the majority and the fate of a deskilled working class forced to serve those élites. Where one offers the prospect of an end to harsh manual labour, the other holds out for a better world outside of, rather than within, work. Even so, it is evident that both Gorz and Castells see social and economic polarization as part of the general direction of change.

One of the main features of the post-industrial society, however, is not its simple lines of division, but rather the cross-cutting nature of the new social movements, as stressed by both Touraine and Castells. The impact of these movements is clearly meant to direct our attention beyond industrial forms of class politics, but it is an open question in the work of the three writers — Touraine, Castells and Gorz — as to the nature of the relationship between the 'old' and the 'new' lines of conflict (see Book 3 (Bocock and Thompson, 1992), Chapter 1, for a discussion of industry and class).

The green movement — cutting across traditional lines of social conflict

There *is,* none the less, complete agreement on one principal feature of the coming society among all the writers that we have discussed: namely, the central importance of knowledge and information in the transition, especially as a source of technological innovation. Information and its uses is regarded as a major resource, which has already begun to reshape activities in the manufacturing and state sectors as well as in private services such as finance and commerce. Strong claims have also been advanced for the importance of information technology as a 'heartland technology'; that is, one capable of generating further innovations at the workplace and beyond. To convey the significance placed upon this dynamic we need only to remind ourselves of the observation by Castells (noted in Section 1.1) that information generation and processing is to office work what mass production was to craft-based manufacture — a radical shift in the structure and organization of the economy. Figure 4.1 provides an impression of the post-industrial changes that could be involved in such a shift.

Of course, if valid, Castells's observation raises a further question as to what it is exactly that we are said to have gone beyond? We know that it is not capitalism, for instance. In the West, a competitive economic system based upon the purchase and sale of commodities is still intact, as are the social relationships which underpin this system. But we also know that there *is* agreement over the passing of industrialism. If post-industrialism or informationalism is therefore a new phase of capitalism, have we then also moved beyond the *modern* economy and its associated ideas of progress? If mass manufacture and mass markets may be regarded as the height of modern industrial progress, how

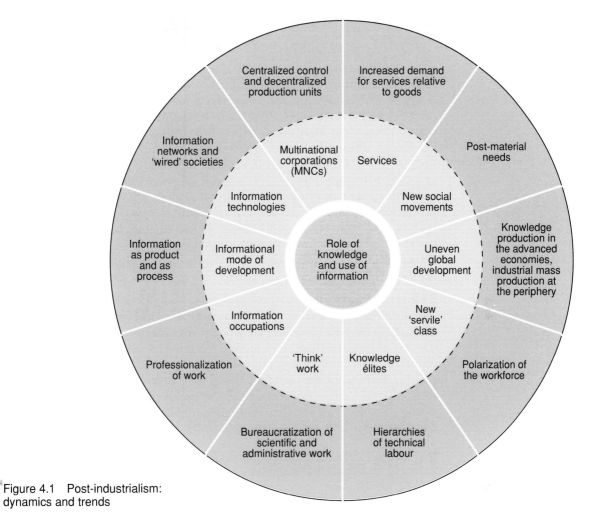

Figure 4.1   Post-industrialism: dynamics and trends

should we then regard the dynamic of information and the emergence of a more divided society? Should we consider these characteristics as a new *form* of economic modernity, or as something that takes us beyond the modern economic era, as Lyotard suggests in his post-modern argument outlined in Chapter 7?

Section 5 will place this question in the context of the global economy and the uneven development of modern societies (and it will resurface in a discussion of Frederic Jameson's (1984) views on late capitalism and post-modernity in the following chapter). Before that, we turn our attention to an alternative account of the direction of economic change — post-Fordism.

3   FROM FORDISM TO POST-FORDISM

Although it is claimed that the first signs of the decline of Fordism as an industrial era were apparent in the late 1960s and early 1970s, at about the time when a post-industrial society was also said to be emerging, the directions of change sketched within the two transitions and the debates surrounding them have taken rather different routes. At the risk of caricature, if the debate over what comes after industrialism focused upon the rise of services and the role of information, the debate over the end of Fordism has largely concerned itself with what kind of manufacturing and product demand has replaced that of mass production and mass markets. With the shift to post-Fordism a new kind of economic era is said to have opened up: one based, as was noted in the chapter Introduction, on flexible forms of economic organization and production, along with a more pluralistic set of lifestyles.

Earlier we referred to mass production as a twentieth-century *form* of industrialism. It is useful to bear this periodization in mind as a means of locating the two debates. Post-Fordist manufacture does not signal the end of industrialism, it is merely regarded as a more recent form of industry. For some writers, however, post-Fordism has taken on a wider set of meanings, as the economic basis for a post-modern culture. This section is primarily concerned with the economic implications of what is said to come after Fordism, although certain political and cultural considerations will be indispensable to the analysis.

3.1   THE REGULATIONIST CONTEXT

Before we explore the different pathways out of Fordism, we need to have a broad sense of what Fordism as an industrial era looks like. (As noted in the chapter Introduction, you will find a full discussion of the concept of 'Fordism' in Book 2 (Allen *et al.*, 1992), Chapter 5.)

ACTIVITY 3   Now turn to **Reading C, 'Fordism and post-Fordism'**, by Robin Murray, and read the *first* section on the characteristics of Fordism (i.e. up to the section headed 'The Break-up of Fordism').

Murray identifies certain structures specific to Fordism. He also provides a broad account of its history. As a way of familiarizing yourself with the concept of Fordism, I would like you to make a short list of what you consider to be the defining characteristics of Fordism as outlined by Murray.

Leaving the historical detail to one side, I picked out the following features:

- The combination of standardized parts, special-purpose machinery, the fragmentation of labour skills, and the moving assembly line.
- Economies of scale reaped through large-scale mass production. (Although this entailed high fixed costs in plant and machinery, the sheer volume of production reduced the cost per car as output rose.)
- Long runs of standarized goods linked to a system of protected national markets.
- A concentration of highly paid, semi-skilled 'mass workers' in large factories.
- A hierarchical, bureaucratic form of work organization, characterized by a centralized management.
- State management of the national economy through a range of 'Keynesian' policies which regulated levels of income, demand and welfare.
- And finally, and most importantly, the link between mass production and mass consumption that enabled the whole process to reproduce itself.

You may have picked out other features which fall under the broad concept of Fordism and, indeed, it is interesting to note the sheer breadth of the vision that comprises Fordism. There is certainly more to this vision than the simple idea that the economy has, in some way, been transformed into something that resembles a giant car plant. In fact, it was Antonio Gramsci, an Italian Marxist writing in the early 1930s, who first used the term 'Fordism', to refer to a new industrial lifestyle based upon the 'American way'. As an industrial era, however, Fordism is primarily a post-war affair, and it was not until the 1970s that the first attempt to systematically construct a 'history' around the concept of Fordism appeared. Michel Aglietta, a member of what is known as the French regulationist school, published his account of Fordism in 1976, and it appeared in English in 1979 under the title *A Theory of Capitalist Regulation: The US Experience*.

In this text, on the basis of evidence drawn from the US economy, Aglietta outlined the structure of Fordism and also pointed to its coming crisis. At that time, in the 1970s, a state of economic uncertainty was evident across the western economies as a slow-down in productivity and declining profitability, which had appeared first in the US in the late 1960s, spread across the other industrial economies, notably those of Europe. Compounded by the 'oil shock' of 1973, which led to a dramatic increase in energy costs in the western nations, the long post-war boom which had lent credibility to the notion of Fordism as an industrial *era* appeared to be at an end. In a moment, we shall take a closer look at the nature of this economic crisis and the *limits* to Fordism. First, however, it would be helpful to say a little more about the regulationist approach.

Let me sketch the background. There are a variety of schools which talk about economic regulation, but the Parisian school, of which Aglietta is a central figure, is probably the best known. What is distinctive about the Parisian school, or for that matter all regulationist approaches, as their title suggests, is a concern with the regulation of the economy. This may sound a rather ordinary concern, yet in the context of much economic theory it is unusual in two respects. First, regulationists assume that the frequent disruptions and recurrent crises that an economy is subject to owe little to the 'hidden hand' of the competitive market for their resolution. There is no short- or long-term tendency towards equilibrium in the market-place. Secondly, and relatedly, they recognize a role for political and cultural relations in attempts to regulate the instability of advanced economies. In particular, this approach stresses the role of *institutions*, such as the state, in attempting to balance the patterns of production and social demand. The pattern of accumulation and growth in the advanced economies is thus secured as much by *social* regulation as it is by economic regulation. What marks out the Parisian regulationist school, however, is their characterization of the processes of growth and accumulation.

Periods of growth and decline in the advanced economies are understood through two key concepts, *a regime of accumulation* and *a mode of regulation. Regimes of accumulation* are periods of growth characterized by whatever it is that ensures a compatibility between what is produced and what is consumed in an economy. Under a Fordist regime of accumulation, for example, production and consumption, as we have seen, are both characterized by mass standards. Production involves large batch, standardized runs (of cars, fridges, washing machines, and the like) that offer rapid productivity gains which, in turn, feed through to workers' incomes and the formation of mass markets. The *wage relation* is regarded as critical, as it influences levels of productivity and the share of profits accruing to industry, as well as shaping the overall level of employment. The wage relation connects the sphere of production with the sphere of consumption, and it is this connection which is said to give a regime of accumulation its distinctive shape. Moreover, it is this connection which enables the multitude of firms to take their investment and production decisions in the knowledge that the markets will not dramatically change in the foreseeable future. Equally significant however is the *labour process*: the tasks that workers perform and the technologies that they use. It is this aspect of production which provides the initial boost in productivity that gets a regime under way. So, for instance, under Fordism, it would have been the mass technologies and the highly specialized, semi-skilled and unskilled workforce which exhibited the most dynamic forms of organization.

A *mode of regulation* is of a rather different order and, for want of a better way of expressing it, it functions as a support framework for growth regimes. It pulls together and directs the wide variety of actions taken by firms, banks, retailers, workers, state employees, and the like, into some kind of regulated network. In other words, it enables a particular regime of accumulation to develop in a particular direction in a more or less stable manner. How this process of regulation occurs is itself complex, although the support framework does include a whole host of cultural styles and political practices, ranging from popular aspirations and social expectations to the more formal interventions of the state, such as the politics of 'Keynesianism'. Under Fordism, for instance, an institutionalized expectation of stable growth, rising consumption levels, and increased social welfare, were said to have made up the 'social cement' of the regime. Thus, even something as basic as the largely unquestioned acceptance of full-time factory work (among men) helped to ensure the stability of the regime. Indeed, it could be asserted that it is the mode of regulation that 'holds together' a particular industrial era, albeit in different ways in different countries.

It is important to note, therefore, that any national economy, whether it be the US, France, Japan, Germany, or the UK, will find its own 'route' through Fordism. A nation's past history, its cultural and political peculiarities, and the nature of its connections with the global economy, all combine to produce a *national mode of growth.* Thus, for example, it is generally assumed that the post-war productivity levels achieved in the UK were never comparable to those achieved under conditions of mass production in the US. In contrast, the welfare benefits system in the UK offered a more developed form of state regulation than in the US. This kind of uneven development is regarded as a common characteristic across national economies.

Having said that, the broad concept of Fordism *is* taken to encompass post-war developments across the advanced economies. In regulationist terms, these developments represent a distinctive period of economic growth in which a certain regime of accumulation *came together* with a supportive mode of regulation. By the early 1970s, however, as we have noted, the cohesion between the two was showing signs of fracture.

Crises are regarded by regulationists as an endemic feature of capitalist economies, although not all economic crises are of the same magnitude. Some offer an opportunity to bring an economy back into balance, while others are regarded as more fundamental; that is, as representing a threat to the basic structure of an economy. In such cases, the whole process of regulation starts to break down and with it the dynamic of capital accumulation.

It is possible to trace the structural crisis of Fordism to a number of factors, although disagreement exists over their relative significance. (See Boyer, 1990, for a comprehensive account of the structural crisis of Fordism.) However, two factors are widely regarded as key to the crisis. The first is rooted in the Fordist labour process and concerns the inability of mass production methods to realise further productivity gains within manufacturing, as well as their limited applicability to areas of the economy such as services. On this view, the *limits* of Fordism had been reached, both in a technical sense and in relation to a mass collective workforce whose resistance to the dull, repetitive rhythms of work had peaked. From a technical standpoint, increasing returns to scale from ever larger mass production complexes were said to have been frustrated by the difficulties experienced in balancing what is produced with what is in demand at any one point in time. Fluctuation in the pace of demand, shifting patterns of taste, delays in re-starting the line and the time taken to re-tool machinery, all contributed towards a trend of declining productivity. And from the point of view of labour, the excessive bureaucratization of control, coupled with the tedium of work had led to increased absenteeism and strife among the workforce. The very characteristics, therefore, which had once contributed to the success of the Fordist regime were now blocking the accumulation process.

The second factor is located at the international level. In essence, it concerns a shift in the post-war pattern of global demand. This, it is argued, occurred partly in response to the steady erosion of the US dollar as an international regulatory currency. As strong economies such as Japan and Germany challenged the hegemony of the US in the world economic order, the impact of increased competitiveness fuelled global instability and enhanced the prospect of international recession. Another related consequence of increased internationalization was the breakdown of oligopolistic pricing methods within national markets. The overall result was further disruption in the post-war economic momentum.

Thus, within the spheres of both production and consumption, the national and international dynamics that had sustained Fordist economic growth were, on this view, beginning to crack, and with them the forms of social regulation that supported the regime. If correct, therefore, the coming era may actually hold the prospect of a resolution to the crisis of Fordism. Broadly speaking, the nature of this resolution has been sketched in two ways — a neo-Fordist resolution and a post-Fordist resolution. We can distinguish them in so far as the first scenario represents an *extension* to the Fordist era, whereas the latter scenario represents a *break* with Fordism. We shall consider each resolution in turn.

Neo-Fordism

As there is nothing certain about the emergence of a new link between production and consumption, nor anything automatic about the rise of a mode of regulation compatible with it, the Parisian regulationists, and Aglietta in particular, are cautious about naming a successor to Fordism. In general, they have spoken about developments on two economic fronts which may possibly transcend the limits to Fordism. The first points to a transformation of the labour process, and the second draws attention to the global shifts in the organization of production.

Changes in the labour process which, in themselves, offer a partial resolution to the crisis of Fordism in the western economies include both increased automation at the workplace and the introduction of new working practices. Technological innovations such as computer-

numerically controlled and computer-integrated manufacturing systems
are held to signify the direction of economic change. Such systems, it is
argued, lead to an overall reduction in the amount of labour required, a
shift in control away from machine operators to skilled technicians,
and, above all, a greater *flexibility* in production scale without incurring
further substantial costs. The ability to switch from mass production to
small-batch production is held to be one of the key features of this
technology. Moreover, this kind of flexible technology finds its
counterpart in the formation of flexible work groups and social
innovations such as 'quality circles'. Taken together, the new
technologies and the new work practices within manufacturing hold out
the prospect of a new lease of life for Fordism — and not only within
the western economies.

Computer-controlled production

One of the implications of the new production technologies is that a
greater decentralization of production is possible. The centralization of
managerial control, combined with the Fordist break-up of the labour
process into discrete elements, has enabled larger firms to move parts of
their production processes to peripheral locations. At first, this
movement of capital took place within the advanced economies,
although by the 1970s it included less developed countries such as
Hong Kong, Taiwan, Singapore, South Korea, and Brazil. This
movement of production did not represent a break with Fordism
however. On the contrary, the search for new locations was based upon
a quest for new mass markets and attempts to maintain productivity
levels by tapping available pools of unskilled, cheap labour. According
to Lipietz (1987), the spread of Fordism across the globe, albeit in an

uneven and partial manner, represents an attempt to overcome the crisis of Fordism at the 'centre' — that is, in the western economies.

In fact, the 'centre/periphery' distinction offers a useful way of summarizing the directions of change that neo-Fordism represents. In the central or core western economies, new technologies are said to be creating a polarization of the workforce that is not dissimilar to Gorz's projection. So while a highly skilled, technical élite amass the advantages gained from increased automation, the majority are either deskilled or unemployed. Meanwhile, at the global periphery, routinized, labour-intensive methods of production predominate. The latter should not be read as an entirely negative scenario, however, as this type of production has created the possibility for economic advance among the newly industrializing countries (witness the Asian economies, for example).

The neo-Fordist scenario is none the less a cautious vision; one based upon the centrality of the labour process in the movement from one regime of accumulation to another. As neo-Fordists move beyond the labour process to consider the cultural and political dimensions of the mode of regulation, their vision tends to become somewhat blurred.

Post-Fordism

Post-Fordism, as noted above, represents a movement *beyond* Fordism. It signifies a qualitative shift in the organization of production and consumption, as well as a break in the mode of regulation. As a thesis, however, post-Fordism is not generally associated with the French regulationist school, although the framework of meaning that informs the thesis clearly binds it to the theoretical stance adopted by the French regulationists.

ACTIVITY 4   You can judge for yourself the closeness of this theoretical relationship and also gauge the breadth of the changes involved in a post-Fordist shift by reading the rest of **Reading C, 'Fordism and post-Fordism'**, by Robin Murray.

As you read the remainder of Reading C, you should focus upon the post-Fordist changes identified by Murray, in respect of:

- the organization of production
- practices of consumption
- forms of regulation.

In the arena of production, it is possible to note a number of features which post-Fordism shares with neo-Fordism. The role of *flexible manufacturing systems* with their ability to switch from economies of scale (mass) to economies of scope (batch) is an important shared feature, and so too is the introduction of new ways of organizing work to improve product quality. In both cases, however, there is a further twist to the post-Fordist characterization. Where neo-Fordists tend to associate the new technologies with job deskilling and an increased centralization of managerial control, post-Fordists, while recognizing this prospect, point to a more positive side of the technologies. Alongside job deskilling, the new technologies are also seen as creating opportunities for enskilling and reskilling. Moreover, they are said to hold out the prospect of a multi-skilled labour force operating in a less hierarchical work environment.

Murray also notes a series of production changes less often considered by neo-Fordists. Across the sectors there have been changes in product life and product innovation, with shorter, flexible runs and a wider range of products on offer; changes in stock control, with just-in-time methods removing the need to hold large amounts of costly stock; and changes in design and marketing in response to an increasingly diverse pattern of consumer demand. It is also interesting to note that services occupy an important 'lead role' for Murray, especially retail services. It is doubtful, however, that the retail sector could match the propulsive role performed by the consumer goods industries in the Fordist era.

Turning to consumption, it is evident that Murray sees a firm link to the changes in the way that goods and services are produced. With the emphasis upon niche markets, segmented markets, and rapidly changing consumer tastes, he notes that cultural expectations and aspirations are in the process of shifting from standardized (Fordist) styles towards a greater acceptance of difference and plurality within the UK and the West more generally. Naturally, it is difficult to gauge the extent of such a trend, but we should remind ourselves that we are concerned with *directions* of change, rather than any complete set of practices.

Similarly, at the national political level we can only catch a glimpse of Murray's account of the displacement of Keynesianism in the UK by a more strident neo-liberal economic strategy; that is, one based upon the economic rationality of the private market. Elsewhere, Jessop (with others, 1988 and 1990) has written about the significance of a neo-liberal strategy for the development of a post-Fordist route out of the economic uncertainty of the 1970s in the UK. In this strategy, we see the outline of an attempt to mobilize certain key social groups within the class structure around a direction of change secured by the competitiveness and morality of the market-place. However, Jessop and Murray are too aware of the contrasts in political strategies across Europe, the US, and Japan in the 1980s to be able to draw general conclusions about the regulatory structures which would support and direct a more flexible regime of accumulation.

Taken as a whole, then, Murray's approach has much in common with the regulationists, in so far as he is trying to think through the connections between the dynamics of accumulation and their social coordination, as well as how the relationships between classes enter into the formation of renewed stability between production and consumption. In terms of substance too, there are shared concerns with another writer who works loosely within a regulationist framework. David Harvey's ideas concerning the complex mix of forces which are said to have led to an altered rhythm and an acceleration in the pace of modern economic life were discussed in Chapter 2 of this book. In *The Condition of Postmodernity* (1989), the argument that the pace of economic life has quickened dramatically since the 1960s is linked closely by Harvey to the dynamics of a more flexible regime of accumulation. Alongside the by now familiar developments in flexible workplace technologies, 'flat' organizational structures, increased cooperation and coordination between firms, and diverse consumer markets, we also find knowledge and information playing an important part in the speed-up of market trading and in coordinating responses to the volatility of global demand. What is distinctive about Harvey's view of the new flexible regime, however, is that he traces many of these developments to what has been happening in the sphere of modern *finance*.

Where others locate the dynamic of the new regime within the flexible modes of production and consumption, Harvey locates it in the emergence of new financial systems. He argues that, since the 1970s, the banking and the financial system has achieved a degree of autonomy relative to industrial production which carries with it the ability to create havoc with the stability of material production as well as to overcome the rigidities of Fordist-type production and consumption. The formation of new financial markets, the introduction of new financial instruments, the opening up of new systems of global coordination between financial centres, have, according to Harvey, carried capitalism into a new era in which the rapidity and scale of capital flows makes it more difficult for nation-states to secure stable accumulation strategies. At the same time, innovation within financial systems has enabled firms, governments, and consumers to adopt more flexible strategies towards the 'blockages' of Fordism. It is in this sense that the emergence of a flexible regime of accumulation can be understood as *one* type of response to the transformation of the global financial system.

3.2   AFTER FORDISM? AN OVERVIEW

As with post-industrialism, it is possible to identify a number of economic and social fronts which take us beyond Fordist mass production and mass consumption. How far beyond is rather a moot question, although all commentators do agree that Fordism, however conceived, is in crisis. Moreover, attempts to overcome this crisis point towards a wider use of flexible production techniques and the promotion of flexible patterns of work organization. Both neo-Fordists, such as Aglietta, and post-Fordists, such as Murray, stress the significance of greater flexibility in the organization of production. Harvey would also agree on this aspect.

At a more detailed level, however, there is less agreement over the kinds of flexibility that are actually taking place within the sphere of production and, indeed, their extent. Aglietta offers a specific account of flexible automation related to changes in the labour process, whereas Murray, in addition, entertains a notion of flexibility around supply networks, product runs, job demarcation boundaries, labour market practices, stock control, and the like. Perhaps more importantly, there is an undercurrent in Murray's account that all the changes under way offer a potentially progressive mode of development, whereas the pitch in Aglietta's account is generally regressive — for the majority of working people at least.

However, the sharpest expression of difference between neo-Fordist and post-Fordist accounts is found in their respective interpretations of the end of Fordism. Neo-Fordism represents an *adjustment* to the problems of Fordism, a way forward that extends the period of Fordism. In contrast, post-Fordism represents a qualitatively new economic direction, a *step beyond* Fordism. As such, post-Fordism signals a new *era*, in much the same way that Castells spoke about an information *age*. This can be gleaned from the breadth of the post-Fordist scenario which attempts to outline the kinds of social regulation that may support the rise of a new flexible regime. It would, however, be an exaggeration to claim that either Murray or Harvey had adequately sketched the lines of a new mode of regulation.

Global Fordism — routinized production at the periphery

At the global level there is perhaps more rather than less that neo-Fordism and post-Fordism hold in common. Lipietz, above all, has drawn attention to the rise of 'global Fordism'; that is, the spread of labour-intensive, routinized production across the globe in response to crisis conditions in the 'core', western economies. Interestingly, this is said to be happening alongside the decline of 'core' economies such as the UK, and the growth of post-Fordist-type regimes in Japan and Germany. And in Harvey too, there is the similar notion of different work regimes existing alongside one another, both within countries and between countries. What happens after Fordism therefore may involve a mix of regimes rather than the straightforward replacement of one mode of development by another.

There is, however, complete agreement over the passing of Fordism, conceived that is as a dynamic of mass manufacture and mass markets. Figure 4.2 provides an impression of what could replace it, if a number of trends were combined.

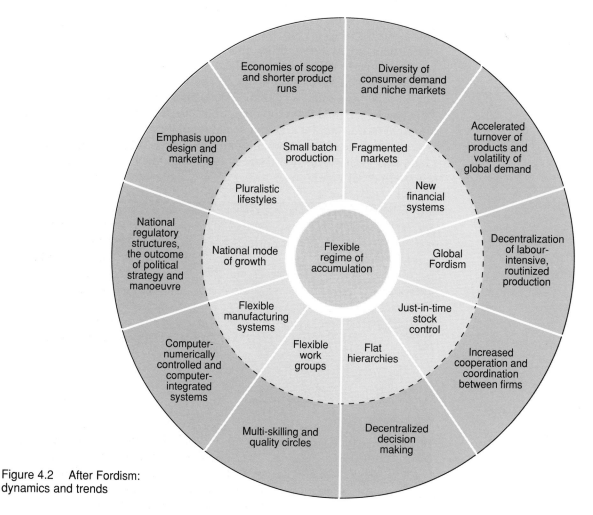

Figure 4.2   After Fordism:
dynamics and trends

On the question of economic modernity, it is harder to discern the common ground. Certainly, all would agree that it is capitalism and its drive for profitability which gives modernity its restless, ceaseless quality. Today, however, it is this very same quality, speeded up, as it were, which according to Harvey represents the economic basis of post-modernism. By this, I take him to mean more than flexibility at the workplace. The economic basis also comprises the rapidity of capital flows, the accelerated turnover of products and consumer tastes, the speed up of communications, and, more generally, a sharp increase in the pace of economic life. Murray too refers to the quickening consumption of images in the 'postmodern market place', although the lines of post-modernism do not form a central part of his analysis. (In the following chapter, Jameson's (1984) account of post-modernism as the cultural logic of late capitalism is explored at length.)

For Aglietta and the Parisian regulationist school, Fordism may well have represented one of the peaks of modernist progress in terms of its scale and pattern of growth, but it is not altogether certain that they would regard a movement beyond this era as involving anything other than a new *form* of economic modernity.

4 ASSESSING ECONOMIC TRANSITIONS

Assuming that you now have a broad sense of the kinds of economic transformation which are said to be under way in the UK economy and beyond, we need to turn our attention to the question of assessment. How do we decide just how far the industrial economies have changed? What are the right questions to ask? This section examines the strengths and weaknesses of the post-industrial and post-Fordist transitions through a consideration of the *scope* and the *pace* of the different developments. It will look at the role of empirical *evidence*, as well as providing an assessment of the *theoretical* strengths of the arguments. The section is thus not so much a debate between possible lines of development, as an assessment of what each argument has to offer. It will ask how successful the claims are in providing us with a sense of what is happening around us and the direction of economic change that we face.

4.1 THE SCOPE OF CHANGE

The tentative nature of change in a period of transition, as noted in the chapter Introduction, leaves us with little choice over the starting point of our assessment. We have to begin with the directions of change suggested by post-industrialism, post-Fordism, and neo-Fordism, for that is all that is available. This will involve more than an exercise in measuring the extent of empirical change, however. A wide assortment of potentially disparate changes, for example, do not add up to a shift in the overall direction of an economy. To assess, say, the direction in which neo-Fordism is pointing we need to identify the *kinds* of change involved, trace the *connections* between them, and then make a *judgement* about which of the changes, if any, are the more robust or decisive. Merely to list the empirical changes or to refer to their magnitude would not settle the issue, as the significance of such trends is essentially a theoretical question.

Consider the example of post-industrialism, which in Bell's hands *connects* the shift in the balance of employment from manufacturing to services, to the shift from blue-collar to white-collar professional work, to the shift in demand from goods to services, to the shift from an economy organized around raw materials and machinery to one organized around knowledge and information technology. Now, in my view, these substantive claims have a certain strength which stems from the actual sequence of connections drawn rather than from any one set of changes. Even though we should not anticipate complete agreement among post-industrial writers about the relative significance of these shifts, few are likely to dispute the sequence of connections drawn. Yet it would be premature to acknowledge the strength of the post-industrial claims.

Before doing so, we would need to satisfy ourselves on three counts.

1   In the first place, we would need to know whether the sequence of connections drawn by Bell and others is correct.

Consider, for example, the firm link drawn by Bell between the growth in service employment and an increase in the demand for services across the major western economies. This link has been challenged on the grounds that service workers are not only employed in the service sector; they are also directly employed in the manufacture and sale of goods (as clerks, accountants, designers, sales people, and the like). Thus, a boost in manufacturing growth is just as likely to lead to a rise in service employment as is an increase in the demand for service products (see Gershuny, 1978). We need to be alert therefore to a mis-specification of connections between changes that are taking place on a number of fronts. The causal chain of the argument may, on closer inspection, turn out to be illusory. The exact same kind of concern may be addressed to the connections drawn by post-Fordists between flexibility in manufacturing systems, product markets, and work organization, on the one hand, and the new institutional forms that comprise a mode of regulation on the other (see Rustin, 1989). Such links, if present, will naturally vary between nations, but in each mode of national growth it is important to trace the emergent patterns of regulation and their relation to processes of economic accumulation.

2   Secondly, we would need to know how widespread are the changes. Are the shifts as well-developed as some writers would have us believe?

Consider the types of flexibility we have spoken about above. How widespread, for instance, is the use of the new computer technologies within manufacturing? Are product markets fragmenting to the extent that Murray and others have indicated? And what of the new patterns of work organization — how pervasive is the influence of multi-skilling, flexible work groups and 'quality circles'? Wood (1989), among others, remains sceptical, for instance, over the extensive adoption of each of these aspects. It is not evident, for example, why the advance of flexibility in one area should be followed by advances in other areas. Market diversification, for example, can be met by the assembly of different products from production runs organized along mass production lines (see Sayer, 1989). The real issue with these developments, however, as it is with the introduction of information technologies, is not the number of cases which can be cited across the industrial economies, but whether such innovations can sustain a new kind of economy. Even if we had extensive empirical data on these developments (which is unlikely as we are discussing *emergent* trends), such data would not amount to a *decisive* answer in favour or against a movement towards a new kind of economy.

3   Our final concern is that we would need to know the geographical scope of the developments.

Take the example of Bell's post-industrial vision. It is strictly a vision of the First World which, interestingly, has its counterpart in a shift to industrialism in the Third World. In *The Coming of Post-Industrial Society*, Bell speaks of a geographical divide between knowledge-production and mass production, with the latter increasingly taking place outside of the advanced economies. However, a more explicit account of this global division of labour is to be found in the work of Lipietz. As we have seen, whilst neo-Fordism is said to have taken hold in the West, more 'primitive' forms of Fordism, shed of their social welfare element, co-exist in less developed economies. Thus, in both Bell's post-industrialism and in Lipietz's neo-Fordism, it is apparent that what is happening in the West is certainly changing the lives of people elsewhere.

This view of global connections is also central to Castells's and Harvey's assessments of uneven global development. Castells argues that, in the coming information age, the internationalization of the economic order is being reconstructed through advances in information technology. Power and knowledge rest with an international, professional élite who control the networks of information through which the global reorganization of production and markets is taking place. For Harvey, it is nothing less than the accelerated speed-up of capitalism which is making the world smaller, so to speak, as the 'old idea' of the 'West and the Rest' breaks down under the impact of the interpenetration of economies and cultures (see Chapter 2).

Clearly there are many examples of such global connections. Whether the dynamics which lie behind these connections are sufficiently robust to support the scope of these claims begs a further issue however — that of *economic dominance*.

Structural reach

By *economic dominance*, I mean that some changes are considered more fundamental than others, more central to the direction of an economy and events beyond. These are the dynamics which drive change. We have encountered a variety of such dynamics: the propulsive effects of the Fordist industries of mass production; Bell's view of knowledge as the 'principle' or driving force of a post-industrial economy; similarly, the importance attached by Castells to the catalytic role of information in an economy; the stress placed upon the new flexible sectors of the economy by post-Fordists; and the speed-up of capital circulation identified by Harvey, which gives causal weight to the new financial systems.

In each of these cases a dominant influence is identified which may manifest itself in one of two ways (see Book 2 (Allen *et al.*, 1992), Chapter 5, for a discussion of economic dominance). Either the influence will be *extensive* (that is, something like information technologies or flexible working arrangements will spread widely across an economy), or the influence will be *structural* (this implies that such dynamics have a *reach* across an economy which is not matched by their widespread adoption within an economy). So, for example, it could be argued that Fordist mass production techniques were structurally dominant in the post-war period because of their ability to generate and transmit growth to other parts of the economy. This did not mean, however, that the whole economy had been turned over to the mass production of consumer durables.

ACTIVITY 5

You need to stand back and to think about this for a while. Most of the dynamics identified above exert a *structural* influence. It is entirely possible, however, that the dynamic chosen is the wrong one or that its effects are much exaggerated (see Thrift, 1989).

I would like you to take the example of, *either* knowledge and information in the coming post-industrial era, *or* flexible accumulation in the post-Fordist transition, and to consider how such dynamics have the potential to *reach* through an economy. You will need to turn back to the relevant sections to recall the diagrammatic representations of the two transitions, as well as to recollect the arguments which lie behind them.

You should also think about the *kinds* of evidence which may undermine the importance of the dynamic that you are considering. Apart from the fact that some post-industrial arguments tend to neglect aspects of manufacturing change, whereas certain post-Fordist accounts tend to play down the significance of developments within the service sector, you should also consider how far, if at all, modern economies are actually characterized by a single, dominant economic dynamic.

4.2 THE PACE AND TEMPO OF CHANGE

This represents the second part of our assessment of economic transitions. Even though we may feel confident about the direction and scope of change, we may still overemphasize its long-term significance. Leaving to one side the fact that there are always continuities present in any period of transition, the pace and tempo of change is often left unstated in assessments of economic change. The price paid for this neglect is a loss of any notion of *historical time.*

The microelectronics revolution — a critical burst of historical time

Following Braudel (1972), we can distinguish between different sorts of historical time. There are rapid, critical periods of time, of the kind talked about by Castells, where sharp bursts of technological change are followed by phases of consolidation as a variety of industries adapt to the new information practices. A similar irregular and disruptive note of change is present in Gorz's descriptions of how industries and occupations contract, expand or disappear. There are periods of medium duration, of up to half a century, which may also experience a disruptive tempo as the groundwork for a transition is laid down. Post-Fordism in the UK, for example, would fit into this medium time period, with the last twenty or so years representing the initial phase of development. There are also periods of long-term change, in which time unfolds in a more gradual manner. Post-industrialists, or rather, early post-industrial accounts, tend to emphasize this conception of historical time. On this view, economies are considered to evolve in a particular sequence, with the most developed economies, those that are knowledge-based, setting out the path of development that others are likely to follow. If this were so, then in the present period the US or Japan would be seen as the 'lead' role model. In more recent versions of post-industrialism, however, this cumulative account of change is played down and the contingent character of transitions emphasized. Finally, there are other sorts of historical time, such as the 'explosive event' that precipitates a war or political upheaval, but our concerns here are mainly with the long term and the medium term.

One of the advantages of thinking about time in these ways, as you may have already realized, is that it enables us to *periodize* the claims of the different versions of change. This is helpful in two ways.

1   The periodization of change provides a temporal yardstick by which we can gauge the length and form of any transition.

Commentators, for example, are often quick to point out that suggested developments have not in fact taken place. But if we know the pace and tempo of the projected changes, and their likely duration, then this may help us to weigh up such comments.

Consider, once again, the post-industrial views of Bell, which date back to 1973. Some of the developments he described concerning the potential impact of information-based activities upon the social structure of a modern economy were strongly criticized at the time for their sweeping nature. It is quite possible, however, that we are only now in a position to see the consequences of the information society across a range of economies. Certainly, Castells is of this view. Alternatively, we may still have some time to wait before the significance of information as an economic dynamic is felt.

2   The periodization of change also offers a further check on the range of trends which suggest a potential economic direction.

Are some of the trends identified cyclical or short-term, perhaps in response to economic recession or recent political developments? Have we been misled by an awkward combination of the familiar and the new? The trend towards the fragmentation of consumer tastes and the significance of niche markets in the current period, for example, is one broad phenomenon that has received sceptical support as a permanent feature of a new economic order. For some, it may well be a short-term response to the economic crisis that started in the 1970s, or simply the temporary outcome of the current pattern of income distribution. It may even be the combined result of the two. Similarly, Harvey's stress upon the accelerated pace of capitalism and the dominance of finance over industrial production may also represent a misreading of the global situation. Gordon (1988), for example, has argued that the recent volatility of financial markets and flows may also be understood as *part of* the contemporary economic crisis, and not as a sign of a new global order opening up before us.

In considering potentially far-reaching changes, therefore, the periodization of change also draws attention to some of the pitfalls that accompany the task of theorizing economic change.

5   CONCLUSION: BEYOND THE MODERN ECONOMY?

The long rise of the modern economy, dating back to its commercial and agrarian roots in the eighteenth century and culminating in the recent phase of mass industry, represents the historical backdrop to the arguments set out in this chapter (see Book 1 (Hall and Gieben, 1992), Chapter 3, and Book 2, (Allen *et al.*, 1992), Chapter 5, for a discussion of these respective economic 'moments'). That we are witnessing a transformation of the present structure of modern western economies is, I would have thought, not in doubt. As we have seen, however, there is considerable disagreement over the direction, scope, and pace of change. Equally, there is much dispute over whether the baggage of concepts associated with industrialism, and with Fordism and mass production can serve to explain what is happening to economic life in the West and beyond.

We have considered some of the strongest claims concerning a coming economic era; namely, those of post-industrialism and post-Fordism (and relatedly neo-Fordism). We noted that the path of development in each of the two scenarios had a different starting point and a different trajectory, as well as being driven by a particular kind of dynamic. For the post-industrialists, it is the dynamic of information and knowledge which is taking us beyond the industrial era and into a world of services centred on information technologies and networked offices. For those who would move us beyond Fordism and mass production, it is the dynamic of flexibility which is taking us towards a more pluralistic, less bureaucratic, more decentralized mode of economic life. However, it is also of interest to note the points at which the lines of direction in the two scenarios intersect. There are at least three areas of common concern which are worth specifying.

The *first* shared concern is that of knowledge and the development of new technologies. Both post-industrial and post-Fordist accounts stress the role of knowledge and innovation in the organization of production, and the rise of 'lead' industries based upon breakthroughs in microelectronic and information technologies. The emphasis placed upon these technologies differs somewhat, as do the consequences derived for society, but, none the less, knowledge as an asset appears to lie behind both post-industrial and flexible futures. Furthermore, it could be argued, following Giddens (1990), that such technological settings, rather than taking us beyond industrialism, represent a new *form* of industry; albeit one that is powered by electricity rather than by coal or steam, and where microcircuit-based machinery organizes the nature and the pace of work. On this view, Castells's observation, that the new technologies represent some kind of shift in the economy on a par with the shift from craft to mass manufacture, points to a *continuation* of the modern economic era rather than a move beyond it. What is perhaps more difficult to think through, however, is how all this meshes with our notions of modern economic progress — ideas that are based upon mass manufacturing and mass standards.

The *second* area of common concern is revealing in this context. In both post-industrial and post-Fordist accounts, there is a tendency towards greater not less economic and social inequality. It is a world of professional élites and multi-skilled workers, on the one hand, and a class of service workers, often employed on a casual or part-time basis, on the other. And far from being an accident of economic development, this segmentation or polarization of the social structure appears to be a *structural* tendency of the new economic order. Low-paid, insecure service work represents the downside of both post-industrial and post-Fordist forms of growth. And in both scenarios it is women who are disproportionately concentrated in this kind of 'servile' work, to use Gorz's term. We can read this tendency towards greater inequality in one of two ways, however. We can regard it as a sign of the limits to modern progress, or we can interpret it as yet another illustration of the 'double-sided' character of modernity — with women comprising most of the new 'servicing' class (see Book 3 (Bocock and Thompson, 1992), Chapter 1 on gender divisions and work).

Finally, the *third* area of common concern is one that perhaps raises the sharpest questions over the character of modern economic life, namely, its globalization. Despite, for example, a difference of emphasis and description in the accounts of Castells and Harvey, both point to aspects of the modern global order which are, in their view, undergoing fundamental change. As noted in Chapter 2, and intimated earlier in this chapter, the accelerated pace of modern life, the 'shrinking' of space, and the extent to which the fortunes of people in diverse places across the globe are increasingly interconnected and interwoven have all called into question our ability to think of modern progress in terms of *national* economic progress, and also in terms of developed and less developed *national* economies. There are two aspects to mull over here.

In the first place, there is the presence of 'backward' enclaves *within* the economies of the First World cities. Alongside the financial and commercial practices of New York and London, for example, we find the sweat shops and outworking practices that are more often associated with Third World economies. Yet they are not opposing developments, and nor are they unrelated. There is no simple equation of finance with post-industrialism and the informal economic practices often undertaken by a migrant workforce with pre-industrialism. On the contrary, they are part and parcel of the same global economic forces which are eroding the identity of the West as the 'Rest', as it were, move to the centres of the modern world. Chapter 6 explores this issue of cultural identity in greater depth.

The second aspect raises a question mark over the very idea that it is possible to discern a dominant direction of economic change within a modern economy. After all, if national economies are increasingly becoming 'sites' across which international forces flow, with some parts of a country passed over by the new growth dynamics, then the new uneven global order will very likely be characterized by *more* than one line of economic direction within and between countries. The idea that a single dominant economic dynamic, such as information or flexible manufacturing, is capable of transforming much of the world economy may therefore represent the thinking of a *modern discourse* whose economic moment has now passed.

REFERENCES

Aglietta, M. (1979) *A Theory of Capitalist Regulation: The US Experience*, London, Verso.

Allen, J., Braham, P. and Lewis, P. (eds) (1992) *Political and Economic Forms of Modernity*, Cambridge, Polity Press.

Bell, D. (1973) *The Coming of Post-Industrial Society*, New York, Basic Books.

Bell, D. (1976) *The Cultural Contradictions of Capitalism*, New York, Basic Books.

Bell, D. (1980) 'The social framework of the information society', in Forester, T. (ed) *The Microelectronics Revolution*, Oxford, Basil Blackwell.

Bocock, R. and Thompson, K. (eds) (1992) *Social and Cultural Forms of Modernity*, Cambridge, Polity Press.

Boyer, R. (1990) *The Regulation School: A Critical Introduction*, New York, Columbia University Press.

Braudel, F. (1972) 'History and the social sciences', in Burke, P. (ed.) *Economy and Society in Early Modern Europe*, London, Routledge and Kegan Paul.

Castells, M. (1989) *The Informational City*, Oxford, Basil Blackwell.

Gershuny, J. I. (1978) *After Industrial Society? Emerging Self-Service Economy*, London and Basingstoke, Macmillan.

Giddens, A. (1990) *The Consequences of Modernity*, Cambridge, Polity Press.

Gordon, D. (1988) 'The global economy: new edifice or crumbling foundations?', *New Left Review*, no.168, pp.24–65.

Gorz, A. (1982) *Farewell to the Working Class: An Essay on Post-Industrial Socialism*, London, Pluto Press.

Gorz, A. (1989) *Critique of Economic Reason*, London, Verso.

Hall, S. and Gieben, B. (eds) (1992) *Formations of Modernity*, Cambridge, Polity Press.

Harvey, D. (1989) *The Condition of Postmodernity*, Oxford, Basil Blackwell.

Jameson, F. (1984) 'Postmodernism, or the cultural logic of late capitalism', *New Left Review*, no.146, pp.53–92.

Jessop, B., Bonnett, K., Bromley, S., and Ling, T. (1988) *Thatcherism: A Tale of Two Nations*, Cambridge, Polity Press.

Jessop, B., Bonnett, K., and Bromley, S. (1990) 'Farewell to Thatcherism? Neo-Liberalism vs New Times', *New Left Review*, no.179, pp.81–202.

Lipietz, A. (1987) *Mirages and Miracles: The Crises of Global Fordism*, London, Verso.

Lyotard, J.-F. (1984) *The Postmodern Condition*, Manchester, Manchester University Press.

Murray, R. (1989) 'Fordism and post-Fordism', in Hall, S. and Jacques, M. (eds) *New Times*, London, Lawrence and Wishart.

Porat, M. (1977) *The Information Economy: Definition and Measurement*, Washington DC, US Dept. of Commerce.

Rustin, M. (1989) 'The politics of post-Fordism: or, the trouble with "New Times"', *New Left Review*, no.175, pp.54–77.

Sayer, A. (1989) 'Post-Fordism in question', *The International Journal of Urban and Regional Research*, vol.13, no.4, pp.667–95.

Thrift, N. (1989) 'New times and spaces? The perils of transition models', *Environment and Planning D: Society and Space*, vol.7, no.2, pp.127–8.

Touraine, A. (1971) *The Post-Industrial Society*, New York, Random House.

Wood, S. (1989) *The Transformation of Work? Skill, Flexibility and the Labour Process*, London, Unwin Hyman.

READING A   # THE INFORMATIONAL MODE OF DEVELOPMENT

Manuel Castells

The New Technological Paradigm

During the two decades from the late 1960s to the late 1980s a series of scientific and technological innovations have converged to constitute a new technological paradigm. The scientific and technical core of this paradigm lies in microelectronics, building on the sequential discoveries of the transistor (1947), the integrated circuit (1957), the planar process (1959), and the microprocessor (1971). ...

Social, economic, and institutional factors have, as I will argue, been decisive in the coming together of these different scientific innovations under the form of a new technological paradigm. ... The new technological paradigm is characterized by two fundamental features. First, the core new technologies are *focused on information processing*. This is the primary distinguishing feature of the emerging technological paradigm. To be sure, information and knowledge have been crucial elements in all technological revolutions, since technology ultimately boils down to the ability to perform new operations, or to perform established practices better, on the basis of the application of new knowledge. All major technological changes are in fact based on new knowledge. However, what differentiates the current process of technological change is that *its raw material itself is information, and so is its outcome*. What an integrated circuit does is to speed up the processing of information while increasing the complexity and the accuracy of the process. What computers do is to organize the sets of instructions required for the handling of information, and, increasingly, for the generation of new information, on the basis of the combination and interaction of stored information. What telecommunications does is to transmit information, making possible flows of information exchange and treatment of information, regardless of distance, at lower cost and with shorter transmission times. What genetic engineering does is to decipher and, eventually, program the code of the living matter, dramatically expanding the realm of controllable information processing.

The output of the new technologies is also information. Their embodiment in goods and services, in decisions, in procedures, is the result of the application of their informational output, not the output itself. In this sense, the new technologies differ from former technological revolutions, and justify calling the new paradigm the 'informational technological paradigm', in spite of the fact that some of the fundamental technologies involved in it (for example, superconductivity) are not information technologies. ...

The second major characteristic of the new technologies is in fact common to all major technological revolutions. The main effects of their innovations are on *processes*, rather than on *products*. There are, of course,

Source: Castells, M. (1989) *The Informational City*, Oxford, Basil Blackwell, pp.12–15, 17–19, 28–32.

major innovations in products, and the surge of new products is a fundamental factor in spurring new economic growth. However, the deepest impact of innovation is associated with the transformation of processes. This was also the case with the two industrial revolutions associated with technical paradigms organized respectively around the steam engine and around electricity. ...

Similarly, in the current informational revolution, what new information technologies are about in the first place is process. A chip has value only as a means of improving the performance of a machine for an end-use function. A computer is a tool for information handling, whose usefulness for the organization or individual using it depends on the purpose of the information-processing activity. A genetically modified cell will take on its actual significance in its interaction with the whole body. While all social and biological activities are in fact processes, some elements of these processes crystallize in material forms that constitute goods and services, the usual content of economic products. Technological revolutions are made up of innovations whose products are in fact processes.

These two major characteristics of the informational technological paradigm have fundamental effects on its impact on society. ...

The Organizational Transition from Industrialism to Informationalism

The main process in this transition is not the shift from goods to services but, as the two main theorists of the 'post-industrial society' proposed many years ago, Alain Touraine in 1969 and Daniel Bell in 1973, the emergence of information processing as the core, fundamental activity conditioning the effectiveness and productivity of all processes of production, distribution, consumption, and management. The new centrality of information processing results from evolution in all the fundamental spheres of the industrial mode of development, under the influence of economic and social factors and structured largely by the mode of production. Specifically, the secular trend toward the increasing role of information results from a series of developments in the spheres of production, of consumption, and of state intervention.

In the sphere of *production*, two major factors have fostered information-processing activities within the industrial mode of development. The first is the emergence of the large corporation as the predominant organizational form of production and management. An economy based on large-scale production and centralized management generated the growing number of information flows that were needed for efficient articulation of the system. The second resides within the production process itself (considering production in the broad sense, that is including production of both goods and services), and is the shift of the productivity sources from capital and labor to 'other factors' (often associated with science, technology, and management) ... The hard core of these information-processing activities is composed of knowledge, which structures and provides adequate meaning to the mass of information required to manage organizations and to increase productivity.

In the sphere of *consumption*, two parallel processes have emphasized the role of information. On the one hand, the constitution of mass markets, and the increasing distance between buyers and sellers, have created the need for specific marketing and effective distribution by firms, thus triggering a flurry of information-gathering systems and information-distributing flows, to establish the connection between the two ends of the market. On the other hand, under the pressure of new social demands, often expressed in social movements, a growing share of the consumption process has been taken over by collective consumption, that is, goods and services directly or indirectly produced and/or managed by the state, as a right rather than as a commodity, giving rise to the welfare state. The formation of the welfare state has produced a gigantic system of information flows affecting most people and most activities, spurring the growth of bureaucracies, the formation of service delivery agencies, and consequently the creation of millions of jobs in information handling.

In the sphere of *state intervention*, the past half-century has seen a huge expansion of government regulation of economic and social activities that has generated a whole new administration, entirely made up of information flows and information-based decision processes. Although variations in the mode of production lead to a bureaucratic cycle, with upswings and downturns in the trend toward regulation, state intervention is in more subtle ways a structural feature of the new mode of development, in a process that Alain Touraine has characterized as 'la société programmée'. This is the process by which the state sets up a framework within which large-scale organizations, both private and public, define strategic goals, which may be geared toward international economic competitiveness or military supremacy, that permeate the entire realm of social activities without necessarily institutionalizing or formalizing the strategic guidance of these activities. ...

These structural trends, emerging and converging in a society largely dominated by the industrial mode of development, pave the way for the transformation of that mode, as information processing, with its core in knowledge generation, detracts from the importance of energy in material production, as well as from the importance of goods-producing in the overall social fabric. However, this transformation of the mode of development could not be accomplished without the surge of innovation in information technologies which, by creating the material basis from which information processing can expand its role, contributes to the change both in the structure of the production process and in the organization of society. It is in this sense that I hypothesize the formation of a new, informational mode of development: on the basis of the convergence through interaction of information technologies and information-processing activities into an articulated techno-organizational system. ...

The Articulation between the Informational Mode of Development and the Restructuring of Capitalism: Reshaping the Techno-Economic Paradigm

... Given the complexity of the articulation process, I will differentiate between the two dimensions that compose the informational mode of development: the *technological* and the *organizational*. Both have been fundamental in giving rise to a new form of capitalism which, in turn, has stimulated and supported the technological revolution and has adopted new organizational forms.

New *information technologies* have been decisive in the implementation of the three fundamental processes of capitalist restructuring.

1 Increasing the rate of profit by various means:

(a) Enhancing productivity by the introduction of microelectronics-based machines that transform the production process.

(b) Making possible the decentralization of production, and the spatial separation of different units of the firm, while reintegrating production and management at the level of the firm by using telecommunications and flexible manufacturing systems.

(c) Enabling management to automate those processes employing labor with a sufficiently high cost level and a sufficiently low skill level to make automation both profitable and feasible. These jobs happened to be those concentrated in the large-scale factories that had become the strongholds of labor unions, and better remunerated labor, during the industrial era.

(d) Positioning capital in a powerful position *vis-à-vis* labor. Automation, flexible manufacturing, and new transportation technologies provide management with a variety of options that considerably weaken the bargaining position of the unions. ...

2 New technologies are also a powerful instrument in weighting the accumulation and domination functions of state intervention. This occurs on two main levels:

(a) On the one hand, rapid technological change makes obsolete the entire existing weapons system, creating the basis for the expansion of the 'warfare state' in a political environment characterized by states striving for military supremacy and therefore engaging in a technological arms race that can only be supported by the resources of the state.

(b) On the other hand, the strategic role played by high technology in economic development draws the state to concentrate on providing the required infrastructure, downplaying its role in redistributional policies.

3 The process of *internationalization of the economy* could never take place without the dramatic breakthroughs in information technologies. Advances in telecommunications, flexible manufacturing that allows simultaneously for standardization and customization, and new transpor-

tation technologies emerging from the use of computers and new materials, have created the material infrastructure for the world economy, as the construction of the railway system provided the basis for the formation of national markets in the nineteenth century. ...

The *organizational* components of the informational mode of development are also fundamental features in the restructuring process. Three major organizational characteristics of informationalism may be distinguished, each one of them affecting the three dimensions of the restructuring process.

1   There is a growing *concentration of knowledge-generation and decision-making processes in high-level organizations* in which both information and the capacity of processing it are concentrated. ... Given the strategic role of knowledge and information control in productivity and profitability, these core centers of corporate organizations are the only truly indispensable components of the system, with most other work, and thus most other workers, being potential candidates for automation from the strictly functional point of view. How far this tendency toward widespread automation is actually taken in practice is a different matter, depending on the dynamics of labour markets and social organization.

This concentration of information power in selected segments of the corporate structure greatly favors the chances of the restructuring process in the three dimensions presented:

(a)   Productive labour can be reduced to its essential component, thus downgrading the objective bargaining power of the large mass of functionally dispensable labor.

(b)   The rise of the technocracy within the state displaces the traditional integrative functions of the politically determined bureaucracy, establishing a tight linkage between the high levels of the state and the corporate world through the intermediary of the scientific establishment. ...

(c)   As technology transfer becomes the key to competition in the international economy, that process is controlled by knowledge holders in the centers of the dominant scientific and corporate organizations. ...

2   The second major organizational characteristic of informationalism concerns the *flexibility* of the system and of the relationships among its units, since flexibility is both a requirement of and a possibility offered by new information technologies. Flexibility acts powerfully as a facilitator of the restructuring process in the following ways:

(a)   It changes capital–labor relationships, transforming a potentially permanent and protected worker status into a flexible arrangement generally adapted to the momentary convenience of management. Thus, temporary workers, part-time jobs, homework, flexitime schedules, indefinite positions in the corporate structure, changing assignments, varying wages and benefits according to performance, etc., are all creative expedients of management that, while they increase tremendously the flexibility and thus productivity of the firm, undermine the collective status of labor *vis-à-vis* capital.

(b) In the restructuring of the state, organizational flexibility contributes to the formation of public–private partnerships and to the blurring of the distinction between the public and private spheres. Segments of the welfare state are being shifted to the private sector, corporations are being brought into the formulation of public policies, and a selective interpenetration of state and capital is diminishing the autonomy of the state ...

(c) Flexibility is also a necessary condition for the formation of the new world economy, since it is the only organizational form that allows constant adaptation of firms to the changing conditions of the world market.

3 A third fundamental organizational characteristic of informationalism is the shift from *centralized* large corporations to *decentralized* networks made up of a plurality of sizes and forms of organizational units. Although networking increases flexibility, it is actually a different characteristic, since there are forms of flexibility that do not require networks. These networks, which could not exist on such a large scale without the medium provided by new information technologies, are the emerging organizational form of our world, and have played a fundamental role in ensuring the restructuring process:

(a) They are the prevalent form of the informal economy, as well as of the sub-contracting practices that have disorganized and reorganized the labor process, enhancing capital's profitability.

(b) They have provided the model for the constitution of the new warfare state ... on the basis of the interaction between different specialized government agencies, the defence industry, high-technology firms, and the scientific establishment.

(c) They are the organizational form used by major multinational corporations that have established variable strategic alliances to compete in the international economy. Unlike the tendency of the industrial mode of development toward oligopolistic concentration, in the informational era large corporations set up specific alliances for given products, processes, and markets: these alliances vary according to time and space, and result in a variable geometry of corporate strategies that follow the logic of the multiple networks where they are engaged rather than the monolithic hierarchy of empire conglomerates. ...

READING B   WORK AND POST-INDUSTRIALISM

André Gorz

In an article which is characteristic of the prevalent economic thinking, Lionel Stoleru writes:

> A wave of technological advances has rendered a whole series of jobs unnecessary and reduced employment on a huge scale without creating an equivalent number of jobs elsewhere. ... It will enable us to produce more and better with less human effort: savings in manufacturing costs and in working time will increase purchasing power and *create new areas of activity elsewhere in the economy (if only in leisure activities).*
> [Gorz's italics]

Stoleru later returns to this last point to make it clear that these new activities will be *paid* activities, *jobs* although they will not be properly 'work' as it has been understood up to now:

> The substitution of robotics and computer communications for human labour ... allows a value to be released which is greater than the wages previously paid out... This value is then available *for remunerating those who have lost their jobs.* Unemployment constitutes a displacement of activity rather than the abolition of jobs.

The interest of this apparently economic text lies in the wealth of different explicit and implicit meanings it contains. ...

From the point of view of economic rationality, the working time saved across the whole of society, thanks to the increasing efficiency of the means used, constitutes working time made available for the production of additional wealth. ...

This can well be seen on the directions most often suggested to ensure 'new growth': they concern, on the one hand, the computerization and robotization of household tasks (for example, 'telephone shopping', automatic, computer-programmed cooking, the electronic cottage), and, on the other, the at least partial industrialization and computerization of services providing catering, cleaning, bodily care, education, childcare and so on. Economic rationalization appears thus destined to penetrate the sphere of 'reproduction' in which domestic labour, which is neither remunerated nor accounted for, nor, more often than not, even measured as regards the time spent on it, is still dominant. The explicit goals of the innovations proposed are to save time, and, more especially, to liberate women or households from household chores.

To say that they will 'create jobs' is a paradoxical way of denying the economic rationality which is, in other respects, their justification: the aim of fast-food chains, domestic robots, home computers, rapid hair-

Source: Gorz, A. (1989) *Critique of Economic Reason*, London, Verso, pp.2–7.

dressing salons and the like, is not to *provide work* but to save it. Where paid labour (that is, jobs) is really necessary in these areas, the quantity of paid labour provided is much lower than the quantity of domestic labour saved. If this were not the case, these products and services would be financially inaccessible and devoid of interest for the vast majority of people: in order to obtain an hour of free time, the average wage earner would have to spend the equivalent of — or possibly more than — the wage she or he earned in one hour of work; he or she would have to work at least an extra hour in order to gain an extra hour of free time; the time saved in performing domestic tasks would have to be spent working (or working extra time) at the factory or the office, and so on. Now the use value of domestic appliances and industrialized services lies precisely, by contrast, in the *net* time they gain for us, and their exchange value in their high productivity per hour: the user spends less time working in order to earn enough to purchase these products or services, than she or he spends in providing these services for him- or herself. This is indeed a liberation of time across the whole of society.

The question we must ask, then, is what meaning we wish to give this new-found free time and what content we wish to give it. ...

Including leisure activities within the economic sphere and assuming that their expansion will generate new economic activities appears at first to be a paradoxical way of avoiding the above question. The rationality governing leisure activities is, in fact, the opposite of the rationality governing economic activities: such activities consume rather than create free time; their aim is not to save time but to spend it. This is holiday time, time for extravagance, time for gratuitous activity which is an end in itself. In short, such time has no utility, nor is it the means to any other end and the categories of instrumental rationality (efficiency, productivity, performance) are not applicable to it, except to pervert it.

To state, as Stoleru does, that leisure activities generate, that they indeed demand, new paid activities is not, however, totally absurd, provided that society is viewed not as a single but as a dual economic entity. And this is, in effect, what the majority of writers do. The continued division of society as they conceive it will be inevitable. The reason for this division will be (as it is already) the unequal distribution of the savings made in working hours: an increasingly large section of the population will continue to be expelled, or else marginalized, from the sphere of economic activities, whilst another section will continue to work as much as, or even more than, it does at present, commanding, as a result of its performances or aptitudes, ever-increasing incomes and economic powers. Unwilling to give up part of their work and the prerogatives and powers that go with their jobs, the members of this professional elite will only be able to increase their leisure time by getting third parties to procure their free time for them. Therefore they will ask these third parties to do in their place all the things everyone is capable of doing, particularly all labour referred to as 'reproduction'. And they will purchase services and appliances which will allow them to save time *even when producing these services and appliances takes more time than the average person will save by using them*. They will thus foster the development, across the whole of society, of activities which have no economic rationality — since the people performing them have to spend more time in doing them than the people benefiting from them actually save — and which only serve the private interests of the members of this professional elite, who are able to purchase time more cheaply than they can sell it personally. These are activities performed by *servants*, whatever the status of the people who do them or method of payment used.

The division of society into classes involved in intense economic activity on the one hand, and a mass of people who are marginalized or excluded from the economic sphere on the other, will allow a sub-system to develop, in which the economic elite will buy leisure time by getting their own personal tasks done for them, at low cost, by other people. The work done by personal servants and enterprises providing personal services makes more time available for this elite and improves their quality of life; the leisure time of this economic elite provides jobs, which are in most cases insecure and underpaid, for a section of the masses excluded from the economic sphere. ...

The unequal distribution of work in the economic sphere, coupled with the unequal distribution of the free time created by technical innovations thus leads to a situation in which one section of the population is able to buy extra spare time from the other and the latter is reduced to serving the former. Social stratification of this type is different from stratification in terms of class. By contrast with the latter, it does not reflect the laws immanent in the functioning of an economic system whose impersonal demands are made as much on managers of capital and company administrators as on paid workers. For a section at least of those who provide personal services, this type of social stratification amounts to subordination to and personal dependence upon the people they serve. A 'servile' class, which had been abolished by the industrialization of the post-war period, is again emerging.

Certain conservative governments, and even a number of trade unions, justify and promote this formidable social regression on the pretext that it permits the 'creation of jobs', that is, that servants increase the amount of time their masters can devote to activities which are highly productive in economic terms — as if the people who do 'odd jobs' were not also capable of productive or creative work; as if those who have services done for them were creative and competent every minute of their working day and were thus irreplaceable; as if it were not the very conception the latter have of their function and rights which is depriving the young people who deliver their hot croissants, newspapers and pizzas of chances of economic and social integration; as if, in a word, the differentiation of economic tasks required such a degree of specialization that the stratification of society — into a mass of operatives, on the one hand, and a class of irreplaceable and over-worked decision-makers and technicians who need a host of helpers to serve them personally in order to do their jobs, on the other — were inevitable.

Certainly, the existence of a servile class is less obvious today than it was during the periods when the affluent classes employed a large number of domestic servants (according to British censuses — in which they were categorized as 'domestic and personal servants' — the latter represented 14 per cent of the working population between 1851 and 1911). The difference is that nowadays these personal services are to a large extent socialized or industrialized: the majority of servants are employed by service enterprises which hire out labour (insecure, part-time employment; piecework; and so on) which is then exploited by private individuals. But this does not alter the basic fact that these people are doing servants' work, that is, work which those who earn a decent living transfer, for their personal advantage and without gains in productivity, on to the people for whom there is no work in the economy.

READING C   FORDISM AND POST-FORDISM

Robin Murray

Fordism is an industrial era whose secret is to be found in the mass production systems pioneered by Henry Ford. These systems were based on four principles from which all else followed:

(a) products were standardised; this meant that each part and each task could also be standardised. Unlike craft production — where each part had to be specially designed, made and fitted — for a run of mass-produced cars, the same headlight could be fitted to the same model in the same way.

(b) if tasks are the same, then some can be mechanised; thus mass production plants developed special-purpose machinery for each model, much of which could not be switched from product to product.

(c) those tasks which remained were subject to scientific management or Taylorism, whereby any task was broken down into its component parts, redesigned by work-study specialists on time-and-motion principles, who then instructed manual workers on how the job should be done.

(d) flowline replaced nodal assembly, so that instead of workers moving to and from the product (the node), the product flowed past the workers.

Ford did not invent these principles. What he did was to combine them in the production of a complex commodity, which undercut craft-made cars as decisively as the handloom weavers had been undercut in the 1830s. Ford's Model T sold for less than a tenth of the price of a craft-built car in the US in 1916, and he took 50 per cent of the market.

This revolutionary production system was to transform sector after sector during the 20th century, from processed food to furniture, clothes, cook-

Source: Murray, R. (1989) 'Fordism and Post-Fordism', in Hall, S. and Jacques, M. (eds) *New Times*, London, Lawrence and Wishart Ltd, pp.38–47.

ers, and even ships after the second world war. The economies came from the scale of production, for although mass production might be more costly to set up because of the purpose-built machinery, once in place the cost of an extra unit was discontinuously cheap.

Many of the structures of Fordism followed from this tension between high fixed costs and low variable ones, and the consequent drive for volume. First, as Ford himself emphasised, mass production presupposes mass consumption. Consumers must be willing to buy standardised products. Mass advertising played a central part in establishing a mass consumption norm. So did the provision of the infrastructure of consumption — housing and roads. To ensure that the road system dominated over rail, General Motors, Standard Oil and Firestone Tyres bought up and then dismantled the electric trolley and transit systems in 44 urban areas.

Second, Fordism was linked to a system of protected national markets, which allowed the mass producers to recoup their fixed costs at home and compete on the basis of marginal costs on the world market, or through the replication of existing models via foreign investment.

Third, mass producers were particularly vulnerable to sudden falls in demand. Ford unsuccessfully tried to offset the effect of the 1930s depression by raising wages. Instalment credit, Keynesian demand and monetary management, and new wage and welfare systems were all more effective in stabilising the markets for mass producers in the postwar period. HP and the dole cheque became as much the symbols of the Fordist age as the tower block and the motorway.

The mass producers not only faced the hazard of changes in consumption. With production concentrated in large factories they were also vulnerable to the new 'mass worker' they had created. Like Taylorism, mass production had taken the skill out of work, it fragmented tasks into a set of repetitive movements, and erected a rigid division between mental and manual labour. It treated human beings as interchangeable parts of a machine, paid according to the job they did rather than who they were.

The result was high labour turnover, shopfloor resistance, and strikes. The mass producers in turn sought constant new reservoirs of labour, particularly from groups facing discrimination, from rural areas and from less developed regions abroad. The contractual core of Taylorism — higher wages in return for managerial control of production — still applied, and a system of industrial unions grew up to bargain over these wage levels. In the USA, and to an extent the UK, a national system of wage bargaining developed in the postwar period, centred on high-profile car industry negotiations, that linked wage rises to productivity growth, and then set wage standards for other large-scale producers and the state. It was a system of collective bargaining that has been described as implementing a Keynesian incomes policy without a Keynesian state. As long as the new labour reservoirs could be tapped, it was a system that held together the distinct wage relation of Fordism.

Taylorism was also characteristic of the structure of management and supplier relations. Fordist bureaucracies are fiercely hierarchical, with links between the divisions and departments being made through the centre rather than at the base. Planning is done by specialists; rulebooks and guidelines are issued for lower management to carry out. If you enter a Ford factory in any part of the world, you will find its layout, materials, even the position of its Coca Cola machines, all similar, set up as they are on the basis of a massive construction manual drawn up in Detroit. Managers themselves complain of deskilling and the lack of room for initiative, as do suppliers who are confined to producing blueprints at a low margin price.

These threads — of production and consumption, of the semi-skilled worker and collective bargaining, of a managed national market and centralised organisation — together make up the fabric of Fordism. They have given rise to an economic culture which extends beyond the complex assembly industries, to agriculture, the service industries and parts of the state. It is marked by its commitment to scale and the standard product (whether it is a Mars bar or an episode of *Dallas*); by a competitive strategy based on cost reduction; by authoritarian relations, centralised planning, and a rigid organisation built round exclusive job descriptions.

These structures and their culture are often equated with industrialism, and regarded as an inevitable part of the modern age. I am suggesting that they are linked to a particular form of industrialism, one that developed in the late 19th century and reached its most dynamic expression in the postwar boom. Its impact can be felt not just in the economy, but in politics (in the mass party) and in much broader cultural fields — whether American football, or classical ballet (Diaghilev was a Taylorist in dance), industrial design or modern architecture. The technological *hubris* of this outlook, its Faustian bargain of dictatorship in production in exchange for mass consumption, and above all its destructiveness in the name of progress and the economy of time, all this places Fordism at the centre of modernism. ...

The Breakup of Fordism

Fordism as a vision — both left and right — had always been challenged, on the shopfloor, in the political party, the seminar room and the studio. In 1968 this challenge exploded in Europe and the USA. It was a cultural as much as an industrial revolt, attacking the central principles of Fordism, its definitions of work and consumption, its shaping of towns and its overriding of nature.

From that time we can see a fracturing of the foundations of predictability on which Fordism was based. Demand became more volatile and fragmented. Productivity growth fell as the result of workplace resistance. The decline in profit drove down investment. Exchange rates were fluctuating, oil prices rose and in 1974 came the greatest slump the West had had since the 1930s.

The consensus response was a Keynesian one, to restore profitability through a managed increase in demand and an incomes policy. For monetarism the route to profitability went through the weakening of labour, a cut in state spending and a reclaiming of the public sector for private accumulation. Economists and politicians were re-fighting the battles of the last slump. Private capital on the other hand was dealing with the present one. It was using new technology and new production principles to make Fordism flexible, and in doing so stood much of the old culture on its head.

In Britain, the groundwork for the new system was laid not in manufacturing but in retailing. Since the 1950s, retailers had been using computers to transform the distribution system. All mass producers have the problem of forecasting demand. If they produce too little they lose market share. If they produce too much, they are left with stocks, which are costly to hold, or have to be sold at a discount. Retailers face this problem not just for a few products, but for thousands. Their answer has been to develop information and supply systems which allow them to order supplies to coincide with demand. Every evening Sainsbury's receives details of the sales of all 12,000 lines from each of its shops; these are turned into orders for warehouse deliveries for the coming night, and replacement production for the following day. With computerised control of stocks in the shop, transport networks, automatic loading and unloading, Sainsbury's flow-line make-to-order system has conquered the Fordist problem of stocks.

They have also overcome the limits of the mass product. For, in contrast to the discount stores which are confined to a few, fast-selling items, Sainsbury's, like the new wave of high street shops, can handle ranges of products geared to segments of the market. Market niching has become the slogan of the high street. Market researchers break down market by age (youth, young adults, 'grey power'), by household types (dinkies, single-gender couple, one-parent families), by income, occupation, housing and, increasingly, by locality. They analyse 'lifestyles', correlating consumption patterns across commodities, from food to clothing, and health and holidays.

The point of this new anthropology of consumption is to target both product and shops to particular segments. ... In modern shops the emphasis has shifted from the manufacturer's economies of scale to the retailer's economies of scope. The economies come from offering an integrated range from which customers choose their own basket of products. There is also an economy of innovation, for the modern retail systems allow new product ideas to be tested in practice, through shop sales, and the successful ones then to be ordered for wider distribution. Innovation has become a leading edge of the new competition. Product life has become shorter, for fashion goods and consumer durables.

A centrepiece of this new retailing is design. Designers produce the innovations. They shape the lifestyles. They design the shops, which are described as 'stages' for the act of shopping. ... With market researchers they have steered the high street from being retailers of goods to retailers of style.

These changes are a response to, and a means of shaping, the shift from mass consumption. Instead of keeping up with the Joneses there has been a move to be different from the Joneses. Many of these differences are vertical, intended to confirm status and class. But some are horizontal centred and round group identities, linked to age, or region or ethnicity. ... Whatever our responses, the revolution in retailing reflects new principles of production, a new pluralism of products and a new importance for innovation. As such it marks a shift to a post-Fordist age.

There have been parallel shifts in manufacturing, not least in response to the retailers' just-in-time system of ordering. ... But the most successful manufacturing regions have been ones which have linked flexible manufacturing systems, with innovative organisation and an emphasis on 'customisation' design and quality. Part of the flexibility has been achieved through new technology, and the introduction of programmable machines which can switch from product to product with little manual resetting and downtime. Benetton's automatic dyeing plant, for example, allows it to change its colours in time with demand. In the car industry, whereas General Motors took nine hours to change the dyes on its presses in the early 1980s, Toyota have lowered the time to two minutes, and have cut the average lot size of body parts from 5,000 to 500 in the process. The line, in short, has become flexible. Instead of using purpose-built machines to make standard products, flexible automation uses general-purpose machines to produce a variety of products.

Japanisation

Manufacturers have also been adopting the retailers' answer to stocks. The pioneer is Toyota which stands to the new era as Ford did to the old, Toyoda, the founder of Toyota, inspired by a visit to an American supermarket, applied the just-in-time system to his component suppliers, ordering on the basis of his daily production plans, and getting the components delivered right beside the line. Most of Toyota's components are still produced on the same day as they are assembled.

Toyoda's prime principle of the elimination of wasteful practices meant going beyond the problem of stocks. His firm has used design and materials technology to simplify complex elements, cutting down the number of parts and operations. It adopted a zero-defect policy, developing machines which stopped automatically, when a fault occurred, as well as statistical quality control techniques. As in retailing, the complex web of processes, inside and outside the plant, were coordinated through computers, a process that economists have called systemation (in contrast to automation). The result of these practices is a discontinuous speed-up in what Marx called the circulation of capital. Toyota turns over its materials and products ten times more quickly than western car producers, saving material and energy in the process.

The key point about the Toyota system, however, is not so much that it speeds up the making of a car. It is in order to make these changes that it has adopted quite different methods of labour control and organisation. Toyoda saw that traditional Taylorism did not work. Central management had no access to all the information needed for continuous innovation. Quality could not be achieved with deskilled manual workers. Taylorism wasted what they called 'the gold in workers' heads'.

Toyota, and the Japanese more generally, having broken the industrial unions in the 1950s, have developed a core of multi-skilled workers whose tasks include not only manufacture and maintenance, but the improvement of the products and processes under their control. Each breakdown is seen as a chance for improvement. Even hourly-paid workers are trained in statistical techniques and monitoring, and register and interpret statistics to identify deviations from a norm — tasks customarily reserved for management in Fordism. Quality circles are a further way of tapping the ideas of the workforce. In post-Fordism, the worker is designed to act as a computer as well as a machine.

As a consequence the Taylorist contract changes. Workers are no longer interchangeable. They gather experience. The Japanese job-for-life and corporate welfare system provides security. For the firm it secures an asset. Continuous training, payment by seniority, a breakdown of job demarcations, are all part of the Japanese core wage relation. The EETPU's [i.e. the electricians' union] lead in embracing private pension schemes, BUPA, internal flexibility, union-organised training and single-company unions are all consistent with this path of post-Fordist industrial relations.

Not the least of the dangers of this path is that it further hardens the divisions between the core and the peripheral workforce. The cost of employing lifetime workers means an incentive to subcontract all jobs not essential to the core. The other side of the Japanese jobs-for-life is a majority of low-paid, fragmented peripheral workers, facing an underfunded and inadequate welfare state. The duality in the labour market, and in the welfare economy, could be taken as a description of Thatcherism. The point is that neither the EETPU's policy nor that of Mrs Thatcher should read as purely political. There is a material basis to both, rooted in changes in production.

There are parallel changes in corporate organisation. With the revision of Taylorism, a layer of management has been stripped away. Greater central control has allowed the decentralisation of work. Day-to-day autonomy has been given to work groups and plant managers. Teams linking departments horizontally have replaced the rigid verticality of Fordist bureaucracies.

It is only a short step from here to sub-contracting and franchising. This is often simply a means of labour control. But in engineering and light consumer industries, networks and semi-independent firms have often proved more innovative than vertically integrated producers. A mark of post-Fordism is close two-way relations between customer and supplier, and between specialised producers in the same industry. Co-operative

competition replaces the competition of the jungle. These new relationships within and between enterprises and on the shopfloor have made
least headway in the countries in which Fordism took fullest root, the
USA and the UK. Here firms have tried to match continental and Japanese
flexibility through automation while retaining Fordist shopfloor, managerial and competitive relations.

Yet in spite of this we can see in this country a culture of post-Fordist
capitalism emerging. Consumption has a new place. As for production the
keyword is flexibility — of plant and machinery, as of products and
labour. Emphasis shifts from scale to scope, and from cost to quality.
Organisations are geared to respond to rather than regulate markets. They
are seen as frameworks for learning as much as instruments of control.
Their hierarchies are flatter and their structures more open. The guerrilla
force takes over from the standing army. All this has liberated the centre
from the tyranny of the immediate. Its task shifts from planning to strategy,
and to the promotion of the instruments of post-Fordist control — systems, software, corporate culture and cash.

CHAPTER 5 SOCIAL PLURALISM AND POST-MODERNITY

Kenneth Thompson

CONTENTS

1   INTRODUCTION

The first half of the twentieth century was dominated by
Modernism — a movement that rejected the legacy of the past, that
was caught up in the early enthusiasm for technological progress,
and that sought to create the world anew. It accompanied and may
even be seen as the cultural equivalent of the Russian Revolution.
Rejecting tradition, it was the culture of innovation and change ...
Fifty years later, however, by the second half of the century, this
dramatic, daring and innovative trend had become the cultural
norm accepted by Western Establishments ... The revolutionary
impulses that had once galvanized politics and culture had clearly
become sclerotic. The Brave New World was in retreat. In its place
has emerged a new movement that seeks to recover tradition, a
world that seems to prefer stability to change. Just as the whole
socialist idea has gone into retreat, so too the great Modernist
project has been largely abandoned. Into this vacuum steps
Postmodernism, an eclectic movement of parody and pastiche that
fits happily into a world where conservation has become the rage,
where new pubs can be built with Victorian fittings, where
Modernist tower blocks are replaced with 'vernacular' retreats into
the archaic ... Postmodernism, of course, can also be portrayed in a
progressive light. Some advocates of the Postmodern believe
Modernism to have been a phallocentric, imperialist affair. In this
light, Postmodernism appears as a form of liberation, a fragmented
movement in which a hundred flowers may bloom. Such people
might also argue that while Modernism was the product of a
particular Western culture, Postmodernism heralds the recognition
of a plurality of cultures.
(Richard Gott, 1986)

The above quotation is from Richard Gott's article 'The crisis of
contemporary culture', which introduced *The Guardian's* three-day
major series *Modernism and Post-modernism* in December, 1986.
Clearly this newspaper thought the subject of an alleged cultural shift
from modernism to post-modernism sufficiently important for it to
devote many pages and several issues to the subject. The reason it was
considered important is indicated by the sub-heading: 'Why did the
revolutionary movement that lit up the early decades of the century
fizzle out? In a major series, *Guardian* critics analyse late twentieth
century malaise' (Gott, 1986, p.10). The subsequent articles made it
even clearer that the cultural 'malaise' represented by the shift from
modernism to post-modernism was regarded as symptomatic of a deeper
social and political malaise.

If post-modernism had simply been about a change in cultural styles in
architecture, films, painting and novels, it is unlikely that it would have
merited such attention. But, as Gott suggests, most of those who write
about the culture of post-modernism believe that, for good or ill, it is
related in some way to the emergence of a new social epoch of post-

modernity. Some of the related social developments have already been discussed in previous chapters: the collapse of communism and the loss of confidence, not only in revolutionary Marxism, but also in social planning as epitomized by post-war housing estates and tower blocks; the alleged economic changes from mass production to flexible specialization, and from mass consumption patterns to lifestyle niches in the marketplace, with a consequent fragmentation of social classes; the perception that the modernist ideas of technological progress and economic growth may be the cause of problems of pollution, waste and wars, rather than the solutions; the decline of the politics of party, parliament and trades unions, and the growth of 'micropolitics' marked by struggles over power at the institutional and local levels, or over single issues.

Demolition of post-war residential tower blocks in Hackney, London

To these possibly epochal changes might be added one that is particularly relevant to the cultural sphere, although it is also involved in the economic, political and social changes, and that is the astonishing growth and pervasiveness of the mass media of communication, particularly the visual (or figural) media of film, television and graphic design. If we are entering a post-modern age, then one of its most distinctive characteristics is a loss of rational and social coherence in favour of cultural images and social forms and identities marked by fragmentation, multiplicity, plurality and indeterminacy.

Do we need post-modern social theories to evaluate these changes, or is there nothing happening that could not be encompassed by theories developed to explain the formations of modernity? (The issue of whether post-modernism marks the end of the 'Enlightenment project' is discussed further in Chapter 7 of this book.) As we will see, the theorists to be discussed take different positions on this question. In the end, the neo-Marxists, Harvey and Jameson, believe that post-modernist developments can be incorporated into a renovated Marxist framework. In contrast, Foucault and Baudrillard eventually proclaimed that all-encompassing theories such as Marxism were incapable of explaining current developments, although both were uncomfortable with the label 'post-modernist' to describe their positions (perhaps in keeping with the fragmentation and diversity of post-modern culture). This chapter will focus on four issues:

1   Is there a distinctive cultural trend towards post-modernism?

2   Is post-modernism related to *economic* developments? For example, can post-modernity be explained as the latest stage in the development of capitalism?

3   What are the *political* implications of post-modernism? Does it mark the end of class-based politics and the emergence of a new kind of politics?

4   Is post-modernism the cultural expression of an increasing *social* pluralism that warrants its description as 'post-modernity' — a new social epoch?

The discussion of these issues is structured as follows:

Section 2 considers David Harvey's description (Reading A) of the culture of post-modernism and his account of the ways in which various theorists have attempted to relate it to economic, political and social processes. Harvey's own position is that of a neo-Marxist who accepts that certain cultural trends have gathered pace to such an extent that they merit the label 'post-modernist', but believes these can ultimately be explained as the result of developments within the capitalist economic system.

Section 3 examines one of the most influential attempts to relate post-modernist culture to political, economic and social developments, that of another neo-Marxist, Frederic Jameson, and his thesis of 'post-modernism as the cultural logic of late capitalism'. Jameson maintains that there *is* a distinctive culture of post-modernism, but that it is nothing more than the cultural logic of the latest stage of capitalism. He admits that the cultural logic of post-modernism may be difficult to map on to the structural developments of capitalism, but he still believes it will be possible once Marxism has assimilated some of the theoretical insights generated by cultural analysts and the new social movements, such as feminism. For him, post-modern culture does not necessarily herald a new epoch:

> The post-modern may well in that sense be little more than a transitional period between two stages of capitalism, in which the earlier forms of the economic are in the process of being restructured on a global scale, including the older forms of labour

> and its traditional organizational institutions and concepts.
> new international proletariat (taking forms we cannot yet in
> will re-emerge from this convulsive upheaval it needs no prophet
> to predict; we ourselves are still in the trough, however, and no
> one can say how long we will stay there.
> (Jameson, 1991, p.417)

In the end, therefore, despite his acknowledgement that there is a
culture of post-modernism and his appreciation of the perspectives
brought by new political movements and a plurality of social groups, it
appears that he still believes in the subordination of these to the Marxist
categories of class analysis. Despite this, as discussed in Section 4, he is
criticized by a more orthodox Marxist such as Callinicos for conceding
too much to those who maintain that we are entering a new cultural and
social epoch, and who claim that overarching theories (or
metanarratives) such as Marxism cannot do justice to the diversity and
fragmentation of post-modernity.

Section 5 considers the case for a constructive view of post-modern
politics as 'New Times'. It focuses on the argument of Hebdige, who,
along with others, such as Laclau and Mouffe, claims that the new
social movements point to the complexity of the contemporary social
field and the range of identities on offer, which are irreducible to class
positions and the logic of production.

Section 6 looks at Baudrillard's account of the distinctive culture of the
present era, which seems to support the case for seeing post-modernity
as a new epoch, even though he rejects the post-modernist culture. He
emphasizes the impact of the mass media in producing a culture based
on images or copies (simulations) in which it is no longer possible to
distinguish the 'real' from the copy that 'improves on the real' (the
'hyperreal'). Having begun by criticizing the consumer economy from a
Marxist perspective, Baudrillard has rapidly lost faith in such attempts
to penetrate beneath the cultural surface to find the causal explanation
in an economic base. Indeed, he seems to have come to the conclusion
that it is impossible to develop general theories or political strategies in
the new epoch. This is a more extreme position than that of Foucault,
another theorist who has also been singled out as a source of post-
modernist theory. Foucault rejected totalizing theories such as Marxism
and psychoanalysis as reductionist and coercive in their practical
implications, prefering microanalyses of the many different discourses
and institutional practices through which power was exercised. But,
unlike Baudrillard, he continued to believe that such analyses could
inform positive political strategies of resistance to power.

Section 7 turns to a selection of more positive or constructive views of
post-modernism and post-modernity. As Richard Gott noted, advocates
of the post-modern believe that modernism tended towards intellectual
and political domination, often in the name of science and progress,
whereas post-modernism can appear as a form of liberation, in which
the fragmentation and plurality of cultures and social groups allow a

hundred flowers to bloom. The perspectives of minority groups — for example, ethnic groups, feminists, gays, sects and cults — are tolerated, and post-modernism may even give rise to unexpected combinations and pastiches of cultural codes and discourses that modernism would have dismissed as 'irrational', 'mindless eclecticism', or 'politically unsound'. (Modernist critics of post-modernism believe that those charges are still justified.) Some examples of these post-modern social forms and perspectives are examined: Judith Stacey's study of post-modern family regimes in California; 'New Age' religions and other efforts to forge new individual and group identities by combining seemingly disparate discourses.

These different figures are therefore taken as representing different facets of the debate on post-modernism and adopt different positions towards it. Both Harvey and Jameson, who provide vivid descriptive accounts of the phenomenon, in the end, wish to retain a neo-Marxist account of developments in 'late capitalism' as providing the best explanatory key to what they acknowledge are the significant cultural trends which post-modernism has set in motion.

Callinicos offers a 'root and branch' rebuttal of post-modernism's claims, and reaffirms the primacy of class politics from a classical Marxist position. Baudrillard believes post-modernism signals the 'death of meaning' in modern culture but, though he is deeply pessimistic about it, he argues that there is no alternative and delights in offering an 'extreme' account of post-modern culture. Hebdige, Laclau, Mouffe and the New Times theorists take a more positive view of the social and cultural pluralism and political possibilities which post-modernism opens up. And the 'New Age' movements examined at the end of the chapter inhabit the post-modern break-up of modern culture but are seeking new, 'post-modern' forms of community and belief to put in the place of 'the end of the grand narratives'.

My own position in these debates is one which welcomes the opening created by the concept of post-modernity, because it allows us to focus on some of the diverse and contradictory trends which were glossed over by sociological theories of modernity and modernization and by orthodox Marxist theories that stressed economic determinism and class polarization. This position does not prejudge the issues to be considered here of whether post-modernity is a distinct period and cultural configuration, and exactly how it is related to economic and political developments.

2 POST-MODERNISM

There are many ways of trying to describe what is meant by post-modernism. Post-modernism is the very loose term used to describe the new aesthetic cultural and intellectual forms and practices which are emerging in the 1980s and 1990s. As the word suggests, 'post-modernism' follows, and is rapidly replacing, modernism, the term used to describe the cultural styles and movements of the first half of the twentieth century. Modernism — including the practices of abstraction, non-representational art in painting, the high-tec functionalism of modern architecture, avant-garde experiments with form in literature and so on — set out in the early years of the twentieth century to challenge nineteenth century realism and to 'shock' bourgeois tastes with its experimental and avant-garde techniques. But, post-modernists argue, eventually it was 'tamed', becoming institutionalized as the International Style, dominating the skylines of every modern city, the 'monuments' of corporate capitalism, the fashionable museums and art galleries and the international art market. Now a new, more populist culture is emerging, closer to everyday life, to the market place, to consumption and to the new popular culture of the media — a culture which renounces purity, mastery of form and élitism, and is more playful, ironic, and eclectic in style.

One of the clearest summaries of some of the issues is provided by David Harvey in his book *The Condition of Postmodernity* (1989), and I would like you to read the lengthy extract from that book. However, before you do this, I would like to make the following points that you should bear in mind:

1   Our main interest in this discussion of the culture of post-modernism is how it relates to social, economic and political processes, rather than in post-modernism as a set of stylistic movements in the arts. Harvey's summary provides a useful overview of the ramifications of the debates about post-modernism in different fields. However, it is not important to understand all the references to post-modernism as a movement in painting, literature and film (architecture is given more attention because of its links to social planning and economic changes). Similarly, we will not pursue questions about changes in philosophy, such as those raised by his references to American pragmatism, post-structuralism and deconstructionism.

2   Concentrate on grasping the general characteristics of post-modernism as a cultural trend involving a multiplicity and mixing of styles and codes, forsaking modernism's attempts to impose a unifying or overarching (meta-) theory or metanarrative. Likewise, in post-modern social theory, the tendency is to follow social analysts like Foucault, who insisted on the plurality of 'power-discourse' formations. It is opposed to all forms of metanarratives (including Marxism, Freudianism, and various totalizing metatheories of history or scientific progress stemming from the Enlightenment), whilst paying close attention to 'other worlds' and 'other voices' (women, gays, blacks, colonized peoples with their own histories).

3   Do post-modernist cultural trends correspond to fundamental trends in social, economic and political processes, which might constitute a

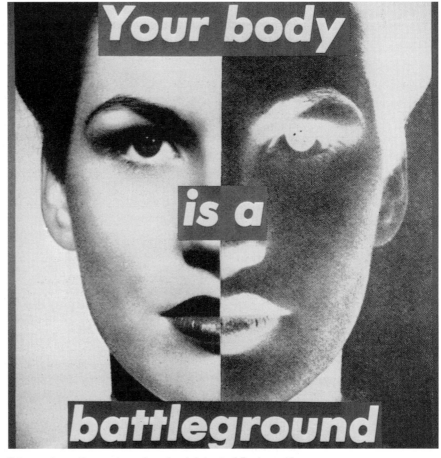

Other voices: the post-modern feminist art of Barbara Kruger

new social epoch of post-modernity — a pluralistic, post-industrial, post-class society of multiple lifestyles and also multiple power-discourses? Or do they merely follow the 'cultural logic of late capitalism', as Frederic Jameson proposes?

4   What are the political implications of post-modernism? Is it neo-conservative, liberating, or simply another form of revolt against established orthodoxies?

ACTIVITY 1

You should now read **Reading A, 'The condition of postmodernity'**, by David Harvey, which you will find at the end of this chapter. Make a summary list of the main ideas that you find useful or interesting. You might then like to compare your list with the one below.

Where do you think Harvey stands in terms of Gott's contrast between those who see post-modernism as symptomatic of social 'malaise' and those who believe it heralds the recognition of a plurality of cultures?

1   In architecture, post-modernism prefers the popular and vernacular styles, symbolized by Las Vegas, rather than the modernist 'soulless' buildings like the Manhattan skyscrapers or the residential tower blocks of post-war urban planning.

2   In philosophy, various schools of thought have intermingled in a wave of reaction against the Enlightenment legacy and its faith in the powers of technology, science and reason. Harvey mentions American Pragmatism, post-Marxist and post-structuralist thought, in this connection. At the same time, in religious thought, there have been attempts to develop a post-modern theology which reaffirms spiritual and moral bases of action neglected by secular modernism, whilst not abandoning the powers of reason. (Sometimes this takes the form of a pastiche of religious ideas and selected elements of science and secular reason as in New Age religion, which we will consider later.)

3   Post-modernism seems to revel in fragmentation, ephemerality and discontinuity, preferring difference over uniformity.

4   Post-modernist thinkers, such as Foucault and Lyotard, attack any notion that there might be a metalanguage, metanarrative or metatheory through which all things can be connected, represented, or explained.

5   There is an emphasis on looking for 'local' factors or partial explanations, such as the micro-politics of power relations in different social contexts and in relation to specific discourses, language games or interpretative communities.

6   Politically, post-modernism entails engaging in multiple, local autonomous struggles for liberation, rejecting the imperialism of an enlightened modernity that presumed to speak for others (colonized peoples, blacks and ethnic groups, religious minorities, women, and the working class) with a unified voice.

7   Post-modernists have a different view of language and communication to that held by modernists. Modernists presupposed a tight and identifiable relation between what was said (the signified or 'message') and how it was being said (the signifier or 'medium'), whereas post-structuralists see these as continually breaking apart and re-attaching in new combinations. 'Deconstructionism' (associated with the work of the French philosopher, Derrida) views cultural life as intersecting 'texts'; deconstructive cultural analysis is concerned with 'reading' texts by deconstructing them or breaking-down the narrative to show how it is composed of different textual elements and fragments.

8   Post-modernism's preoccupation with the fragmentation and instability of language carries over into a conception of the post-modern personality as 'schizophrenic' (not in the clinical sense, but in relation to a fragmented sense of identity). Words gain their meaning from being part of a sequential chain of linked 'signifiers' in a sentence. If the links become unstable and the sequence disjointed, then there will be a fragmentation of meaning, manifested in an inability to think things through — including an inability to think through one's own biography and to unify the past, present and future in one's psychic life.

Experience is reduced to a 'series of pure and unrelated presences in time' and the experiences of the present become overwhelmingly vivid as they are communicated by mass media images and sensational spectacles (not just in entertainment, but also political, military and scientific). The immediacy of events and the sensationalism of the spectacle become the stuff of which consciousness is forged.

9   The other side of loss of linear or sequential ideas of time and the search for instantaneous impact is a parallel loss of depth. Jameson emphasizes the 'depthlessness' and concern for surface appearance of contemporary culture.

10   High-brow authority over cultural taste collapses and is replaced by popular culture and consumerism.

11   Some social and cultural analysts of post-modernism take a positive and constructive view, insisting that various groups, such as youth and ethnic groups, develop their own sub-cultures by using consumer culture and fashion to construct a sense of their own public identities.

12   Finally, some Marxists, such as Jameson, maintain that post-modernism is simply the cultural logic of late capitalism.

Harvey's own view on the links between the economy and post-modernity is that there is a close relationship, although he admits it may be difficult to prove that it is a causal relationship. He sees links between Fordism (e.g. assembly-line mass production) and modernism, as the dominant economic and cultural trends in the period up to 1970, and a similar association between post-Fordism (e.g. flexible accumulation in which international financial markets come to dominate the economic order and Japanese productive organization the industrial) and post-modernism in the subsequent period. (Debates about the extent of such trends in the economic sphere were discussed in Chapter 4.) Speed-up of communication, transport, fashion cycles, commodity life-spans, and the associated shrinking of distances and spaces — what he calls 'time-space compression' — has radically affected the codes of transmission of social values and meanings. He gives a good example in the case of food: supermarkets and restaurants in cities such as London or Los Angeles now offer foods from all over the world. The cuisines of the world are now assembled in one place in the same way that the world's geographical complexity is reduced to a series of images on a television screen each evening. On television, as in Disneyland, it is now possible to experience the world's geography vicariously through images or 'simulacra'. In some cases these reproductions may fit the stereotype even better than the original (just as Indian curries in a British supermarket may come closer to our ideal than those served in Bombay!): they are 'hyperreal'.

Harvey does not insist on a distinct break between modernity and post-modernity. He agrees that the conditions of post-modern time-space compression exaggerate tendencies that have been present in capitalist modernization in the past, generated by successive waves of compression arising from the pressures of capital accumulation, with its perpetual search to annihilate space through time and reduce turnover time. However, Harvey tends towards the view that there has been a change in the 'mode of regulation' of capitalist economies as a result of the first major post-war slump in 1973. (This view was discussed in Chapter 4.) That slump inaugurated a period of extremely rapid change, flux and uncertainty. However, he is cautious about reaching a final judgement on whether or not the new systems of production and marketing, characterized by more flexible labour processes and markets, of geographical mobility and rapid shifts in consumption patterns, warrant the title of a new regime of accumulation, and whether the revival of entrepreneurialism and neo-conservatism, coupled with the cultural turn of post-modernism, warrant the title of a new mode of regulation. He notes many signs of continuity rather than rupture with the Fordist era (Harvey, 1989, p.170) and even concedes that the cultural traits of modernism and post-modernism may simply represent opposing dynamic tendencies that have always existed within capitalism, which would explain why similar cultural forces were described in the previous *fin de siécle* in cities such as Vienna. As the sociologist Simmel remarked, it is in such places and at such times of fragmentation and economic insecurity that the desire for stable values leads to a heightened desire for charismatic authority and sacred attachments through family, religion and state (Simmel, 1900). Harvey remarks that there is abundant evidence of a revival of support for such institutions and values throughout the western world since about 1970. The resulting cultural configuration or pastiche of novel and nostalgic elements is what gives post-modernity its paradoxical and intriguing character.

3 POST-MODERNISM AS THE CULTURAL LOGIC OF LATE CAPITALISM

3.1 CULTURE AND ECONOMY

In his essay, 'Post-modernism or the cultural logic of late capitalism' (1984), Jameson presents the thesis that post-modern culture logically corresponds to a stage in the development of capitalism. He rejects the idea of the conservative sociologist Daniel Bell that we are living in a post-industrial society (Bell, 1973), or that class conflict has ended. Adapting the ideas of the Marxist economist, Ernest Mandel, Jameson distinguishes three periods in the development of capitalism: market capitalism, characterized by the growth of industrial capital in largely national markets (from about 1700 to 1850); monopoly capitalism in the age of imperialism, when European nation-states developed international markets, exploiting the raw materials and cheap labour of their colonial territories; and, most recently (Mandel dates it from 1945,

Jameson from the 1960s), the phase of late capitalism, of multinational corporations with global markets and mass consumption. Furthermore, in Jameson's account of late capitalism, increasingly it is culture itself that is 'commodified' and consumed:

> Where an older Marxist social theory saw cultural forms as part of the ideological veil or distorting mirror preventing the real economic relations in a society from being seen, this theory sees the production, exchange, marketing and consumption of cultural forms — considered in their widest sense and therefore including advertising, TV and the mass media generally — as a central focus and expression of economic activity. Here, images, styles and representations are not the promotional accessories to economic products, they are the products themselves. In a similar way, the explosion of information technology makes information not merely a lubricant of the cycles of exchange and profit, but itself the most important of commodities. If it is possible to imagine this nostalgically as a final greedy swallowing-up of culture by the forces of commodity capitalism then this is in itself to reproduce a notion of the autonomy or separateness of culture which, Jameson wants us to believe, is itself out of date.
> (Connor, 1989, p.46)

According to Jameson, a better way of modelling this situation is as 'an explosion: a prodigious expansion of culture throughout the social realm, to the point at which everything in our social life — from economic value and state power to practices and the very structure of the psyche itself — can be said to have become "cultural"' (Jameson, 1984, p.87). His key point about the post-modern economic phase is that culture has become integrated into commodity production and this makes it different from modernism in the earlier stages of capitalism.

> What has happened is that aesthetic production today has become integrated into commodity production generally, the frantic economic urgency of producing fresh waves of ever more novel-seeming goods (from clothing to airplanes), at ever greater rates of turnover, now assigns an increasingly essential structural function and position to aesthetic innovation and experimentation.
> (Jameson, 1984, p.56)

Whereas modernist culture could be judged against certain dominant standards (hence the distinction between high culture and low or popular culture), and might even be oppositional or shocking, post-modernist culture is totally commodified and tends to be judged in terms of what gives immediate pleasure and makes money. Indeed, Jameson admits that his ideas about post-modernism emerged in response to architectural debates where, more decisively than in the other arts or media, post-modernist positions occupied the space left as a result of the criticisms of high modernism, which was credited with the destruction of the fabric of the traditional city and older neighbourhoods. Hence, his references to Robert Venturi's influential manifesto *Learning from Las Vegas* (Venturi *et al.*, 1977), which pointed out the popular success of buildings which purists would regard as 'fake' and 'tacky'. He notes that post-modernists have been fascinated by the whole 'degraded' landscape of schlock and kitsch, of TV series and Readers' Digest culture, of advertising and motels, of the television late show and the grade B Hollywood films, of so-called 'para-literature' with its airport paperback categories of the Gothic and the romance, the popular biography, the murder mystery and science fiction or fantasy novel (Jameson, pp.54–5).

Excalibur Castle Hotel in Las Vegas, Nevada

The constitutive stylistic features of post-modernist culture for Jameson are: a fondness for pastiche; the 'flat' multiplication and collage of styles, as opposed to the 'deep' expressive aesthetics of unique style characteristic of modernism; retreat from the idea of the unified personality to the 'schizoid' experience of the loss of self in undifferentiated time. He gives a good example from mass culture: nostalgia films (what the French call *la mode retro* — retrospective styling), such as *American Graffiti*, which in 1973 set out to recapture the atmosphere and stylistic peculiarities of the 1950s United States of the Eisenhower era, as does Polanski's film, *Chinatown*, for the 1930s. They are not the same as the older historical novel or film, which sought to represent historical events, but rather they approach the past through stylistic connotation, conveying 'pastness' by the glossy qualities of the image and fashion. Pastiche does not set out to interpret the past or to judge it against some standard, but simply plays images off against each other to achieve its effects and with no clear reference to an external or 'deeper' reality. This superficial pastiche of images ('signifiers') with no referent except other signifiers, also has a kind of 'schizophrenic' character because the individual loses all sense of time as the experiences of the present are overwhelmingly vivid.

Not only does post-modern culture disrupt our sense of time and historical distancing, post-modern architecture also produces 'something like a mutation in built space itself', which leaves us disoriented because 'we do not yet possess the perceptual equipment to match this new hyperspace' (Jameson, 1984, p.80). Jameson's famous example is that of the Bonaventure Hotel, built in the new Los Angeles downtown by the architect and developer John Portman. Although some architectural experts describe it as 'late-modernist', Jameson calls it post-modernist because it meets his criteria of being populist and it produces a disorienting sense of 'decentred hyperspace': there is no single, focal point to give one a sense of direction, just as there is no sense of proportion in the spatial arrangements. Its reflector glass skin achieves a 'peculiar and placeless dissociation of the Bonaventure from its neighbourhood', the elevators are like great Japanese lanterns or gondolas, passing inside and outside the building and splashing down into an internal moat, whilst the vast internal spaces are confusingly laid out, 'transcending the capacities of the individual human body to locate itself' (Jameson, 1984, p.83). (The reader might be amused to note that this populist-style hotel declared bankruptcy just before this author and BBC colleagues arrived to make a television programme to accompany this book, thus threatening to make it the first monument to post-modernity!)

The Bonaventure Hotel

3.2   CULTURE AND POLITICS

We now move on to the second issue, the question of whether post-modernism is also related to the end of the primacy of class-based politics as the result of an increased social pluralism — a multiplicity of social groups and sources of identity, giving rise to different political interests. Jameson agrees that one of the most profoundly post-modern phenomena is the emergence of a whole range of small-group, non-class political practices — micropolitics. However, Jameson criticizes those whom he describes as 'post-modernist ideologues' who claim that these new social movements (women, gays, blacks, ecologists, regional autonomists, etc.) 'arise in the void left by the disappearance of social classes and in the rubble of the political movements organized around those' (Jameson, 1991, p.319). According to Jameson, the conditions that give rise to these social movements or groups are real social changes, but they are nothing to do with the disappearance of classes and class conflicts.

> How classes could be expected to disappear, save in the unique special-case scenario of socialism, has never been clear to me; but the global restructuration of production and the introduction of radically new technologies — that have flung workers in archaic factories out of work, displaced new kinds of industry to unexpected parts of the world, and recruited work forces different from the traditional ones in a variety of features, from gender to skill and nationality — explain why so many people have been willing to think so, at least for a time. Thus the new social movements and the newly emergent global proletariat both result from the prodigious expansion of capitalism in its third (or 'multinational') stage; both are in that sense 'post-modern', at least in terms of the account of post-modernism offered here.
> (Jameson, 1991, p.319)

Despite his criticisms of those he labels as 'post-modern ideologues' Jameson is careful to avoid the impression that he is advocating a return to a base-superstructure deterministic type of explanation of the new social movements:

> Two positions must be distinguished here, which are both wrong. On the one hand, for a properly post-modern 'cynical reason' the new social movements are simply the result — the concomitants and the products — of capitalism itself in its final and most unfettered stage. On the other hand, for a radical-liberal populism such movements are always to be seen as the local victories and the painful achievements and conquests of small groups of people in struggle (who are themselves figures for class struggle in general, as that had determined all the institutions of history, very much including capitalism itself). In short, and no longer to put so fine a point on it, are the 'new social movements' consequences

and after effects of late capitalism? Are they new units generated by the system itself in its interminable inner self-differentiation and self-reproduction? Or are they very precisely new 'agents of history' who spring into being in resistance to the system as forms of opposition to it, forcing it against the direction of its own internal logic into new reforms and internal modifications? But this is precisely a false opposition, about which it would be just as satisfactory to say that both positions are right; the crucial issue is the theoretical dilemma, replicated in both, of some seeming explanatory choice between the alternatives of agency and system. In reality, however, there is no such choice, and both explanations or models — absolutely inconsistent with each other — are also incommensurable with each other and must be rigorously separated at the same time that they are deployed simultaneously. (Jameson, 1991, p.326)

The position taken by Jameson on this dilemma as it related to the issue of the 'new social movements' and their relationship to capitalism leaves him open to the charge that he wants to 'have his cake and eat it'. He maintains that there is the simultaneous possibility of active political commitment working through such partial and limited movements and, at the same time, of continuing to develop a more totalizing and systematic social theory, 'and not some sterile choice between those two things' (*ibid.*, p.320). In other words, he believes it is right to take part in non-class-based social movements, but his Marxist systematic analysis would also insist that such alliances (or the 'Rainbow Coalition') are generally not as durable as those organized around class and the development of class consciousness. It is for this reason that he prefers the example of Jesse Jackson's attempt to develop a Rainbow Coalition in American politics during the 1980s, because 'he rarely makes a speech in which working-class experience is not "constructed" as the mediation around which the equivalence of the coalition is to find its active cohesion' (*ibid.*, p.331). Whereas, the post-modern approach of Ernesto Laclau and Chantal Mouffe in *Hegemony and Socialist Strategy* (1985) is criticized because, although they provide a good description of the way in which alliance politics function — in the establishing of an axis of equivalence along which the parties line up — the equivalence could be in terms of non-class issues such as abortion or nuclear energy, and so lacks durability.

The political problem, as Jameson sees it, is that people can identify with *groups*, as represented through the media, but they cannot identify with large, amorphous classes. Consequently, in the era of post-modernism, it is virtually impossible for the metanarrative of class conflict and of the eventual triumph of the proletariat to succeed in encompassing all developments. Classes can no longer function or be represented as the 'agents' or 'subjects' of history. On the other hand, whilst the plurality of protest groups and social movements can attract allegiance and offer an identity, their 'very lively social struggles of the current period are largely dispersed and anarchic' (Jameson, 1991, p.349). It is difficult to unite them in some metanarrativeof alliance and combined struggle because there is not a single enemy group against which they can struggle. Late capitalism has become such an impersonal system that it is difficult to develop convincing representations of a 'ruling class' as an identifiable group. An actual group of influential businessmen, such as those who advised and backed President Ronald Reagan in the late 1970s and 1980s, is more likely to be regarded as a local network of cronies (in southern California and the Sun Belt) engaged in conspiracy, rather than bringing discredit on business or being regarded as representatives of the ruling class (Jameson, 1991).

According to Jameson, the different groups should unite against a common enemy, which he calls corporate capitalism. But this entity is dispersed throughout the whole social system and culture: there are many levels and centres of power. Furthermore, post-modern culture itself would have to be identified as decadent and simply a ruling-class culture, which is difficult to do convincingly because of its seeming popularity and the pleasures that consumption offers. Opposition to it can seem puritanical or a form of out-of-date élitism. Despite these problems, Jameson maintains his faith in the Marxist metanarrative of history and a belief in the eventual emergence of a global class struggle combining the many local groups at present engaged in dispersed power struggles:

> I'm convinced that this new post-modern global form of capitalism will now have a new class logic about it, but it has not yet completely emerged because labour has not yet reconstituted itself on a global scale, and so there is a crisis in what classes and class consciousness are. It's very clear that agency on the Left is not there in those older forms but the Marxist narrative assures us that some form of agency will reconstitute itself and that is the sense in which I still find myself committed to the Marxist logic.
> (Jameson, 1991, p.31)

As he himself admits, although this belief is supported by the logic of the Marxist metanarrative, his faith is based on individual belief and 'could just be an aberrant personal religion of some sort' (*ibid.*). His own brilliant analysis of the fragmented post-modern culture makes clear how difficult it is for such metanarratives to survive in contemporary society.

4   REJECTIONS OF POST-MODERNISM

Outright rejections of the thesis that we are entering a post-modern epoch take several forms. Perhaps the most outright rejection is that voiced by orthodox Marxists who seek to reaffirm the revolutionary socialist tradition and the primacy of class-based politics against those they regard as 'revisionists' or proponents of more pluralistic 'New Times'. Such rejection is to be found in the work of Callinicos, especially in his aptly titled book *Against Post-modernism: a Marxist critique* (1989). Callinicos describes his approach as

> continuing in a very minor key Marx's critique of religion, where he treats Christianity in particular not simply, as the Enlightenment had, as a set of false beliefs, but as the distorted expression of real needs denied by class society. Similarly I seek here not simply to demonstrate the intellectual inadequacy of post-modernism, understood as the claim, justified by appeal to post-modern art, post-structural philosophy, and the theory of post-industrial society, that we are entering a post-modern epoch, but to set it in historical context. Post-modernism, then, is best seen as a symptom.
> (Callinicos, 1989, p.6)

It is interesting that Callinicos should treat post-modernism as Marx treated religion, merely as a symptom of something more 'real', by which he means economic conditions associated with capitalism, and as a set of political attitudes reflecting those conditions. Thus, 'post-modernist' ideas are said to be a reflection of opportunities for an 'over consumptionist lifestyle offered upper white-collar strata by capitalism in the 1980s and political disillusionment in the aftermath of 1968' (Callinicos, 1989, p.7).

Jean-François Lyotard in France, and Ernesto Laclau and Chantal Mouffe in Britain, are cited as examples of leading 'post-Marxists' who argue that socialists should abandon 'classism' — the classical Marxist stress upon the class struggle as the driving force of history, and of the working-class as the agency of socialist change. The resulting fusion of post-modernism and post-Marxism was exemplified in the 1980s by the magazine *Marxism Today*, which expressed the idea that we are living in 'New Times', as follows:

> Unless the Left can come to terms with those New Times, it must live on the sidelines...At the heart of New Times is the shift from the old mass-production Fordist economy to a new, more flexible, post-Fordist order based on computers, information technology and robotics. But New Times are about more than economic change. Our world is being remade. Mass production, the mass consumer, the big city, the big-brother state, the sprawling housing estate, and the nation-state are in decline: flexibility, diversity, differentiation, mobility, communication, decentralization and internationalization are in the ascendant. In the process our own identities, our sense of self, our own subjectivities are being transformed. We are in transition to a new era.
> (*Marxism Today*, October 1988)

Callinicos's criticisms of the thesis of New Times and the era of post-modernity include detailed arguments about the extent to which Fordist mass production has declined (an issue discussed in Chapter 4 of this book), and whether post-modernist cultural trends are any different from modernism. He makes a strong case against the thesis that there has been a decisive shift from a modern to a post-modern era, although the case against the more moderate thesis of a gradual change is less conclusive. However, the crux of his argument is directed against any distraction from the predominant importance of class conflict.

The response of those who argue that we are in New Times or a post-modern era is that other social positions and identities have become more important or 'real' for people, irrespective of whether or not that is a distraction from their supposed class interests and so a form of 'false consciousness'. Capitalism may be a major cause of some problems addressed by feminists, ecologists, New Age religionists, fundamentalists, and other groups, but they define their concerns differently. And, as one of the early American sociologists, William I.Thomas, pointed out: 'If men (*sic*) define situations as real, they are real in their consequences'. In other words, we have to take their reasoning seriously, not prejudge the question of the most significant factors in each situation. This is particularly important in a period where there is an apparent increase in social pluralism and new cultural formations. (It is still possible to follow Callinicos's example and to question the *degree* of social pluralism or cultural novelty, provided the evidence is considered in an open-minded way and takes account of the views of the people being studied, particularly their judgements as to where their interests and allegiances lie.)

5   RECONSTRUCTIONS IN POST-MODERNITY OR NEW TIMES

Most of the theorists who have written about post-modernity have viewed it as some kind of transition period in which older systems of production are giving way to newer ones, as in the change from Fordist to post-Fordist production; services are overtaking manufacturing occupations; supranational forms of organization are increasing at the expense of national forms; 'civil society' is expanding and becoming more diversified, not only in terms of different consumer groups and lifestyles, but also with respect to a pluralization of social life in which ordinary people in industrialized societies have a greater range of positions and identities available in their everyday working, social, familial and sexual lives. There are different opinions about the extent of these changes (particularly about whether they only apply to industrialized countries and to the better-off two-thirds of the people in those countries) and also about whether they are capable of being subsumed under the logic of a new stage of global capitalism. However, leaving aside the question of whether it is possible to predict a future stage of social development in the way that the Enlightenment project envisaged, there is no doubt that analyses of post-modernity or New Times are attempting to develop new concepts and categories that are adequate to the rich kaleidoscope of contemporary social life and that they have succeeded in opening up fresh and stimulating debates.

What distinguishes those I have called the 'constructive post-modernists' from some other post-modernists and critics of post-modernism is their tendency to look for positive developments through their efforts to create new 'emancipatory narratives', new identities, original syntheses and rearticulations of otherwise divergent or fragmented elements. Dick Hebdige provides a good description of some of these developments in Britain during the 1980s, particularly those that sought to use popular culture and the media. His comments are made from the political point of view of a committed socialist who is concerned about the political implications of these developments, but they have a wider relevance irrespective of any political project. In reading the following quotation from Hebdige's article, *After the Masses*, you should form your own judgements about the social significance of such efforts to construct new identities and communities. Do they justify a more positive view of post-modernity or New Times than is allowed by the outright critics of the idea of post-modernism such as Callinicos?

In the following extract from Hebdige's article, he begins by showing how consumer identities and lifestyles constitute social types and categories that could be used in a more positive way by sociologists so as to develop a 'sociology of aspiration' (what people desire to be). He does not envisage this as a substitute for class analysis, but he believes it is another important dimension of social stratification that has become more significant in these New Times.

> One of the features of post-Fordist production is the leading role given to market research, packaging and presentation. While it doesn't literally *produce* the social, it's none the less the case that marketing has provided the dominant and most pervasive classifications of 'social types' in the 1980s (the yuppie is the most obvious example). We use these categories as a kind of social shorthand even if we are reluctant to find ourselves reflected in them. We live in a world and in bodies which are deeply scored by the power relations of race and class, sexuality and gender but we also live — whether or not we know it consciously — in a world of style-setters, innovators, sloanes, preppies, empty nesters (working couples with grown up families), dinkies (dual-income-no-kids), casuals, sensibles, the constrained majority, and today's prime targets, the pre-teens and woofies (well-off-older folk).
>
> These are the types outlined in commercial lifestyling and 'psychographics' — forms of research which don't present descriptions of living, breathing individuals so much as

hypothetical 'analogues' of 'aspirational clusters'. In other words the new intensive but speculative forms of market research are designed to offer a social map of desire which can be used to determine where exactly which products should be 'pitched' and 'niched'. All these types could no doubt be translated back into the old language (it would perhaps be relatively easy to return them to the axis of social class) but everything specific would be lost in the translation.

It is clear that such research methods and the marketing initiative associated with them have been developed precisely to cut across the old social-sexual polarities. The parameters are designed to be transcultural and transnational (the spread of 'psychographics' in the UK is linked to the drive to go pan-European in preparation for 1992). We may find such forms of knowledge immoral, objectionable or sinister — a waste of time and resources which are unforgiveable in a world where people are starving and in a country where people are still sleeping in the streets — but the fact is that they do actively create and sustain one *version* of the social. They depend for their success on the accurate outlining and anticipation (through observation and interviews with 'target' subjects) not just of what (some) people think they want but of *what they'd like to be*. A sociology of aspiration might begin by combining the considerable *critical* and *diagnostic* resources available within existing versions of sociology and cultural studies with the *descriptive* and *predictive* knowledge available within the new intensive market research to get a more adequate picture of what *everybody* says they want and what they want to be in all its radical plurality.
(Hebdige, 1989, pp.89–90)

The key point that Hebdige is making in this discussion of lifestyles and consumer groups is that these are social phenomena that are no less real than previously privileged sociological categories such as 'class', and they are now more important and complex than in earlier periods. (See Book 3 (Bocock and Thompson, 1992), Chapter 3.) Consequently, the Left has to take them more seriously and accept 'what certain forms of post-modernism recommend: a scepticism towards imposed general, "rational" solutions: a relaxation of the old critical and judgemental postures, although without retreating from its principles' (*ibid.*).

The second set of new collectivities that requires positive appraisal according to Hebdige, are those that actively use the mass media to construct an identity. Unlike more pessimistic post-modernist analysts, and the critics of post-modernism, Hebdige emphasizes the capacity of people to develop new communities and identities through popular culture and the mass media, rather than being passive masses.

It may well be true that the two great collective identities through which the masses came together to 'make history' in the last two hundred years — the first associated with nation, the second with class — are breaking down today in the overdeveloped world. But new 'emancipation narratives' are being written round collectives other than the imaginary community of nation or the international brotherhood of socialist *man*. This is true even in popular culture and the 'depthless' field of the media upon which Baudrillard operates.

Within the transfigured 'public realm', established by transnational communication networks, new forms, both of alliance and contestation, are possible. One of the things ignored in the more 'fatal' versions of new times is the binding power of the new transnational media systems: the power they have to move people not just to buy the products of the culture industries but to buy *into* networks that offer forms of community and alliance which can transcend the confines of class, race, gender, regional and national culture. Popular music offers many examples of this kind of bonding. Some of these 'communities of affect' (rather than 'communities of interest') are explicitly utopian. The simultaneously most spectacular yet most participatory examples to date of the kind of bonding, made possible across transnational communication systems have been the televised events organized round Band Aid, Sport Aid, Live Aid and the Free Mandela movement. This is where you see the optimistic will in action. Televangelism is another less engaging example of this kind of mobilization specific to the media age.

Rather than 'psychic autism' (Baudrillard) or the waning of affect (Jameson) such phenomena suggest the possibility of a new kind of politics existing primarily in and through the airwaves and organized around issues of universal moral concern. Such crusades are likely to be extended in the 1990s. Once again the desire to feel and to feel *connected* to a transitory mass of other people, to engage in transitory and *superficial* alliances of this kind is not intrinsically either good or bad. Instead it has to be *articulated*. Jimmy Swaggart managed to articulate the yearning for community and righteousness one way. Jerry Dammers, founder of the Two Tone movement and co-organizer of the Mandela concert, helped to direct the flow of similar desires in a radically different direction.
(Hebdige, 1989, pp.90–1)

This discussion of new forms of 'communities of affect' or emotionally based collectivities takes us beyond the consumer identities and their related images as focused on by theorists such as Jameson and Baudrillard. They cannot be 'read-off' or understood simply as the 'cultural logic of late capitalism' (Jameson).

The remaining two alternatives draw different conclusions about the implications of the increasing and diverse social pluralism that has attracted the label 'post-modernity'. The first position, which we will discuss next, is represented by Jean Baudrillard, who maintains that in

Live Aid Concert

the post-modern era 'appearances are everything'. The second position, to be discussed later, is that of the various constructive post-modernists, who hold that it is possible to combine cultural codes that were thought to be irreconcilable or contradictory according to Enlightenment thought (including radical Enlightenment theory, such as Marxism). An example of this in practice would be the varied 'post-modern' family regimes described by Judith Stacey the American sociologist in *Brave New Families* (1990) with their surprising linkings and crossover codes involving fundamentalist religion, left-wing politics, feminism, patriarchalism, and other seemingly incongruent elements. Other examples include New Age religion and various charismatic movements.

6   POST-MODERNITY: CONSUMPTION AND APPEARANCES

Baudrillard's account of the post-modern era is significant for the light that it throws on two aspects that distinguish it from earlier eras: the proliferation of communications through the mass media, particularly television, and the full emergence of consumer society. The new mass media use a montage of images (unlike print) and juxtapose or collapse time–space distancing. The result is that culture is now dominated by simulations — objects and discourses that have no firm origin, no referent, no ground or foundation. Signs get their meanings from their relations with each other, rather than by reference to some independent reality or standard. There is a multiplicity of constantly shifting cultural codes, with no fixed metacode to which they all relate and against which they can be judged. Similarly, with respect to the economy, activities and styles of consumption often play a larger role in defining people's identities and consciousness than position in the production system. Baudrillard rejects Marxism and other structuralist theories that deny the surface 'appearance' of things in favour of a hidden underlying structure. Such interpretative strategies all privilege some form of rationality. Like the philosopher Nietzsche, Baudrillard criticizes such claims to 'truth' and favours a model based on what he calls 'seduction'. Seduction plays on the surface; it is the surface appearance that is effective in determining action, not some latent or hidden structure as claimed by Marxism or Freudianism.

Baudrillard's position has become progressively more radically opposed to the Enlightenment tradition of rational thought and its project of promoting progress through scientific means. In his early works, *Le Système des Objets* (The System of Objects) (1968) and *La Société de Consommation* (Consumer Society) (1970), he simply sought to extend the Marxist critique of capitalism to areas beyond the scope of the theory of the mode of production, so as to take account of the meaning and communicational structure of commodities in post-war society. He explored the possibility that consumption had become the chief basis of the social order and of the classification system that encodes behaviour and groups. Such classifications could not be explained by reference to some other structure, such as the mode of production and economic classes, or by reference to 'real' needs or use value. Consumer objects constituted a system of signs that took their meaning from the play of differences between the signs, and these were inexhaustible in their ability to incite desire (or to seduce). Consequently, like many social and literary theorists who took a 'linguistic turn' in the 1960s, he moved steadily in the direction of analysing linguistic or symbolic codes purely in terms of their internal relationships and without reference to some external objects that they might be supposed to represent. In his later work, *Simulacres et Simulations* (1981), Baudrillard's theory of commodity culture removes any distinction between object and representation. In their place he pictures a social world constructed out of models or 'simulacra' which have no foundation in any reality except their own.

> A simulation is different from a fiction or lie in that it not only presents an absence as a presence, the imaginary as the real, it also undermines any contrast to the real, absorbing the real within itself. Instead of a 'real' economy of commodities that is somehow bypassed by an 'unreal' myriad of advertising images, Baudrillard now discerns only a hyperreality, a world of self-referential signs. He has moved from the TV ad which, however, never completely erases the commodity it solicits, to the TV newscast which creates the news if only to be able to narrate it, or the soap opera whose daily events are both referent and reality for many viewers.
> (Poster (ed.), 1988, p.6)

Main Street, Disneyland, Los Angeles, simulates idealized reality. A newer development, City Walk, L.A., aims to go further and mimic the city in which it is located, but without the poverty, danger and dirt. It is a cross between a shopping mall and a real street, 'based on the assumption that a city's essence can be distilled, enhanced and artfully packaged like so much synthetic perfume' (*Los Angeles Times*, 29 February 1992). Developers said there would be no real litter, but 'candy wrappers will be embedded in the terrazzo flooring, as if discarded by previous visitors' (*ibid.*).

A good example of Baudrillard's use of the concepts of simulation and hyperreality is to be found in his statements about Disneyland in Los Angeles. He describes it as a perfect model of the ways in which simulation works. At first glance it appears to be simply a play of illusions and phantasms, such as pirates, the frontier, future worlds, etc. 'This imaginary world is supposed to be what makes the operation successful. But what draws the crowds is undoubtedly much more the social microcosm, the miniaturized and *religious* revelling in real America, in its delights and drawbacks' (Poster (ed.), 1988, p.171). In Disneyland, all of America's values are exalted in miniature and comic-strip form. It is not just a question of Disneyland providing an idealized digest of American life and values, which works ideologically to conceal 'real' contradictions in American society.

> Disneyland is presented as imaginary in order to make us believe that the rest is real, when in fact all of Los Angeles and the America surrounding it are no longer real, but of the order of the hyperreal and simulation. It is no longer a question of a false representation of reality (ideology), but of concealing the fact that the real is no longer real, and thus of saving the reality principle … It is meant to be an infantile world, in order to make us believe

that the adults are elsewhere, in the 'real' world, and to conceal the fact that real childishness is everywhere, particularly among those adults who go there to act the child in order to foster illusions of their real childishness.
(Poster (ed.), 1988, p.172)

Although this is a rather paradoxical statement — suggesting that there is no 'real' Los Angeles or America — it does make sense if we accept it as an exaggerated version of the point that society itself is increasingly composed of constructed images (simulacra). Nowhere is this more clearly demonstrated than in Los Angeles, the site of Hollywood and Disneyland. However, critics of Baudrillard on the political left, whilst echoing some of his ideas about simulation and hyperreality, accuse him of lapsing into political apathy. One critic said that Baudrillard's version of California, in his short book *America* (1988), was 'Reaganized and yuppified' and that in it 'there are no migrant workers, no Chicano barrios, no Central American refugees, no Vietnamese refugees or Asians, not even any blacks ...' (Kellner, 1989, pp.171–2).

Baudrillard would probably respond that such groups are themselves co-opted into the world of simulacra and hyperreality, of which Disneyland and Hollywood are merely the most extreme examples. He notes sarcastically that, because America imagines itself as an 'achieved utopia', minorities and the poor must disappear from view: it is only bad taste if they continue to show themselves (Baudrillard, 1988, p.111).

ACTIVITY 2   You should now take stock of the implications of the radical post-modernist position represented by Baudrillard. I suggest you make a summary of this position, referring to the preceding discussion. (You might also see the earlier references to Baudrillard and consumption in Book 3 (Bocock and Thompson, 1992), Chapter 3.) What would you consider to be the main contributions of this approach and what do you think are its deficiencies?

It is difficult to form a conclusive judgement about Baudrillard's contribution, partly because of the rather convoluted expressions he uses, but also because he seems to adopt an extreme position in order to shock his readers and perhaps jolt them out of what he would regard as their complacency or dogmatism. Nevertheless, he does focus on some important features of contemporary social life that distinguish the present period from earlier epochs and so might justify the label 'post-modernity', although he rejects the label 'post-modernist' for his own position.

The key contribution is to make us aware of how radically social life and our perceptions have been changed by the development of endlessly differentiated consumer lifestyles, the constant stream of television images, and the expanded capacity of the media to seduce us in a strange new world of 'hyperreality': a world of simulations which is immune to rationalist critique, whether Marxist, liberal or any other metatheory of reality. Baudrillard's radical, post-modernist message, is that the media images do not merely represent reality: they *are* reality, because their meaning derives from their position within a system of signs, not from some referent in a 'real' world outside that system. Whereas earlier sociologists, such as the founders of Symbolic Interactionism, George Herbert Mead (1863–1931) and Charles H.Cooley (1864–1929) emphasized the development of the individual's self concept through primary group interaction (family and other significant relationships) and seeing ourselves through the eyes of those 'significant others', Baudrillard emphasizes the influence of the mechanically reproduced images of the media. For Baudrillard, the mass media are not a means of communication because there is no feedback or exchange of information. (He regards media surveys and opinion polls as just another media spectacle.) The only political strategy he can recommend to the masses (a term which encompasses everyone, not as in the older distinction between élite and masses) is to refuse to take the media seriously; that is, to refuse to play the game and so merely regard the media as nothing but spectacles.

Needless to say, Baudrillard's position is thought to be far too accepting of the status quo by those who believe the media do distort reality, or reflect a reality that must be changed. Critical theorists, such as Jurgen Habermas, believe that it is possible to establish rational criteria for judging the adequacy of representations of reality, and they are prepared to advocate social changes that would create the conditions for non-distorted communication and debate in civil society. (This is discussed further by Gregor McLennan in Chapter 7 of this book.) Others such as Hebdige, argue that groups and social movements can offer resistance by resignifying the meanings that are presented to them by the media and in consumer objects. We will turn to some examples of other strategies in the next section, which focuses on efforts to combine different cultural codes in everyday life.

7 NEW CONNECTIONS OF CONSTRUCTIVE POST-MODERNISM

Hebdige's comment that some of the media-related movements were sometimes explicitly utopian, and usually sought to provide a bond of moral community, gives us a link to the ideas of other writers who have taken a constructive approach to post-modernism. These are the various scholars from different disciplines who have discerned post-modernist trends that constitute a challenge to the negative aspects of modernism, such as its materialism, secularism, individualism, patriarchy, scientism, anthropocentrism and ecological vandalism. Constructive post-modern thought seeks new connections and syntheses that might offer alternatives to the negative aspects of modernism. The kinds of phenomena studied include some that modernist thought would have regarded as marginal or antithetical to modern life: the sacred, charisma, passion, spirituality, cosmic meaning and unity, enchantment, community and so-called 'feminine' qualities such as 'love' and 'romance'. Some of these were emphasized in the nineteenth century Romantic Movement, which was a reaction against assumed negative aspects of Enlightenment thought and modernity. However, there is an important difference in that constructive post-modernism does not have a romanticized view of the pre-modern, but seeks to combine the benefits of modernity with values and qualities that it believes were devalued by modernism as an ideology (*materialistic* capitalism is viewed as a contributory factor, but not the sole cause).

Judith Stacey's book *Brave New Families* (1990) describes the varied pattern of family regimes in an area of California, Silicon Valley, where there seems to be surprising linkings and crossovers involving fundamentalist religion, left-wing politics, feminism, patriarchalism, and various other seemingly incongruent elements. On the basis of her case studies of these extremely complicated family patterns, in which some of the women were finding that membership of a 'born again' religious movement provided 'a flexible resource for reconstituting gender and kinship relationships in post-modern and post-feminist directions' (p.18), she came to the conclusion:

> We are living, I believe, through a transitional and contested period of family history, a period *after* the modern family order, but before what we cannot foretell. Precisely because it is not possible to characterize with a single term the competing sets of family cultures that co-exist at present, I identify this family regime as post-modern. The post-modern family is not a new model of family life, not the next stage in an orderly progression of family history, but the stage when the belief in a logical progression of stages breaks down. Rupturing evolutionary models of family history and incorporating both experimental and nostalgic elements, 'the' post-modern family lurches forward and backward into an uncertain future.
> (Stacey, 1990, p.18)

The various 'post-modern' family forms that Stacey found in Silicon Valley were marked by differences rather than uniformities. At first glance they resembled the traditional, extended family household, but on closer examination they were found to be composed of various mixtures of friends and relatives, and the members of the household subscribed to sets of beliefs and rationalities that would traditionally have been regarded as incongruous. They do not conform to any single cultural code or form of social organization, and in that sense they are 'disorganized'. But for these Californians, who had experienced rapid and acute economic and cultural change, they represent pragmatic attempts to hold together their different subject positions (e.g. as partner, mother, feminist, worker, political liberal and religious fundamentalist) and to provide a buffer against the effects of further disruptive changes.

It is just such reactions to modernity that we need to focus on in our discussion of post-modernity. These reactions are interesting, not only because they represent new and often surprising combinations and crossovers of codes and discourses, but also because they offer a challenge to the grand theories and concepts derived from the Enlightenment tradition concerning the course of social development. On the whole, such tendencies or movements are not seeking to turn the clock back to a pre-modern 'golden age', as did some conservative reactionaries in responding to the emergence of the modern age. They are efforts to articulate new identities, communities, and even utopias, in the face of increasing ephemerality and social life that lacks foundation — a society of spectacles and fashions, fragmentation of work and class identities, destruction of local communities and natural resources.

Another example of constructive post-modernism that combines elements of religion, psychology and business, is that of 'New Age' religions. Heelas has traced these to the distinctive view of the self that began to take root in the 1960s and to what the sociologist Talcott Parsons (1975) called 'the expressive revolution', which is concerned with discovering one's 'true' nature, delving within in order to experience the riches of 'life' itself, and which is all about authenticity, liberation, creativity and natural wisdom (Heelas, 1991). Many people have been content with a more psychological version of expressivism, seeking self-development or self-actualization, in which importance is attached to getting in touch with feelings and being oneself. Others, however, have become involved with a more utopian version of the quest within. For these New Age or self-religionists, the key belief is that God lies within. 'Rather than the self being quasi-sacralized' as in the more psychological wing of expressivism, it is now accorded an explicitly sacred status (Heelas, 1991, p.1). In many respects the contemporary New Age religion is the direct descendant of the late 1960s and early 1970s hippie counter-culture, but New Age religionists do not think that it is necessary to 'drop out' in order to avoid the 'iron cage' of modernity. Whereas, prior to the 1960s, this kind of quest for actualization of a sacred self was limited to small numbers of cultural sophisticates (Heelas mentions literary figures like Rousseau, Goethe, Whitman and Emerson), it then began to enter popular culture and subsequently spread through the agency of therapists, counsellors, healers in alternative medicine, management trainers (especially in Human Resource Management), educationalists, and some of the authors addressing feminist and environmentalist issues. The persuasiveness of self-religiosity may owe much to the failure of the ideology of progress to produce collectivist solutions by way of reforming institutions, leaving people to seek perfection and utopia within themselves. If this also serves to motivate them to perform their

work and other institutional roles more effectively, then institutional
encouragement is likely to be forthcoming. Large companies in Britain,
America and other countries have been prepared to spend considerable
sums of money on training courses based on techniques deriving from
the early self-religionist, Gurdjieff, or contemporary gurus such as
Erhard's Seminars Training (EST). Perhaps the fears of Daniel Bell about
'a disjunction between the kind of organization and the norms
demanded in the economic realm, and the norms of self-realization that
are now central in the culture' (Bell, 1976, p.15) will be dispelled by the
New Age religionists. Alternatively, future economic crises may force a
reversion to materialistic concerns at the expense of the quest for
actualization of the sacred self: New Age religion may then be revealed
as a temporary 'yuppie religion'.

Let us take another example: the televangelists that Hebdige mentions.
They are part of an upsurge of fundamentalist and charismatic religious
movements that have appeared across the globe and across religious
boundaries — not only across Christian denominational boundaries, but
also other religions such as Islam and Judaism. They accept and use
many of the techniques and facilities made possible by modernity,
whilst rejecting various aspects of modernist ideology. According to the
secularization thesis and theories of social deprivation, such movements
should have been diminishing and have had a residual appeal confined
to the poor. But, as an article on the televangelists Jim and Tammy
Baaker pointed out, this was not the case:

> Many, if not most, academic discussions of fundamentalist religion
> or televangelism in the nineteen-eighties rested on the premise that
> fundamentalism was a reaction against modernity on the part of
> the dispossessed, the uneducated, the minority of Americans left
> behind by the modern world. To theorists of fundamentalism, the
> donors to a televangelist such as Baaker had to be poor rural folk,
> elderly women living on Social Security: people outside the
> mainstream of middle-class American society. How a minority of
> poor rural folk managed to contribute such huge sums to the
> telepreachers — the total had risen to a billion five hundred
> million dollars annually by 1986 — was a question that most
> theorists never bothered to address. Of course, anyone who
> actually looked at Baaker's audiences in his high-tech television
> studios would see hundreds of well-dressed and extremely
> respectable looking people of all ages: a cross-section one might
> imagine of the American middle class.
> (Fitzgerald, 1990, p.48)

Nor were these involvements merely transitory and limited to passive
television viewing. Over a hundred thousand of Baaker's supporters
contributed a thousand dollars each for 'lifetime partnerships' in his
community/theme park called Heritage USA. Other televangelists built
universities, hospitals, hotels, television studios, and community
centres. One of them, Pat Robertson, campaigned unsuccessfully in

1988 for the Presidency of the United States and was even thought to be a serious threat to the eventual winner, George Bush, at one stage. There are many explanations offered to account for this upsurge of fundamentalism, and its attractiveness to a wide cross-section of people. (Some of these explanations were referred to in Book 3 (Bocock and Thompson, 1992), Chapter 7, when the secularization thesis was discussed.) The point being made here is that it represents one of the forms taken by constructive post-modernism, combining elements of modernity with values that seemed to be excluded in the ideology of modernism.

The two concepts in classical sociology that might have been usefully developed to account for these trends — charisma and the sacred — were thought to refer to fringe phenomena destined to decline under the impact of science and the process of rationalization. Even Max Weber and Émile Durkheim, who developed the concepts, tended to think of them as being undercut by modernity.

Weber limited the concept of charisma to the relationship between outstanding leaders and their followers; and he said the opportunities for leaders to exercise a charismatic sway over their followers were destined to decline under the deadening force of rationalization and bureaucracy. Durkheim did not use the term charisma, but he attributed a kind of charismatic force to the sacred, which was a quality of the suprapersonal community: the sense of the social as timeless, all-encompassing, vital, emotionally compelling, evoking deep commitment and a sense of surpassing value. Durkheim saw such experiences of self-transcendence as being engendered by emotionally charged group rituals, and these were less likely to occur in modern society. However, he believed they had to occur to some extent in all societies, and the lack of such opportunities in his own time could only be because it was a 'transitional era'. Since Durkheim's lifetime (he died in 1917) there has been a significant development that he could not have foreseen: the growth of the mass media, which made possible a new sense of 'collective effervescence' and imagined community. However, it is also the case that the apparent pluralization of sources of identity and imagined communities owes much to mass media representations or simulations. It is one of the strengths of theories of post-modernity that they emphasize these processes, as we saw in our discussions of Jameson, Baudrillard and Hebdige.

Even mundane areas of life can give a mild taste of the collective effervescence and social communion offered by charisma. Identification with local or national sports teams, or with entertainment idols and their styles, can function in that way. Another alternative to membership of charismatic movements with an explicitly religious nature is found in the strong attachment fostered between individuals and the nation. In times of national crisis, this attachment may be strengthened by the rise of a charismatic leader who is thought to embody the potent characteristic of the threatened sacred nation. In the culture of everyday life, even the act of buying can be an exercise in community, as the shopping mall becomes an arena in which to congregate with others and to enjoy a pleasurable disjuncture of ordinary awareness within a group (Jacobs, 1984). In the shopping mall the personalized images that have been connected to the products — images of sexual power, glamour, or national pride — serve to convince shoppers that while purchasing goods they are simultaneously participating together in a shared experience of a more vital and sensual world (Lindholm, 1990).

However, it can be argued that in contemporary western societies, the major alternative forms of charisma are found not in public, secular realms of capitalist consumption, nor in the worship of the nation, nor in entertainment, nor in religion, either orthodox or magical. Instead, people experience merger and self-loss, fundamental meaning and identity, in more intimate circumstances. For example, it is in the supposedly private community of the family or home, whatever form or regime it takes, that people look for a 'haven in a heartless world' (Lasch, 1977). But because so much is now required of the family in terms of personal fulfilment, and because the social pressures on the family are so great (the need for two incomes, housing shortages, social mobility, low status of housework), many are disappointed at what is actually delivered. Lindholm, in his study of charismatic communities and movements, suggests that it is for this reason that many countercultural communes, such as the Manson group who committed several brutal murders in California in 1969, call themselves 'families' and attempt to live out in the commune a fantasy of what they believed families ought to be (Lindholm, 1990, p.182).

The challenge that 'reconstructive post-modernists' face is to develop a sociological paradigm, developing further ideas that were only touched on by earlier theorists such as Weber and Durkheim, which will do justice to the non-rational aspects of the social. Concepts such as charisma and the sacred point to the fact that society is based upon a deeply evocative communion of self and other, and the Enlightenment privileging of reason has distracted sociological attention from that fundamental dimension of social life. Such a paradigm also has political and policy implications because it focuses, not merely on the ownership and distribution of wealth, but also on the conditions which would permit a pluralistic and multiplex society to tolerate and even promote numerous middle-level communal groups offering a satisfying sense of commitment and emotional gratification.

8   CONCLUSION

It is difficult to make an overall assessment of the many and diverse elements that have been included under the label of post-modernity or post-modernism. To some extent this may be because it is not yet established as a distinct period or a single tendency. In many respects the label is more usefully seen as indicating a number of developments that do not seem to fit in with the Enlightenment's metanarratives about progress, rationalization and secularization, which were continued in sociological convergence theories of modernity and modernization maintaining that all societies were evolving in the same direction, and in Marxist scientific materialist theories of increasing class polarization and class consciousness.

Post-modernism, as it relates to aesthetics, supports this reading, as it refers to a tendency towards pastiches of incongruent cultural codes, without any single articulating principle or theoretical foundation. It is very much a question of indiscriminate populism: 'anything goes' or 'whatever turns you on'. Of course, there are limits to this apparent free for all — not least the fact that things are seldom free; indeed, culture is increasingly commodified. In that respect there are definite ties between culture and economic developments. However, capitalism as an economic system is now so firmly established, despite its cycles of booms and slumps, that it can afford to allow a high level of social and cultural pluralism. If anything, it is in the interests of capitalism to foster the dynamic tendencies of social and cultural pluralism because they encourage innovation and develop more niche markets and flexible specialization. As we have seen, even socially innovative phenomena such as Band Aid and New Age religion, which are motivated by autonomous moral principles that may appear to be antithetical to materialistic and commercial values, may be reconciled with and even co-opted into the economic system. This may be viewed negatively, or it can be interpreted more positively as indicating that there is scope within late capitalism for increased social and cultural variety and pluralism. Consequently, there are different views about how post-modernism should be judged in political terms. If, as Jameson and others believe, post-modernism indicates that we are in a transitional phase before the emergence of a new epoch, then it is too soon to make a final judgement about its potentially progressive or reactionary qualities. There is still room for debate, and that may be the best thing to come out of the current fascination with post-modernism and post-modernity. This is the conclusion of some (though not at all) feminists, for example Janet Flax, who welcome the space opened up for new and partial standpoints:

> Feminist theories, like other forms of postmodernism, should encourage us to tolerate and interpret ambivalence, ambiguity, and multiplicity as well as to expose the roots of our needs for imposing order and structure no matter how arbitrary and oppressive these needs may be. If we do our work well, 'reality' will appear even more unstable, complex, and disorderly than it does now.
> (Flax, 1987, p.643)

REFERENCES

Baudrillard, J. (1968) *Le Système des Objets*, Paris, Gallimard.

Baudrillard, J. (1970) *La Société de Consommation*, Paris, Gallimard.

Baudrillard, J. (1981) *Simulacres et Simulations*, Paris, Galilee, part translated as *Simulations*, New York, Semiotext(e), 1983.

Baudrillard, J. (1988) *America,* London, Verso. Originally published in French, 1986.

Bell, D. (1973) *The Coming of Post-Industrial Society*, New York, Basic Books.

Bell, D. (1976) *The Cultural Contradictions of Capitalism*, London, Heinemann.

Bocock, R. and Thompson, K. (eds) (1992) *Social and Cultural Forms of Modernity*, Cambridge, Polity Press.

Callinicos, A. (1989) *Against Post-modernism: a Marxist Critique,* Cambridge, Polity Press.

Connor, S. (1989) *Post-modernist Culture*, Oxford, Blackwell.

Fitzgerald, F. (1990) 'Reflections: Jim and Tammy' *The New Yorker*, April 1990, pp.45–87.

Flax, J. (1987) 'Post-modernism and gender relations in feminist theory', *Signs: Journal of Women in Culture and Society*, Vol.12, No.4, pp.621–43.

Gott, R. (1986) 'Modernism and post-modernism: the crisis of contemporary culture', *The Guardian,* 1 December, 1986, p.10.

Harvey, D. (1989) *The Condition of Postmodernity*, Oxford, Blackwell.

Hebdige, D. (1989) 'After the masses', in Hall, S. and Jacques, M. (eds), *New Times,* London, Lawrence and Wishart.

Heelas, P. (1991) 'The sacralization of the self and new age capitalism' in Abercrombie N. and Warde, A. (eds), *Social Change in Contemporary Britain*, Cambridge, Polity Press.

Jacobs, J. (1984) *The Mall*, Prospect Heights, Illinois, Waveland.

Jameson, F. (1984) 'Post-modernism or the cultural logic of late capitalism', *New Left Review*, No.146, pp.53–92.

Jameson, F. (1991) *Postmodernism or The Cultural Logic of Late Capitalism,* London, Verso.

Kellner, D. (1989) *Jean Baudrillard: From Marxism to Postmodernism and Beyond,* Cambridge, Polity Press.

Laclau, E. and Mouffe, C. (1985) *Hegemony and Socialist Strategy*, London, Verso.

Lasch, C. (1977) *Haven in a Heartless World*, New York, Basic Books.

Lindholm, C. (1990) *Charisma*, Oxford, Blackwell.

Marxism Today (1988) October.

Parsons, T. (1975) *The Educational and Expressive Revolutions*, London, London School of Economics.

Poster, M. (ed.) (1988) *Jean Baudrillard: Selected works*, Cambridge, Polity Press.

Simmel, G. (1900) *Die Philosophie des Geldes*, Leipzig: Duncker and Humblot, translated as *The Philosophy of Money*, London, Routledge, 1978.

Stacey, J. (1990) *Brave New Families*, New York, Basic Books.

Venturi, R. *et al.* (1977) *Learning from Las Vegas*, revised edition, Cambridge, M.I.T. Press.

READING A   THE CONDITION OF POSTMODERNITY

David Harvey

Over the last two decades 'postmodernism' has become a concept to be wrestled with, and such a battleground of conflicting opinions and political forces that it can no longer be ignored. 'The culture of the advanced capitalist societies' announce the editors of *PRECIS 6* (1987), 'has undergone a profound shift in the *structure of feeling*.' Most, I think, would now agree with Huyssens's (1984) more cautious statement:

> What appears on one level as the latest fad, advertising pitch and hollow spectacle is part of a slowly emerging cultural transformation in Western societies, a change in sensibility for which the term 'postmodern' is actually, at least for now, wholly adequate. The nature and depth of that transformation are debatable, but transformation it is. I don't want to be misunderstood as claiming that there is a wholesale paradigm shift of the cultural, social, and economic orders; any such claim clearly would be overblown. But in an important sector of our culture there is a noticeable shift in sensibility, practices and discourse formations which distinguishes a post-modern set of assumptions, experiences and propositions from that of a preceding period.

With respect to architecture, for example, Charles Jencks dates the symbolic end of modernism and the passage to the postmodern as 3.32 p.m. on 15 July 1972, when the Pruitt-Igoe housing development in St.Louis (a prize-winning version of Le Corbusier's 'machine for modern living') was dynamited as an uninhabitable environment for the low-income people it housed. Thereafter, the ideas of the CIAM, Le Corbusier, and the other apostles of 'high modernism' increasingly gave way before an onslaught of diverse possibilities of which those set forth in the influential *Learning from Las Vegas* by Venturi, Scott Brown, and Izenour (also published in 1972) proved to be but one powerful cutting edge. The point of that work, as its title implies, was to insist that architects had more to learn from the study of popular and vernacular landscapes (such as those of suburbs and commercial strips) than from the pursuit of some abstract, theoretical, and doctrinaire ideals. It was time, they said, to build for people rather than for Man. The glass towers, concrete blocks, and steel slabs that seemed set fair to steamroller over every urban landscape from Paris to Tokyo and from Rio to Montreal, denouncing all ornament as crime, all individualism as sentimentality, all romanticism as kitsch, have progressively given way to ornamented tower blocks, imitation mediaeval squares and fishing villages, custom-designed or vernacular housing, renovated factories and warehouses, and rehabilitated landscapes of all kinds, all in the name of procuring some more 'satisfying' urban environment. So popular has this quest become that no less a figure than Prince

Source: Harvey, D. (1989) *The Condition of Postmodernity*, Oxford, Blackwell, pp.39–65.

Charles has weighed in with vigorous denunciations of the errors of post-war urban redevelopment and the developer destruction that has done more to wreck London, he claims, than the Luftwaffe's attacks in World War II.

In planning circles we can track a similar evolution. Douglas Lee's influential article 'Requiem for large-scale planning models' appeared in a 1973 issue of the *Journal of the American Institute of Planners* and correctly predicted the demise of what he saw as the futile efforts of the 1960s to develop large-scale, comprehensive, and integrated planning models (many of them specified with all the rigour that computerized mathematical modelling could then command) for metropolitan regions. Shortly thereafter, the *New York Times* (13 June 1976) described as 'mainstream' the radical planners (inspired by Jane Jacobs) who had mounted such a violent attack upon the soulless sins of modernist urban planning in the 1960s. It is nowadays the norm to seek out 'pluralistic' and 'organic' strategies for approaching urban development as a 'collage' of highly differentiated spaces and mixtures, rather than pursuing grandiose plans based on functional zoning of different activities. ...

Shifts of this sort can be documented across a whole range of diverse fields. The postmodern novel, McHale (1987) argues, is characterized by a shift from an 'epistemological' to an 'ontological' dominant. By this he means a shift from the kind of perspectivism that allowed the modernist to get a better bearing on the meaning of a complex but nevertheless singular reality, to the foregrounding of questions as to how radically different realities may coexist, collide, and interpenetrate. The boundary between fiction and science fiction has, as a consequence, effectively dissolved, while postmodernist characters often seem confused as to which world they are in, and how they should act with respect to it. Even to reduce the problem of perspective to autobiography, says one of Borges' characters, is to enter the labyrinth: 'Who was I? Today's self, bewildered, yesterday's, forgotten; tomorrow's, unpredictable?' The question marks tell it all.

In philosophy, the intermingling of a revived American pragmatism with the post-Marxist and poststructuralist wave that struck Paris after 1968 produced what Bernstein (1985, p.25) calls a 'rage against humanism and the Enlightenment legacy.' This spilled over into a vigorous denunciation of abstract reason and a deep aversion to any project that sought universal human emancipation through mobilization of the powers of technology, science, and reason. Here, also, no less a person than Pope John Paul II has entered the fray on the side of the postmodern. The Pope 'does not attack Marxism or liberal secularism because they are the wave of the future,' says Rocco Buttiglione, a theologian close to the Pope, but because the 'philosophies of the twentieth century have lost their appeal, their time has already passed.' The moral crisis of our time is a crisis of Enlightenment thought. For while the latter may indeed have allowed man to emancipate himself 'from community and tradition of the Middle Ages in which his individual freedom was submerged,' the Enlightenment affirmation of 'self without God' in the end negated itself because reason, a means, was left, in the absence of God's truth, without any spiritual or moral goal. If lust and power are 'the only values that don't need the light of reason to be discovered,' then reason had to become a mere instrument to subjugate others (*Baltimore Sun*, 9 September 1987). The postmodern theological project is to reaffirm God's truth without abandoning the powers of reason.

With such illustrious (and centrist) figures as the Prince of Wales and Pope John Paul II resorting to postmodernist rhetoric and argumentation, there can be little doubt as to the breadth of change that has occurred in 'the structure of feeling' in the 1980s. Yet there is still abundant confusion as to what the new 'structure of feeling' might entail. Modernist sentiments may have been undermined, deconstructed, surpassed, or bypassed, but there is little certitude as to the coherence or meaning of the systems of thought that may have replaced them. Such uncertainty makes it peculiarly difficult to evaluate, interpret, and explain the shift that everyone agrees has occurred.

Does postmodernism, for example, represent a radical break with modernism, or is it simply a revolt within modernism against a certain form of 'high modernism' as represented, say, in the architecture of Mies van der Rohe and the blank surfaces of minimalist abstract expressionist painting? Is postmodernism a style (in which case we can reasonably trace its precursors back to Dada, Nietzsche, or even, as Kroker and Cook (1986) prefer, to St. Augustine's *Confessions* in the fourth century) or should we view it strictly as a periodizing concept (in which case we debate whether it originated in the 1950s, 1960s, or 1970s)? Does it have a revolutionary potential by virtue of its opposition to all forms of meta-narratives (including Marxism, Freudianism, and all forms of Enlightenment reason) and its close attention to 'other worlds' and to 'other voices' that have for too long been silenced (women, gays, blacks, colonized peoples with their own histories)? Or is it simply the commercialization and domestication of modernism, and a reduction of the latter's already tarnished aspirations to a *laissez-faire*, 'anything goes' market eclecticism? Does it, therefore, undermine or integrate with neo-conservative politics? And do we attach its rise to some radical restructuring of capitalism, the emergence of some 'postindustrial' society, view it, even, as the 'art of an inflationary era' or as the 'cultural logic of late capitalism' (as Newman and Jameson have proposed)? ...

I begin with what appears to be the most startling fact about postmodernism: its total acceptance of the ephemerality, fragmentation, discontinuity, and the chaotic that formed the one half of Baudelaire's conception of modernity. But postmodernism responds to the fact of that in a very particular way. It does not try to transcend it, counteract it, or even to define the 'eternal and immutable' elements that might lie within it. Postmodernism swims, even wallows, in the fragmentary and the chaotic currents of change as if that is all there is. Foucault (1984, pxiii) instructs us, for example, to 'develop action, thought, and desires by proliferation, juxtaposition, and disjunction,' and 'to prefer what is positive and multiple, difference over uniformity, flows over unities, mobile arrangements over systems. Believe that what is productive is not sedentary but nomadic.' To the degree that it does try to legitimate itself by reference to the past, therefore, postmodernism typically harks back to that wing of thought, Nietzsche in particular, that emphasizes the deep chaos of modern life and its intractability before rational thought. This does not imply, however, that postmodernism is simply a version of modernism; real revolutions in sensibility can occur when latent and dominated ideas in one period become explicit and dominant in another. Nevertheless, the continuity of the condition of fragmentation, ephemerality, discontinuity, and chaotic change in both modernist and postmodernist thought is important. I shall make much of it in what follows.

Embracing the fragmentation and ephemerality in an affirmative fashion implies a whole host of consequences ... . To begin with, we find writers like Foucault and Lyotard explicitly attacking any notion that there might be a meta-language, meta-narrative, or meta-theory through which all things can be connected or represented. Universal and eternal truths, if they exist at all, cannot be specified. Condemning meta-narratives (broad interpretative schemas like those deployed by Marx or Freud), as 'totalizing', they insist upon the plurality of 'power-discourse' formations (Foucault), or of 'language games' (Lyotard). Lyotard in fact defines the postmodern simply as 'incredulity towards meta-narratives.'

Foucault's ideas — particularly as developed in his early works — deserve attention since they have been a fecund source for post-modernist argument. The relation between power and knowledge is there a central theme. But Foucault (1972, p.159) breaks with the notion that power is ultimately located within the state, and abjures us to 'conduct an *ascending* analysis of power, starting, that is, from its infinitesimal mechanisms, which each have their own history, their own trajectory, their own techniques and tactics, and then see how these mechanisms of power have been — and continue to be — invested, colonized, utilized, involuted, transformed, displaced, extended, etc. by ever more general mechanisms and by forms of global domination.' Close scrutiny of the micro-politics of power relations in different localities, contexts, and social situations leads him to conclude that there is an intimate relation between the systems of knowledge ('discourses') which codify techniques and practices for the exercise of social control and domination within particular localized contexts. The prison, the asylum, the hospital, the university, the school, the psychiatrist's office, are all examples of sites where a dispersed and piecemeal organization of power is built up independently of any systematic strategy of class domination. What happens at each site cannot be understood by appeal to some overarching general theory. Indeed the only irreducible in Foucault's scheme of things is the human body, for that is the 'site' at which all forms of repression are ultimately registered. So while there are, in Foucault's celebrated dictum, 'no relations of power without resistances' he equally insists that no utopian scheme can ever hope to escape the power-knowledge relation in non-repressive ways. He here echoes Max Weber's pessimism as to our ability to avoid the 'iron cage' of repressive bureaucratic-technical rationality. More particularly, he interprets Soviet repression as the inevitable outcome of a utopian revolutionary theory (Marxism) which appealed to the same techniques and knowledge systems as those embedded in the capitalist system it sought to replace. The only way open to 'eliminate the fascism in our heads' is to explore and build upon the open qualities of human discourse, and thereby intervene in the way knowledge is produced and constituted at the particular sites where a localized power-discourse prevails. Foucault's work with homosexuals and prisoners was not aimed at producing reforms in state practices, but dedicated to the cultivation and enhancement of localized resistance to the institutions, techniques, and discourses of organized repression.

Foucault evidently believed that it was only through such a multi-faceted and pluralistic attack upon localized practices of repression that any global challenge to capitalism might be mounted without replicating all the multiple repressions of capitalism in a new form. His ideas appeal to the various social movements that sprang into existence during the 1960s (feminists, gays, ethnic and religious groupings, regional autonomists, etc.) as well as to those disillusioned with the practices of communism and the politics of communist parties. Yet it leaves open, particularly so in the deliberate rejection of any holistic theory of capitalism, the question of the path whereby such localized struggles might add up to a progressive, rather than regressive, attack upon the central forms of capitalist exploitation and repression. Localized struggles of the sort that Foucault appears to encourage have not generally had the effect of challenging capitalism, though Foucault might reasonably respond that only struggles fought in such a way as to challenge all forms of power-discourse might have such a result.

Lyotard, for his part, puts a similar argument, though on a rather different basis. He takes the modernist preoccupation with language and pushes it to extremes of dispersal. While 'the social bond is linguistic,' he argues, it 'is not woven with a single thread' but by an 'indeterminate number' of 'language games.' Each of us lives 'at the intersection of many of these' and we do not necessarily establish 'stable language combinations and the properties of the ones we do establish are not necessarily communicable.' As a consequence, 'the social subject itself seems to dissolve in this dissemination of language games.' Interestingly, Lyotard here employs a lengthy metaphor of Wittgenstein's (the pioneer of the theory of language games), to illuminate the condition of postmodern knowledge: 'Our language can be seen as an ancient city: a maze of little streets and squares, of old and new houses, and of houses with additions from different periods; and this surrounded by a multitude of new boroughs with straight regular streets and uniform houses.'

The 'atomization of the social into flexible networks of language games' suggests that each of us may resort to a quite different set of codes depending upon the situation in which we find ourselves (at home, at work, at church, in the street or pub, at a memorial service, etc.). To the degree that Lyotard (like Foucault) accepts that 'knowledge is the principal force of production' these days, so the problem is to define the locus of that power when it is evidently 'dispersed in clouds of narrative elements' within a heterogeneity of language games. Lyotard (again like Foucault) accepts the potential open qualities of ordinary conversations in which rules can bend and shift so as 'to encourage the greatest flexibility of utterance.' He makes much of the seeming contradiction between this openness and the rigidities with which institutions (Foucault's 'non-discursive domains') circumscribe what is or is not admissible within their boundaries. The realms of law, of the academy, of science and bureaucratic government, of military and political control, of electoral politics, and corporate power, all circumscribe what can be said and how it can be said in important ways. But the 'limits the institution imposes on potential language "moves" are never established once and for all.' They are 'themselves the stakes and provisional results of language strategies, within the institution and without.' We ought not, therefore, to reify institutions prematurely, but to recognize how the differentiated performance of language games creates institutional languages and powers in the first place. If 'there are many different language games — a heterogeneity of elements' we have then also to recognize that they can 'only give rise to institutions in patches — local determinism.'

Such 'local determinisms' have been understood by others (e.g. Fish, 1980) as 'interpretative communities,' made up of both producers and consumers of particular kinds of knowledge, of texts, often operating within a particular institutional context (such as the university, the legal system, religious groupings), within particular divisions of cultural labour (such as architecture, painting, theatre, dance), or within particular places (neighbourhoods, nations, etc.). Individuals and groups are held to control mutually within these domains what they consider to be valid knowledge.

To the degree that multiple sources of oppression in society and multiple foci of resistance to domination can be identified, so this kind of thinking has been taken up in radical politics, even imported into the heart of Marxism itself. We thus find Aronowitz arguing in *The Crisis of Historical Materialism* that 'the multiple, local, autonomous struggles for liberation occurring throughout the post-modern world make all incarnations of master discourses absolutely illegitimate' (Bove, 1986, p.18). Aronowitz is here seduced, I suspect, by the most liberative and therefore most appealing aspect of postmodern thought — its concern with 'otherness'. Huyssens (1984) particularly castigates the imperialism of an enlightened modernity that presumed to speak for others (colonized peoples, blacks and minorities, religious groups, women, the working class) with a unified voice. The very title of Carol Gilligan's *In a Different Voice* (1982) — a feminist work which challenges the male bias in setting out fixed stages in the moral development of personality — illustrates a process of counter-attack upon such universalizing presumptions. The idea that all groups have a right to speak for themselves, in their own voice, and have that voice accepted as authentic and legitimate is essential to the pluralistic stance of postmodernism. Foucault's work with marginal and interstitial groups has influenced a whole host of researchers, in fields as diverse as criminology and anthropology, into new ways to reconstruct and represent the voices and experiences of their subjects. Huyssens, for his part, emphasizes the opening given in postmodernism to understanding difference and otherness, as well as the liberatory potential it offers for a whole host of new social movements (women, gays, blacks, ecologists, regional autonomists, etc.). Curiously, most movements of this sort, though they have definitely helped change 'the structure of feeling', pay scant attention to postmodernist arguments, and some feminists (e.g. Hartsock, 1987) are hostile for reasons that we will later consider.

Interestingly, we can detect this same preoccupation with 'otherness' and 'other worlds' in postmodernist fiction. McHale, in emphasizing the pluralism of the worlds that coexist within postmodernist fiction, finds Foucault's concept of a *heterotopia* a perfectly appropriate image to capture what that fiction is striving to depict. By heterotopia, Foucault means the coexistence in 'an impossible space' of a 'large number of fragmentary possible worlds' or, more simply, incommensurable spaces that are juxtaposed or superimposed upon each other. Characters no longer contemplate how they can unravel or unmask a central mystery, but are forced to ask, 'Which world is this? What is to be done in it? Which of myselves is to do it?' instead. The same shift can be detected in cinema. In a modernist classic like *Citizen Kane* a reporter seeks to unravel the mystery of Kane's life and character by collecting multiple reminiscences and perspectives from those who had known him. In the more postmodernist format of the contemporary cinema we find, in a film like *Blue Velvet*, the central character revolving between two quite incongruous worlds — that of a conventional 1950s small-town America with its high school, drugstore culture, and a bizarre, violent, sex-crazed underworld of drugs, dementia, and sexual perversion. It seems impossible that these two worlds should exist in the same space, and the central character moves between them, unsure which is the true reality, until the two worlds collide in a terrible denouement. A postmodernist painter like David Salle likewise tends to 'collage together incompatible source materials as an alternative to choosing between them' (Taylor, 1987). Pfeil (1988) even goes so far as to depict the total field of postmodernism as 'a distilled representation of the whole antagonistic, voracious world of otherness'.

But to accept the fragmentation, the pluralism, and the authenticity of other voices and other worlds poses the acute problem of communication and the means of exercising power through command thereof. Most postmodernist thinkers are fascinated by the new possibilities for information and knowledge production, analysis, and transfer. Lyotard (1984), for example, firmly locates his arguments in the context of new technologies of communication and, drawing upon Bell's and Touraine's theses of the passage to a 'postindustrial' information-based society, situates the rise of postmodern thought in the heart of what he sees as a dramatic social and political transition in the languages of communication in advanced capitalist societies. He looks closely at the new technologies for the production, dissemination and use of that knowledge as a 'principal force of production'. The problem, however, is that knowledge can now be coded in all kinds of ways, some of which are more accessible than others. There is more than a hint in Lyotard's work, therefore, that modernism has changed because the technical and social conditions of communication have changed.

Postmodernists tend to accept, also, a rather different theory as to what language and communication are all about. Whereas modernists had presupposed that there was a tight and identifiable relation between what was being said (the signified or 'message') and how it was being said (the signifier or 'medium'), poststructuralist thinking sees these as 'continually breaking apart and re-attaching in new combinations'. 'Deconstructionism' (a movement initiated by Derrida's reading of Martin Heidegger in the late 1960s) here enters the picture as a powerful stimulus to post-modernist ways of thought. Deconstructionism is less a philosophical position than a way of thinking about and 'reading' texts. Writers who create texts or use words do so on the basis of all the other texts and words they have encountered, while readers deal with them in the same way. Cultural life is then viewed as a series of texts intersecting with other texts, producing more texts (including that of the literary critic, who aims to produce another piece of literature in which texts under consideration are intersecting freely with other texts that happen to have affected his or her thinking). This intertextual weaving has a life of its own. Whatever we write conveys meanings we do not or could not possibly intend, and our words cannot say what we mean. It is vain to try and master a text because the perpetual interweaving of texts and meaning is beyond our control. Language works through us. Recognizing that, the deconstructionist impulse is to look inside one text for another, dissolve one text into another, or build one text into another.

Derrida considers, therefore, collage/montage as the primary form of post-modern discourse. The inherent heterogeneity of that (be it in painting, writing, architecture) stimulates us, the receivers of the text or image, 'to produce a signification which could be neither univocal nor stable'. Both producers and consumers of 'text' (cultural artefacts) participate in the production of significations and meanings (hence Hassan's emphasis upon 'process', 'performance', 'happening', and 'participation' in the post-modernist style). Minimizing the authority of the cultural producer creates the opportunity for popular participation and democratic determinations of cultural values, but at the price of a certain incoherence or, more problematic, vulnerability to mass-market manipulation. However this may be, the cultural producer merely creates raw materials (fragments and elements), leaving it open to consumers to recombine those elements in any way they wish. ...

There is more than a hint of this sort of thinking within the modernist tradition (directly from surrealism, for example) and there is a danger here of thinking of the meta-narratives in the Enlightenment tradition as more fixed and stable than they truly were. Marx, as Ollman (1971) observes, deployed his concepts relationally, so that terms like value, labour, capital, are 'continually breaking apart and re-attaching in new combinations' in an open-ended struggle to come to terms with the totalizing processes of capitalism. Benjamin, a complex thinker in the Marxist tradition, worked the idea of collage/montage to perfection, in order to try and capture the many layered and fragmented relations between economy, politics, and culture without ever abandoning the standpoint of a totality of practices that constitute capitalism. Taylor (1987, pp.53–65) likewise concludes, after reviewing the historical evidence of its use (particularly by Picasso), that collage is a far from adequate indicator of difference between modernist and postmodernist painting.

But if, as the postmodernists insist, we cannot aspire to any unified representation of the world, or picture it as a totality full of connections and differentiations rather than as perpetually shifting fragments, then how can we possibly aspire to act coherently with respect to the world? The simple postmodernist answer is that since coherent representation and action are either repressive or illusionary (and therefore doomed to be self-dissolving and self-defeating), we should not even try to engage in some global project. Pragmatism (of the Dewey sort) then becomes the only possible philosophy of action. We thus find Rorty (1985, p.173), one of the major US philosophers in the postmodern movement, dismissing 'the canonical sequence of philosophers from Descartes to Nietzsche as a distraction from the history of concrete social engineering which made the contemporary North American culture what it is now, with all its glories and all its dangers'. Action can be conceived of and decided only within the confines of some local determinism, some interpretative community, and its purported meanings and anticipated effects are bound to break down when taken out of these isolated domains, even when coherent within them. We similarly find Lyotard (1984, p.66) arguing that 'consensus has become an outmoded and suspect value' but then adding, rather surprisingly, that since 'justice as a value is neither outmoded nor suspect', (how it could remain such a universal, untouched by the diversity of language games, he does not tell us), we 'must arrive at an idea and practice of justice that is not linked to that of consensus'.

It is precisely this kind of relativism and defeatism that Habermas seeks to combat in his defence of the Enlightenment project. While Habermas is more than willing to admit what he calls 'the deformed realization of reason in history' and the dangers that attach to the simplified imposition of some meta-narrative on complex relations and events, he also insists that 'theory can locate a gentle, but obstinate, a never silent although seldom redeemed claim to reason, a claim that must be recognized de facto whenever and wherever there is to be consensual action'. He, too, turns to the question of language and in *The Theory of Communicative Action* insists upon the dialogical qualities of human communication in which speaker and hearer are necessarily oriented to the task of reciprocal understanding. Out of this, Habermas argues, consensual and normative statements do arise, thus grounding the role of universalizing reason in daily life. It is this that allows 'communicative reason' to operate 'in history as an avenging force'. Habermas's critics are, however, more numerous than his defenders.

The portrait of postmodernism I have so far sketched in seems to depend for its validity upon a particular way of experiencing, interpreting, and being in the world. This brings us to what is, perhaps, the most problematic facet of postmodernism, its psychological presuppositions with respect to personality, motivation, and behaviour. Preoccupation with the fragmentation and instability of language and discourses carries over directly, for example, into a certain conception of personality. Encapsulated, this conception focuses on schizophrenia (not, it should be emphasized, in its narrow clinical sense), rather than on alienation and paranoia. ... Jameson (1984b) explores this theme to very telling effect. He uses Lacan's description of schizophrenia as a linguistic disorder, as a breakdown in the signifying chain of meaning that creates a simple sentence. When the signifying chain snaps, then 'we have schizophrenia in the form of a rubble of distinct and unrelated signifiers'. If personal identity is forged through 'a certain temporal unification of the past and future with the present before me', and if sentences move through the same trajectory, then an inability to unify past, present, and future in the sentence betokens a similar inability to 'unify the past, present and future of our own biographical experience or psychic life'. ...

A number of consequences follow from the domination of this motif in postmodernist thought. We can no longer conceive of the individual as alienated in the classical Marxist sense, because to be alienated presupposes a coherent rather than a fragmented sense of self from which to be alienated. It is only in terms of such a centred sense of personal identity that individuals can pursue projects over time, or think cogently about the production of a future significantly better than time present and time past. Modernism was very much about the pursuit of better futures, even if perpetual frustration of that aim was conducive to paranoia. But postmodernism typically strips away that possibility by concentrating upon the schizophrenic circumstances induced by fragmentation and all those instabilities (including those of language) that prevent us even picturing coherently, let alone devising strategies to produce, some radically different future. Modernism, of course, was not without its schizoid moments — particularly when it sought to combine myth with heroic modernity — and there has been a sufficient history of the 'deformation of reason' and of 'reactionary modernisms' to suggest that the schizophrenic circumstance, though for the most part dominated, was always latent within the modernist movement. Nevertheless, there is good reason to believe that 'alienation of the subject is displaced by fragmentation of the subject' in postmodern aesthetics (Jameson, 1984a, p.63). If, as Marx insisted, it takes the alienated individual to pursue the Enlightenment project with a tenacity and coherence sufficient to bring us to some better future, then loss of the alienated subject would seen to preclude the conscious construction of alternative social futures.

The reduction of experience to 'a series of pure and related presents' further implies that the 'experience of the present becomes powerfully, overwhelmingly vivid and "material": the world comes before the schizophrenic with heightened intensity, bearing the mysterious and oppressive charge of affect, glowing with hallucinatory energy' (Jameson, 1984b, p.120). The image, the appearance, the spectacle can all be experienced with an intensity (joy or terror) made possible only by their appreciation as pure and unrelated presents in time. So what does it matter 'if the world thereby momentarily loses its depth and threatens to become a glossy skin, a stereoscopic illusion, a rush of filmic images without density?' (Jameson, 1984b). The immediacy of events, the sensationalism of the spectacle (political, scientific, military, as well as those of entertainment), become the stuff of which consciousness is forged.

Such a breakdown of the temporal order of things also gives rise to a peculiar treatment of the past. Eschewing the idea of progress, postmodernism abandons all sense of historical continuity and memory, while simultaneously developing an incredible ability to plunder history and absorb whatever it finds there as some aspect of the present. Postmodernist architecture, for example, takes bits and pieces from the past quite eclectically and mixes them together at will. ...

The collapse of time horizons and the preoccupation with instantaneity have in part arisen through the contemporary emphasis in cultural production on events, spectacles, happenings, and media images. Cultural producers have learned to explore and use new technologies, the media, and ultimately multi-media possibilities. The effect, however, has been to re-emphasize the fleeting qualities of modern life and even to celebrate them. But it has also permitted a *rapprochement,* in spite of Barthes's interventions, between popular culture and what once remained isolated as 'high culture'. Such a *rapprochement* has been sought before, though nearly always in a more revolutionary mode, as movements like Dada and early surrealism, constructivism, and expressionism tried to bring their art to the people as part and parcel of the modernist project of social transformation. Such avant-gardist movements possessed a strong faith in their own aims as well as immense faith in new technologies. The closing of the gap between popular culture and cultural production in the contemporary period, while strongly dependent on new technologies of communication, seems to lack any avant-gardist or revolutionary impulse, leading many to accuse postmodernism of simple and direct surrender to commodification, commercialization, and the market (Foster, 1985). However this may be, much of postmodernism is consciously anti-auratic and anti-avant-garde and seeks to explore media and cultural arenas open to all. It is no accident that Sherman, for example, uses photography and evokes pop images as if from film stills in the poses she assumes.

This raises the most difficult of all questions about the postmodern movement, namely its relationship with, and integration into, the culture of daily life. Although much of the discussion of it proceeds in the abstract, and therefore in the not very accessible terms that I have been forced to use here, there are innumerable points of contact between producers of cultural artefacts and the general public: architecture, advertising, fashion, films, staging of multi-media events, grand spectacles, political campaigns, as well as the ubiquitous television. It is not always clear who is influencing whom in this process.

Venturi et al (1972, p.155) recommend that we learn our architectural aesthetics from the Las Vegas strip or from much-maligned suburbs like

Levittown, simply because people evidently like such environments. 'One does not have to agree with hard hat politics', they go on to say, 'to support the rights of the middle-middle class to their own architectural aesthetics, and we have found that Levittown-type aesthetics are shared by most members of the middle-middle class, black as well as white, liberal as well as conservative'. There is absolutely nothing wrong, they insist, with giving people what they want, and Venturi himself was even quoted in the *New York Times* (22 October 1972), in an article fittingly entitled 'Mickey Mouse teaches the architects', saying 'Disney World is nearer to what people want than what architects have ever given them'. Disneyland, he asserts, is 'the symbolic American utopia'.

There are those, however, who see such a concession of high culture to Disneyland aesthetics as a matter of necessity rather than choice. Daniel Bell (1978, p.20), for example, depicts postmodernism as the exhaustion of modernism through the institutionalization of creative and rebellious impulses by what he calls 'the cultural mass' (the millions of people working in broadcast media, films, theatre, universities, publishing houses, advertising and communications industries, etc. who process and influence the reception of serious cultural products and produce the popular materials for the wider mass-culture audience). The degeneration of high-brow authority over cultural taste in the 1960s, and its replacement by pop art, pop culture, ephemeral fashion, and mass taste is seen as a sign of the mindless hedonism of capitalist consumerism.

Iain Chambers (1986; 1987) interprets a similar process rather differently. Working-class youth in Britain found enough money in their pockets during the postwar boom to participate in the capitalist consumer culture, and actively used fashion to construct a sense of their own public identities, even defined their own pop-art forms, in the face of a fashion industry that sought to impose taste through advertising and media pressures. The consequent democratization of taste across a variety of sub-cultures (from inner-city macho male to college campuses) is interpreted as the outcome of a vital struggle that pitched the rights of even the relatively under-privileged to shape their own identities in the face of a powerfully organized commercialism. The urban-based cultural ferments that began in the early 1960s and continue to this very day lie, in Chambers's view, at the root of the postmodern turn:

> Post-modernism, whatever form its intellectualizing might take, has been fundamentally anticipated in the metropolitan cultures of the last twenty years: among the electronic signifiers of cinema, television and video, in recording studios and record players, in fashion and youth styles, in all those sounds, images and diverse histories that are daily mixed, recycled and 'scratched' together on that giant screen which is the contemporary city.

It is hard, also, not to attribute some kind of shaping role to the proliferation of television use. After all, the average American is now reputed to watch television for more than seven hours a day, and television and video ownership (the latter now covering at least half of all US households) is now so widespread throughout the capitalist world that some effects must surely be registered. Postmodernist concerns with surface, for example, can be traced to the necessary format of television images. Television is also, as Taylor (1987, pp.103–5) points out, 'the first cultural medium in the whole of history to present the artistic achievements of the past as a stitched-together collage of equi-important and simultaneously existing phenomena, largely divorced from geography and material history and transported to the living rooms and studios of the West in a more or less uninterrupted flow'. It posits a viewer, furthermore, 'who shares the medium's own perception of history as an endless reserve of equal events'. It is hardly surprising that the artist's relation to history (the peculiar historicism we have already noted) has shifted, that in the era of mass television there has emerged an attachment to surfaces rather than roots, to collage rather than in-depth work, to superimposed quoted images rather than worked surfaces, to a collapsed sense of time and space rather than solidly achieved cultural artefact. And these are all vital aspects of artistic practice in the post-modern condition.

To point to the potency of such a force in shaping culture as a total way of life it is not necessary to lapse, however, into a simple-minded technological determinism of the 'television causes postmodernism' variety. For television is itself a product of late capitalism and, as such, has to be seen in the context of the promotion of a culture of consumerism. This directs our attention to the production of needs and wants, the mobilization of desire and fantasy, of the politics of distraction as part and parcel of the push to sustain sufficient buoyancy of demand in consumer markets to keep capitalist production profitable. Charles Newman (1984, p.9) sees much of the postmodernist aesthetic as a response to the inflationary surge of late capitalism. 'Inflation', he argues, 'affects the ideas exchange just as surely as it does commercial markets'. Thus 'we are witness to continual internecine warfare and spasmodic changes in fashion, the simultaneous display of all past styles in their infinite mutations, and the continuous circulation of diverse and contradictory intellectual elites, which signal the reign of the cult of creativity in all areas of behaviour, an unprecedented non-judgemental receptivity to Art, a tolerance which finally amounts to indifference'. From this standpoint, Newman concludes, 'the vaunted fragmentation of art is no longer an aesthetic choice: it is simply a cultural aspect of the economic and social fabric'.

This would certainly go some way to explain the postmodernist thrust to integrate into popular culture through the kind of frank, even crass, commercialization that modernists tended to eschew by their deep resistance to the idea (though never quite the fact) of commodification of their production. There are those however, who attribute the exhaustion of high modernism precisely to its absorption as the formal aesthetics of corporate capitalism and the bureaucratic state. Postmodernism then signals nothing more than a logical extension of the power of the market over the whole range of cultural production. Crimp (1987, p.85) waxes quite acerbic on this point:

What we have seen in the last several years is the virtual takeover of art by big corporate interests. For whatever role capital played in the art of modernism, the current phenomenon is new precisely because of its scope. Corporations have become the major patrons of art in every respect. They form huge collections. They fund every major museum exhibition. ... Auction houses have become lending institutions, giving a completely new value to art as collateral. And all of this affects not only the inflation of value of old masters but art production itself. ... [The corporations] are buying cheap and in quantity, counting on the escalation of the value of young artists. ... The return to painting and sculpture of a traditional cast is the return to commodity production, and I would suggest that, whereas traditionally art had an ambiguous commodity status, it now has a thoroughly unambiguous one.

The growth of a museum culture (in Britain a museum opens every three weeks, and in Japan over 500 have opened up in the last fifteen years) and a burgeoning 'heritage industry' that took off in the early 1970s, add another populist (though this time very middle-class) twist to the commercialization of history and cultural forms. 'Post-modernism and the heritage industry are linked', says Hewison (1987, p.135), since 'both conspire to create a shallow screen that intervenes between our present lives and our history'. History becomes a 'contemporary creation, more costume drama and re-enactment than critical discourse'. We are, he concludes, quoting Jameson, 'condemned to seek History by way of our own pop images and simulacra of that history which itself remains for ever out of reach'. The house is viewed no longer as a machine but as 'an antique for living in'.

The invocation of Jameson brings us, finally, to his daring thesis that postmodernism is nothing more than the cultural logic of late capitalism. Following Mandel (1975), he argues that we have moved into a new era since the early 1960s in which the production of culture 'has become integrated into commodity production generally: the frantic urgency of producing fresh waves of ever more novel seeming goods (from clothes to airplanes), at ever greater rates of turnover, now assigns an increasingly essential structural function to aesthetic innovation and experimentation'. The struggles that were once exclusively waged in the arena of production have, as a consequence, now spilled outwards to make of cultural production an arena of fierce social conflict. Such a shift entails a definite change in consumer habits and attitudes as well as a new role for aesthetic definitions and interventions. While some would argue that the counter-cultural movements of the 1960s created an environment of unfulfilled needs and repressed desires that postmodernist popular cultural production has merely set out to satisfy as best it can in commodity form, others would suggest that capitalism, in order to sustain its markets, has been forced to produce desire and so titillate individual sensibilities as to create a new aesthetical over and against traditional forms of high culture. In either case, I think it important to accept the proposition that the cultural evolution which has taken place since the early 1960s, and which asserted itself as hegemonic in the early 1970s, has not occurred in a social, economic or political vacuum. The deployment of advertising as 'the official art of capitalism' brings advertising strategies into art, and art into advertising strategies ... It is interesting, therefore, to ruminate upon the stylistic shift that Hassan (1985) sets up in relation to the forces that emanate from mass-consumer culture: the mobilization of fashion, pop art, television and other forms of media image, and the variety of urban life styles that have become part and parcel of daily life under capitalism. Whatever else we do with the concept, we should not read postmodernism as some autonomous artistic current. Its rootedness in daily life is one of its most patently transparent features. ...

References

Aronowitz, S. (1981) *The Crisis of Historical Materialism*, New York.

Baltimore Sun, 9 September 1987.

Bell, D. (1978) *The Cultural Contradictions of Capitalism*, New York.

Bernstein, R. J. (ed.) (1985) *Habermas and Modernity*, Cambridge, Polity Press.

Bove, P. (1986) 'The ineluctability of difference: scientific pluralism and the critical intelligence' in Arac, J. (ed) *Postmodernism and Politics*, Manchester.

Chambers, I. (1986) *Popular Culture: The Metropolitan Experience*, London.

Chambers, I. (1987) 'Maps for the metropolis: a possible guide to the present', *Cultural Studies*, 1, pp.1–22.

Crimp, D. (1987) 'Art in the 80s: the myth of autonomy', *PRECIS* 6, p.83–91.

Fish, S. (1980) *Is There a Text in This Class? The Authority of Interpretive Communities*, Cambridge, Mass.

Foster, H. (1985) *Recodings: Art, Spectacle, Cultural Politics*, Port Townsend, Washington.

Foucault, M. (1972) *Power/Knowledge*, New York.

Foucault, M. (1984) *The Foucault Reader* (ed. P. Rabinow), Harmondsworth.

Gilligan, C. (1982) *In a Different Voice: Psychological Theory and Women's Development*, Cambridge, Mass.

Habermas, J. (1985/8) *The Theory of Communicative Action*: vol. 1, London, Heinemann/Blackwell and vol.2, Cambridge, Polity Press.

Hartsock, N. (1987) 'Rethinking modernism: minority versus majority theories,' *Cultural Critique*, 7, pp.187–206.

Hassan, I. (1985) 'The culture of postmodernism', *Theory, Culture and Society*, 2 (3), pp.119–32.

Hewison, R. (1987) *The Heritage Industry*, London.

Huyssens, A. (1984) 'Mapping the post-modern,' *New German Critique*, 33, pp.5–52.

Jameson, F. (1984a) 'The politics of theory: ideological positions in the post-modernism debate,' *New German Critique,* 33, pp.53–65.

Jameson, F. (1984b) 'Postmodernism, or the cultural logic of late capitalism,' *New Left Review*, 146, pp.53–92.

Jencks, C. (1984) *The Language of Post-modern Architecture*, London.

Kroker, A. and Cook, D. (1986) *The Postmodern Scene: Excremental Culture and Hyper-aesthetics*, New York.

Lee, D. (1973) 'Requiem for large-scale planning models,' *Journal of the American Institute of Planners*, 39, pp.117–42.

Lyotard, J. (1984) *The Postmodern Condition: A Report on Knowledge*, Manchester, Manchester University Press.

Mandel, E. (1975) *Late Capitalism*, London.

McHale, B. (1987) *Postmodernist Fiction*, London.

Los Angeles Times, 29 February 1992

New York Times, 13 June 1976.

New York Times, 22 October 1972.

Newman, C. (1984) 'The postmodern aura: the act of fiction in an age of inflation,' *Salmagundi,* 63, 4, pp.3–199.

Ollman, B. (1971) *Alienation*, Cambridge.

Pfeil, F. (1988) 'Postmodernism as a "structure of feeling"', in Nelson, C. and Grossberg, L. (eds) *Marxism and the Interpretation of Culture,* Urbana, Illinois.

PRECIS 6 (1987) *The culture of fragments*, Columbia University Graduate School of Architecture, New York.

Rorty, R. (1985) 'Habermas and Lyotard on postmodernity', in Bernstein, R. (ed.) *Habermas and Modernity,* Oxford.

Taylor, B. (1987) *Modernism, Post-modernism, Realism: A Critical Perspective for Art*, Winchester.

Venturi, R., Scott Brown, D., and Izenour, S. (1972) *Learning from Las Vegas,* Cambridge, Mass.

CHAPTER 6 THE QUESTION OF CULTURAL IDENTITY

Stuart Hall

CONTENTS

1   INTRODUCTION: IDENTITY IN QUESTION

The question of 'identity' is being vigorously debated in social theory. In essence, the argument is that the old identities which stabilized the social world for so long are in decline, giving rise to new identities and fragmenting the modern individual as a unified subject. This so-called 'crisis of identity' is seen as part of a wider process of change which is dislocating the central structures and processes of modern societies and undermining the frameworks which gave individuals stable anchorage in the social world.

The aim of this chapter is to explore some of these questions about cultural identity in late-modernity and to assess whether a 'crisis of identities' exists, what it consists of, and in which directions it is moving. The chapter addresses such questions as: What do we mean by a 'crisis of identity'? What recent developments in modern societies have precipitated it? What form does it take? What are its potential consequences? The first part of this chapter (Sections 1–2) deals with shifts in the concepts of identity and the subject. The second part (Sections 3–6) develops this argument with respect to *cultural identities* — those aspects of our identities which arise from our 'belonging' to distinctive ethnic, racial, linguistic, religious and, above all, national cultures.

Several of the chapters in this volume approach their central concern from a number of different positions, framing it within a debate, as if between different protagonists. This chapter works somewhat differently. It is written from a position basically sympathetic to the claim that modern identities are being 'de-centred'; that is, dislocated or fragmented. Its aim is to explore this claim, to see what it entails, to qualify it, and to discuss what may be its likely consequences. In the course of the argument, this chapter modifies the claim by introducing certain complexities and examining some contradictory features which the 'de-centring' claim, in its simpler forms, neglects.

Accordingly, the formulations in this chapter are provisional and open to contestation. Opinion within the sociological fraternity is still deeply divided about these issues. The trends are too recent and too ambiguous, and the very concept we are dealing with — identity — too complex, too underdeveloped, and too little understood in contemporary social science to be definitively tested. As with many of the other phenomena examined in this volume, it is impossible to offer conclusive statements or to make secure judgements about the theoretical claims and propositions being advanced. You should bear this in mind as you read the rest of the chapter.

For those theorists who believe that modern identities are breaking up, the argument runs something like this. A distinctive type of structural change is transforming modern societies in the late twentieth century.

This is fragmenting the cultural landscapes of class, gender, ethnicity, race, and nationality which gave us firm locations individuals. These transformations are also shifting our per identities, undermining our sense of ourselves as integrated subjects. This loss of a stable 'sense of self' is sometimes called the dislocation or de-centring of the subject. This set of double displacements — de-centring individuals both from their place in the social and cultural world, and from themselves — constitutes a 'crisis of identity' for the individual. As the cultural critic, Kobena Mercer, observes, 'identity only becomes an issue when it is in crisis, when something assumed to be fixed, coherent and stable is displaced by the experience of doubt and uncertainty' (Mercer, 1990, p.43).

Many of these processes of change have been discussed at length in earlier chapters. Taken together, they represent a process of transformation so fundamental and wide-ranging that we are bound to ask if it is not modernity itself which is being transformed. This chapter adds a new dimension to the argument: the claim that, in what is sometimes described as our post-modern world, we are also 'post' any fixed or essentialist conception of identity — something which, since the Enlightenment, has been taken to define the very core or essence of our being, and to ground our existence as human subjects. In order to explore this claim, I shall look first at definitions of identity and at the character of change in late-modernity.

1.1   THREE CONCEPTS OF IDENTITY

For the purposes of exposition, I shall distinguish three very different conceptions of identity: those of the (a) Enlightenment subject (b) sociological subject, and (c) post-modern subject. The Enlightenment subject was based on a conception of the human person as a fully centred, unified individual, endowed with the capacities of reason, consciousness and action, whose 'centre' consisted of an inner core which first emerged when the subject was born, and unfolded with it, while remaining essentially the same — continuous or 'identical' with itself — throughout the individual's existence. The essential centre of the self was a person's identity. I shall say more about this in a moment, but you can see that this was a very 'individualist' conception of the subject and 'his' (for Enlightenment subjects were usually described as male) identity.

The notion of the sociological subject reflected the growing complexity of the modern world and the awareness that this inner core of the subject was not autonomous and self-sufficient, but was formed in relation to 'significant others', who mediated to the subject the values, meanings and symbols — the culture — of the worlds he/she inhabited. G.H. Mead, C.H. Cooley, and the symbolic interactionists are the key figures in sociology who elaborated this 'interactive' conception of identity and the self (see *Penguin Dictionary of Sociology:* MEAD,

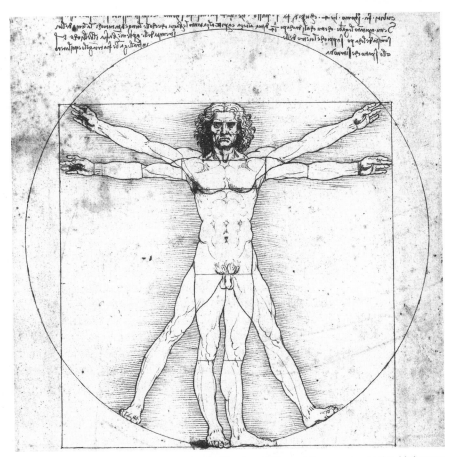

Renaissance thinkers, like Leonardo da Vinci, put Man at the centre of the Universe

GEORGE H.; SYMBOLIC INTERACTIONISM). According to this view, which has become the classic sociological conception of the issue, identity is formed in the 'interaction' between self and society. The subject still has an inner core or essence that is 'the real me', but this is formed and modified in a continuous dialogue with the cultural worlds 'outside' and the identities which they offer.

Identity, in this sociological conception, bridges the gap between the 'inside' and the 'outside' — between the personal and the public worlds. The fact that we project 'ourselves' into these cultural identities, at the same time internalizing their meanings and values, making them 'part of us', helps to align our subjective feelings with the objective places we occupy in the social and cultural world. Identity thus stitches (or, to use a current medical metaphor, 'sutures') the subject into the structure. It stabilizes both subjects and the cultural worlds they inhabit, making both reciprocally more unified and predictable.

Yet these are exactly what are now said to be 'shifting'. The subject, previously experienced as having a unified and stable identity, is becoming fragmented; composed, not of a single, but of several, sometimes contradictory or unresolved, identities. Correspondingly, the identities which composed the social landscapes 'out there', and which ensured our subjective conformity with the objective 'needs' of the culture, are breaking up as a result of structural and institutional change. The very process of identification, through which we project ourselves into our cultural identities, has become more open-ended, variable and problematic.

This produces the post-modern subject, conceptualized as having no fixed, essential or permanent identity. Identity becomes a 'moveable feast': formed and transformed continuously in relation to the ways we are represented or addressed in the cultural systems which surround us (Hall, 1987). It is historically, not biologically, defined. The subject assumes different identities at different times, identities which are not unified around a coherent 'self'. Within us are contradictory identities, pulling in different directions, so that our identifications are continuously being shifted about. If we feel we have a unified identity from birth to death, it is only because we construct a comforting story or 'narrative of the self' about ourselves (see Hall, 1990). The fully unified, completed, secure and coherent identity is a fantasy. Instead, as the systems of meaning and cultural representation multiply, we are confronted by a bewildering, fleeting multiplicity of possible identities, any one of which we could identify with — at least temporarily.

You should bear in mind that the above three conceptions of the subject are, to some extent, simplifications. As the argument develops, they will become more complex and qualified. Nevertheless, they are worth holding on to as crude pegs around which to develop the argument of this chapter.

1.2   THE CHARACTER OF CHANGE IN LATE-MODERNITY

A further aspect of the issue of identity relates to the character of change in late-modernity; in particular, to that process of change known as 'globalization' (discussed in earlier chapters, especially Chapter 2), and its impact on cultural identity.

In essence, the argument here is that change in late-modernity has a very specific character. As Marx said about modernity, '[it is a] constant revolutionizing of production, uninterrupted disturbance of all social relations, everlasting uncertainty and agitation. ... All fixed, fast-frozen relationships, with their train of venerable ideas and opinions, are swept away, all new-formed ones become obsolete before they can ossify. All that is solid melts into air. ... ' (Marx and Engels, 1973, p.70).

Modern societies are therefore by definition societies of constant, rapid and permanent change. This is the principal distinction between 'traditional' and 'modern' societies. Anthony Giddens argues that, 'In traditional societies, the past is honoured and symbols are valued because they contain and perpetuate the experience of generations.

Tradition is a means of handling time and space, which inserts any particular activity or experience within the continuity of past, present and future, these in turn being structured by recurrent social practices' (Giddens, 1990, pp.37–8). Modernity, by contrast, is not only defined as the experience of living with rapid, extensive and continuous change, but is a highly reflexive form of life in which 'social practices are constantly examined and reformed in the light of incoming information about those very practices, thus constitutively altering their character' (ibid., pp.37–8).

Giddens cites in particular the *pace of change* and the *scope of change* — 'as different areas of the globe are drawn into interconnection with one another, waves of social transformation crash across virtually the whole of the earth's surface' — and the *nature of modern institutions* (Giddens, 1990, p.6). The latter are either radically new as compared with traditional societies (e.g. the nation-state or the commodification of products and wage labour), or have a specious continuity with earlier forms (e.g. the city) but are organized on quite different principles. More significant are the transformations of time and space, and what he calls the 'disembedding of the social system' — 'the "lifting out" of social relations from local contexts of interaction and their restructuring across indefinite spans of time–space' (ibid., p.21). We will take up all these themes later. However, the general point we would stress is that of *discontinuities*.

> The modes of life brought into being by modernity have swept us away from all traditional types of social order in quite unprecedented fashion. In both their extensionality ['external aspects'] and their intensionality ['internal aspects'] the transformations involved in modernity are more profound than most sorts of change characteristic of prior periods. On the extensional plane they have served to establish forms of social interconnection which span the globe; in intensional terms they have come to alter some of the most intimate and personal features of our day-to-day existence.
> (Giddens, 1990, p.21)

David Harvey speaks of modernity as not only entailing 'a ruthless break with any or all preceding conditions', but as 'characterized by a never-ending process of internal ruptures and fragmentations within itself' (1989, p.12). Ernesto Laclau (1990) uses the concept of 'dislocation'. A dislocated structure is one whose centre is displaced and not replaced by another, but by 'a plurality of power centres'. Modern societies, Laclau argues, have no centre, no single articulating or organizing principle, and do not develop according to the unfolding of a single 'cause' or 'law'. Society is not, as sociologists often thought, a unified and well-bounded whole, a totality, producing itself through evolutionary change from within itself, like the unfolding of a daffodil from its bulb. It is constantly being 'de-centred' or dislocated by forces outside itself.

Late-modern societies, he argues, are characterized by 'difference'; they are cut through by different social divisions and social antagonisms which produce a variety of different 'subject positions' — i.e. identities — for individuals. If such societies hold together at all, it is not because they are unified, but because their different elements and identities can, under certain circumstances, be articulated together. But this articulation is always partial: the structure of identity remains open. Without this, Laclau argues, there would be no history.

This is a very different, and far more troubled and provisional, conception of identity than the earlier two (see Section 1.1). We should add that, far from being dismayed by all this, Laclau argues that dislocation has positive features. It unhinges the stable identities of the past, but it also opens up the possibility of new articulations — the forging of new identities, the production of new subjects, and what he calls the 'recomposition of the structure around particular nodal points of articulation' (Laclau, 1990, p.40).

Giddens, Harvey and Laclau offer somewhat different readings of the nature of change in the post-modern world, but their emphasis on discontinuity, fragmentation, rupture and dislocation contains a common thread. You should bear this in mind when we come to consider what some theorists claim to be the impact of the contemporary change that is known as 'globalization'.

1.3 WHAT IS AT STAKE IN THE QUESTION OF IDENTITIES?

So far the arguments may seem rather abstract. To give you some sense of how they apply to a concrete situation, and what is 'at stake' in these contested definitions of identity and change, let us take an example which highlights the *political* consequences of the fragmentation or 'pluralization' of identities.

In 1991, President Bush, anxious to restore a conservative majority to the US Supreme Court, nominated Clarence Thomas, a black judge of conservative political views. In Bush's judgement, white voters (who may have been prejudiced about a black judge) were likely to support Thomas because he was conservative on equal-rights legislation, and black voters (who support liberal policies on race) would support Thomas because he was black. In short, the President was 'playing the identities game'.

During the Senate 'hearings' on the appointment, Judge Thomas was accused of sexual harassment by a black woman, Anita Hill, a former junior colleague of Thomas's. The hearings caused a public scandal and polarized American society. Some blacks supported Thomas on racial grounds; others opposed him on sexual grounds. Black women were divided, depending on whether their 'identities' as blacks or as women prevailed. Black men were also divided, depending on whether their sexism overrode their liberalism. White men were divided, depending, not only on their politics, but on how they identified themselves with respect to racism and sexism. White conservative women supported Thomas, not only on political grounds, but because of their opposition to feminism. White feminists, often liberal on race, opposed Thomas on sexual grounds. And because Judge Thomas is a member of the judicial élite and Anita Hall, at the time of the alleged incident, a junior employee, there were issues of social class position at work in these arguments too.

The question of Judge Thomas's guilt or innocence is not at issue here; what is, is the 'play of identities' and its political consequences. Consider:

- The identities were contradictory. They cross-cut or 'dislocated' each other.

- The contradictions operated both 'outside', in society, cutting across settled constituencies, *and* 'inside' the heads of each individual.

- No single identity — e.g. that of social class — could align all the different identities into one, overarching 'master identity', on which a politics could be securely grounded. People no longer identify their social interests exclusively in class terms; class cannot serve as a discursive device or mobilizing category through which all the diverse social interests and identities of people can be reconciled and represented.

- Increasingly, the political landscapes of the modern world are fractured in this way by competing and dislocating identifications — arising, especially, from the erosion of the 'master identity' of class and the emerging identities belonging to the new political ground defined by the the new social movements: feminism, black struggles, national liberation, anti-nuclear and ecological movements (Mercer, 1990).

- Since identity shifts according to how the subject is addressed or represented, identification is not automatic, but can be won or lost. It has become politicized. This is sometimes described as a shift from a politics of (class) identity to a politics of *difference.*

I can now briefly outline the shape of the rest of the chapter. First, I shall look in somewhat more depth at how the concept of identity is said to have shifted, from that of the Enlightenment subject to that of the sociological and then the 'post-modern' subject. Thereafter, the chapter will explore that aspect of modern cultural identity which is formed through one's membership of a *national* culture — and how the processes of dislocating change, encapsulated by the concept of 'globalization', are affecting it.

2   THE BIRTH AND DEATH OF THE MODERN SUBJECT

In this section I shall outline the account offered by some contemporary theorists of the main shifts that have occurred in the way the subject and identity are conceptualized in modern thought. My aim is to trace the stages through which a particular version of 'the human subject' — with certain fixed human capacities and a stable sense of its own identity and place in the order of things — first emerged in the modern age; how it became 'centred' in the discourses and practices which shaped modern societies; how it acquired a more sociological or interactive definition; and how it is being 'de-centred' in late-modernity. The main focus of this section is conceptual. It is concerned with *changing conceptions* of the human subject as a discursive figure, whose unified form and rational identity, I shall argue, were presupposed by, and essential to, both the discourses of modern thought and the processes which shaped modernity.

To try to map the history of the notion of the modern subject is an exceedingly difficult exercise. The idea that identities were fully unified and coherent, and have now become totally dislocated, is a highly simplistic way of telling the story of the modern subject, and I adopt it here as a device entirely for the purpose of convenient exposition. Even those who hold broadly to the notion of a de-centring of identity would not subscribe to it in this simplified form, and you should bear this qualification in mind as you read this section. However, this simple formulation does have the advantage of enabling me (in the brief space of this chapter) to sketch a crude picture of how, according to the proponents of the de-centring view, the conceptualization of the modern subject has shifted at *three* strategic points during modernity. These shifts underline the basic claim that conceptualizations of the subject change, and therefore have a history. Since the modern subject emerged at a particular time (its 'birth') and has a history, it follows that it can also change and, indeed, that under certain circumstances we can even contemplate its 'death'.

It is now a commonplace that the modern age gave rise to a new and decisive form of *individualism,* at the centre of which stood a new conception of the individual subject and its identity. This does not mean that people were not individuals in pre-modern times, but that individuality was both 'lived', 'experienced' and 'conceptualized' differently. The transformations (discussed in earlier volumes in this series) which ushered in modernity, tore the individual free from its stable moorings in traditions and structures. Since these were believed to be divinely ordained, they were held not to be subject to fundamental change. One's status, rank and position in the 'great chain of being' — the secular and divine order of things — overshadowed any sense that one was a sovereign individual. The birth of the 'sovereign individual' between the Renaissance humanism of the sixteenth century and the

Enlightenment of the eighteenth century represented a significant break with the past. Some argue that it was the engine which set the whole social system of 'modernity' in motion.

Raymond Williams notes that the modern history of the individual subject brings together two distinct meanings: on the one hand, the subject is 'indivisible' — an entity which is unified within itself and cannot be further divided; on the other, it is also an entity which is 'singular, distinctive, unique' (see Williams, 1976, pp.133-5: INDIVIDUAL). Many major movements in Western thought and culture contributed to the emergence of this new conception: The Reformation and Protestantism, which set the individual conscience free from the religious institutions of the Church and exposed it directly to the eye of God; Renaissance humanism, which placed Man (*sic*) at the centre of the universe; the scientific revolutions, which endowed Man with the faculty and capacities to inquire into, investigate and unravel the mysteries of Nature; and the Enlightenment, centred on the image of rational, scientific Man, freed from dogma and intolerance, before whom the whole of human history was laid out for understanding and mastery.

Much of the history of Western philosophy consists of reflections on, or refinements of, this conception of the subject, its powers and capacities. One major figure who gave this conception its primary formulation was the French philosopher, René Descartes (1596–1650). Sometimes seen as 'the father of modern philosophy', Descartes was a mathematician and scientist, the founder of analytic geometry and optics, and deeply influenced by the 'new science' of the seventeenth century. He was afflicted by that profound doubt which followed the displacement of God from the centre of the universe; and the fact that the modern subject was 'born' amidst metaphysical doubt and scepticism reminds us that it was *never* as settled and unified as this way of describing it suggests (see Forester, 1987). Descartes settled accounts with God by making him the Prime Mover of all creation; thereafter he explained the rest of the material world entirely in mechanical and mathematical terms.

Descartes postulated two distinct substances — spatial substance (matter) and thinking substance (mind). He thus re-focused that great *dualism* between 'mind' and 'matter' which has troubled Western philosophy ever since. Things must be explained, he believed, by reducing them to their essentials — the fewest possible, ultimately, irreducible elements. At the centre of 'mind' he placed the individual subject, constituted by its capacity to reason and think. 'Cogito, ergo sum' was Descartes' watchword: 'I *think*, therefore I am' (my emphasis). Ever since, this conception of the rational, cogitative and conscious subject at the centre of knowledge has been known as 'the Cartesian subject'.

Another critical contribution was made by John Locke who, in his *Essay Concerning Human Understanding*, defined the individual in terms of 'the sameness of a rational being' — that is, an identity which remained the same and which was continuous with its subject: 'as far as this consciousness can be extended backwards to any past action or thought, so far reaches the identity of that person' (Locke, 1967, pp.212–13). This conceptual figure or discursive device — the 'sovereign individual' — was embedded in each of the key processes and practices which made the modern world. He (*sic*) was the 'subject' of modernity in two senses: the origin or 'subject' of reason, knowledge, and practice; and the one who bore the consequences of these practices — who was 'subjected to' them (see Foucault, 1986; also *Penguin Dictionary of Sociology:* SUBJECT.)

Some have questioned whether capitalism actually required a conception of sovereign individuals of this kind (Abercrombie *et al.*, 1986). Nevertheless, the rise of a more individualist conception of the subject is widely accepted. Raymond Williams summarizes this embedding of the modern subject in the practices and discourses of modernity in the following passage:

> The emergence of notions of **individuality**, in the modern sense, can be related to the break-up of the medieval social, economic and religious order. In the general movement against feudalism there was a new stress on a man's personal existence over and above his place or function in a rigid hierarchical society. There was a related stress, in Protestantism, on a man's direct and individual relation to God, as opposed to this relation mediated by the Church. But it was not until the late seventeenth and eighteenth centuries that a new mode of analysis, in logic and mathematics, postulated the individual as the substantial entity (cf. Leibniz's 'monads'), from which other categories and especially collective categories were derived. The political thought of the Enlightenment mainly followed this model. Argument began from individuals, who had an initial and primary existence, and laws and forms of society were derived from them: by submission, as in Hobbes; by contract or consent, or by the new version of natural law, in liberal thought. In classical economics, trade was described in a model which postulated separate individuals who [possessed property and] decided, at some starting point, to enter into economic or commercial relations. In utilitarian ethics, separate individuals calculated the consequences of this or that action which they might undertake.
> (Williams, 1976, pp.135–6)

It was just possible in the eighteenth century to imagine the great processes of modern life as centred upon the individual subject-of-reason. But as modern societies grew more complex, they acquired a more collective and social form. Classic liberal theories of government based on individual rights and consent were obliged to come to terms with the structures of the nation-state and the great masses which make up a modern democracy. The classic laws of political economy, property, contract and exchange had to operate, after industrialization, amidst the great class formations of modern capitalism. The individual entrepreneur of Adam Smith's *Wealth of Nations* or even of Marx's *Capital* was transformed into the corporate conglomerates of the modern economy. The individual citizen became enmeshed in the bureaucratic administrative machineries of the modern state.

A more *social* conception of the subject then emerged. The individual came to be seen as more located and 'placed' within these great supporting structures and formations of modern society. Two major developments contributed to articulating a broader set of conceptual foundations for the modern subject. The first was Darwinian biology. The human subject was 'biologized' — reason was given a basis in Nature, and mind a 'ground' in the physical development of the human brain.

The second development emerged with the rise of new social sciences. However, the transformations which this set in motion were uneven. These were:

1   The 'sovereign individual', with 'his' wants, needs, desires and interests remained the pivotal figure in the discourses of both modern economics and the law.

2   The dualism typical of Cartesian thought was institutionalized in the split in the social sciences between psychology and the other disciplines. The study of the individual and its mental processes became psychology's special and privileged object of study.

3   Sociology, however, provided a critique of the 'rational individualism' of the Cartesian subject. It located the individual in group processes and the collective norms which, it argued, underpin any contract between individual subjects. It therefore developed an alternative account of how individuals are formed subjectively through their membership of, and participation in, wider social relationships; and, conversely, how processes and structures are sustained by the roles which individuals play in them. This 'internalizing' of the outside in the subject, and 'externalizing' of the inside through action in the social world (as discussed earlier), is the primary sociological account of the modern subject, and is encapsulated in the theory of socialization. As was noted above, G.H. Mead and the symbolic interactionists adopted a radically interactive view of this process. The integration of the individual into society has been a long-term concern of sociology. Theorists like Goffman were highly attentive to the way 'the self' is presented in different social situations, and how conflicts between these different social roles are negotiated. At a more macro-sociological level, Parsons studied the 'fit' or complementarity between 'the self' and the social system. Nevertheless, some critics would claim that mainstream sociology has retained something of Descartes' dualism, especially in its tendency to construct the problem as a relation between two connected, but separate, entities: here, 'the individual *and* society'.

This interactive sociological model, with its stable reciprocity between 'inside' and 'outside', is very much a product of the first half of the twentieth century, when the social sciences assumed their current disciplinary form. However, in the very same period, a more disturbed and disturbing picture of the subject and identity was beginning to emerge in the aesthetic and intellectual movements associated with the rise of Modernism (see Book 3 (Bocock and Thompson, 1992), Chapter 9).

Here we find the figure of the isolated, exiled or estranged individual, framed against the background of the anonymous and impersonal crowd or metropolis. Examples include the poet Baudelaire's famous portrait of the 'Painter of Modern Life', who sets up his house 'in the heart of the multitude, amid the ebb and flow of motion, in the midst of the fugitive and the infinite' and who 'becomes one flesh with the crowd', enters into the crowd 'as though it were an immense reservoir of electrical energy'; the *flaneur* (or 'idle stroller'), who wanders amid the new shopping arcades watching the passing spectacle of the metropolis, whom Walter Benjamin celebrated in his essay on Baudelaire's Paris, and whose counterpart in late-modernity is probably the tourist (cf. Urry, 1990); 'K', the anonymous victim confronted by a faceless bureaucracy in Kafka's novel, *The Trial*; and that host of estranged figures in twentieth century literature and social criticism who are meant to represent the unique experience of modernity. Several such 'exemplary instances of modernity', as Frisby calls them, people the pages of major turn-of-the-century social theorists like George Simmel, Alfred Schutz and Siegfried Kracauer (all of whom tried to capture the essential features of modernity in famous essays on 'The Stranger' or 'Outsider') (see Frisby, 1985, p.109). These images proved prophetic of what was to befall the Cartesian and sociological subjects in late-modernity.

2.1   DE-CENTRING THE SUBJECT

Those who hold that modern identities are being fragmented argue that what has happened in late-modernity to the conception of the modern subject is not simply its estrangement, but its dislocation. They trace this dislocation through a series of ruptures in the discourses of modern knowledge. In this section, I shall offer a brief sketch of **five** great advances in social theory and the human sciences which have occurred in, or had their major impact upon, thought in the period of late-modernity (the second half of the twentieth century), and whose main effect, it is argued, has been the final de-centring of the Cartesian subject.

The first major de-centring concerns the traditions of Marxist thinking. Marx's writing belongs, of course, to the nineteenth and not the twentieth century. But one of the ways in which his work was recovered and re-read in the 1960s was in the light of his argument that 'men (*sic*) make history, but only on the basis of conditions which are not of their own making'. His re-readers interpreted this to mean that individuals could not in any true sense be the 'authors' or agents of history since they could only act on the basis of the historical conditions made by others into which they were born, and using the resources (material and culture) provided to them from previous generations.

Marxism, properly understood, they argued, displaced any notion of individual agency. The Marxist structuralist, Louis Althusser (1918–89) (whose theories of ideology are discussed by Kenneth Thompson: see Book 3 (Bocock and Thompson, 1992), Chapter 7; see also *Penguin Dictionary of Sociology:* ALTHUSSER) argued that, by putting social relations (modes of production, exploitation of labour power, the circuits of capital) rather than an abstract notion of Man at the centre of his theoretical system, Marx displaced two key propositions of modern philosophy: '(1) that there is a universal essence of man; (2) that this essence is the attribute of "each single individual" who is its real subject':

> These two postulates are complementary and indissoluble. But their existence and their unity presuppose a whole empiricist–idealist world outlook. By rejecting the essence of man as his theoretical basis, Marx rejected the whole of this organic system of postulates. He drove the philosophical category of *the subject*, of *empiricism*, of the *ideal essence* from all the domains in which they had been supreme. Not only from political economy (rejection of the myth of *homo economicus*, that is, of the individual with definite faculties and needs as the subject of the classical economy); not just from history; … not just from ethics (rejection of the Kantian ethical idea); but also from philosophy itself.
> (Althusser, 1966, p.228)

This 'total theoretical revolution' was, of course, fiercely contested by many humanistic theorists who give greater weight in historical explanation to human agency. We need not argue here about whether Althusser was wholly or partly right, or entirely wrong. The fact is that, though his work has been extensively criticized, his 'theoretical anti-humanism' (that is, a way of thinking opposed to theories which derive their argument from some notion of a universal essence of Man lodged in each individual subject) has had considerable impact on many branches of modern thought.

The second of the great 'de-centrings' in twentieth-century Western thought comes from Freud's 'discovery' of the unconscious. Freud's theory that our identities, our sexuality, and the structure of our desires are formed on the basis of the psychic and symbolic processes of the unconscious, which function according to a 'logic' very different from that of Reason, plays havoc with the concept of the knowing and rational subject with a fixed and unified identity — the subject of Descartes' 'I think, therefore I am'. This aspect of Freud's work has also had a profound impact on modern thought in the last three decades. Psychoanalytic thinkers like Jacques Lacan, for example, (whose work on the unconscious foundations of femininity is discussed by Helen Crowley: see Book 3 (Bocock and Thompson, 1992), Chapter 2) read Freud as saying that the image of the self as 'whole' and unified is something which the infant only gradually, partially, and with great difficulty, *learns*. It does not grow naturally from inside the core of the infant's being, but is formed in relation to others; especially in the complex unconscious psychic negotiations in early childhood between the child and the powerful fantasies which it has of its parental figures. In what Lacan calls the 'mirror phase' of development, the infant who is not yet coordinated, and possesses no self image as a 'whole' person, sees or 'imagines' itself reflected — either literally in the mirror, or figuratively, in the 'mirror' of the other's look — as a 'whole person' (Lacan, 1977). (Incidentally, Althusser borrowed this metaphor from Lacan, when trying to describe the operation of ideology; see Book 3 (Bocock and Thompson, 1992), Chapter 7.) This is close in some ways to Mead's and Cooley's 'looking glass' conception of the interactive self; except that for them socialization was a matter of conscious learning, whereas for Freud subjectivity was the product of unconscious psychic processes.

This formation of the self in the 'look' of the Other, according to Lacan, opens the child's relation with symbolic systems outside itself, and is thus the moment of the child's entry into the various systems of symbolic representation — including language, culture and sexual difference. The contradictory and unresolved feelings which accompany this difficult entry — the splitting of love and hate for the father, the conflict between the wish to please and the impulse to reject the mother, the division of the self into its 'good' and 'bad' parts, the disavowal of the masculine/feminine parts of oneself, and so on — which are key aspects of this 'unconscious formation of the subject', and which leave the subject 'divided', remain with one for life. However, though the subject is always split or divided it experiences its own identity as being held together and 'resolved', or unified, as a result of the fantasy of itself as a unified 'person' which it formed in the mirror phase. This, according to this kind of psychoanalytic thinking, is the contradictory origin of 'identity'.

Thus, identity is actually something formed through unconscious processes over time, rather than being innate in consciousness at birth. There is always something 'imaginary' or fantasized about its unity. It always remains incomplete, is always 'in process', always 'being formed'. The 'feminine' parts of the male self, for example, which are disavowed, remain with him and find unconscious expressions in many unacknowledged ways in adult life. Thus, rather than speaking of identity as a finished thing, we should speak of *identification*, and see it as an on-going process. Identity arises, not so much from the fullness of identity which is already inside us as individuals, but from a *lack* of wholeness which is 'filled' from *outside us,* by the ways we imagine ourselves to be seen by *others*. Psychoanalytically, the reason why we continually search for 'identity', constructing biographies which knit together the different parts of our divided selves into a unity, is to recapture this fantasized pleasure of fullness (plenitude).

Again, Freud's work, and that of the psychoanalytic thinkers like Lacan who read him in this way, has been widely contested. By definition, unconscious processes cannot be easily seen or examined. They have to be inferred by the elaborate psychoanalytic techniques of reconstruction and interpretation and are not easily amenable to 'proof'. Nevertheless, their general impact on modern ways of thought has been very considerable. Much modern thinking about subjective and psychic life is 'post-Freudian', in the sense that it takes Freud's work on the unconscious for granted, even when it rejects some of his specific hypotheses. Again, you can appreciate the damage which this way of thinking does to notions of the rational subject and identity as fixed and stable.

The third de-centring I shall examine is associated with the work of the structural linguist, Ferdinand de Saussure (see Book 1 (Hall and Gieben, 1992), Chapter 5, for a discussion of his theories of language). Saussure argued that we are not in any absolute sense the 'authors' of the statements we make or of the meanings we express in language. We can only use language to produce meanings by positioning ourselves within the rules of language and the systems of meaning of our culture. Language is a social, not an individual system. It pre-exists us. We cannot in any simple sense be its authors. To speak a language is not only to express our innermost, original thoughts, it is also to activate the vast range of meanings which are already embedded in our language and cultural systems.

Further, the meanings of words are not fixed in a one-to-one relation to objects or events in the world outside language. Meaning arises in the relations of similarity and difference which words have to other words within the language code. We know what 'night' is because it is *not* 'day'. Notice the analogy here between language and identity. I know who 'I' am in relation to 'the other' (e.g. my mother) whom I cannot be. As Lacan would say, identity, like the unconscious, 'is structured like language'. What modern philosophers of language, like Jacques Derrida, who have been influenced by Saussure and the 'linguistic turn', argue is that, despite his/her best efforts the individual speaker can never finally fix meaning — including the meaning of his or her identity. Words are 'multi-accentual'. They always carry echoes of other meanings which they trigger off, despite one's best efforts to close meaning down. Our statements are underpinned by propositions and premises of which we are not aware, but which are, so to speak, carried along in the bloodstream of our language. Everything we say has a 'before' and an 'after' — a 'margin' in which others may write. Meaning is inherently unstable: it aims for closure (identity), but is constantly disrupted (by difference). It is constantly sliding away from us. There are always supplementary meanings over which we have no control, which will arise and subvert our attempts to create fixed and stable worlds (see Derrida, 1981).

The fourth major de-centring of identity and the subject occurs in the work of the French philosopher and historian, Michel Foucault. In a series of studies (some of which have been referred to in other volumes in this series: for example, Book 1 (Hall and Gieben, 1992), Chapter 6; Book 3 (Bocock and Thompson, 1992), Chapters 4 and 5), Foucault has produced a sort of 'genealogy of the modern subject'. Foucault isolates a new type of power, evolving through the nineteenth century, and coming to full flower at the beginning of this century, which he calls 'disciplinary power'. Disciplinary power is concerned with the regulation, surveillance and government of, first, the human species or whole populations, and secondly, the individual and the body. Its sites are those new institutions which developed throughout the nineteenth century and which 'police' and discipline modern populations — in workshops, barracks, schools, prisons, hospitals, clinics, and so on (see, for example, *Madness and Civilization* (1967), *Birth of the Clinic* (1973) and *Discipline and Punish* (1975)).

The aim of 'disciplinary power' is to bring 'the lives, deaths, activities, work, miseries and joys of the individual', as well as his/her moral and physical health, sexual practices and family life under stricter discipline and control; bringing to bear on them the power of administrative regimes, the expertise of the professional, and the knowledge provided by the 'disciplines' of the social sciences. Its basic object is to produce 'a human being who can be treated as a "docile body"' (Dreyfus and Rabinow, 1982, p.135).

What is particularly interesting from the point of view of the history of the modern subject is that, though Foucault's disciplinary power is the product of the new large-scale regulating *collective* institutions of late-modernity, its techniques involve an application of power and knowledge which further 'individualizes' the subject and bears down more intensely on his/her body:

> In a disciplinary regime, individualization is descending. Through surveillance, constant observation, all those subject to control are individualized. … Not only has power now brought individuality into the field of observation, but power fixes that objective individuality in the field of writing. A vast, meticulous documentary apparatus becomes an essential component of the growth of power [in modern societies]. This accumulation of individual documentation in a systematic ordering makes 'possible the measurement of overall phenomena, the description of groups, the characterization of collective facts, the calculation of gaps between individuals, their distribution in a given population'.
> (Dreyfus and Rabinow, 1982, p.159, quoting Foucault)

It is not necessary to accept every detail of Foucault's picture of the all-encompassing character of the 'disciplinary regimes' of modern administrative power to understand the paradox that, the more collective and organized is the nature of the institutions of late-modernity, the greater the isolation, surveillance and individuation of the individual subject.

The fifth de-centring which proponents of this position cite is the impact of feminism, both as theoretical critique and as a social movement. Feminism belongs with that company of 'new social movements', all of which surfaced during the 1960s — the great watershed of late-modernity — alongside the student upheavals, the anti-war and counter-cultural youth movements, the civil-rights struggles, the 'Third-World' revolutionary movements, the peace movements, and the rest associated with '1968'. What is important about this historical moment is that:

- These movements were opposed to the corporate liberal politics of the West as well as the 'Stalinist' politics of the East.
- They affirmed the 'subjective' as well as the 'objective' dimensions of politics.
- They were suspicious of all bureaucratic forms of organization and favoured spontaneity and acts of political will.
- As argued earlier, all these movements had a powerful *cultural* emphasis and form. They espoused the 'theatre' of revolution.
- They reflected the weakening or break-up of class politics, and the mass political organizations associated with it, and their fragmentation into various and separate social movements.
- Each movement appealed to the social *identity* of its supporters. Thus feminism appealed to women, sexual politics to gays and lesbians, racial struggles to blacks, anti-war to peaceniks, and so on. This is the historical birth of what came to be know as *identity politics* — one identity per movement.

But feminism also had a more direct relation to the conceptual de-centring of the Cartesian and the sociological subject:

- It questioned the classic distinction between 'inside' and 'outside', 'private' and 'public'. Feminism's slogan was 'the personal is political'.
- It therefore opened up to political contestation whole new arenas of social life — the family, sexuality, housework, the domestic division of labour, child-rearing, etc. (This is discussed further in Book 3 (Bocock and Thompson, 1992), Chapter 2.)
- It also exposed, as a political and social question, the issue of how we are formed and produced as gendered subjects. That is to say, it politicized subjectivity, identity and the process of identification (as men/women, mothers/fathers, sons/daughters).
- What began as a movement directed at challenging the social *position* of women, expanded to include the *formation* of sexual and gendered identities.
- Feminism challenged the notion that men and women were part of the same identity — 'Mankind' — replacing it with *the question of sexual difference*.

In this section, then, I have tried to map the conceptual shifts by which, according to some theorists, the Enlightenment 'subject', with a fixed and stable identity, was de-centred into the open, contradictory, unfinished, fragmented identities of the post-modern subject. I have traced this through *five* great de-centrings. Let me remind you again that a great many social scientists and intellectuals do not accept the conceptual or intellectual implications (as outlined above) of these developments in modern thought. However, few would now deny their deeply unsettling effects on late-modern ideas and, particularly, on how the subject and the issue of identity have come to be conceptualized.

3   NATIONAL CULTURES AS 'IMAGINED COMMUNITIES'

Having traced the conceptual shifts by which the late-modern or post-modern conceptions of the subject and identity have emerged, I shall now turn to the question of how this 'fragmented subject' is placed in terms of its *cultural* identities. The particular cultural identity I am concerned with is that of *national* identity (though other aspects are implicated in the story). What is happening to cultural identity in late-modernity? Specifically, how are national cultural identities being affected or displaced by the process of globalization?

In the modern world, the national cultures into which we are born are one of the principal sources of cultural identity. In defining ourselves we sometimes say we are English or Welsh or Indian or Jamaican. Of course, this is to speak metaphorically. These identities are not literally imprinted in our genes. However, we do think of them as if they are part of our essential natures. The conservative philosopher, Roger Scruton argues that:

> The condition of man (*sic*) requires that the individual, while he exists and acts as an autonomous being, does so only because he can first identify himself as something greater — as a member of a society, group, class, state or nation, of some arrangement to which he may not attach a name, but which he recognizes instinctively as home.
> (Scruton, 1986, p.156)

Ernest Gellner, from a more liberal position, also believes that without a sense of national identification the modern subject would experience a deep sense of subjective loss:

> The idea of a man (*sic*) without a nation seems to impose a [great] strain on the modern imagination. A man must have a nationality as he must have a nose and two ears. All this seems obvious, though, alas, it is not true. But that it should have come to seem so

very obviously true is indeed an aspect, perhaps the very core, of the problem of nationalism. Having a nation is not an inherent attribute of humanity, but it has now come to appear as such. (Gellner, 1983, p.6)

The argument we will be considering here is that, in fact, national identities are not things we are born with, but are formed and transformed within and in relation to *representation*. We only know what it is to be 'English' because of the way 'Englishness' has come to be represented, as a set of meanings, by English national culture. It follows that a nation is not only a political entity but something which produces meanings — *a system of cultural representation*. People are not only legal citizens of a nation; they participate in the *idea* of the nation as represented in its national culture. A nation is a symbolic community and it is this which accounts for its 'power to generate a sense of identity and allegiance' (Schwarz, 1986, p.106).

National cultures are a distinctly modern form. The allegiance and identification which, in a pre-modern age or in more traditional societies, were given to tribe, people, religion and region, came gradually in Western societies to be transferred to the *national* culture. Regional and ethnic differences were gradually subsumed beneath what Gellner calls the 'political roof' of the nation-state, which thus became a powerful source of meanings for modern cultural identities.

The formation of a national culture helped to create standards of universal literacy, generalized a single vernacular language as the dominant medium of communication throughout the nation, created a homogeneous culture and maintained national cultural institutions, such as a national education system (see Geoffrey Whitty's discussion of this in Book 3 (Bocock and Thompson, 1992), Chapter 6). In these and other ways, national culture became a key feature of industrialization and an engine of modernity. Nevertheless, there are other aspects to a national culture which pull it in a different direction, bringing to the fore what Homi Bhabha calls 'the particular ambivalence that haunts the idea of the nation' (Bhabha, 1990, p.1). Some of these ambiguities are explored in Section 4. First, Section 3.1 will consider how a national culture functions as a system of representation, and Section 3.2 whether national identities are really as unified and homogeneous as they represent themselves to be. It is only when these two questions have been answered, that we can properly consider the claim that national identities were once centred, coherent, and whole, but are now being dislocated by the processes of globalization.

3.1 NARRATING THE NATION: AN IMAGINED COMMUNITY

National cultures are composed not only of cultural institutions, but of symbols and representations. A national culture is a *discourse* — a way of constructing meanings which influences and organizes both our actions and our conception of ourselves (see *Penguin Dictionary of Sociology:* DISCOURSE; also Book 1 (Hall and Gieben, 1992), Chapter 6). National cultures construct identities by producing meanings about 'the nation' with which we can *identify;* these are contained in the stories which are told about it, memories which connect its present with its past, and images which are constructed of it. As Benedict Anderson (1983) has argued, national identity is an 'imagined community' (see the discussion of this idea by Kenneth Thompson in Book 3 (Bocock and Thompson, 1992), Chapter 7).

Anderson argues that the differences between nations lie in the different ways in which they are imagined. Or, as that great British patriot Enoch Powell put it, 'the life of nations no less than that of men is lived largely in the imagination' (Powell, 1969, p.245). But how is the modern nation imagined? What representational strategies are deployed to construct our commonsense views of national belonging or identity? What are the representations of, say, 'England' which win the identifications and define the identities of 'English' people? 'Nations', Homi Bhabha has remarked, 'like narratives, lose their origins in the myths of time and only fully realize their horizons in the mind's eye' (Bhabha, 1990, p.1). How is the narrative of the national culture told?

Of the many aspects which a comprehensive answer to that question would include, I have selected *five* main elements.

1   First, there is the *narrative of the nation*, as it is told and retold in national histories, literatures, the media and popular culture. These provide a set of stories, images, landscapes, scenarios, historical events, national symbols and rituals which stand for, or *represent,* the shared experiences, sorrows, and triumphs and disasters which give meaning to the nation. As members of such an 'imagined community', we see ourselves in our mind's eye sharing in this narrative. It lends significance and importance to our humdrum existence, connecting our everyday lives with a national destiny that preexisted us and will outlive us. From England's green and pleasant land, its gentle, rolling countryside, rose-trellised cottages and country house gardens — Shakespeare's 'sceptered isle' — to public ceremonials like the Trooping of the Colour and Poppy Day, the discourse of 'Englishness' represents what 'England' *is*, gives meaning to the identity of 'being English' and fixes 'England' as a focus of identification in English (and Anglophile) hearts. As Bill Schwarz observes:

> These make up the threads that bind us invisibly to the past. Just as English nationalism is denied, so is the fact of its turbulent and contested history. What we get instead ... is an emphasis on tradition and heritage, above all on *continuity* so that our present political culture is seen as the flowering of a long organic evolution.
> (Schwarz, 1986, p.155)

Jubilee year, 1977

2   Secondly, there is the emphasis on *origins, continuity, tradition and timelessness*. National identity is represented as primordial — 'there, in the very nature of things', sometimes slumbering, but ever ready to be 'awoken' from its 'long, persistent and mysterious somnolence' to resume its unbroken existence (Gellner, 1983, p.48). The essentials of the national character remain unchanged through all the vicissitudes of history. It is there from birth, unified and continuous, 'changeless' throughout all the changes, eternal. Mrs Thatcher remarked at the time of the Falklands War that there were some people 'who thought we could no longer do the great things which we once did ... that Britain was no longer the nation that had built an Empire and ruled a quarter of the world. ... Well they were wrong ... Britain has not changed' (quoted in Barnett, 1982, p.63).

3   A third discursive strategy is what Hobsbawm and Ranger call *the invention of tradition*: 'Traditions which appear or claim to be old are often quite recent in origin and sometimes invented. ... "Invented tradition" [means] a set of practices, ... of a ritual or symbolic nature which seek to inculcate certain values and norms of behaviours by repetition which automatically implies continuity with a suitable historical past'. For example, 'Nothing appears more ancient, and linked to an immemorial past, than the pageantry which surrounds British monarchy and its public ceremonial manifestations. Yet ... in its modern form it is the product of the late nineteenth and twentieth centuries' (Hobsbawm and Ranger, 1983, p.1).

4   A fourth example of the narrative of national culture is that of a *foundational myth*: a story which locates the origin of the nation, the people and their national character so early that they are lost in the

mists of, not 'real', but 'mythic' time — like basing the definition of the English as 'free-born' on the Anglo-Saxon parliament. Invented traditions make the confusions and disasters of history intelligible, converting disarray into 'community' (e.g. the Blitz or evacuation during World War II) and disasters into triumphs (e.g. Dunkirk). Myths of origin also help disenfranchised peoples to 'conceive and express their resentment and its contents in intelligible terms' (Hobsbawm and Ranger, 1983, p.1). They provide a narrative in terms of which an alternative history or counter-narrative, which pre-dates the ruptures of colonization, can be constructed (e.g. Rastafarianism for the dispossessed poor of Kingston, Jamaica; see Hall, 1985). New nations are then founded on these myths. (I say 'myths' because, as was the case with many African nations which emerged after decolonization, what preceded colonization was not 'one nation, one people', but many different tribal cultures and societies.)

5   National identity is also often symbolically grounded on the idea of a *pure, original people or 'folk'*. But, in the realities of national development, it is rarely this primordial folk who persist or exercise power. As Gellner wryly observes, 'When [the Ruritanians] donned folk costume and trekked over the hills, composing poems in the forest clearings, they did not also dream of one day becoming powerful bureaucrats, ambassadors and ministers' (1983, p.61).

The discourse of national culture is thus not as modern as it appears to be. It constructs identities which are ambiguously placed between past and future. It straddles the temptation to return to former glories and the drive to go forwards ever deeper into modernity. Sometimes national cultures are tempted to turn the clock back, to retreat defensively to that 'lost time' when the nation was 'great', and to restore past identities. This is the regressive, the anachronistic, element in the national cultural story. But often this very return to the past conceals a struggle to mobilize 'the people' to purify their ranks, to expel the 'others' who threaten their identity, and to gird their loins for a new march forwards. During the 1980s, the rhetoric of Thatcherism sometimes inhabited both these aspects of what Tom Nairn calls the 'Janus-face' of nationalism (Nairn, 1977): looking back to past imperial glories and 'Victorian values' while simultaneously undertaking a kind of modernization in preparation for a new stage of global capitalist competition. Something of the same kind may be going on now in Eastern Europe. Areas breaking away from the old Soviet Union reaffirm their essential ethnic identities and claim nationhood, buttressed by (sometimes extremely dubious) 'stories' of mythic origins, religious orthodoxy, and racial purity. Yet they may be also using the nation as the form in which to compete with other ethnic 'nations', and so to gain entry to the rich 'club' of the West. As Immanuel Wallerstein has acutely observed, 'the nationalisms of the modern world are the ambiguous expression [of a desire] for ... assimilation into the universal ... and simultaneously for ... adhering to the particular, the reinvention of differences. Indeed it is a universalism through particularism and particularism through universalism' (Wallerstein, 1984, pp.166–7).

3.2 DECONSTRUCTING THE 'NATIONAL CULTURE': IDENTITY AND DIFFERENCE

Section 3.1 considered how a national culture functions as a source of cultural meanings, a focus of identification, and a system of representation. This section now turns to the question of whether national cultures and the national identities they construct are actually *unified.* In his famous essay on the topic, Ernest Renan said that three things constitute the spiritual principle of the unity of a nation: ' ... the possession in common of a rich legacy of memories, ... the desire to live together, [and] the will to perpetuate the heritage that one has received in an undivided form' (Renan, 1990, p.19). You should bear in mind these three resonant concepts of what constitutes a national culture as an 'imagined community': *memories* from the past; the *desire* to live together; the perpetuation of the *heritage.*

Timothy Brennan reminds us that the word *nation* refers 'both to the modern nation-state and to something more ancient and nebulous — the *natio* —a local community, domicile, family, condition of belonging' (Brennan, 1990, p.45). National identities represented precisely the result of bringing these two halves of the national equation together — offering both membership of the political nation-state and identification with the national culture: 'to make culture and polity congruent' and to endow 'reasonably homogeneous cultures, each with its own political roof' (Gellner, 1983, p.43). Gellner clearly establishes this impulse to *unify* in national cultures:

> ... culture is now the necessary shared medium, the life-blood, or perhaps rather the minimal shared atmosphere, within which alone the members of the society can breathe and survive and produce. For a given society it must be one in which they can all breathe and speak and produce; so it must be the *same* culture. (Gellner, 1983, pp.37–8)

To put it crudely, however different its members may be in terms of class, gender or race, a national culture seeks to unify them into one cultural identity, to represent them all as belonging to the same great national family. But is national identity a unifying identity of this kind, which cancels or subsumes cultural difference?

Such an idea is open to doubt, for several reasons. A national culture has never been simply a point of allegiance, bonding and symbolic identification. It is also a structure of cultural power. Consider the following points:

1   Most modern nations consist of disparate cultures which were only unified by a lengthy process of violent conquest — that is, by the forcible suppression of cultural difference. 'The British people' are the product of a series of such conquests — Celtic, Roman, Saxon, Viking and Norman. Throughout Europe the story is repeated *ad nauseam.* Each conquest subjugated conquered peoples and their cultures,

customs, languages and traditions and tried to impose a more unified cultural hegemony. As Ernest Renan has remarked, these violent beginnings which stand at the origins of modern nations have first to be 'forgotten' before allegiance to a more unified, homogeneous national identity could begin to be forged. Thus 'British' culture still does not consist of an equal partnership between the component cultures of the UK, but of the effective hegemony of 'English', a southern-based culture which represents itself as the essential British culture, over Scottish, Welsh, and Irish and, indeed, other regional cultures. Matthew Arnold, who tried to fix the essential character of the English people from their literature, claimed when considering the Celts that such 'provincial nationalisms had to be swallowed up at the level of the political and licensed as cultural contributors to English culture' (Dodd, 1986, p.12).

2   Secondly, nations are always composed of different social classes, and gender and ethnic groups. Modern British nationalism was the product of a very concerted effort, in the late Victorian and high imperial period, to unify the classes across social divisions by providing them with an alternative point of identification —common membership of 'the family of the nation'. The same point can be made about gender. National identities are strongly gendered. The meanings and values of 'Englishness' have powerful masculine associations. Women play a secondary role as guardians of hearth, kith and kin, and as 'mothers' of the nation's 'sons'.

3   Thirdly, modern Western nations were also the centres of empires or of neo-imperial spheres of influence, exercising cultural hegemony over the cultures of the colonized. Some historians now argue that it was in this process of comparison between the 'virtues' of 'Englishness' and the negative features of other cultures that many of the distinctive characteristics of English identities were first defined (see C. Hall, 1992).

Instead of thinking of national cultures as unified, we should think of them as constituting a *discursive device* which represents difference as unity or identity. They are cross-cut by deep internal divisions and differences, and 'unified' only through the exercise of different forms of cultural power. Yet — as in the fantasies of the 'whole' self of which Lacanian psychoanalysis speaks — national identities continue to be represented as *unified*.

One way of unifying them has been to represent them as the expression of the underlying culture of 'one people'. Ethnicity is the term we give to cultural features — language, religion, custom, traditions, feeling for 'place' — which are shared by a people. It is therefore tempting to try to use ethnicity in this 'foundational' way. But this belief turns out, in the modern world, to be a myth. Western Europe has no nations which are composed of only one people, one culture or ethnicity. *Modern nations are all cultural hybrids.*

It is even more difficult to try to unify national identity around race. First, because — contrary to widespread belief — race is not a biological or genetic category with any scientific validity. There are different genetic strains and 'pools', but they are as widely dispersed *within* what are called 'races' as they are *between* one 'race' and another. Genetic difference — the last refuge of racist ideologies — cannot be used to distinguish one people from another. Race is a *discursive* not a biological category. That is to say, it is the organizing category of those ways of speaking, systems of representation, and social practices (discourses) which utilize a loose, often unspecified set of differences in physical characteristics — skin colour, hair texture, physical and bodily features etc. — as *symbolic markers* in order to differentiate one group socially from another.

Of course the unscientific character of the term 'race' does not undermine 'how racial logics and racial frames of reference are articulated and deployed, and with what consequences' (Donald and Rattansi, 1992, p.1). In recent years, biological notions of races as a distinct species (notions which underpinned extreme forms of nationalist ideology and discourse in earlier periods: Victorian eugenics, European race theories, fascism) have been replaced by *cultural* definitions of race, which allow race to play a significant role in discourses about the nation and national identity. Paul Gilroy has commented on the links between 'cultural racism' and 'the idea of race and the ideas of nation, nationality, and national belonging':

> We increasingly face a racism which avoids being recognized as such because it is able to line up 'race' with nationhood, patriotism and nationalism. A racism which has taken a necessary distance from crude ideas of biological inferiority and superiority now seeks to present an imaginary definition of the nation as a unified *cultural* community. It constructs and defends an image of national culture — homogeneous in its whiteness yet precarious and perpetually vulnerable to attack from enemies within and without. ... This is a racism that answers the social and political turbulence of crisis and crisis management by the recovery of national greatness in the imagination. Its dream-like construction of our sceptered isle as an ethnically purified one provides special comfort against the ravages of [national] decline.
> (Gilroy, 1992, p.87)

But even when 'race' is used in this broader discursive way, modern nations stubbornly refuse to be resolved into it. As Renan observed, 'the leading nations of Europe are nations of essentially mixed blood': 'France is [at once] Celtic, Iberic and Germanic. Germany is Germanic, Celtic and Slav. Italy is the country where ... Gauls, Etruscans, Pelagians and Greeks, not to mention many other elements, intersect in an indecipherable mixture. The British Isles, considered as a whole, present a mixture of Celtic and Germanic blood, the proportions of which are singularly difficult to define' (Renan, 1990, pp.14–15). And these are relatively simple 'mixtures' as compared with those to be found in Central and Eastern Europe.

This brief examination undermines the idea of the nation as a unified cultural identity. National identities do not subsume all other forms of difference into themselves and are not free of the play of power, internal divisions and contradictions, cross-cutting allegiances and difference. So when we come to consider whether national identities are being dislocated, we must bear in mind the way national cultures help to 'stitch up' differences into one identity.

4   GLOBALIZATION

The previous section qualified the idea that national identities have ever been as unified or homogeneous as they are represented to be. Nevertheless, in modern history, national cultures have dominated 'modernity' and national identities have tended to win out over other, more particularistic sources of cultural identification.

What, then, is so powerfully dislocating national cultural identities now, at the end of the twentieth century? The answer is, a complex of processes and forces of change, which for convenience can be summed up under the term 'globalization'. This concept was extensively discussed by Anthony McGrew in Chapter 2 of this volume. As he argued, 'globalization' refers to those processes, operating on a global scale, which cut across national boundaries, integrating and connecting communities and organizations in new space–time combinations, making the world in reality and in experience more interconnected. Globalization implies a movement away from the classical sociological idea of a 'society' as a well-bounded system, and its replacement by a perspective which concentrates on 'how social life is ordered across time and space' (Giddens, 1990, p.64). These new temporal and spatial features, resulting in the compression of distances and time-scales, are among the most significant aspects of globalization affecting cultural identities, and they are discussed in greater detail below.

Remember that globalization is not a recent phenomenon: 'Modernity is inherently globalizing' (Giddens, 1990, p.63). As David Held argued (Book 1 (Hall and Gieben, 1992), Chapter 2), nation-states were never as autonomous or as sovereign as they claimed to be. And, as Wallerstein reminds us, capitalism 'was from the beginning an affair of the world economy and not of nation states. Capital has never allowed its aspirations to be determined by national boundaries' (Wallerstein, 1979, p.19). So *both* the trend towards national autonomy and the trend towards globalization are deeply rooted in modernity (see Wallerstein, 1991, p.98).

You should bear in mind these two contradictory tendencies within globalization. Nevertheless, it is generally agreed that, since the 1970s, both the scope and pace of global integration have greatly increased, accelerating the flows and linkages between nations. In this and the

Capitalism — 'an affair of the world economy'

next section, I shall attempt to track the consequences of these aspects of globalization on cultural identities, examining *three* possible consequences:

1   National identities are being *eroded* as a result of the growth of cultural homogenization and 'the global post-modern'.

2   National and other 'local' or particularistic identities are being *strengthened* by the resistance to globalization.

3   National identities are declining but *new* identities of hybridity are taking their place.

4.1   TIME–SPACE COMPRESSION AND IDENTITY

What impact has the latest phase of globalization had on national identities? You will remember from Chapter 2 that one of its main features is 'time–space compression' — the speeding up of global processes, so that the world feels smaller and distances shorter, so that events in one place impact immediately on people and places a very long distance away. David Harvey argues that:

> As space appears to shrink to a 'global' village of telecommunications and a 'spaceship earth' of economic and ecological inter-dependencies — to use just two familiar and everyday images — and as time horizons shorten to the point where the present is all there is, so we have to learn to cope with an overwhelming sense of compression of our spatial and temporal worlds.
> (Harvey, 1989, p.240)

What is important for our argument about the impact of globa
identity is that time and space are also the basic coordinates c
systems of *representation*. Every medium of representation —
drawing, painting, photography, figuring through art or the
telecommunications systems — must translate its subject into spatial
and temporal dimensions. Thus, narrative translates events into a
beginning–middle–end time sequence; and visual systems of
representation translate three-dimensional objects into two dimensions.
Different cultural epochs have different ways of combining these time–
space coordinates. Harvey contrasts the rational ordering of space and
time of the Enlightenment (with its regular sense of order, symmetry
and balance) with the broken and fragmented time–space coordinates of
the Modernist movements of the late nineteenth and early twentieth
centuries. We can see new space–time relationships being defined in
developments as different as Einstein's theory of relativity, the cubist
paintings of Picasso and Braque, the works of the Surrealists and
Dadaists, the experiments with time and narrative in the novels of
Marcel Proust and James Joyce, and the use of montage techniques in
the early cinema of Vertov and Eisenstein.

Section 3 argued that identity is deeply implicated in representation.
Thus, the shaping and reshaping of time–space relationships within
different systems of representation have profound effects on how
identities are located and represented. The male subject, represented in
eighteenth-century paintings surveying his property, in the form of the
well-regulated and controlled classical spatial forms of the Georgian
crescent (Bath) or English country residence (Blenheim Palace), or
seeing himself located in the spacious, controlled forms of Nature of a
Capability Brown formal garden or parkland, has a very different sense
of cultural identity from the subject who sees 'himself/herself' mirrored
in the fragmented, fractured 'faces' which look out from the broken
planes and surfaces of one of Picasso's cubist canvases. All identities are
located in symbolic space and time. They have what Edward Said calls
their 'imaginary geographies' (Said, 1990): their characteristic
'landscapes', their sense of 'place', 'home', or *heimat*, as well as their
placings in time — in invented traditions which bind past and present,
in myths of origin which project the present back into the past, and in
the narratives of the nation which connect the individual to larger, more
significant national historic events.

Another way of thinking about this is in terms of what Giddens (1990)
calls the separation of space from place. 'Place' is specific, concrete,
known, familiar, bounded: the site of specific social practices which
have shaped and formed us, and with which our identities are closely
bound up.

> In premodern societies, space and place largely coincided, since the
> spatial dimensions of social life are, for most of the population ...
> dominated by 'presence' — by localised activity. ... Modernity
> increasingly tears space away from place by fostering relations
> between 'absent' others, locationally distant from any given

situation of face-to-face interaction. In conditions of modernity ... locales are thoroughly penetrated by and shaped in terms of social influences quite distant from them. What structures the locale is not simply that which is present on the scene; the 'visible form' of the locale conceals the distanced relations which determine its nature. (Giddens, 1990, p.18)

Places remain fixed; they are where we have 'roots'. Yet space can be 'crossed' in the twinkling of an eye — by jet, fax or satellite. Harvey calls this 'the annihilation of space through time' (1989, p.205).

4.2 TOWARDS THE GLOBAL POST-MODERN?

Some theorists argue that the general effect of these globalizing processes has been to weaken or undermine national forms of cultural identity. They argue that there is evidence of a loosening of strong identifications with the national culture, and a strengthening of other cultural ties and allegiances, 'above' and 'below' the level of the nation-state. National identities remain strong, especially with respect to such things as legal and citizenship rights, but local, regional and community identities have become more significant. Above the level of the national culture, 'global' identifications begin to displace, and sometimes over-ride, national ones.

Some cultural theorists argue that the trend towards greater global interdependence is leading to the break-down of *all* strong cultural identities and is producing that fragmentation of cultural codes, that multiplicity of styles, emphasis on the ephemeral, the fleeting, the impermanent, and on difference and cultural pluralism which Kenneth Thompson described in Chapter 5, but on a global scale — what we might call *the global post-modern*. Cultural flows and global consumerism between nations create the possibilities of 'shared identities' — as 'customers' for the same goods, 'clients' for the same services, 'audiences' for the same messages and images — between people who are far removed from one another in time and space. As national cultures become more exposed to outside influences it is difficult to preserve cultural identities intact, or to prevent them from becoming weakened through cultural bombardment and infiltration.

People in small, apparently remote villages in poor, 'Third World' countries can receive in the privacy of their homes the messages and images of the rich, consumer cultures of the West, purveyed through TV sets or the transistor radio, which bind them into the 'global village' of the new communications networks. Jeans and trainers — the 'uniform' of the young in Western youth culture — are as ubiquitous in South-East Asia as in Europe or the US, not only because of the growth of the world-wide marketing of the youth consumer image, but because they are often actually produced in Taiwan or Hong Kong or South Korea for the New York, Los Angeles, London or Rome high-street shop. It is hard to think of 'Indian cooking' as something distinctive of the ethnic

Entering the 'global village'

traditions of the Asian sub-continent when there is an Indian restaurant in the centre of every city and town in Britain.

The more social life becomes mediated by the global marketing of styles, places and images, by international travel, and by globally networked media images and communications systems, the more *identities* become detached — disembedded — from specific times, places, histories, and traditions, and appear 'free-floating'. We are confronted by a range of different identities, each appealing to us, or rather to different parts of ourselves, from which it seems possible to choose. It is the spread of consumerism, whether as reality or dream, which has contributed to this 'cultural supermarket' effect. Within the discourse of global consumerism, differences and cultural distinctions which hitherto defined *identity* become reducible to a sort of international *lingua franca* or global currency into which all specific traditions and distinct identities can be translated. This phenomenon is known as 'cultural homogenization'.

ACTIVITY 1   You should now read **Reading A, 'Global culture'**, by Kevin Robins, which you will find at the end of this chapter. As you read, note:
- First, the account Robins offers of trends towards 'global standardization';
- Then, the turn in the argument: 'global standardization' also involves the 'marketing' of difference;
- Finally, what Robins then says about the growth of a new global–local nexus.

To some extent, what is being debated is the tension between the 'global' and the 'local' in the transformation of identities. National identities, as we have seen, represent attachment to particular places, events, symbols, histories. They represent what is sometimes called a *particularistic* form of attachment or belonging. There has always been a tension between these and more *universalistic* identifications — for example, to 'humanity' rather than to 'Englishness'. This tension has persisted throughout modernity: the growth of nation-states, national economies and national cultures continuing to provide a focus for the first; the expansion of the world market and modernity as a global system providing the focus for the second. With Section 5, which examines how globalization in its most recent forms impacts on identities, you may find it helpful to think of such impact in terms of new ways of articulating the particularistic and the universalistic aspects of identity, or new ways of negotiating the tension between the two.

5   THE GLOBAL, THE LOCAL AND THE RETURN OF ETHNICITY

Are national identities being 'homogenized'? Cultural homogenization is the anguished cry of those who are convinced that globalization threatens to undermine national identities and the 'unity' of national cultures. However, as a view of the future of identities in a post-modern world this picture is too simplistic, exaggerated and one-sided as it stands.

We can pick up at least *three* major qualifications or counter-tendencies. The first arises from Kevin Robins's argument and the observation that, alongside the tendency towards global homogenization, there is also a fascination with *difference* and the marketing of ethnicity and 'otherness'. There is a new interest in 'the local' together with the impact of 'the global'. Globalization (in the form of flexible specialization and 'niche' marketing) actually exploits local differentiation. Thus, instead of thinking of the global *replacing* the local, it would be more accurate to think of a new articulation between 'the global' and 'the local'. This 'local' is not, of course, to be confused with older identities, firmly rooted in well-bounded localities. Rather, it operates within the logic of globalization. However, it seems unlikely that globalization will simply destroy national identities. It is more likely to produce, simultaneously, *new* 'global' *and new* 'local' identifications.

The second qualification to the argument about the global homogenization of identities is that globalization is very unevenly distributed around the globe, between regions and between different strata of the population *within* regions. This is what Doreen Massey calls globalization's 'power geometry'.

ACTIVITY 2   You should now read **Reading B, 'A global sense of place'**, by Doreen
Massey. Note her examples of the ways in which the *same* processes
affect groups and places *differently*.

The third point in the critique of cultural homogenization is the
question of who is most affected by it. Since there is an uneven
direction to the flow, and since unequal relations of cultural power
between 'the West' and 'the Rest' persist, globalization — though by
definition something which affects the whole globe — may appear to be
essentially a Western phenomenon.

Kevin Robins reminds us:

> For all that it has projected itself as transhistorical and
> transnational, as the transcendent and universalizing force of
> modernization and modernity, global capitalism has in reality been
> about westernization — the export of western commodities, values,
> priorities, ways of life. In a process of unequal cultural encounter,
> 'foreign' populations have been compelled to be the subjects and
> subalterns of western empire, while, no less significantly, the west
> has come face to face with the 'alien' and 'exotic' culture of its
> 'Other'. Globalization, as it dissolves the barriers of distance,
> makes the encounter of colonial centre and colonized periphery
> immediate and intense.
> (Robins, 1991, p.25)

In the latest form of globalization, it is still the images, artefacts and
identities of Western modernity, produced by the cultural industries of
'Western' societies (including Japan) which dominate the global
networks. The proliferation of identity choices is more extensive at the
'centre' of the global system than at its peripheries. The patterns of
unequal cultural exchange, familiar from earlier phases of globalization,
persist into late-modernity. If you want to sample the exotic cuisines of
other cultures in one place, it would be better to eat in Manhattan, Paris
or London than in Calcutta or Delhi.

On the other hand, societies of the periphery have *always* been open to
Western cultural influences and are now more so. The idea that these
are 'closed' places — ethnically pure, culturally traditional, undisturbed
until yesterday by the ruptures of modernity — is a Western fantasy
about 'otherness': a 'colonial fantasy' maintained *about* the periphery *by*
the West, which tends to like its natives 'pure' and its exotic places
'untouched'. Nevertheless, the evidence suggests that globalization is
impacting everywhere, including the West, and the 'periphery' is
experiencing its pluralizing impact too, though at a slower, more
uneven pace.

The global post-modern

5.1   'THE REST' IN 'THE WEST'

The preceding pages have presented three qualifications to the first of
the three possible consequences of globalization: i.e. the
homogenization of global identities. These are that:

(a)   Globalization can go hand in hand with a strengthening of local
      identities, though this is still within the logic of time–space
      compression;

(b)   Globalization is an uneven process and has its own 'power
      geometry';

(c)   Globalization retains some aspects of Western global domination,
      but cultural identities everywhere are being relativized by the
      impact of time–space compression.

Perhaps the most striking example of this third point is the
phenomenon of migration. After World War II, the decolonizing
European powers thought they could pull out of their colonial spheres
of influence, leaving the consequences of imperialism behind them. But
global interdependence now works both ways. The movements of
Western styles, images, commodities and consumer identities outwards
has been matched by a momentous movement of peoples from the
peripheries to the centre in one of the largest and most sustained
periods of 'unplanned' migration in recent history. Driven by poverty,
drought, famine, economic undevelopment and crop failure, civil war
and political unrest, regional conflict and arbitrary changes of political
regime, the accumulating foreign indebtedness of their governments to
Western banks, very large numbers of the poorer peoples of the globe
have taken the 'message' of global consumerism at face value, and
moved towards the places where 'the goodies' come from and where the

chances of survival are higher. In the era of global communica
West is only a one-way airline charter ticket away.

There have been continuous, large-scale, legal and 'illegal' migra
into the US from many poor countries of Latin America, and the
Caribbean basin (Cuba, Haiti, Puerto Rico, the Dominican Republic, the
islands of the British Caribbean), as well as substantial numbers of
'economic migrants' and political refugees from South-East Asia and the
Far East — Chinese, Koreans, Vietnamese, Cambodians, Indians,
Pakistanis, Japanese. Canada has a substantial minority Caribbean
population. One consequence is a dramatic shift in the 'ethnic mix' of
the US population — the first since the mass migrations of the early part
of this century. In 1980, one in every five Americans came from an
African-American, Asian-American or American-Indian background. In
1990, the figure was one in four. In many major cities (including Los
Angeles, San Francisco, New York, Chicago, and Miami), whites are
now a minority. In the 1980s, the population of California grew by 5.6
million, 43 per cent of which were people of colour — that is, including
Hispanics and Asians, as well as African-Americans (compared to 33
per cent in 1980) — and one-fifth is foreign born. By 1995 one-third of
American public school students are expected to be 'non-white' (US
Census, 1991, quoted in Platt, 1991).

Over the same period, there has been a parallel 'migration' into Europe
of Arabs from the Maghreb (Morocco, Algeria, Tunisia), and Africans
from Senegal and Zaire into France and Belgium; of Turks and North
Africans into Germany; of Asians from the ex-Dutch East and West
Indies and Surinam into the Netherlands; of North Africans into Italy;
and, of course, of people from the Caribbean and from India, Pakistan,
Bangladesh, Kenya, Uganda and Sri Lanka into the UK. There are
political refugees from Somalia, Ethiopia, the Sudan and Sri Lanka and
other places in small numbers everywhere.

This formation of ethnic-minority 'enclaves' within the nation-states of
the West has led to a 'pluralization' of national cultures and national
identities.

5.2   THE DIALECTIC OF IDENTITIES

How has this situation played itself out in Britain in terms of identity?
The first effect has been to contest the settled contours of national
identity, and to expose its closures to the pressures of difference,
'otherness' and cultural diversity. This is happening, to different
degrees, in all the Western national cultures and as a consequence it has
brought the whole issue of national identity and the cultural
'centredness' of the West into the open.

> Older certainties and hierarchies of British identity have been
> called into question in a world of dissolving boundaries and
> disrupted continuities. In a country that it is now a container of

> African and Asian cultures, the sense of what it is to be British can
> never again have the old confidence and surety. Other sources of
> identity are no less fragile. What does it mean to be European in a
> continent coloured not only by the cultures of its former colonies,
> but also by American and now Japanese cultures? Is not the very
> category of identity itself problematical? Is it at all possible, in
> global times, to regain a coherent and integral sense of identity?
> Continuity and historicity of identity are challenged by the
> immediacy and intensity of global cultural confrontations. The
> comforts of Tradition are fundamentally challenged by the
> imperative to forge a new self-interpretation based upon the
> responsibilities of cultural Translation.
> (Robins, 1991, p.41)

Another effect has been to trigger a widening of the field of identities,
and a proliferation of new identity-positions together with a degree of
polarization amongst and between them. These developments constitute
the second and third possible consequences of globalization I referred to
earlier (Section 4) — the possibility that globalization might lead to a
strengthening of local identities, or to the production of *new identities*.

The strengthening of local identities can be seen in the strong defensive
reaction of those members of dominant ethnic groups who feel
threatened by the presence of other cultures. In the UK, for example,
such defensiveness has produced a revamped Englishness, an aggressive
little Englandism, and a retreat to ethnic absolutism in an attempt to
shore up the nation and rebuild 'an identity that coheres, is unified and
filters out threats in social experience' (Sennett, 1971, p.15). This is
often grounded in what I have earlier called 'cultural racism', and is
evident now in legitimate political parties of both Left and Right, and in
more extremist political movements throughout Western Europe.

It is sometimes matched by a strategic retreat to more defensive
identities amongst the minority communities themselves in response to
the experience of cultural racism and exclusion. Such strategies include
re-identification with cultures of origin (in the Caribbean, India,
Bangladesh, Pakistan); the construction of strong counter-ethnicities —
as in the symbolic identification of second-generation Afro-Caribbean
youth, through the symbols and motifs of Rastafarianism, with their
African origin and heritage; or the revival of cultural traditionalism,
religious orthodoxy and political separatism, for example, amongst
some sections of the Muslim community.

There is also some evidence of the third possible consequences of
globalization — the production of *new* identities. A good example is
those new identities which have emerged in the 1970s, grouped around
the signifier 'black', which in the British context provides a new focus
of identification for *both* Afro-Caribbean and Asian communities. What
these communities have in common, which they represent through
taking on the 'black' identity, is not that they are culturally, ethnically,
linguistically or even physically the same, but that they are seen and
treated as 'the same' (i.e. non-white, 'other') by the dominant culture. It

is their exclusion which provides what Laclau and Mouffe call the common 'axis of equivalence' of this new identity. However, despite the fact that efforts are made to give this 'black' identity a single or unified content, it continues to exist as an identity *alongside a wide range of other differences.* Afro-Caribbean and Indian people continue to maintain different cultural traditions. 'Black' is thus an example, not only of the *political* character of new identities — i.e. their *positional* and conjunctural character (their formation in and for specific times and places) — but also of the way identity and difference are inextricably articulated or knitted together in different identities, the one never wholly obliterating the other.

As a tentative conclusion it would appear then that globalization *does* have the effect of contesting and dislocating the centred and 'closed' identities of a national culture. It does have a pluralizing impact on identities, producing a variety of possibilities and new positions of identification, and making identities more positional, more political, more plural and diverse; less fixed, unified or trans-historical. However, its general impact remains contradictory. Some identities gravitate towards what Robins calls 'Tradition', attempting to restore their former purity and recover the unities and certainties which are felt as being lost. Others accept that identity is subject to the play of history, politics, representation and difference, so that they are unlikely ever again to be unitary or 'pure'; and these consequently gravitate towards what Robins (following Homi Bhabha) calls 'Translation'.

Section 6 will now briefly sketch this contradictory movement between Tradition and Translation on a wider, global canvas and ask what it tells us about the way identities need to be conceptualized in relation to modernity's futures.

Asian cultural identities maintained in a European context

6   FUNDAMENTALISM, DIASPORA AND HYBRIDITY

Where identities are concerned, this oscillation between Tradition and Translation (which was briefly traced above in relation to Britain) is becoming more evident on a global canvas. Everywhere, cultural identities are emerging which are not fixed, but poised, *in transition*, between different positions; which draw on different cultural traditions at the same time; and which are the product of those complicated cross-overs and cultural mixes which are increasingly common in a globalized world. It may be tempting to think of identity in the age of globalization as destined to end up in one place or another: either returning to its 'roots' or disappearing through assimilation and homogenization. But this may be a false dilemma.

For there is another possibility: that of 'Translation'. This describes those identity formations which cut across and intersect natural frontiers, and which are composed of people who have been *dispersed* forever from their homelands. Such people retain strong links with their places of origin and their traditions, but they are without the illusion of a return to the past. They are obliged to come to terms with the new cultures they inhabit, without simply assimilating to them and losing their identities completely. They bear upon them the traces of the particular cultures, traditions, languages and histories by which they were shaped. The difference is that they are not and will never be *unified* in the old sense, because they are irrevocably the product of several interlocking histories and cultures, belong at one and the same time to several 'homes' (and to no one particular 'home'). People belonging to such *cultures of hybridity* have had to renounce the dream or ambition of rediscovering any kind of 'lost' cultural purity, or ethnic absolutism. They are irrevocably *translated*. The word 'translation', Salman Rushdie notes, 'comes etymologically from the Latin for "bearing across"'. Migrant writers like him, who belong to two worlds at once, 'having been borne across the world ... are translated men' (Rushdie, 1991). They are the products of the new *diasporas* created by the post-colonial migrations. They must learn to inhabit at least two identities, to speak two cultural languages, to translate and negotiate between them. Cultures of hybridity are one of the distinctly novel types of identity produced in the era of late-modernity, and there are more and more examples of them to be discovered.

ACTIVITY 3   You should now read **Reading C, 'Diaspora cultures'**, by Paul Gilroy. The author here highlights the question of 'diaspora identities' through a study of 'black British' culture of the 1980s.

Some people argue that 'hybridity' and syncretism — the fusion between different cultural traditions — is a powerful creative source, creating new forms that are more appropriate to late-modernity than the old, embattled national identities of the past. Others, however, argue that hybridity, with the indeterminacy, 'double consciousness', and relativism it implies, also has its costs and dangers. Salman Rushdie's novel about migration, Islam, and the prophet Mohammed, *The Satanic Verses,* with its deep immersion in Islamic culture *and* its secular consciousness of the exiled 'translated man', so offended the Iranian fundamentalists that they passed sentence of death on him for blasphemy. It also outraged many British Muslims. In defending his novel, Rushdie offered a strong and compelling defence of 'hybridity'.

> Standing at the centre of the novel is a group of characters most of whom are British Muslims, or not particularly religious persons of Muslim background, struggling with just the sort of great problems that have arisen to surround the book, problems of hybridization and ghettoization, of reconciling the old and the new. Those who oppose the novel most vociferously today are of the opinion that intermingling with different cultures will inevitably weaken and ruin their own. I am of the opposite opinion. *The Satanic Verses* celebrates hybridity, impurity, intermingling, the transformation that comes of new and unexpected combinations of human beings, cultures, ideas, politics, movies, songs. It rejoices in mongrelization and fears the absolutism of the Pure. *Mélange,* hotchpotch, a bit of this and a bit of that is *how newness enters the world.* It is the great possibility that mass migration gives the world, and I have tried to embrace it. *The Satanic Verses* is for change-by-fusion, change-by-conjoining. It is a love-song to our mongrel selves.
> (Rushdie, 1991, p.394)

However, the *Satanic Verses* may well have become trapped between the irreconcilable forces of Tradition and Translation. This is the view offered by the sympathetic, but critical, Bhiku Parekh in Reading D.

ACTIVITY 4   You should now read **Reading D, 'Between holy text and moral void'**, by Bhiku Parekh.

On the other hand, there are equally powerful attempts to reconstruct purified identities, to restore coherence, 'closure' and Tradition, in the face of hybridity and diversity. Two examples are the resurgence of nationalism in Eastern Europe and the rise of fundamentalism.

In an era when regional integration in the economic and political fields, and the breaking down of national sovereignty, are moving very rapidly in Western Europe, the collapse of the communist regimes in Eastern Europe and the break-up of the old Soviet Union have been followed by a powerful revival of ethnic nationalism, fuelled by ideas of both racial purity and religious orthodoxy. The ambition to create new, culturally

The tension between
Tradition and
Translation

and ethnically unified nation-states (which I have suggested above
never really existed in Western national cultures) was the driving force
behind the break-away movements in the Baltic states of Estonia, Latvia
and Lithuania, the disintegration of Yugoslavia and the move to
independence of many former Soviet Republics, from Georgia, the
Ukraine, Russia and Armenia to Kurdistan, Uzbekistan and the 'Muslim'
Asian republics of the old Soviet state. Much the same process has been
taking place in the 'nations' of Central Europe which were carved out of
the disintegration of the Austro-Hungarian and Ottoman Empires at the
end of the First World War.

These new would-be 'nations' try to construct states that are unified in
both ethnic and religious terms, and to create political entities around
homogeneous cultural identities. The problem is that they contain
within their 'borders' minorities who identify themselves with different
cultures. Thus, for example, there are 'ethnic' Russian minorities in the
Baltic Republics and the Ukraine, ethnic Poles in Lithuania, an
Armenian enclave (Nagorno-Karabakh) in Azerbaijan, Turkic-Christian
minorities amongst the Russian majorities of Moldavia, and large
numbers of Muslims in the southern republics of the old Soviet Union
who share more, in cultural and religious terms, with their Middle-
Eastern Islamic neighbours than with many of their 'countrymen'.

The other significant form of the revival of particularistic nationalism and ethnic and religious absolutism is, of course, the phenomenon of 'fundamentalism'. This is evident everywhere (for example, in the revived little-Englandism referred to earlier), though its most striking example is to be found in some Islamic states in the Middle East. Beginning with the Iranian Revolution, fundamentalist Islamic movements, which seek to create religious states in which the political principles of organization are aligned with the religious doctrines and laws of the *Koran*, have arisen in many, hitherto secular Islamic societies. In fact, this trend is difficult to interpret. Some analysts see it as a reaction to the 'forced' character of Western modernization; certainly, Iranian fundamentalism was a direct response to the efforts of the Shah in the 1970s to adopt Western models and cultural values wholesale. Some interpret it as a response to being left out of 'globalization'. The reaffirmation of cultural 'roots' and the return to orthodoxy has long been one of the most powerful sources of counter-identification amongst many Third World and post-colonial societies and regions (one thinks here of the roles of nationalism and national culture in the Indian, African and Asian independence movements). Others see the roots of Islamic fundamentalism in the failure of Islamic states to throw up successful and effective 'modernizing' leaderships or secular, modern parties. In conditions of extensive poverty and relative economic under-development (fundamentalism is stronger in the poorer Islamic states of the region), a restoration of the Islamic faith is a powerful mobilizing and binding political and ideological force, especially where democratic traditions are weak.

The trend towards 'global homogenization', then, is matched by a powerful revival of 'ethnicity', sometimes of the more hybrid or symbolic varieties, but also frequently of the exclusive or 'essentialist' varieties cited above. Bauman has referred to this 'resurgence of ethnicity' as one of the main reasons why the more extreme, free-ranging or indeterminate versions of what happens to identity under the impact of the 'global post-modern' requires serious qualification.

> The 'resurgence of ethnicity' ... puts in the forefront the unanticipated flourishing of ethnic loyalties inside national minorities. By the same token, it casts a shadow on what seems to be the deep cause of the phenomenon: the growing separation between the membership of body politic and ethnic membership (or more generally, cultural conformity) which removes much of its original attraction from the programme of cultural assimilation. ... Ethnicity has become one of the many categories or tokens, or 'tribal poles', around which flexible and sanction-free communities are formed and in reference to which individual identities are constructed and asserted. There are now, therefore, [many] fewer centrifugal forces which once weakened ethnic integrity. There is instead a powerful demand for pronounced, though symbolic rather than institutionalized, ethnic distinctiveness.
> (Bauman, 1990, p.167)

The resurgence of nationalism and other forms of particularism at the end of the twentieth century, alongside and intimately linked to globalization, is of course a remarkable reversal, a most unexpected turn of events. Nothing in the modernizing Enlightenment perspectives or ideologies of the West — neither liberalism nor indeed Marxism, which for all its opposition to liberalism also saw capitalism as the unwitting agent of 'modernity' — foresaw such an outcome.

Both liberalism and Marxism, in their different ways, implied that the attachment to the local and the particular would gradually give way to more universalistic and cosmopolitan or international values and identities; that nationalism and ethnicity were archaic forms of attachment — the sorts of thing which would be 'melted away' by the revolutionizing force of modernity. According to these 'metanarratives' of modernity, the irrational attachments to the local and the particular, to tradition and roots, to national myths and 'imagined communities', would gradually be replaced by more rational and universalistic identities. Yet globalization seems to be producing neither simply the triumph of 'the global' nor the persistence, in its old nationalistic form, of 'the local'. The displacements or distractions of globalization turn out to be more varied and more contradictory than either its protagonists or opponents suggest. However, this also suggests that, though powered in many ways by the West, globalization may turn out to be part of that slow and uneven but continuing story of the de-centring of the West.

REFERENCES

Abercrombie, N., Hill, S. and Turner, B. (1986) *Sovereign Individuals of Capitalism*, London, Allen and Unwin.

Abercrombie, N., Hill, S. and Turner, B. (eds) (1988) *The Penguin Dictionary of Sociology*, 2nd edn, Harmondsworth, Penguin.

Althusser, L. (1966) *For Marx*, London, Verso.

Anderson, B. (1983) *Imagined Communities*, London, Verso.

Barnett, A. (1982) *Iron Britannia*, London, Allison and Busby.

Bauman, Z. (1990) 'Modernity and ambivalence', in Featherstone, M. (ed.), *Global Culture*, London, Sage.

Bhabha, H. (ed.) (1990) *Narrating the Nation,* London, Routledge.

Bocock, R. and Thompson, K. (eds) (1992) *Social and Cultural Forms of Modernity*, Cambridge, Polity Press.

Brennan, T. (1990) 'The national longing for form', in Bhabha, H. (ed.) *Narrating The Nation*, London, Routledge.

Derrida, J. (1981) *Writing and Difference*, London, Routledge.

Dodd, P. (1986) 'Englishness and the national culture', in Colls, R. and Dodd, P. (eds) *Englishness: Politics and Culture, 1880–1920*, London, Croom Helm.

Donald, J. and Rattansi, A. (eds) (1992) *'Race', Culture and Difference*, London, Sage.

Dreyfus, H. and Rabinow, P. (1982) *Michel Foucault: Beyond Structuralism and Hermeneutics*, Brighton, Harvester.

Forester, J. (1987) 'A brief history of the subject', in *Identity: The Real Me*, ICA Document 6, London, Institute for Contemporary Arts.

Foucault, M. (1967) *Madness and Civilization*, London, Tavistock.

Foucault, M. (1973) *Birth of the Clinic*, London, Tavistock.

Foucault, M. (1975) *Discipline and Punish*, London, Allen Lane.

Foucault, M. (1986) 'The subject and power', in Dreyfus, J. and Rabinow, P., *Michel Foucault: Beyond Structuralism and Hermeneutics*, Brighton, Harvester.

Frisby, D. (1985) *Fragments of Modernity*, Cambridge, Polity Press.

Gellner, E. (1983) *Nations and Nationalism*, Oxford, Blackwell.

Giddens, A. (1990) *The Consequences of Modernity*, Cambridge, Polity Press.

Gilroy, P. (1992) 'The end of anti-racism', in Donald, J. and Rattansi, A. (eds) *'Race', Culture and Difference*, London, Sage.

Gilroy. P. (1987) *There ain't no Black in the Union Jack,* London, Hutchinson.

Hall, C. (1992) *White, Male and Middle Class: Explorations in Feminism and History*, Cambridge, Polity Press.

Hall, S. (1985) 'Religious cults and social movements in Jamaica', in Bocock, R. and Thompson, K. (eds) *Religion and Ideology*, Manchester, Manchester University Press.

Hall, S. (1987) 'Minimal Selves', in *Identity: The Real Me,* ICA Document 6, London, Institute for Contemporary Arts.

Hall, S. (1990) 'Cultural identity and diaspora', in Rutherford, J. (ed.), *Identity*, London, Lawrence and Wishart.

Hall, S. and Gieben, B. (eds) (1992) *Formations of Modernity*, Cambridge, Polity Press.

Harvey, D. (1989) *The Condition of Post-Modernity*, Oxford, Oxford University Press.

Hobsbawm, E. and Ranger, T. (eds) (1983) *The Invention of Tradition*, Cambridge, Cambridge University Press.

Lacan, J. (1977) 'The mirror stage as formative of the function of the I', in *Écrits*, London, Tavistock.

Laclau, E. (1990) *New Reflections on the Revolution of our Time*, London, Verso.

Locke, J. (1967) *An Essay Concerning Human Understanding*, London, Fontana.

Marx, K. and Engels, F. (1973) *The Communist Manifesto,* in *Revolutions of 1848,* Harmondsworth, Penguin Books.

Massey, D. (1991) 'A global sense of place', *Marxism Today*, June.

Mercer, K. (1990) 'Welcome to the jungle', in Rutherford, J. (ed.), *Identity*, London, Lawrence and Wishart.

Nairn, T. (1977) *The Break-up of Britain*, London, Verso.

Parekh, B. (1989) 'Between holy text and moral void', *New Statesman and Society*, 23 March.

Penguin Dictionary of Sociology: see Abercrombie *et al.* (1988).

Platt, A. (1991) *Defending the Canon*, Fernand Braudel Centre and Institute of Global Studies, Binghamton, State University of New York.

Powell, E. (1969) *Freedom and Reality*, Farnham, Elliot Right Way Books.

Renan, E. (1990) 'What is a nation?', in Bhabha, H. (ed.) *Narrating the Nation*, London, Routledge.

Robins, K. (1991) 'Tradition and translation: national culture in its global context', in Corner, J. and Harvey, S. (eds), *Enterprise and Heritage: Crosscurrents of National Culture*, London, Routledge.

Rushdie, S. (1991) *Imaginary Homelands*, London, Granta Books.

Said, E. (1990) 'Narrative and geography', *New Left Review* No.180, March/April, pp.81–100.

Schwarz, B. (1986) 'Conservatism, nationalism and imperialism', in Donald, J. and Hall, S. (eds), *Politics and Ideology*, Milton Keynes, Open University Press.

Scruton, R. (1986) 'Authority and allegiance', in Donald, J. and Hall, S. (eds) *Politics and Ideology*, Milton Keynes, Open University Press.

Sennett, R. (1971) *The Ideas of Disorder*, Harmondsworth, Penguin.

Urry, J. (1990) *The Tourist Gaze*, London, Sage.

Wallerstein, I. (1979) *The Capitalist Economy*, Cambridge, Cambridge University Press.

Wallerstein, I. (1984) *The Politics of the World Economy*, Cambridge, Cambridge University Press.

Wallerstein, I. (1991) 'The national and the universal', in King, A. (ed.), *Culture, Globalization and the World System*, London, Macmillan.

Williams, R. (1976) *Keywords*, London, Fontana.

READING A   GLOBAL CULTURE

Kevin Robins

The historical development of capitalist economies has always had profound implications for cultures, identities, and ways of life. The globalization of economic activity is now associated with a further wave of cultural transformation, with a process of cultural globalization. At one level, this is about the manufacture of universal cultural products — a process which has, of course, been developing for a long time. In the new cultural industries, there is a belief — to use Saatchi [and Saatchi] terminology — in 'world cultural convergence'; a belief in the convergence of lifestyle, culture, and behaviour among consumer segments across the world. This faith in the emergence of a 'shared culture' and a common 'world awareness' appears to be vindicated by the success of products like *Dallas* or *Batman* and by attractions like Disneyland. According to the president of the new Euro Disneyland, 'Disney's characters are universal'. 'You try and convince an Italian child', he challenges, 'that Topolino — the Italian name for Mickey Mouse — is American' (Shamoon, 1989).

As in the wider economy, global standardization in the cultural industries reflects, of course, the drive to achieve ever greater economies of scale. More precisely, it is about achieving both scale and scope economies by targeting the shared habits and tastes of particular market segments at the global level, rather than by marketing, on the basis of geographical proximity, to different national audiences. The global cultural industries are increasingly driven to recover their escalating costs over the maximum market base, over pan-regional and world markets. They are driven by the very same globalizing logic that is reshaping the economy as a whole.

The new merchants of universal culture aspire towards a borderless world. Sky and BSB (which merged their activities in October 1990) beam out their products to a 'world without frontiers'; satellite footprints spill over the former integrity of national territories. With the globalization of culture, the link between culture and territory becomes significantly broken. A representative of Cable News Network (CNN) describes the phenomenon:

> There has been a cultural and social revolution as a consequence of the globalisation of the economy. A blue-collar worker in America is affected as much as a party boss in Moscow or an executive in Tokyo. This means that what we do for America has validity outside America. Our news is global news.
> (Quoted in Fraser, 1989)

What is being created is a new electronic cultural space, a 'placeless' geography of image and simulation. ... This new global arena of culture is

Source: Robins, K. (1991) 'Tradition and translation: national culture in its global context', in Corner, J. and Harvey, S. (eds), *Enterprise and Heritage: Crosscurrents of National Culture*, London, Routledge, pp.28–31, 33–6.

a world of instantaneous and depthless communication, a world in which space and time horizons have become compressed and collapsed.

The creators of this universal cultural space are the new global cultural corporations. In an environment of enormous opportunities and escalating costs, what is clearer than ever before is the relation between size and power. What we are seeing in the cultural industries is a recognition of the advantages of scale, and in this sphere too, it is giving rise to an explosion of mergers, acquisitions, and strategic alliances. The most dynamic actors are rapidly restructuring to ensure strategic control of a range of cultural products across world markets. ...

If the origination of world-standardized cultural products is one key strategy, the process of globalization is, in fact, more complex and diverse. In reality, it is not possible to eradicate or transcend difference. Here, too, the principle of equidistance prevails: the resourceful global conglomerate exploits local difference and particularity. Cultural products are assembled from all over the world and turned into commodities for a new 'cosmopolitan' market-place: world music and tourism; ethnic arts, fashion, and cuisine; Third World writing and cinema. The local and 'exotic' are torn out of place and time to be repackaged for the world bazaar. So-called world culture may reflect a new valuation of difference and particularity, but it is also very much about making a profit from it. Theodore Levitt explains this globalization of ethnicity. The global growth of ethnic markets, he suggests, is an example of the global standardization of segments:

> Everywhere there is Chinese food, pitta bread, country and western music, pizza, and jazz. The global pervasiveness of ethnic forms represents the cosmopolitanisation of speciality. Again, globalisation does not mean the end of segments. It means, instead, their expansion to worldwide proportions.
> (Levitt, 1983, pp.30–1)

Now it is the turn of African music, Thai cuisine, Aboriginal painting, and so on, to be absorbed into the world market and to become cosmopolitan specialities.

Global–local nexus

Globalization is about the compression of time and space horizons and the creation of a world of instantaneity and depthlessness. Global space is a space of flows, an electronic space, a decentred space, a space in which frontiers and boundaries have become permeable. Within this global arena, economies and cultures are thrown into intense and immediate contact with each other — with each 'Other' (an 'Other' that is no longer simply 'out there', but also within).

I have argued that this is the force shaping our times. Many commentators, however, suggest that something quite different is happening: that the new geographies are, in fact, about the renaissance of locality and region. There has been a great surge of interest recently in local economies and local economic strategies. The case for the local or regional economy as the key unit of production has been forcefully made by the 'flexible specialization' thesis. ... This perspective stresses the central and prefigurative importance of localized production complexes. Crucial to their success, it is suggested, are strong local institutions and infrastructures: relations of trust based on face-to-face contact; a 'productive community' historically rooted in a particular place; a strong sense of local pride and attachment. ...

Whilst globalization may be the prevailing force of our times, this does not mean that localism is without significance. If I have emphasized processes of de-localization, associated especially with the development of new information and communications networks, this should not be seen as an absolute tendency. The particularity of place and culture can never be done away with, can never be absolutely transcended. Globalization is, in fact, also associated with new dynamics of *re*-localization. It is about the achievement of a new global–local nexus, about new and intricate relations between global space and local space. Globalization is like putting together a jigsaw puzzle: it is a matter of inserting a multiplicity of localities into the overall picture of a new global system.

We should not idealize the local, however. We should not invest our hopes for the future in the redemptive qualities of local economies, local cultures, local identities. It is important to see the local as a relational, and relative, concept. If once it was significant in relation to the national sphere, now its meaning is being recast in the context of globalization. For the global corporation, the global–local nexus is of key and strategic importance. According to Olivetti's Carlo de Benedetti, in the face of ever-higher development costs, '*globalisation* is the only possible answer'. 'Marketers', he continues, 'must sell the latest product everywhere at once — and that means producing *locally*' (quoted in Scobie, 1988). Similarly, the mighty Sony describes its operational strategy as 'global localisation' (Wagstyl, 1989). NBC's vice-president, J.B. Holston III, is also resolutely 'for localism', and recognizes that globalization is 'not just about putting factories into countries, it's being part of that culture too' (Brown, 1989, p.44).

What is being acknowledged is that globalization entails a corporate presence in, and understanding of, the 'local' arena. But the 'local' in this sense does not correspond to any specific territorial configuration. The global–local nexus is about the relation between globalizing and particularizing dynamics in the strategy of the global corporation, and the 'local' should be seen as a fluid and relational space, constituted only in and through its relation to the global. ...

The global–local nexus is ... not straightforwardly about a renaissance of local cultures. There are those who argue that the old and rigid hegemony of national cultures is now being eroded from below by burgeoning local and regional cultures. Modern times are characterized, it is suggested, by a process of cultural decentralization and by the sudden resurgence of place-bound traditions, languages and ways of life. It is important not to devalue the perceived and felt vitality of local cultures and identities. But again, their significance can only be understood in the context of a broader and encompassing process. Local cultures are over-shadowed by an emerging 'world culture' — and still, of course, by resilient national and nationalist cultures.

References

Brown, C. (1989) 'Holston exports', *Broadcast*, 13 October.

Fraser, N. (1989) 'Keeping the world covered', *Observer*, 12 November.

Levitt, T. (1983) *The Marketing Imagination*, London, Macmillan.

Scobie, W. (1988) 'Carlo, suitor to La Grande Dame', *Observer*, 14 February.

Shamoon, S. (1989) 'Mickey the Euro mouse', *Observer*, 17 September.

Wagstyl, S. (1989) 'Chief of Sony tells why it bought a part of America's soul', *Financial Times*, 4 October.

READING B   A GLOBAL SENSE OF PLACE

Doreen Massey

... Time–space compression needs differentiating socially. This is not just a moral or political point about inequality, although that would be sufficient reason to mention it; it is also a conceptual point.

Imagine for a moment that you are on a satellite, further out and beyond all actual satellites; you can see 'planet earth' from a distance and, rarely for someone with only peaceful intentions, you are equipped with the kind of technology which allows you to see the colours of people's eyes and the numbers on their numberplates. You can see all the movement and tune in to all the communication that is going on. Furthest out are the satellites, then aeroplanes, the long haul between London and Tokyo, and the hop from San Salvador to Guatemala City. Some of this is people moving, some of it is physical trade, some is media broadcasting. There are faxes, e-mail, film-distribution networks, financial flows and transactions. Look in closer and there are ships and trains, steam trains slogging laboriously up hills somewhere in Asia. Look in closer still and there are lorries and cars and buses, and on down further, somewhere in sub-Sahara Africa, there's a woman on foot who still spends hours a day collecting water.

Now, I want to make one simple point here, and that is about what one might call the *power-geometry* of it all; the power-geometry of time–space compression. For different social groups, and different individuals, are placed in very distinct ways in relation to these flows and interconnections. This point concerns not merely the issue of who moves and who doesn't, although that is an important element of it; it is also about power in relation *to* the flows and the movement. Different social groups have

Source: Massey, D. (1991) 'A global sense of place', *Marxism Today*, June, pp.25–26.

distinct relationships to this anyway differentiated mobility: some people are more in charge of it than others; some initiate flows and movement, others don't; some are more on the receiving-end of it than others; some are effectively imprisoned by it.

In a sense, at the end of all the spectra are those who are both doing the moving and the communicating and who are in some way in a position of control in relation to it — the jet-setters, the ones sending and receiving the faxes and the e-mail, holding the international conference calls, the ones distributing the films, controlling the news, organising the investments and the international currency transactions. There are the groups who are really in a sense in charge of time–space compression, who can really use it and turn it to advantage, whose power and influence it very definitely increases. On its more prosaic fringes this group probably includes a fair number of Western academics and journalists — those, in other words, who write most about it.

But there are also groups who are also doing a lot of physical moving, but who are not 'in charge' of the process in the same way at all. The refugees from El Salvador or Guatemala and the undocumented migrant workers from Michoacán in Mexico, crowding into Tijuana to make a perhaps fatal dash for it across the border into the US to grab a chance of a new life. Here the experience of movement, and indeed of a confusing plurality of cultures, is very different. And there are those from India, Pakistan, Bangladesh, the Caribbean, who come half way round the world only to get held up in an interrogation room at Heathrow.

Or — a different case again — there are those who are simply on the receiving end of time–space compression. The pensioner in a bed-sit in any inner city in this country, eating British working-class-style fish and chips from a Chinese take-away, watching a US film on a Japanese television; and not daring to go out after dark. And anyway the public transport's been cut.

Or — one final example to illustrate a different kind of complexity — there are the people who live in the *favelas* of Rio, who know global football like the back of their hand, and have produced some of its players; who have contributed massively to global music, who gave us the samba and produced the lambada that everyone was dancing to last year in the clubs of Paris and London; and who have never, or hardly ever, been to downtown Rio. At one level they have been tremendous contributors to what we call time–space compression; and at another level they are imprisoned in it.

This is, in other words, a highly complex social differentiation. There are differences in the degree of movement and communication, but also in the degree of control and of initiation. The ways in which people are placed within 'time–space compression' are highly complicated and extremely varied. ...

READING C   DIASPORA CULTURES

Paul Gilroy

It bears repetition that 'race', ethnicity, nation and culture are not inter-changeable terms. The cultural forms discussed below cannot be contained neatly within the structures of the nation-state. This quality can be used to reveal an additional failing in the rigid, pseudobiological definition of national cultures which has been introduced by ethnic absolutism. Black Britain defines itself crucially as part of a diaspora. Its unique cultures draw inspiration from those developed by black populations elsewhere. In particular, the culture and politics of black America and the Caribbean have become raw materials for creative processes which redefine what it means to be black, adapting it to distinctively British experiences and meanings. Black culture is actively made and re-made. ...

As black styles, musics, dress, dance, fashion and languages became a determining force shaping the style, music, dress, fashion and language of urban Britain as a whole, blacks have been structured into the mechanisms of this society in a number of different ways. Not all of them are reducible to the disabling effects of racial subordination. This is part of the explanation of how ... youth cultures ... became repositories of anti-racist feeling. Blacks born, nurtured and schooled in this country are, in significant measure, British even as their presence redefines the meaning of the term. The language and structures of racial politics, locked as they are into a circular journey between immigration as problem and repatriation as solution, prevent this from being seen. Yet recognizing it and grasping its significance is essential to the development of anti-racism in general and in particular for understanding the social movements for racial equality that helped to create the space in which 'youth culture' could form. The contingent and partial belonging to Britain which blacks enjoy, their ambiguous assimilation, must be examined in detail for it is closely associated with specific forms of exclusion. If we are to comprehend the cultural dynamics of 'race' we must be able to identify its limits. This, in turn, necessitates consideration of how blacks define and represent themselves in a complex combination of resistances and negotiations, which does far more than provide a direct answer to the brutal forms in which racial subordination is imposed.

Black expressive cultures affirm while they protest. The assimilation of blacks is not a process of acculturation but of cultural syncretism. ... Accordingly, their self-definitions and cultural expressions draw on a plurality of black histories and politics. In the context of modern Britain this has produced a diaspora dimension to black life. Here, non-European traditional elements, mediated by the histories of Afro-America and the Caribbean, have contributed to the formation of new and distinct black cultures amidst the decadent peculiarities of the Welsh, Irish, Scots and English. These non-European elements must be noted and their distinc-

Source: Gilroy, P. (1987) *There ain't no Black in the Union Jack*, London, Hutchinson, pp.154–6.

tive resonance must be accounted for. Some derive from the immediate history of Empire and colonization in Africa, the Caribbean and the Indian sub-continent from where post-war settlers brought both the methods and the memories of their battles for citizenship, justice and independence. Others create material for the processes of cultural syncretism from extended and still-evolving relationships between the black populations of the over-developed world and their siblings in racial subordination elsewhere.

The effects of these ties and the penetration of black forms into the dominant culture mean that it is impossible to theorize black culture in Britain without developing a new perspective on British culture *as a whole*. This must be able to see behind contemporary manifestations into the cultural struggles which characterized the imperial and colonial period. An intricate web of cultural and political connections binds blacks here to blacks elsewhere. At the same time, they are linked into the social relations of this country. Both dimensions have to be examined and the contradictions and continuities which exist between them must be brought out.

READING D   BETWEEN HOLY TEXT AND MORAL VOID

Bhikhu Parekh

The central life experiences of immigrants cast them in a highly ambiguous relationship with the sacred. Lacking roots in an ongoing way of life, unable to feel in their bones the deepest joys and agonies of their adopted home, cut off from the social well-springs of meaning and value, their lives lack depth and richness, the commonest source of the experience of sacredness. Their dignity as human beings is constantly mocked by the hostile 'host' society; their sacred family ties are brutally snapped by evil immigration laws; their children leave home every morning and return speaking a language increasingly unintelligible and even hurtful to them. Thanks to all this, their predominant mood is one of doubt and suspicion, a subdued rage at the hypocrisy of a society that says one thing but does the opposite.

Different immigrants respond to these experiences and moods differently and evolve different strategies of physical and moral survival. Of these, two are relevant to our discussion. At one extreme, there is total cynicism. All people stink, are imposters, ruthless, cheats, predators, manipulators. None can be trusted, not even, or rather especially not, fellow-immigrants. Everything in this world is superficial and crude, and can be mocked, deflated, perverted, turned upside-down. At the other extreme, there is a retreat to the familiar certainties of the past.

The meaning of life is deemed to be permanently and incorrigibly revealed in a sacred text, body of rituals, or a pool of inherited and inviolable

Source: Parekh, B. (1989) 'Between holy text and moral void', *New Statesman and Society*, 23 March, pp.30–1.

traditions. Even if these are perceived to be irrelevant or inapplicable in the new environment, they are uniquely the immigrant's own in a society that has stripped him or her of all else, the only thing that *distinguishes* them, gives them a past, roots in the present and the confidence to face the future. The holy text or traditions give certainty in a world of moral void; they are a sure protection against the dehumanising impact of cynicism. At one extreme, then, deep and self-destructive doubt; at the other, an impenetrable and intolerant certainty. One has lost a sense of sacredness, the other has a surfeit of it.

All immigrants, however reflective and introspective they may be, harbour bits of both tendencies (and many others), nervously holding them in a precarious balance, turning to one when the other fails or becomes unbearable. Rushdie is no exception. He writes about the tension between these tendencies without fully appreciating that it lies at the very centre of his being and both enriches and distorts his perception of his subject matter.

This is evident in *The Satanic Verses*. An immensely daring and persistently probing exploration of the human condition, which only a rootless immigrant can undertake, lies ill at ease with timid obeisance to the latest literary and political fashions; profound seriousness lapses suddenly and without warning into pointless playfulness. The sacred is interlaced with flippancy, the holy with the profane. Intensely delicate explorations of human relationships and emotions are shadowed by an almost childlike urge to shock, hurt and offend.

As an immigrant, Rushdie sometimes seems to resent that everyone around him is not an immigrant; on other occasions, he is profoundly pleased that the natives have their roots intact and showers benediction. At a different level, he is both drawn towards and repelled by his fellow-immigrants. He both fights them and fights for them; both resents them and delights in their world of certainties; cares for them but also tramples on their dearest memories and sentiments. He loves them as real human beings, yet he also turns them into an abstract cause; and his holy anti-racism goes hand-in-hand with touches of contempt for them.

It is this that at least partly explains the current tension between him and the Muslims. The tension is a result of the conflict between two very different approaches to the predicament of an exile. Unlike the white onlookers who understand neither, the contestants know that nothing less than their fundamental existential choices, and even sanity, are at stake. The vast majority of Muslims have chosen one way of coping with their predicament; Rushdie another. They give meaning to their poor and empty lives by holding on to the holy and its rocklike certainties; he doubts almost everything, including the very search for meaning. Their approach has little room for doubt; Rushdie's has only a limited space for the holy, or even the sacred, and he is deeply nervous in its presence. They solace each other within a common fellowship and lead individually heteronomous lives within an autonomous group; Rushdie's quest for personal autonomy leads to an ambiguous relationship with the white society and especially its literary establishment. The inescapable conflict between the two exploded the moment he produced a full-scale exploration of the sacred in *The Satanic Verses*.

CHAPTER 7 THE ENLIGHTENMENT PROJECT REVISITED

Gregor McLennan

CONTENTS

1   INTRODUCTION: THE POST-MODERN CONDITION

The previous chapters of this book have outlined a series of debates about the changing structures and dynamics of modern (mainly western) society. Sometimes these debates are about social processes such as market diversification, occupational restructuring, and economic or political 'globalization'. Sometimes the focus appears to be rather more political, cultural and experiential: our changing sense of personal identity and political allegiance, for example. Of course, the overall key question has been whether 'modernity' is passing, or has already passed, into a state of 'post-modernity'.

This chapter is about the changing nature of modern social *thought*. An examination of this topic confirms, perhaps even more than in other topic areas, how *radical* the challenge of 'post-modernity' is. This is because the crisis and (supposed) surpassing of modernity is not merely a matter of economic, political and cultural *processes;* it is also the crisis of a whole way of *understanding* the social world, a long-established way of 'knowing' society. Post-modern theorists say that a changing social world requires an entirely different way of *reflecting* on our existence today. In other words, they argue that, just as social *conditions* change, so too do the *concepts* and *categories* that we use to make sense of society. As social scientists, we thus need to 'deconstruct' fundamentally the way we habitually look at the social world. This means examining and perhaps even discarding some of the basic ideas and aspirations of social science, ideas which go back to the Enlightenment of the eighteenth century. That is why the title of this chapter invites us to 'revisit' the whole Enlightenment project for social science.

Notice that in speaking of an 'Enlightenment project' we are not implying a totally unified theory or organized intellectual movement, though it is true that the phrase does tend to suggest something very deliberate and coherent. Such a degree of unity and purpose did not exist even amongst the original *philosophes*; and today those who share a desire to preserve something of the Enlightenment heritage do not necessarily share a particular belief system or an 'ism' in the way, for example, that Marxists or feminists do. So there is something slightly misleading about the term 'Enlightenment project'.

And yet it is also undeniable that there is a cluster of underlying assumptions and expectations about the nature of modern social theory which are shared by a significant number of social scientists and which stem from classical eighteenth- and nineteenth-century scientific aspirations. Today, these assumptions are being put under the theoretical microscope, and whether the decision is finally to preserve or reject them, one thing is clear: that they form a very *strong* and *distinctive* cluster of beliefs and expectations about the role of knowledge in the improvement of the human condition. In that sense, the idea of a 'project' — a general aspiration — seems a more appropriate label to use for the Enlightenment heritage than a blander term such as 'outlook' or 'perspective'.

But in what sense are the ideas of the 'Enlightenment project' coming under attack? Take, for example, one manifestly central idea: the scientific study of something called 'society'. From the outset, this proposition implies that a fairly coherent and uniform set of interrelated phenomena, one which exists 'out there', as it were, is readily amenable to sociological reflection 'in here'. In sociological knowledge, therefore, the real state of a singular being (society) gets mentally appropriated by means of abstract sociological concepts and appropriate methods of investigation.

But, at this point, the post-modernist comes along and says: Hold on, are we really sure that we can make even this initial distinction between what is 'out there' and what is 'in here'? Moreover, what gives us the right, he or she asks, to see society as a totality, as a unified and coherent being? Why isn't it just a motley collection of unrelated bits and pieces? And how can we ever tell if our concepts genuinely do 'grasp' or 'reflect' this thing called society accurately? Indeed, who is to say what 'knowledge' of society really amounts to?

Such a provocative trail of questions is not exclusive to post-modernists — many other social scientists have posed them too. But post-modernists are especially convinced that now more than ever before we need to be openly *un*certain about the status of all the concepts and results of social science. This concern to unsettle the basic concepts of sociology explains why one of the key texts for this chapter, Lyotard's *The Postmodern Condition*, is actually subtitled 'A report on *knowledge*' rather than, say, 'a report on social change'. Truly to begin to understand post-modern society, in other words, it is not enough to register and reflect on changes in social conditions: the very form and content of sociological reflection itself must be fundamentally reoriented.

It is important at this point to clarify the relation between social science and philosophy or epistemology (i.e. the theory of knowledge). You could say, to begin with, that only philosophers are interested *primarily* in epistemological questions such as 'what is knowledge?' or 'what is truth?' Social scientists, by contrast, are primarily interested in finding out about human society and in developing theories about its structure and dynamics. However, social scientists do become embroiled in philosophical questions as a 'secondary' pursuit. This is because it is impossible to understand society by merely looking and seeing what is there. We need *theories* of society for deep understanding. And yet, as is well known, very *different* theories and interpretations are usually available to be drawn upon in any sociological area; and these different theories often present us with very different 'facts', different 'pictures', and different *versions* of what society is really all about.

So although social scientists are interested primarily in *society,* they become interested in questions about truth, knowledge and validity because theories must be judged between and *justified.* And the process of justification inevitably raises the question about how we *know* one theory or version of society is better or truer than another. Moreover, when it is realized that many of the apparently 'hard' terms of sociology — such as 'class', 'social action' or 'interaction', and even 'society' itself — are organizing *concepts* as much as palpable entities, then once again social science is plunged into a secondary concern with epistemology. We want to ask: Why *that* concept rather than some other? What *is* the relation between sociological concepts and social reality? — And so on.

2   A DEBATE: POST-MODERNITY VERSUS ENLIGHTENMENT

The Enlightenment occurred at the threshold of typically modern Western society, and it gave a definitive shape to many of the ideas and procedures of modern western social science (see Book 1 (Hall and Gieben, 1992), Chapter 1). The post-modernist challenge to the Enlightenment model of social knowledge involves either rejecting entirely, or at least seriously questioning, the following typical Enlightenment tenets:

- The view that our knowledge of society, like society itself, is *holistic, cumulative,* and broadly *progressive* in character.
- That we can attain *rational* knowledge of society.
- That such knowledge is *universal* and thus *objective.*
- That sociological knowledge is both *different* from, and *superior* to, 'distorted' forms of thought, such as ideology, religion, common sense, superstition and prejudice.
- That social scientific knowledge, once validated and acted upon, can lead to mental liberation and social betterment amongst humanity generally.

In sum, the post-modernist thesis is that, not only have the structures of modern *society* begun to change dramatically, but also that the foundations of modern social *thought* have become obsolete and dogmatic.

There are three main possible responses to that critical thesis. One is to accept it as valid and consequently to embark upon a search for a distinctly 'non-Enlightenment' rationale for sociological enquiry. The second response is to try to refute the post-modernist challenge and in various ways defend the Enlightenment project. A third response is to attempt something of a compromise; for example, we might accept that, as a result of post-modernist criticisms, the Enlightenment project now looks rather weak or dogmatic or in crisis; we may also perhaps feel that post-modernism itself has few *constructive* answers to the sorts of difficult questions it raises.

The pattern of this chapter follows the logic of the debate as just sketched out. The next two sections present brief extracts from Lyotard and Habermas, respectively. Then I look at responses to the debate between these two which are roughly speaking pro-Habermas, pro-Lyotard, and neutral. Finally, I engage in an evaluative overview which includes summaries of how the debate affects two of the most influential traditions of social science thinking, namely Marxism and feminism.

3 LYOTARD: ABANDONING THE METANARRATIVES OF MODERNITY

Let us begin by analysing a short reading from a key figure in the anti-Enlightenment camp, Jean-François Lyotard. Lyotard's book *The Postmodern Condition* was first published in France in 1979 and translated into English in 1984, causing something of a sensation within social philosophy. Here is how that book opens.

ACTIVITY 1   You should now read **Reading A, 'Abandoning the metanarratives of modernity'**, by Jean-François Lyotard, which you will find at the end of this chapter.

As I read this text, Lyotard seems to be defining what he calls the 'postmodern age' in terms of the kinds of technological and social changes referred to in earlier chapters of this volume. This is not, however, the 'postmodern condition' as such. For Lyotard, this latter term is reserved for the condition or status of *knowledge* about society, knowledge of ourselves in the post-modern age. It thus concerns the basic conceptual frameworks that we adopt in order to understand modern life. This focus on knowledge involves developing an *epistemological* rather than a substantive slant on the issue of whether modernity is passing (has passed) into post-modernity. (Epistemological = concerning concepts of knowledge; substantive = concerning matters of empirical substance.)

Lyotard asserts that the main feature of the Enlightenment approach to knowledge is its concern to be scientifically legitimate. Science in this sense implies 'objective' and 'impartial' knowledge of the world, and stands in sharp contrast to what Lyotard terms 'narratives'; that is, the myriad *stories* or 'fables' that we invent in order to give meaning and significance to our lives. These stories or narratives may be personal, political, moral, mythical, religious, or whatever. But the point, as far as the Enlightenment view of knowledge is concerned, is that narratives as such do not deliver *real* knowledge (i.e. universally valid principles or laws), be they laws of nature or laws of society. Rather, narratives exist to provide existential or ideological comforts to us as we go through life, and they are irremediably tainted — as compared with scientific truths — by their essentially local, social and personal contexts. The governing assumption of Enlightenment thought, for Lyotard, is altogether loftier than this, namely that society 'out there' can be progressively 'captured' by social scientific knowledge without any recourse whatsoever to the taints and comforts of personal and social narratives.

However, the dramatic assertion which Lyotard then makes is that this whole Enlightenment picture of 'pure' knowledge is itself nothing but a very powerful *myth*: in effect precisely a narrative of sorts. Now, whilst the scientific concern with objective knowledge may not, as such, be a comforting story, nevertheless that concern is invariably justified or 'legitimated' by reference to higher-level storylines, and these Lyotard terms 'metanarratives'. Amongst the main influential metanarratives of the last 200 years which have served to legitimate the myth of objective Science, Lyotard mentions the heroic legends of 'the creation of wealth', the 'working subject' and 'the dialectics of Spirit'.

What Lyotard is getting at here is that aspirations to scientific knowledge are never quite as pure as Enlightenment thought makes out. Scientific progress, for example, is often seen as a necessary and crucial part of the drive for industrial and commercial growth ('the creation of wealth'). And economic growth is often in turn seen as the precondition of human well-being and civilization. Marxist theorists would present a somewhat different metanarrative, saying that science ultimately serves, or ought to serve, the liberation of humanity (i.e. 'the working subject') from exploitation, labour and toil. Other philosophers have conceived human progress in terms of the progress of *ideas themselves*, forming a potential spiral of spiritual emancipation ('the dialectics of Spirit').

So it seems after all that many supposedly objective aspirations to science inevitably tend to be framed by some kind of metanarrative involving distinctly value-laden notions of social progress and human emancipation. Emancipation here is, if you like, the end of the story, and it is science that enables us to perceive clearly the essence of that story of humanity's progress.

Science alone, however, cannot provide the whole of the metanarrative, for that, according to Lyotard, is the job of the discourse known as *philosophy*. It is philosophy rather than science as such which decides what is to be classed as 'real' science and what is to be stigmatized as 'mere' narrative; it is philosophy which exists to inform us of what the true essence and end points of the story of human Progress and Knowledge are; and it is philosophy which judges what counts as true and what does not.

Now, Lyotard proposes further that this modernist conception of knowledge, which features such a cosy partnership between the pursuit of science and the legitimating discourse of philosophy, should be abandoned completely. Instead of pursuing the truth, we should openly embrace the postmodern condition of uncertainty and 'agonistics' (i.e. rhetorical jousting). There are two prongs to Lyotard's attack here.

One is really a point of logic, and is already implicit in what I have said so far. If the objective grandeur of 'science' actually always turns out to rest upon some sort of metanarrative or other — none of which can be 'objectively' proved or refuted, but each acting as the philosophical rationalization of human ideologies — then the very claim to objectivity and value-neutrality is spurious, deceitful and self-cancelling. Further, if the mantle of 'objectivity' is simply unavailable, then no one metanarrative is inherently 'privileged' over any other. But if *this is* so, then we need to be very sceptical about the ultimate truth-claims of *all* metanarratives. Lyotard thus defines the condition of post-modernity as 'incredulity toward metanarratives', whether the latter are to do with the historical march of Reason, Civilization, Wealth, or the Proletariat.

Lyotard's second prong of argumentation is more sociological than philosophical. He refers to the significant changes going on in the whole mode of collecting and communicating social information. And ultimately 'knowledge' is about just that: the storage of, and 'aura' surrounding, certain kinds of discourse and information. If this is so, he then implies, there is simply no place today for a view of knowledge which sees it as a privileged unified body of mental 'thought' which exists in the collective Mind, and which is guarded preciously by an élite of scientists, philosophers and academics. Rather, the reality of knowledge today is a huge array of 'moves' within pragmatic 'discourses' or 'language games', all targeted towards very specific audiences, each having its own criterion of accreditation and each increasingly treated in practice as an economic *commodity* to be bought and sold according to its market demand.

Moreover, the advanced technology of computerized information storage encourages us to treat knowledge as a set of resources and services which we can draw upon, and pass on, for particular social purposes. To view knowledge pragmatically and realistically in this way is virtually to destroy the sacred 'aura' of modernist conceptions of knowledge and science. But note also that to 'deconstruct' knowledge, to de-sanctify it, to remove it from the hereditary possession of philosophers, scholars and scientists, is not necessarily to wholly *devalue* it, in Lyotard's eyes. On the contrary, by adopting the post-modern view of knowledge as a kaleidoscopic array of limited and transient language games, we can see how deep at the heart of post-modern society, knowledges (in the plural, not the singular) actually lie. The control of information, for example, is quite central nowadays to economic production, political opinion-forming and military control alike. Nothing could be more significant than that.

4   HABERMAS: DEFENDING MODERNITY AND ENLIGHTENMENT

In Lyotard's contribution, Jürgen Habermas was cited as someone still very much concerned to 'legitimate' knowledge in the classical Enlightenment sense. Habermas has been developing over the decades, and in great volume, a defence of 'the Enlightenment project' as he understands it. Whilst much of this intellectual labour pre-dates Lyotard's broadside, it is useful here to see Habermas's views as a kind of *response* to post-modernists like Lyotard.

ACTIVITY 2   You should now read **Reading B1, 'Modernity: an incomplete project'**, and **Reading B2, 'The philosophical discourse of modernity'**, by Jürgen Habermas.

In these statements, Habermas elaborates a little further than Lyotard on the origins of Enlightenment aspirations. He reminds us that part of the Enlightenment project was the separating out of three main forms of human thinking — science, morality and art — forms which had previously been rolled up together as a whole world-view under the hegemony of religious or metaphysical principles. In that sense, the Enlightenment project was far less 'holistic' than Lyotard and post-modernists frequently imply.

Habermas sees three different types of rationality developing according to that separation of cognitive spheres. 'Experts' in each sphere come to dominate access to it, and serve to protect specialist knowledge from the clutches of the wider public. In a sense, Habermas is admitting that the Enlightenment project was only ever an *ideal*, not a reality, because from the outset a kind of 'separatist' culture evolved which compartmentalized and professionalized the different spheres of knowledge. Indeed, Habermas goes as far as to suggest that the original fragmentation ('splitting off') of rationality does tend to lead to the kind of atomized, pragmatic forms of knowledge that are highlighted by post-modernists such as Lyotard. To that extent, Habermas does not dispute that the use of knowledge *has* become computerized, compartmentalized, commodified and fragmented. Nor does he have any innocent faith in the *actual* prospects for pure Enlightenment. As he says, the brutal history of the twentieth century has shattered such optimism.

What, then, *is* the dispute between these two thinkers? Firstly, Habermas wants to emphasize the relative blinkeredness and backwardness of the epoch of *pre-modernity*. In that context, he pleads, we should remember the *positive* role of the original Enlightenment epoch.

Secondly, Habermas feels that we have met the likes of Lyotard before in the history of modern philosophy and modern art. Indeed, the history of modernity in its widest sense must be conceived as *including* 'those extravagant programs which have tried to negate modernity'. Whilst agreeing to *learn* something from anti-modernist movements (such as Lyotard now offers and such as the German philosopher Friedrich Nietzsche offered in the nineteenth century), Habermas believes that such movements have 'failed' intellectually. In the second extract particularly, Habermas basically accuses the 'radical critique of reason' or 'Nietzscheanism' of throwing the baby out with the bath water: so totally negative is this critique that its proponents forget the many ambivalent aspects of modernity, and indeed forget about its *positive* connotations, notably 'the prospect of a self-conscious practice, in which the solidary self-determination of all was to be joined with the self-realization of each'.

Thirdly, such a (misplaced) total critique of Enlightenment and modernity inevitably results, politically speaking, in disillusionment and conservatism. By contrast, if we hold on to the original *intentions* of the Enlightenment, then the search for some degree of universality and objectivity remains wedded to the hope that knowledge might 'promote ... the justice of institutions and even the happiness of human beings'. Habermas believes that we can retain the *hope* without falling prey to naïve *expectations*; and in any case, he thinks, the alternative seems to be nothing less than despair. In that sense alone, the Enlightenment project has some running left in it yet.

But true to his dislike of purely negative critique, Habermas does not rest his case for upholding the Enlightenment project solely on the (in his view) demerits of post-modernist arguments. In addition, and at great length, he has constructed a theory of what he calls *communicative action* or *communicative reason*. This theory (elements of which I shall return to) is designed to be both analytically valid as an account of the conditions of meaningful social interaction, and politically progressive as a yardstick for emancipated relationships.

The story so far

Lyotard has criticized both the logical inconsistency and the sociological *naïveté* of Enlightenment or modernist epistemology. Instead, he articulates a post-modernist conception of local pragmatic language games and incredulity towards all metanarratives. In response, Habermas accepts the failures of the original Enlightenment project and the precise way in which the Enlightenment belief in science was presented. Nevertheless, he sees the Enlightenment project as historically progressive *vis-à-vis* pre-modernity, and regards its intentions as still progressive today given the prospect of post-modernist conservatism. In that belief he has attempted to construct a positive theory of communicative reason, one in which an ideal of egalitarian, rational and undistorted interaction between social agents is preserved and promoted.

5   A PROBLEM WITH POST-MODERNISM: ITS RELATIVISM

It could be argued that the central issue of the whole debate about the fate of the Enlightenment project hangs on the question of relativism. Today, many would accept the idea that the morals and manners of a society are very much specific to that particular type of society. In that sense, cultural relativism seems a sound basis from which to conduct social investigations. However, whether the adoption of *cultural relativism* as a sensible basis for social observation necessarily requires the acceptance of *cognitive relativism* (i.e. the view that there can be no such things as universal principles of validity, truth or rationality) is hotly disputed. Critics of the Enlightenment project are convinced that the connection between the two types of relativism cannot be broken, and that a more genuine enlightenment is created by simply accepting relativism right across the board. Against this, defenders of the Enlightenment project feel that cultural relativism does not necessarily entail cognitive relativism, for otherwise we would have to renounce any commitment to principled intellectual enquiry. As we see from our next reading, that is the one main fear which affects those who are broadly pro-Habermas and anti-Lyotard.

ACTIVITY 3   You should now read **Reading C, 'Habermas: autonomy and solidarity',** by Peter Dews.

Like some of the other Readings in this chapter, Dews's presentation might appear somewhat formidable at first, principally due to the roll-call of famous names featured in it. Not only Habermas and Lyotard take a bow, but also Nietzsche, Wittgenstein and Feyerabend. However, it is a *crucial* 'study skill' in approaching debates in social theory to take a deep breath and 'read past' the cited protagonists in order to grasp the main lines of the argument at issue — *no matter which particular 'name' happens to occupy centre stage in the exchanges.*

And in fact, if you are able to take the risk of overcoming your sense of inadequacy (which I assure you is both shared by others and usually quite unmerited!), then a piece such as Dews's offers a very concise encapsulation of the whole skirmish about relativism. Let's look at his discussion, step by step.

Dews begins by saying that, for Lyotard and Nietzsche, the world is conceived as a 'plurality' — a vast array of very different people, ideas, beliefs and standards of judgement. He further suggests that, for Lyotard, this plurality is irreducible; that is to say, any attempt to give it some kind of hidden unity or ultimate meaning is really to 'violate' that plurality. Lyotard's own version of plurality-in-the-world, as we have already seen, involves treating the social world as an almost infinite series of small-scale discourses or 'language games'. The latter are very definitely 'heterogenous' — that is, intrinsically different and non-comparable — so almost by definition they cannot be boxed up together as if they have exactly the same or even a similar purpose or meaning.

Habermas, however (according to Lyotard), tries to do precisely this: he tries to 'enforce' the myriad local language-games into a similar mould, whereby they all reveal the same hidden meaning. This, for Lyotard, is Habermas's cardinal 'error'.

Dews's response identifies 'three distinct levels' of counter-critique, by means of which Lyotard's case can be dismissed. One, he states, is philosophical. (When writers refer to an argument as being philosophical, they usually mean that there is some point of *logic* to be made, or that there is something to do with the very definitions of the *concepts* used by another writer, which renders the theory under review flawed or perhaps even self-contradictory.)

In this instance, Dews takes Lyotard to task for creating a 'chronic confusion' between two distinct ideas. From the fact that there exist a great many different discourses or 'language games', Lyotard wrongly infers that there can be no possible common standards of consistency or validity which cut across all discourses, *in spite of* the notable differences between them. But Dews contends that this is a false inference — that the second idea does not logically follow from the first.

Dews further contends that, contrary to what Lyotard asserts, Habermas is perfectly willing to accept that multiple discourses exist in complex modern societies. Habermas himself, of course, tends to emphasize just *three* main types of discourse (science, art and morality), but we can readily think of many other language games in society, each governed by conventions and terms which are rather peculiar to itself. Commerce, for example, might involve a distinct species of language game, as might sport, work, leisure, shopping, love and war. And each of these 'games' will probably vary with different socio-cultural contexts (e.g. 'East' and 'West'), thus adding a further layer to the complexity of discourses within society.

All the same, Habermas and Dews want to hold on to the possibility that all that complexity does not obliterate the need for some overarching notions of validity which govern all mini-discourses. This does *not* mean that all discourses appeal to exactly the same criterion of validity. Each language game permits very different sorts of valid 'moves'. But still, within *any* language game, all participants must be equally clear about the governing rules, and must in a sense 'agree' to abide by them, even if only to register further disagreement. For Habermas, all linguistic communication implies an 'agreement' of this sort. When two speakers engage with one another, even if only to disagree, they *take for granted* certain assumptions about the organization of speech, and necessarily assume that they could reach an agreement, if they were to debate specific issues with one another under conditions free of distorting factors (i.e. free of domination). This notion is the core of what Habermas calls 'the ideal of rational discourse' embedded in communicative action; and it is at the core of his positive theory. (For a fuller account, see Bernstein, 1985.)

Dews terms his second set of arguments 'political', in that he accuses Lyotard of political complacency and conservatism by his very use of the term 'language game'. A language game is never just a matter of mere talk or specialist terminology. Rather, 'games' are spheres of action involving the exchange of attitudes, values, behaviour and strategy. Games thus also give rise to *conflict*. For example, although young boys frequently play 'war games', war itself is a kind of 'game' — that is, a pattern of structured interaction between people with its own rules of cooperation and conflict (the 'first strikes', the 'retaliation', the 'truce', the 'lull in the fighting', etc.). War, then, is a game like many other forms of social interaction, but a game which is not at all 'in pretence'; it is very much for real.

Dews seems to believe that something as grave as, say, war should not really be termed a 'game' at all, nor that such literally action-packed games should be reduced to their *linguistic* element. So he objects to the very idea of society as made up entirely of language games. He prefers the term 'social practice', which has a proper ring of gravity about it. Of course, social practices still very much involve language, but they are not *reducible* to their linguistic aspect. Lyotard's usage, for Dews, has more than a hint of liberal complacency about it, almost as though a cosy chat or an 'agonistic' dispute about semantics were sufficient to progress such vital social 'language games' as dealing with pollution, deindustrialization, or alcoholism.

The second part of Dews's 'political' objection is, in fact, an extension of his earlier 'philosophical' point, and it is here that Dews most fully raises the question of relativism. Dews starts this point by asserting that Lyotard's position *is* in effect a relativist one; he then lodges the charge that Lyotard's position is invalid because it shares the pitfall of all relativism: self-contradiction.

Let us probe these objections more closely. The first step arises because Lyotard claims that all language games are intrinsically separate from one another — they all have different underlying rules, logics and motivations which absolutely cannot be reduced to one another, nor can they all be subsumed under some higher abstract idea such as 'truth'. It would seem to follow from this that no discourse, or human participant within it, can genuinely *communicate* with any other. Discourses are 'incommensurable' in that sense — they simply cannot be compared or judged one against the other. It would seem that, as participants within discourses, we must be 'locked' inside them, forever debarred from saying anything 'objective' at all about whether one discourse is better or worse than any other; or whether anything is right or wrong, full stop.

A classic example of this relativist dilemma is the debate about 'other cultures'. Here the question is: how *can* a modern, western, scientific culture (discourse) judge — or even properly *understand* — a so-called 'alien' or 'primitive' tribal culture, when the standards and meanings prevalent within the one discourse simply do not have any direct equivalents within the other? Better, then, say the relativists, just to accept such interesting differences between cultures/discourses and try as best we can to understand them in a sympathetic, non-judgemental way. What we *cannot* do is match them against fictitious abstract notions such as Truth, Beauty, etc., since each culture has its own standards in these matters. It follows that no-one is ever in a position to assert the truth and validity of any particular set of 'universal' principles with which to make comparative judgements across societies. And from this it follows that no culture is truly universal: all of us are, always, 'locked' into the norms of our own very transient and specific 'slot' located within space and history. To imagine otherwise, say the relativists, is mere illusion, a wholly false bid by mere humans to attain the impossible 'God's eye view' of the world.

For 'objectivists', however, this relativist argument is specious, and its conclusion is an unnecessary caricature. For one thing, to recognize that we can come to *understand* something of another culture/discourse immediately is, paradoxically, to accept that *some* things can be asserted as meaningful across very different cultures. And, secondly, if meanings and concepts *can* come to be shared, then perhaps so can some cross-cultural concepts of truth and validity, however difficult and complex those inevitably must be. Thirdly, to say that discursive values are always radically and necessarily unmatchable looks itself suspiciously like an *absolute* claim to validity, and this is something which relativists hold to be impossible. But in that case, relativism becomes self-contradictory and therefore unpersuasive.

This introduction to the relativism versus objectivism debate was indispensable, since Dews relishes finding the 'nemesis of all relativism' in Lyotard's specific version of it. The latter says that any attempt to impose 'homogeneity' on the infinity of 'heteromorphous' language games is both impossible and 'terroristic'. Dews replies that this itself is an absolute and terroristic claim which must apply to all language games. Therefore, some principles of verbal and intellectual exchange are universal after all. But this is just the conclusion Lyotard was most concerned to avoid!

Dews's third argument is 'historical' in focus. Lyotard's position seems to imply that in post-modern times we are moving out of an age of uniformity, collectivity and universality and into one characterized by individuation, fragmentation and difference. In response, Dews wants to avoid any sharp contrast between these clusters of concepts, pointing out that, in fact, the whole period of modernity has witnessed *both* individualization and universality. Indeed, he thinks (along with Habermas) that the more separate from one another people or societies or language games become, the *more* they tend to rely on abstract general principles, and the explicit formalization of social rules. Lyotard's vision of pluralism has no place for this important phenomenon of increasing abstract universality. As a result, his post-modern world looks merely 'particularistic'; that is, one in which people are simply atomized and fragmented. Dews implies that this is not a very good or very 'emancipated' condition to advocate. Further, Dews says, relativism encourages intellectual and human indifference: if all cognitive and moral values are relative to specific discourses/language/cultures, then why make any big claims at all about what is right, just or true? Why bother to hold any views about anything?

Throughout this line of thought, Dews (and Habermas), though not seeking to find a grandiose 'God's eye view' of society, do nevertheless seem to believe that arguments about what is true and good *can* be productively engaged in, within and across cultures. They also believe that some important measure of agreement can be reached about how to decide what is true and good. For the moment, Lyotard looks to be in trouble.

6 A PROBLEM WITH ENLIGHTENMENT: ITS HUBRIS

In the last section, you probably felt that the weight of argument was swinging towards Dews and Habermas and against Lyotard. Partly this is because we took as our starting point Dews's own summary of Lyotard, and such summaries in academic and political debate often have distinctly unfavourable 'conclusions' already written between the lines.

So now we need to put the boot on the other foot. What if Dews is caricaturing Lyotard and post-modernism every bit as much as he claims Lyotard caricatures Habermas? And what if some parallel undesirable political conclusion can be seen to follow from the adoption of hardline 'objectivist' arguments against relativism?

The next reading, by Zygmunt Bauman, contrasts strongly with that of Peter Dews, in being broadly pro-Lyotard.

ACTIVITY 4   You should now read **Reading D, 'Legislators and interpreters'**, by Zygmunt Bauman.

In this reading, the tone is a good deal 'softer', less polemical than in the earlier extracts. The 'argument' is progressed not in a crisp, point-scoring way, but by generating a sense of reflectiveness in the face of a complex intellectual situation, a situation where reflectiveness rather than point-scoring is more appropriate, in his view, because it is likely to confront us for 'a long, long time'.

Bauman's place in the debate over the Enlightenment project is not immediately obvious, due to his refusal to endorse, or even discuss at length the opposite 'extremes' of outright Enlightenment or outright relativism. His very starting point is that 'the two-centuries-old philosophical voyage to certainty and universal criteria of perfection and "good life" seems to be a wasted effort'. In a sense he is ruling out right from the start those elements in Dews's and Habermas's argument which continue to suggest that a 'God's eye view' of the world remains feasible. The chief flaw in all modernist philosophy and social theory is its *hubris*: the Western 'pretensions to universality'.

As a sociologist, Bauman cannot take these philosophical pretensions at face value. Behind all attempts to 'legislate' what is eternally true, universal and rational, he implies, lies an ideological drive, whether consciously followed or not: the need constantly to rationalize and elevate the norms of our own type of society. In other words, whilst philosophers and scientists, often in good faith, have striven after disembodied truth and rationality, it is the *culture* and *society* of western science and philosophy that is ultimately being defended, not timeless mental values. To that extent, Bauman accepts Lyotard's claim that science and truth are always embedded in ideological metanarratives. The 'unstoppable march of Reason' is thus really only a front for cultural imperialism, and the hubristic seeking-after-truth in Western philosophy is geared to producing the 'comforting' mirage of universality, not its reality. Reason could therefore be seen as merely one form of distinguishing 'the West' from 'the Rest' (in the terms used earlier in this series; see Book 1 (Hall and Gieben, 1992), Chapter 6).

Bauman makes it clear that he sees the *attraction* of the search for pure Reason, but the rationalist philosophers he most respects are those like Ernest Gellner, who is cited and discussed. Gellner is thought to be at least open to the idea that all that searching is inevitably in vain, and that its best rationale is *not* Truth in the end but a half-hearted belief that modern western society — for all its crimes and faults — contains more potential for ultimate good than other alternatives. In other words, the best objectivists, for Bauman, are those who concede that 'science' rests on a moral metanarrative which cannot be finally demonstrated as valid for all times and places.

Bauman further sees the traditional identity of the western intellectual as today entering a stage of terminal crisis. His/her role as 'legislator' for scientific truth and the good society must therefore be abandoned in the face of the manifest failure of intellectuals to be successful legislators in practice: history simply does not follow any single pattern or intellectually-derived blueprint. Instead, we are witnessing an increasing *pluralization* of the life-world (to use a favourite term of Habermas). In that 'irreversibly plural' world, the proper role for intellectuals, Bauman feels, is the appropriately humble one of *interpreting* different cultural traditions and the linkages between them.

Notice here that, in espousing relativism and in debunking the hubris of western universalist philosophy, Bauman makes clear his dissatisfaction with some expressions of a similar stance — Lyotard is not mentioned but he is surely in Bauman's sights here. The problems with outright post-modernism, he implies, are threefold. It is too vociferously stated to make a proper impact on serious but hesitant 'legislators'; it is self-defeating in that the dream of the non-absolute is stated in 'absolutist terms'; and any role for the intellectual seems rather futile if we are confronted by a 'hopelessly plural' world that we can do nothing with.

Bauman's 'interpreter' figure is modest, but not self-negating. Indeed, by retaining an important, if greatly reduced role for intellectuals, Bauman concedes that he too may be engaged in nothing more than a subtle defence of the Western intellectual mode. Moreover, the importance of that role is thought to consist in promoting understanding between different cultures and traditions, an understanding which will 'urgently' contribute to a better life in common amongst the peoples of the world. In that sense, even the figure of the interpreter holds on to aspects of the Enlightenment project.

Having said that, the brunt of Bauman's discussion is clearly aimed *towards* an acceptance of a post-modern conception of social knowledge and simultaneously it is aimed mostly *against* the kind of objectivism which 'refuse[s] to admit realities' which strongly support relativism.

7   POST-MODERNITY AS 'REFLEXIVITY'

At this point in these deliberations, a summary would perhaps be welcome, especially one which is neither particularly pro-Enlightenment nor particularly enamoured of post-modernism. Such a standpoint can be found in the writings of Anthony Giddens, the British social theorist. In the following extract, Giddens encapsulates the debate in a clear and helpful way, and manages to throw in one or two points which we have not considered much so far. Since Giddens's prose is not that heavy going, at least by comparison with some of the earlier readings, I will not elaborately rehearse his arguments. Indeed, you should by now be seeing yourself as a competent critical reader — whatever 'gaps' you may feel still remain in your understanding. As such, you should also be beginning to form your own overall perspectives or preferences in the post-modernity debate.

ACTIVITY 5   You should now read **Reading E, 'The consequences of modernity'**, by Anthony Giddens.

1   Take brief notes on what Giddens takes to be unacceptable in (a) post-modernism and (b) Enlightenment 'foundationalism'.

2   How does Giddens propose that we should understand the supposed move from modernity to post-modernity?

3   Why does Giddens bring in the issue of the 'decline of the West'?

My own response to these questions would be on the following lines. First of all, Giddens has *three* very brief, but quite decisively phrased, criticisms of post-modernism *à la* Lyotard. He wants to dismiss outright as 'unworthy of serious intellectual consideration' the idea that with the coming of post-modernism we must relinquish any claim to proper *knowledge* of society, and claim instead merely fragmentary opinions, insights, or language games. If this really were true, Giddens wagers, then books like *The Postmodern Condition* would just not get written, and their authors would be out jogging rather than engaging in philosophical argumentation.

Giddens further comments that to see society and social knowledge as moving from modernity to post-modernity is, whether we like it or not, to give the history of society a recognizable 'shape' or intellectual story line — even if the current phase of that overall shape is held to be pretty *shapeless.* In other words, whilst post-modernism seems to celebrate intellectual and social indeterminacy, its very self-definition inevitably confers a degree of unity and coherence upon social evolution — yet unity, coherence, and evolution are just the sort of values post-modernism wants to abandon. The post-modern perspective thus seems rather contradictory. Now Giddens tells us that this point about self-contradiction is rather 'obvious' and 'well known', but he is really being too modest here. The point, I would say, has *not* been put in quite as crisp a way before, nor (in my view) to such clear effect. This demonstrates how, in social theory, important contributions can be made as much by reformulating or *clarifying* commonly held theoretical views as by 'inventing' totally novel concepts.

Giddens's third point against post-modernism is that it advocates nothing that was not already present in Nietzsche's work written a hundred odd years ago; so it cannot be said to be new. But in that case, he goes on, we have to admit *either* that post-modernism has (paradoxically) been around for a very long time, or (more plausibly) that modernism for that length of time has contained *within itself* a post-modern 'moment' or aspect. Either way, modernity is more complex than post-modernists make out. (You will probably recognize this kind of point as familiar from previous readings.)

These are emphatic arguments, lucidly stated. However, for all that, Giddens does *not* end up wholeheartedly backing the Enlightenment project. Like Zygmunt Bauman, Giddens is highly suspicious of 'foundationalism'; that is, the philosophical attempt to find and exhibit the essential foundations of our knowledge of the world, thus grounding it in a set of indubitable truths and methods. He mentions a number of such foundationalist ventures in his piece: for example, some philosophers (rationalists) have tried to invoke the power of reason itself, whilst others ('logical positivists') have appealed to the certainty of empirical sense-perception in an effort to 'stabilize' scientific and social scientific categories. But these categories, Giddens implies, and indeed the very business of scientific enquiry, are always changing, are never stable. There is simply no point in chasing after epistemological certainty in this way. There are no indubitable 'foundations' to be discovered in humanity's quest for understanding.

Nor is there any necessary 'progress', whether in knowledge or in society. Giddens dislikes the very idea that history has a hidden essential meaning and *direction* (he calls this 'teleology'). He insists that we need to start feeling more comfortable with the fact that there are *always* going to be conflicting views of progress, that there are always going to be different ways of construing the essence and goal of history in the first place. If the Enlightenment was really only about substituting for religious certainty the belief in a sort of secular 'providence', then it cannot be accepted as a 'reasonable' project at all.

This brings us to Giddens's own way of conceiving 'post-modernism'. In fact, he declares, the Enlightenment is *not* best regarded as supplying a new 'providential view of history'. From the very beginning, Giddens asserts, any tendency for the appeal to reason to become itself dogmatic and faith-like, was sure to be rigorously questioned in the very name of reason. In a sense, critical reason involves questioning *all* faiths, all pre-given 'foundations' for knowledge and society. This is the critical 'voice' or 'moment' *within* modern thought itself, a voice which is suspicious of reason and progress and which has become louder and more persistent through the nineteenth and twentieth centuries. The label that Giddens gives to this inherently self-critical aspect of the Enlightenment project, and of the experience of modernity more generally, is 'reflexivity'.

To be typically modern, Giddens reckons, is not so much to be convinced of rational progress as to be thoroughly 'unsettled' by the way in which reason and progress can be used for very different political and social purposes. The experience of modernity is thus as much about intellectual puzzlement and existential doubt as it is about intellectual conviction in the powers of reason. Such self-questioning, or *reflexivity*, is *inherent* in modernity, Giddens maintains, as indeed can be seen by the very endlessness of debates about whether knowledge has any foundations or not!

Note here that, by introducing the concept of 'reflexivity', Giddens aims to widen the debate, to take it outside of the limited academic sphere. That is because he is sure that reflexivity (i.e. increasing self-questioning, together with proliferating sources of *information*) also bears on the thinking and everyday lives of most 'modern' people. In the streets as well as in the seminar rooms, he implies, people are increasingly self-aware rather than playing fixed roles, are troubled rather than certain, are aware that there may be *many* certainties within and across cultures, not just a few. Later in his book, he compares the experience of modernity to that of riding a scarcely controllable juggernaut. This is a far cry from taking our place aboard the 'A train' of history, guaranteed of controlled progress.

Overall, Giddens thinks that post-modernism, minus the sensationalism, is getting at *something* important in contemporary experience and intellectual reflection. However, he thinks that that 'something' is best understood as 'radicalized modernity', modernity coming to terms with its own intrinsic reflexivity, rather than being a new phase of post-modernity as such.

Finally, Giddens touches on another crucial issue in our debate which Bauman also raised. He connects the rise and fall of Enlightened reason with the rise and decline of western civilization more generally. After all, when we speak of Enlightenment society and thought, we are normally referring to the product of only a handful of modern nation-states in north-west Europe — nations which also first discovered the powers of capitalist industrialization. So, for all its emphasis on the 'higher' pursuits of philosophy and culture, the Enlightenment project can also be seen sociologically as the inner conscience of the wider *western, industrial, capitalist* project.

The march of reason is thus also the march of this particular type of society, its intellectual 'reflection' if you like. Such societies depend absolutely on technological advance which, in turn, thrives on unfettered competition and exchange in the realm of scientific ideas and inventions. Arguably, these cultural 'needs' or reflections of modern industrial society also, in turn, tend to generate an underlying *philosophical* rationale: hence the Enlightenment project, characterized by reason, progress and historical advance. These intellectual 'tools' are of course also very much a part of what distinguishes the 'West' from 'the Rest' and sets it *above* other cultures.

Such a view of Enlightenment should not be seen as straightforward cynicism. It is a way of saying that *all* intellectual works are cultural products; that all cultural products inevitably reflect something of the type of material society which gives them birth; and that western thought and society are no exception. How vain, when you come to think about it, is the claim to have 'unlocked' the secret of universal reason, a claim made by a tiny handful of people and states amongst the vastness of the world's peoples and cultures? What about Chinese science and culture? What about Eastern ways of knowing? What about peasant practical wisdom? Why should western 'scientific' ideas automatically be granted *cultural* dominance? Just because the West has often sought to impose itself on the rest of humanity does not mean that its core ideas have universal validity. Looked at in this way, the increasing *questioning* of modernist ideas from within a 'radicalized modernity' parallels the more general weakening of western imperialism. The cultural decline of these 'advanced' nations means that a correspondingly more significant place must be taken by other peoples, other cultures and other philosophical ideas than 'western' ones — whether these others be conceived as 'Eastern', 'Southern', 'non-white', 'Third World', 'peripheral' or whatever.

8 EVALUATION

In Giddens's hands, we seem to have struck a happy compromise between Enlightenment and post-modernism. The 'extremes' of both apparent alternatives have been debunked, and the problem area has been more subtly redefined so as to include the good bits of both poles of opinion. What more, we might ask, needs to be said? Isn't that simply the end of the story? However, before accepting Giddens's views as the last word on the matter, we should at least make an effort to pose some tricky questions for him too: for example, is not Giddens in the end just trying to have his cake and eat it?

In taking a little from each camp and in giving nothing away, is not Giddens himself displaying signs of indecisive *ambivalence* or even confusion in his own mind? Such a line of suspicious questioning seems justified in the light of Giddens's presentation of the intellectual history of modernity as constantly oscillating between the poles or 'voices' of Enlightenment and anti-Enlightenment. This is after all a predicament which he feels has today reached an all-time degree of *intensity*, and which he affirms is shared by philosophers and lay actors alike (which presumably includes himself). In that sense, the intractability of the Enlightenment debate is not *resolved* by Giddens at all; instead, he seems to be proposing that we should come to *accept* it as part of the fabric of life in 'radicalized modernity'.

So, whilst some readers will be attracted to Giddens's way of handling the post-modernity/Enlightenment debate, others may find it somewhat indecisive and unsatisfactory, and will be the more eager to press for definite intellectual commitment one way or the other. 'Which side are you on?', we might want to ask. As an alternative conclusion, one could perhaps return here to Dews and Habermas, on the one hand, or Lyotard and Bauman on the other. The former pair share Giddens's suspicion of post-modernism and his concern to preserve something of modernity and something of the classical sociological project. But why, then, Dews might ask, is Giddens so hesitant — here and in his other work — to specify some basic 'foundations' for social theory? And why is he so vehemently opposed (as Habermas is not) to some kind of evolutionary perspective on society?

Post-modernists, of course, would merely reverse the weighting of these critical questions. If Giddens is so against objectivists and evolutionism, how can he claim to stage even a partial defence of modernist thought, since objectivism and evolutionism are widely acknowledged to be at the heart of classical Enlightenment social theory? Again, whilst Giddens appears wholly committed to reflexivity, he never fully tackles the crucial issue of relativism, to which it is closely related. At least the post-modernists grab the bull by the horns on this matter.

Looked at in this way, you could reasonably maintain that Giddens does not so much 'advance' the debate as cloud it; and the original positions he appeared to have moved 'beyond' can themselves be made to look, on reflection, more principled and honourable by comparison. This sequence of criticism would also note with disapproval that Giddens's subtle 'middle way' leaves the political ramifications of the debate rather unclear also. Theoretical views certainly tend to reflect more general ideological themes; but they also surely exist to enhance and articulate them in an influential way. By that criterion, Giddens's thinking on post-modernity — whether for good or ill — does not pack much of a punch.

In other words, Giddens's approach will, for some readers, shine through as a sensitive synthesis with little political dogma coming along as baggage; whereas, for others, it will merely express vacillation and ambivalence. The influence of our own *prior* theoretical and ideological leanings in assessing a position is clearly pertinent here. Those who are already committed to a theoretical tradition or stance are likely to be predisposed towards the side of a debate which tends to confirm that allegiance; whereas wholly 'open-minded' readers are perhaps liable to be a little naïve and impressionable.

Before concluding therefore, let us look at two possible responses to the Enlightenment debate which are certainly anchored more firmly within particular traditions of theory and politics than that of Giddens: namely, Marxism and feminism. The strengths and weaknesses of such 'committed' responses should leave us more aware of the range of available evaluative options.

8.1   THE MARXIST RESOLUTION

Theoretically, Marxism is chiefly about the *class analysis* of modern capitalist societies. Essentially, for Marxists, capitalism exists and thrives on the basis of the exploitation of labour by capital, of workers by capitalists. The dynamics of technological growth can generally be explained by reference to the labour–capital relation and the ceaseless drive for profits that is built into the structure of economic calculation. That economic structure broadly determines the social priorities, political formations, and ideological ambience of capitalist society.

More generally, Marxist theory sees human history as a succession of social formations, each governed by its dominant mode of economic production. In successive modes of production, masters have exploited slaves, feudal lords have exploited peasants, and nowadays capitalists exploit workers. Further, each mode of production 'governs' the social, political and cultural character of its epoch and also the character of social *transitions* between successive modes of production. Marx held that each mode of production could expand and subsist only so far, technologically and socially speaking, before severe and inbuilt 'contradictions' arose. Such contradictions and the social crises they encourage impel society into revolutionary change towards some other, historically more appropriate, economic and social structure.

Understood thus, classical Marxism is an Enlightenment project in three main senses. Firstly, class analysis strives to be 'objective' in some sense. Whatever the social and intellectual beliefs of the epoch happen to be, Marx argued, the ultimate rationale for what we do and how we think stems from the logic of the mode of production and from the social relations or class struggles which characterize that mode. The salient 'subjective' aspects of social life in any epoch can thus generally be related to more objective socio-economic factors. Marxist analysis in that sense seeks to be 'scientific' and is committed to the project of rationally unmasking the various ideological 'distortions' which cloud the real driving forces in modern society.

Secondly, when we widen the picture to cover human history in its entirety, it is clear that, for Marxists, history is seen as having an inner logic and dynamic which impels it forward. History is thus assumed to have a significant evolutionary shape; it is relatively coherent, unified, progressive, and rational — not in the sense of *reasonable*, given its frightful story of oppression, but certainly in terms of having an *explicable rationale*.

Thirdly, in Marxism, as in the original Enlightenment idea, scientific knowledge of human society is thought capable of leading to social and spiritual *emancipation* if used correctly. Now the initial impulse in Marxism, which sets its whole *intellectual* endeavour into motion, is in fact a profound sense of the human waste and injustice of class exploitation. Marxism thus begins with a strong commitment to right the wrongs of capitalist and other class-based societies, to help workers and other oppressed groups free themselves so that they can aspire to a better, individually fulfilling, peaceful and cooperative society. From this ethical impulse grows Marxist 'scientific' analysis, which, in turn, confers an 'objective' status on Marxist political practice.

It now appears evident why post-modernism is anathema to traditional Marxism. Post-modernism 'deconstructs' and even mocks the notions of science, objectivity, progress and emancipation that Marxism requires in some version or other. Post-modernism is sceptical of metanarratives, whereas the Marxist 'story' of the liberation of humanity from oppression and ignorance *via* the class struggle provides just such a powerful tale. Post-modernism dissolves the idea of society as possessing some kind of hidden core of meaning into the 'play' of innumerable language games; whereas the category of 'mode of production' provides a clear core concept for seeing society as a totality in spite of its many complex facets. Post-modernism (its opponents feel) can lead to liberal complacency or (worse still) to ultra-conservative nihilism, whereas Marxism must retain a firm sense of (faith in) socialist hope.

In fact, given this antagonism, Marxists would not be altogether happy about Habermas himself being taken to be the prime defender of Enlightenment. Here it needs to be remembered that Habermas regards (regarded) himself as a sort of Marxist. Over the years, however, he has come to share some standard reservations about classical Marxism and has given these a distinctive twist of his own. In particular, Habermas doubts whether the Marxist focus on labour and production can be broad enough to encompass the special features of cultural and political life. The state, for example, has become so enmeshed in economic life that to see the state as a 'mere' superstructure of the economic base is dangerously schematic. Indeed, for Habermas, the whole sphere of moral and political discourse, the sphere which crucially *legitimates* dominant socio-economic structures, possesses today an autonomy and force which traditional Marxism cannot really come to terms with. This argument places not only the state, but also science and technology and the whole apparatus of discourse, argument and proof, at the leading edge of social development.

These very substantial 'revisions' of Marxism prompt Habermas to recast the whole trajectory of social evolution as an ongoing social *learning* process, rather than simply as a succession of class societies or as the historical development of productive *labour*. All this helps explain why a theory of 'communicative reason' has become crucial to Habermas's thinking. In a sense, Habermas reworks the Marxist story of human development (that of the logic, fettering and emancipation of labour) into a story about the logic, distortion and (potential) fulfilment of communicative reason.

By way of response to this critique, orthodox Marxists would first probably want to accuse Habermas of exaggerating the autonomy of reason, morality and the process of communicative interaction. Indeed, in Habermas's hands these aspects of society almost lose all anchorage in the material structures and class relationships of modern life. In that respect, Habermas might be seen as being almost as 'idealist' and as 'superstructuralist' as the post-modernists he opposes.

Secondly, in spite of Habermas's desire to rescue the Enlightenment notions of validity, rationality and truth, he himself operates with a 'pragmatist' concept of truth. In other words, he sees truth and validity as being the *product* of interactive communication between social actors. He does not see truth in absolute terms, as something inherent in the world which human discourse strives to capture; instead, truth is what human beings, in the process of everyday communicative exchange, come to agree upon. But here it appears that Habermas once again shares a great deal (i.e. relativism) with the post-modernists. And once again, because classical Marxism is firmly anti-relativist in flavour, it seems that the latter, and not Habermas, is the more committed defender of Enlightenment values.

All in all, the classical Marxist would strive to adjudicate the debate between Habermas and Lyotard along the lines of 'a plague on both your houses' — though with the moral points definitely going to Habermas. Furthermore, Marxists are liable to see non-Marxist attempts to transcend this debate (such as that of Giddens) as being a kind of fudging or abstention from the serious issues that the debate does succeed in posing. Not surprisingly, the conclusion would be that

Marxism should be respected as the most developed and clear defence of 'radical Enlightenment' (see Callinicos, 1990).

But wait a minute. What of the fact — often cited in social science texts — that there are several variants of Marxism? And is not the entire Marxist tradition in the throes of a major crisis, both theoretically and politically? Politically speaking, the period since the mid-1980s has witnessed the most dramatic collapse of regimes which have claimed to be based on Marxist ideas. Furthermore, many on the Left as well as the Right have long felt that the characteristics and complexities of advanced capitalist society itself are no longer best or exclusively understood in classical Marxist terms. Even Marxism's most fruitful analytical category — 'mode of production' — is regarded by many neo-Marxists as being only one of *several* necessary concepts for comprehending human interaction and struggle. (The others might include gender relations, ethnicity, generation, culture, etc.)

The 'classical' or 'fundamentalist' Marxist would no doubt seek to come back on these apparent weaknesses in Marxism, seeking to show the misplacedness or irrelevance of such 'revisions'. However, as a matter of fact it is clear that Marxism does admit of many variations, some of which entertain serious doubts, not only about the comprehensiveness and validity of classical Marxism, but also about the Enlightenment form in which classical Marxism is undoubtedly cast. These quasi-Marxists feel that Marxism itself has to become more *pluralistic* in its analytic strategy because society and politics themselves are more multi-levelled or pluralistic than Marxists traditionally concede. Such 'revisionist' Marxists will thus accept a great deal of the post-modernist critique of Enlightenment. They will find themselves asking: Who is to say, in the end, which 'grand narrative' is 'objectively' correct? And why continually strive to present Marxism itself as scientific and objectively true, with other views cast in the role of 'distorted' and 'ideological' thought? Is this not indeed precisely *replacing* real science — which ought to be open, relativistic and hesitant — with a blind *faith* in (Marxist) reason? The vulnerable world of the late twentieth century would seem to be too important a context for Marxists to persist in elevating themselves into omniscient 'legislators' (in Bauman's terms).

According to this train of thought, the initial *firmness* of the Marxist 'line' on our debate can fairly quickly be seen to crumble into a series of dilemmas and problems for Marxism itself. If nothing else, this testifies to the vitality and importance of the 'fate of Enlightenment' debate. No sooner has it been resolved than it breaks out again. A similar message can emerge from a consideration of the stance of another radical tradition, namely feminism.

8.2 FEMINIST DILEMMAS

In some ways, we might expect feminism to provide the most decisive of interventions in the kind of debate we have been following. For one thing, feminism is a confident, committed and historically ascendant perspective; it therefore remains unsullied (as Marxism is not) by the historical record, and is continually fired (as liberalism is not) by the strength of male resistance to feminist claims and insights.

From the point of view of this chapter, the feminist critique of the philosophical *style* of reasoning is particularly notable. The point here is that, on the surface, it is philosophy's concern for very *abstract* debate, for purely *logical* forms of demonstration and proof, that distinguishes it from other disciplines. Philosophers deal, not in people or things, but in ideas and disembodied argument. In that sense, nothing could seem further removed from the biases of gender, class or whatever. Moreover, it is presumed from the outset in philosophical discussion, as part of the occupational culture, so to speak, that the participants in philosophical enquiry will, on entering its lofty portals, willingly *shed* their worldly characteristics in order to engage in a pure meeting of minds. These minds may well happen to be predominantly male, but they might also happen to be female: their being male or female is really quite *incidental* to the process of rational enquiry that they embark upon.

However, feminists above all have come to challenge this picture of the philosophical realm as a depersonalized sphere of reason. On the contrary, they ask, is it not *precisely* characteristic of the strivings of a typically *male* outlook to try desperately to shake off worldly connections and responsibilities so as to presume to speak in the name of reason itself?

The ideal of scientific rationality (as espoused in many versions of the Enlightenment project) is but one expression of this male striving for pure reason. Such an ideal stems in the first place from a sharp contrast between, on the one hand, the individual mind or pure ego and, on the other hand, the messy, living world of nature and society. Through a process of interrogation (scientific research) and reflection (philosophy), the pure ego comes to *comprehend* and then *control* nature. The process of intellectual and physical 'mastery' is then complete, and the philosopher-king can congratulate himself on his absolute powers of reason and technique. He has come to *know* and indeed even to *possess* the previously mysterious and threatening 'other' — the concrete, intuitive world of nature.

In short, from a feminist characterization, the austere business of philosophical enquiry *could* be made out as nothing more or less than the very grandest of Boy's Games. Far from being disinterested and cooperative, philosophical debate is often nit-picking, egoistic, and competitive. The picture of pure reason it depicts reveals a world of isolated man, the hunter after truth, 'probing', 'interrogating' and finally 'possessing' the secrets of nature (where nature is usually described in female terms). And the overall aim is ultimately *control*; that is, power. Such a picture of rationality, far from being presuppositionless (as philosophers have always supposed), is arguable teeming with unquestioned assumptions, assumptions which are essentially 'masculinist'.

This interpretation of philosophical endeavour is undoubtedly insightful and hard-hitting. However, if all claims to 'truth' and 'reason' are part of the great Boy's Game that we know as philosophy, then what of the arguments of feminism itself: are they *not* to be judged as fair, good, forceful, reasonable and true in something like the normal (male?) meanings of those terms?

In our final reading, this pressing question for feminist philosophy is explored further.

ACTIVITY 6   You should now read **Reading F, 'Feminist epistemology: an impossible project?'**, by Margareta Hallberg.

Hallberg gives an admirably concise résumé of the dilemmas for feminist philosophy. It is also a very honest résumé: she declares herself in the end *uncertain* about just how to resolve these issues. Indeed, although she states that she cannot see any feasible way of 'grounding' feminist epistemology (thus sharing the post-modern gripe against Enlightenment), she is also manifestly reluctant to give up altogether the objectivist Enlightenment goal of *progressively* enlarging our shared total knowledge, of *demonstrating* rather than merely asserting better arguments, and of holding that good arguments of any kind tell us something positive about the real world 'outside' the speaker's chosen discourse.

Thus, the author concludes that the problems she raises cannot be resolved at the theoretical level: the three tensions identified (objectivism versus relativism, female versus male thinking, unity versus difference) are inherent. Moreover, Hallberg accepts that the most obvious *practical* concept which might be thought to help resolve the issue, namely the common *experience* of women, is just too vague and questionable to bear the theoretical burden placed upon it. As in the case of Marxism — though with different theoretical bearings — an apparently firm and holistic resolution of the Enlightenment debate becomes once again entangled in complications.

9   CONCLUSION

In this chapter I have presented a range of commentaries on the Enlightenment project revisited. In each case the aim has been, not only to give you an understanding of the key themes, but also to give you access to a number of evaluative options. The idea is that you will at least feel you have seriously engaged in an intriguing but sometimes complex theoretical exchange. Additionally, it is hoped that you will by now feel in a position to decide whether, for example, you would defend something like the Enlightenment ideal of social science; or whether you are a relativist or not; or whether or not you favour a holistic social theory (such as Marxism).

However, one of the things which emerges from debates such as this is that the way in which issues are initially framed and subsequently conducted strongly influences how we finally judge them; and, as I mentioned earlier, none of us comes to these debates entirely free of value commitments, stylistic and political preferences, and so on. Given that, it seems appropriate to finish by making two sets of points about my own way of framing issues. In making these points, the idea is that you are encouraged even further to ask yourself 'What do I really make of all this?' — and then, crucially, to try to *answer* that question.

One point concerns the style in which the chapter has been couched, namely that of a 'debate'. Now, in a sense this rhetorical strategy might already be thought to favour an Enlightenment rather than a post-modern perspective. This is because post-modernists might say that a debate format, rather like a law court, encourages spectators to be *judges*, rationally weighing up the pros and cons, in the light of the evidence, and then deciding who has the *truth* of the matter. But post-modernists would prefer to bracket off the whole question of 'truth' and 'rationality' altogether, and choose to speak instead of various rhetorical exchanges, contributions and discussions. Furthermore, they would say that we choose amongst these various strategies as much on aesthetic and emotive grounds as on purely intellectual ones (and that these latter in any pure sense are really just a figment of the academic imagination).

So one conclusion which is available, but which I have not seriously opened up to you, is that the whole 'debate' format is a bit of a trick, an academic rhetorical ploy which you need not feel obliged to follow. However, such a conclusion is acceptable, paradoxically, only on condition that it is thoroughly *argued through*, and not merely *asserted*. Also, as long as we are *aware* that we are deploying a particular rhetorical format (in this case the debate format), then arguably we have met the minimum condition for 'reflexivity' in this area.

The second point has to do with my own favoured position within the debate. Here again it is possible that I have manoeuvred the discussion in a direction that I personally favour; and so, if I am to be truly fair to the reader, I should at least declare my hand — if only to offer a conclusion that you can 'bounce off' in forming your own.

Of the options posed, my own view comes closest to that of Dews. In other words, I favour a broadly pro-Enlightenment perspective, mainly because, like many closet objectivists, I too am perturbed at the prospect of full-scale relativism. It seems to me that without some universal concepts, without some attempt to see the social world as an evolving totality, without some aspiration to better humanity through improving knowledge, I see no purpose whatever in doing social science at all. Indeed, in a back-handed way, I think many avowed post-modernists are themselves actually in the business of seeking to improve our self-critical faculties and thus contributing to a better totalizing perspective on the nature and direction of society.

In favouring this broadly Enlightenment stance, I should add that much of the original motivation for this came from a general allegiance to Marxism as, in my view, the best available theoretical and political tradition. Like many other quasi-Marxists, I would now want to qualify this as follows:

1   The pro-Enlightenment stance can and should be defended *independently* of any preference for particular social theories (including Marxism).

2   The attraction of Marxism today lies as much in the fact that it is an Enlightenment *type* of theory as it does in its particular substantive or theoretical claims. In other words, the *form* of Marxism as a totalizing, determinate social theory seems to me as important as its specific claims about class struggle or the influence of the modes of production at any given time.

By focusing on the type of theory Marxism is, modern Marxists allow themselves an 'escape clause' which enables them to embrace in principle the contributions of other traditions (for instance feminism) in the hope that a new 'synthesis' can emerge to satisfy the continuing Enlightenment cravings of many social scientists. I choose these emotive words (embrace, hope, satisfy, craving) deliberately: for one central lesson Enlighteners have learned from post-modernists (and I am no exception) is that the ultimate motivation for 'rational' progress in knowledge and society is as much emotive, linguistic and social as it is purely cognitive. How else could it be where engaged human beings are the subject as well as the object of knowledge? In that sense, the strategy of the chapter has not been to steer you unilaterally down the Enlightenment road; rather it has been to highlight the mixed blessings of all the various options. My main intention will have been fulfilled, in other words, if I have made you feel something of the intellectual and moral *ambivalence* that is a central element of the experience of (post-)modernity.

REFERENCES

Bauman, Z. (1988) *Legislators and Interpreters*, Cambridge, Polity Press.

Bernstein, R. (ed.) (1985) *Habermas and Modernity*, Cambridge, Polity Press.

Callinicos, A. (1990) 'Reactionary postmodernism', in Boyne, R. and Rattansi, A. (eds) *Postmodernism and Society*, London, Macmillan.

Dews, P. (1986) *Habermas: Autonomy and Solidarity*, London, Verso.

Giddens, A. (1990) *The Consequences of Modernity*, Cambridge, Polity Press.

Habermas, J. (1985) 'Modernity: an incomplete project', in Foster, H. (ed.) *Postmodern Culture*, London, Pluto Press.

Habermas, J. (1987) 'The normative content of modernity', in *The Philosophical Discourse of Modernity*, Cambridge, Polity Press.

Hallberg, M. (1989) 'Feminist epistemology: an impossible project?' in *Radical Philosophy*, no.53, Autumn, pp.3–7.

Hall, S. and Gieben, B. (eds) (1992) *Formations of Modernity*, Cambridge, Polity Press.

Lyotard, J.-F. (1984) *The Postmodern Condition: A Report on Knowledge*, Manchester, Manchester University Press.

READING A   ABANDONING THE METANARRATIVES OF
MODERNITY

Jean-François Lyotard

The object of this study is the condition of knowledge in the most highly developed societies. I have decided to use the word *postmodern* to describe that condition. The word is in current use on the American continent among sociologists and critics; it designates the state of our culture following the transformations which, since the end of the nineteenth century, have altered the game rules for science, literature, and the arts. The present study will place these transformations in the context of the crisis of narratives.

Science has always been in conflict with narratives. Judged by the yardstick of science, the majority of them prove to be fables. But to the extent that science does not restrict itself to stating useful regularities and seeks the truth, it is obliged to legitimate the rules of its own game. It then produces a discourse of legitimation with respect to its own status, a discourse called philosophy. I will use the term *modern* to designate any science that legitimates itself with reference to a metadiscourse of this kind making an explicit appeal to some grand narrative, such as the dialectics of Spirit, the hermeneutics of meaning, the emancipation of the rational or working subject, or the creation of wealth. For example, the rule of consensus between the sender and addressee of a statement with truth-value is deemed acceptable if it is cast in terms of a possible unanimity between rational minds: this is the Enlightenment narrative, in which the hero of knowledge works towards a good ethico-political end — universal peace. As can be seen from this example, if a metanarrative implying a philosophy of history is used to legitimate knowledge, questions are raised concerning the validity of the institutions governing the social bond: these must be legitimated as well. Thus justice is consigned to the grand narrative in the same way as truth.

Simplifying to the extreme, I define *postmodern* as incredulity toward metanarratives. This incredulity is undoubtedly a product of progress in the sciences: but that progress in turn presupposes it. To the obsolescence of the metanarrative apparatus of legitimation corresponds, most notably, the crisis of metaphysical philosophy and of the university institution which in the past relied on it. The narrative function is losing its functors, its great hero, its great dangers, its great voyages, its great goal. It is being dispersed in clouds of narrative language elements — narrative, but also denotative, prescriptive, descriptive, and so on. Conveyed within each cloud are pragmatic valencies specific to its kind. Each of us lives at the intersection of many of these. However, we do not necessarily establish stable language combinations, and the properties of the ones we do establish are not necessarily communicable. ...

Source: Lyotard, J.-F. (1984) *The Postmodern Condition: A Report on Knowledge*, Manchester, Manchester University Press, pp.xxiii–xxv and 3–11.

... Where, after the metanarratives, can legitimacy reside? The operativity criterion is technological; it has no relevance for judging what is true or just. Is legitimacy to be found in consensus obtained through discussion, as Jürgen Habermas thinks? Such consensus does violence to the heterogeneity of language games. And invention is always born of dissension. Postmodern knowledge is not simply a tool of the authorities; it refines our sensitivity to differences and reinforces our ability to tolerate the incommensurable. ...

1   The Field: Knowledge in Computerized Societies

Our working hypothesis is that the status of knowledge is altered as societies enter what is known as the postindustrial age and cultures enter what is known as the postmodern age. This transition has been under way since at least the end of the 1950s, which for Europe marks the completion of reconstruction. The pace is faster or slower depending on the country, and within countries it varies according to the sector of activity: the general situation is one of temporal disjunction which makes sketching an overview difficult. A portion of the description would necessarily be conjectural. At any rate, we know that it is unwise to put too much faith in futurology.

Rather than painting a picture that would inevitably remain incomplete, I will take as my point of departure a single feature, one that immediately defines our object of study. Scientific knowledge is a kind of discourse. And it is fair to say that for the last forty years the 'leading' sciences and technologies have had to do with language: phonology and theories of linguistics, problems of communication and cybernetics, modern theories of algebra and informatics, computers and their languages, problems of translation and the search for areas of compatibility among computer languages, problems of information storage and data banks, telematics and the perfection of intelligent terminals, paradoxology. The facts speak for themselves (and this list is not exhaustive).

These technological transformations can be expected to have a considerable impact on knowledge. Its two principal functions — research and the transmission of acquired learning — are already feeling the effect, or will in the future. With respect to the first function, genetics provides an example that is accessible to the layman: it owes its theoretical paradigm to cybernetics. Many other examples could be cited. As for the second function, it is common knowledge that the miniaturization and commercialization of machines is already changing the way in which learning is acquired, classified, made available, and exploited. It is reasonable to suppose that the proliferation of information-processing machines is having, and will continue to have, as much of an effect on the circulation of learning as did advancements in human circulation (transportation systems) and later, in the circulation of sounds and visual images (the media).

The nature of knowledge cannot survive unchanged within this context of general transformation. It can fit into the new channels, and become operational, only if learning is translated into quantities of information. We can predict that anything in the constituted body of knowledge that is not translatable in this way will be abandoned and that the direction of new research will be dictated by the possibility of its eventual results being translatable into computer language. The 'producers' and users of knowledge must now, and will have to, possess the means of translating into these languages whatever they want to invent or learn. Research on translating machines is already well advanced. Along with the hegemony of computers comes a certain logic, and therefore a certain set of prescriptions determining which statements are accepted as 'knowledge' statements.

We may thus expect a thorough exteriorization of knowledge with respect to the 'knower', at whatever point he or she may occupy in the knowledge process. The old principle that the acquisition of knowledge is indissociable from the training (*Bildung*) of minds, or even of individuals, is becoming obsolete and will become ever more so. The relationship of the suppliers and users of knowledge to the knowledge they supply and use is now tending, and will increasingly tend, to assume the form already taken by the relationship of commodity producers and consumers to the commodities they produce and consume — that is, the form of value. Knowledge is and will be produced in order to be sold, it is and will be consumed in order to be valorized in a new production: in both cases, the goal is exchange. Knowledge ceases to be an end in itself, it loses its 'use-value'.

It is widely accepted that knowledge has become the principle force of production over the last few decades; this has already had a noticeable effect on the composition of the work force of the most highly developed countries and constitutes the major bottleneck for the developing countries. In the postindustrial and postmodern age, science will maintain and no doubt strengthen its preeminence in the arsenal of productive capacities of the nation-states. Indeed, this situation is one of the reasons leading to the conclusion that the gap between developed and developing countries will grow ever wider in the future.

But this aspect of the problem should not be allowed to overshadow the other, which is complementary to it. Knowledge in the form of an informational commodity indispensable to productive power is already, and will continue to be, a major — perhaps *the* major — stake in the worldwide competition for power. It is conceiveable that the nation-states will one day fight for control of information, just as they battled in the past for control over territory, and afterwards for control of access to and exploitation of raw materials and cheap labor. ...

2   The Problem: Legitimation

... That scientific and technical knowledge is cumulative is never questioned. At most, what is debated is the form that accumulation takes — some picture it as regular, continuous, and unanimous, others as periodic, discontinuous, and conflictual.

But these truisms are fallacious. In the first place, scientific knowledge does not represent the totality of knowledge; it has always existed in addition to, and in competition and conflict with, another kind of knowledge, which I will call narrative in the interests of simplicity (its characteristics will be described later). I do not mean to say that narrative knowledge can prevail over science, but its model is related to ideas of internal equilibrium and conviviality next to which contemporary scientific knowledge cuts a poor figure, especially if it is to undergo an exteriorization with respect to the 'knower' and an alienation from its user even greater than has previously been the case. The resulting demoralization of researchers and teachers is far from negligible; it is well known that during the 1960s, in all of the most highly developed societies, it reached such explosive dimensions among those preparing to practise these professions — the students — that there was noticeable decrease in productivity at laboratories and universities unable to protect themselves from its contamination. Expecting this, with hope or fear, to lead to a revolution (as was then often the case) is out of the question: it will not change the order of things in postindustrial society overnight. But this doubt on the part of scientists must be taken into account as a major factor in evaluating the present and future status of scientific knowledge. ...

... The question of the legitimacy of science has been indissociably linked to that of the legitimation of the legislator since the time of Plato. From this point of view, the right to decide what is true is not independent of the right to decide what is just, even if the statements consigned to these two authorities differ in nature. The point is that there is a strict interlinkage between the kind of language called science and the kind called ethics and politics: they both stem from the same perspective, the same 'choice' if you will — the choice called the Occident.

When we examine the current status of scientific knowledge — at a time when science seems more completely subordinated to the prevailing powers than ever before and, along with the new technologies, is in danger of becoming a major stake in their conflicts — the question of double legitimation, far from receding into the background, necessarily comes to the fore. For it appears in its most complete form, that of reversion, revealing that knowledge and power are simply two sides of the same question: who decides what knowledge is, and who knows what needs to be decided? In the computer age, the question of knowledge is now more than ever a question of government.

3 The Method: Language Games

The reader will already have noticed that in analyzing this problem within the framework set forth, I have favoured a certain procedure: emphasizing facts of language and in particular their pragmatic aspect. ...

It is useful to make the following three observations about language games. The first is that their rules do not carry within themselves their own legitimation, but are the object of a contract, explicit or not, between players (which is not to say that the players invent the rules). The second is that if there are no rules, there is no game, that even an infinitesimal modification of one rule alters the nature of the game, that a 'move' or utterance that does not satisfy the rules does not belong to the game they define. The third remark is suggested by what has just been said: every utterance should be thought of as a 'move' in a game.

The last observation brings us to the first principle underlying our method as a whole: to speak is to fight, in the sense of playing, and speech acts fall within the domain of a general agonistics. This does not necessarily mean that one plays in order to win. A move can be made for the sheer pleasure of its invention: what else is involved in that labor of language harassment undertaken by popular speech and by literature? Great joy is had in the endless invention of turns of phrase, of words and meanings, the process behind the evolution of language on the level of *parole*. But undoubtedly even this pleasure depends on a feeling of success won at the expense of an adversary — at least one adversary, and a formidable one: the accepted language, or connotation.

This idea of an agonistics of language should not make us lose sight of the second principle, which stands as a complement to it and governs our analysis: that the observable social bond is composed of language 'moves'.

READING B1   MODERNITY: AN INCOMPLETE PROJECT

Jürgen Habermas

The idea of modernity is intimately tied to the development of European art, but what I call 'the project of modernity' comes only into focus when we dispense with the usual concentration upon art. Let me start a different analysis by recalling an idea from Max Weber. He characterized cultural modernity as the separation of the substantive reason expressed in religion and metaphysics into three autonomous spheres. They are: science, morality and art. These came to be differentiated because the unified world-views of religion and metaphysics fell apart. Since the 18th century, the problems inherited from these older world-views could be arranged so as to fall under specific aspects of validity: truth, normative rightness, authenticity and beauty. They could then be handled as questions of knowledge, or of justice and morality, or of taste. Scientific discourse, theories of morality, jurisprudence, and the production and criticism of art could in turn be institutionalized. Each domain of culture could be made to correspond to cultural professions in which problems could be dealt with as the concern of special experts. This professionalized treatment of the cultural tradition brings to the fore the intrinsic structures of each of the three dimensions of culture. There appear the structures of cognitive-instrumental, of moral-practical and of aesthetic-expressive rationality, each of these under the control of specialists who seem more adept at being logical in these particular ways than other people are. As a result, the distance grows between the culture of the experts and that of the larger public. What accrues to culture through specialized treatment and reflec-

Source: Habermas, J. (1985) 'Modernity: an incomplete project', in Foster, H. (ed.) *Postmodern Culture*, London, Pluto Press, pp.8–15.

tion does not immediately and necessarily become the property of everyday praxis. With cultural rationalization of this sort, the threat increases that the life-world, whose traditional substance has already been devalued, will become more and more impoverished.

The project of modernity formulated in the 18th century by the philosophers of the Enlightenment consisted in their efforts to develop objective science, universal morality and law, and autonomous art according to their inner logic. At the same time, this project intended to release the cognitive potentials of each of these domains from their esoteric forms. The Enlightenment philosophers wanted to utilize this accumulation of specialized culture for the enrichment of everyday life — that is to say, for the rational organization of everyday social life.

Enlightenment thinkers of the cast of mind of Condorcet still had the extravagant expectation that the arts and sciences would promote not only the control of natural forces but also understanding of the world and of the self, moral progress, the justice of institutions and even the happiness of human beings. The 20th century has shattered this optimism. The differentiation of science, morality and art has come to mean the autonomy of the segments treated by the specialist and their separation from the hermeneutics of everyday communication. This splitting off is the problem that has given rise to efforts to 'negate' the culture of expertise. But the problem won't go away: should we try to hold on to the *intentions* of the Enlightenment, feeble as they may be, or should we declare the entire project of modernity a lost cause?...

I think that instead of giving up modernity and its project as a lost cause, we should learn from the mistakes of those extravagant programs which have tried to negate modernity. ...

The disillusionment with the very failures of those programs that called for the negation of art and philosophy has come to serve as a pretense for conservative positions. Let me briefly distinguish the antimodernism of the 'young conservatives' from the premodernism of the 'old conservatives' and from the postmodernism of the neoconservatives. ...

This typology is like any other, of course, a simplification, but it may not prove totally useless for the analysis of contemporary intellectual and political confrontations. I fear that the ideas of antimodernity, together with an additional touch of premodernity, are becoming popular in the circles of alternative culture.

READING B2   THE PHILOSOPHICAL DISCOURSE OF MODERNITY

Jürgen Habermas

The radical critique of reason exacts a high price for taking leave of modernity. In the first place, these discourses can and want to give no account of their own position. Negative dialectics, genealogy, and deconstruction alike avoid those categories in accord with which modern knowledge has been differentiated — by no means accidentally — and on the basis of which we today understand texts. They cannot be unequivocally classified with either philosophy or science, with moral and legal theory, or with literature and art. At the same time, they resist any return to forms of religious thought, whether dogmatic or heretical. So an incongruity arises between these 'theories' which raise validity claims only to renounce them, and the kind of institutionalization they undergo within the business of science. ... That the self-referential critique of reason is located everywhere and nowhere, so to speak, in discourses without a place, renders it almost immune to competing interpretations. ...

The variations of a critique of reason with reckless disregard for its own foundations are related to one another in another respect as well. ... Not only the devastating consequences of an objectifying relation-to-self are condemned along with this principle of modernity, but also the *other* connotations once associated with subjectivity as an unredeemed promise: the prospect of a self-conscious practice, in which the solidary self-determination of all was to be joined with the self-realization of each. What is thrown out is precisely what a modernity reassuring itself once meant by the concepts of self-consciousness, self-determination, and self-realization.

A further defect of these discourses is explained by their totalizing repudiation of modern forms of life: Although they are interesting in regard to fundamentals, they remain undifferentiated in their results. The criteria according to which Hegel and Marx, and even Max Weber and Lukács, distinguished between emancipatory-reconciling aspects of social rationalization and repressive-alienating aspects have been blunted. In the meantime, critique has taken hold of and demolished the sorts of concepts by which those aspects could be distinguished from one another so that their paradoxical entanglement became visible. Enlightenment and manipulation, the conscious and the unconscious, forces of production and forces of destruction, expressive self-realization and repressive desublimation, effects that ensure freedom and those that remove it, truth and ideology — now all these moments flow into one another. They are not linked to one another as, say, conflicting elements in a disastrous functional context — unwilling accomplices in a contradictory process permeated by oppositional conflict. Now the differences and oppositions are so undermined and even collapsed that critique can no longer discern

Source: Habermas, J. (1987) 'The normative content of modernity', in *The Philosophical Discourse of Modernity,* Cambridge, Polity Press, pp.336–40.

contrasts, shadings, and ambivalent tones within the flat and faded land-scape of a totally administered, calculated, and power-laden world. ...

To Nietzscheanism, the differentiation of science and morality appears as the formative process of a reason that at once usurps and stifles the poetic, world-disclosing power of art. Cultural modernity seems a realm of hor-rors, marked by the totalitarian traits of a subject-centered reason that structurally overburdens itself. Three simple facts are filtered out of this picture: First, the fact that those aesthetic experiences in the light of which true nature is supposed to reveal itself to an exclusive reason are due to the same process of differentiation as science and morality. Then the fact that cultural modernity also owes its division into special discourses for ques-tions of taste, truth, and justice to an increase in knowledge that is hard to dispute. And especially the fact that it is only the modalities of inter-change between these knowledge systems and everyday practice that determine whether the gains from such abstraction affect the lifeworld destructively.

READING C HABERMAS: AUTONOMY AND SOLIDARITY

Peter Dews

In the work of influential contemporary thinkers such as Lyotard and Feyerabend — behind whom, of course, stands the figure of Nietzsche — the very notions of 'truth', 'objectivity', 'consensus', are seen as possessing a coercive moment, as implying the enforced unification of plurality. In his more recent writings Lyotard has sought to break out of this coercion by adopting the Wittgensteinian notion of language-games, which are inherently multiple and irreducible to any universal model of language. Habermas's error can then be portrayed as the belief that 'humanity as a collective (universal) subject seeks its common emancipation through the regularization of the "moves" permitted in all the language-games'. The Critical Theorist's 'narrative of emancipation' unfortunately relies on a *telos* of collective agreement which 'does violence to the heterogeneity of language-games' (Lyotard, 1984, pp.66 and xxv).

There are three distinct levels at which this critique of Habermas must be criticized in its turn. Firstly, at the philosophical level, Lyotard's argu-ments depend on a chronic confusion between *language-games* and *val-idity-claims*. He fails to distinguish between the differentiation of the life-world into three distinct spheres of value, concerned respectively with cognitive, moral and aesthetic questions, and what Habermas terms a 'pluralization of diverging universes of discourse [which] belongs to specifically modern experience'. ... Thus, while admitting the plurality of language-games in contemporary culture, it is possible to argue that val-idity-claims (which are not themselves a specific kind of linguistic activity, but arise within different linguistic activities) *cut across* this mul-

Source: Dews, P. (1986) 'Introduction' to *Habermas: Autonomy and Solidarity*, London, Verso, pp.22–7.

tiplicity. In other words, there will be clashes of viewpoint concerning cognitive, moral and aesthetic questions, but we cannot claim that these conflicts are *in principle* unamenable to discussion, and to possible resolution. Habermas makes a similar point in the course of his critique of Max Weber, who, like Lyotard, tends to run together value-contents and aspects of validity. 'Weber goes too far', Habermas suggests, 'when he infers from the loss of the substantial unity of reason a polytheism of gods and demons struggling with one another, with their irreducibility rooted in a pluralism of incompatible validity-claims. The unity of rationality, in the multiplicity of value-spheres, rationalized according to their inner logics, is secured precisely at the formal level of the argumentative redemption of validity claims' (Habermas, 1984, p.249).

Secondly, on the political level, Lyotard's position is unsatisfactory insofar as it does not even address the issue of social conflict. One of the principal reasons for this is the anodyne connotations of the term 'language-game', which Lyotard employs with excessive laxity. Had he employed an alternative term such as 'social practices', and had he considered that this category would include activities such as pumping pollutants into the environment, closing down industries in depressed areas, and driving under the influence of alcohol, he would have found it less plausible to portray conflict merely as a kind of verbal jousting ('agonistics') internal to each language-game. A further important reason is that, as soon as Lyotard attempts to address the problem of the reciprocal relations of 'language-games' he is confronted with the nemesis of all relativism. For to argue that 'the recognition of the heteromorphous nature of language-games' implies 'the renunciation of terror, which assumes that they are isomorphic and tries to make them so' (Lyotard, 1984, p.66), is again to rely on an equivocation, between 'recognition' as the registering of a state of affairs, or as an acknowledgment of validity. Unless such recognition, in the second sense, is more than simply one language-game among others, it is difficult to comprehend how Lyotard can claim priority for it. Had Lyotard reflected a little further on this, he would have appreciated that Habermas's theory of consensus has nothing to do with the homogenization of language-games, or with the establishment of the supremacy of one language-game, but rather with the condition of possibility of plurality: the regulation of the effects of social practices on each other in the light of the freely expressed interests of all those concerned.

But not only is Lyotard's position philosophically and politically dubious, it is also historically inaccurate, insofar as it fails to perceive that the universalization of principles and the individualization of lifestyles are two sides of the same process. In modern societies, Habermas suggests, the co-ordination of action becomes increasingly dependent on explicit, argumentatively attained agreement, rather than on the background consensus of the life-world. But, to the extent that this is the case, concrete life-forms and general life-world structures increasingly separate out from each other. It is possible for a proliferation of subcultures to take place precisely because the need for agreement on basic rules of social interaction is satisfied at ever higher levels of abstraction. Because he entirely neglects this universalistic component of modern consciousness, Lyotard equates an emancipatory pluralism with a retreat into fragmented and particularistic forms of consciousness. ...

The incoherences and omissions of Lyotard's thought, considered as the paradigm for a self-proclaimed postmodern philosophy, point towards some of the general, underlying problems with post-structuralist-inspired accounts of postmodernity. ... [I]n considering Lyotard's attitude to the philosophy of history, the Nietzschean influence on post-structuralism ensures that the metaphysical character of theories is equated with their systematicity. For Habermas, however, it is not systematicity as such which poses the problem, but the fact that philosophical systems — interpretations of the world as a whole — were based upon a fundamental principle immunized against critical probing, that philosophy traditionally conceived itself as a discourse operating at a level entirely distinct from that of empirical confirmation or disconfirmation. Habermas shares with the post-structuralists a sense of the crisis of philosophy after Hegel, of its struggle to step over into another medium. But he continues the materialist argument of the original Frankfurt School in suggesting that this medium must consist of a practically-oriented collaboration between philosophy and empirical social science. Through such a co-operation philosophy preserves the social and human sciences from empiricist and elementarist myopia, while the sciences lend philosophy a substantive, but non-dogmatic, content. For Habermas, in other words, it is not the *universality* of philosophical truth-claims which is to be abandoned, but rather their non-fallibilist aspect. Post-structuralism, however, through its critique of the universal, is driven into an abandonment of systematic cognitive claims, indeed frequently into a quasi-aesthetic suspension of truth-claims as such. The result of this manoeuvre, however, is that genuine attempts at social and cultural analysis become vulnerable to anecdotal and inadequately theorized evidence, a fact which explains the constitutive vagueness and portentousness of general accounts of postmodernity.

References

Habermas, J. (1984) *The Theory of Communicative Action*, vol.1, trans. by McCarthy, T., Boston.

Lyotard, J.-F. (1984) *The Postmodern Condition: A Report on Knowledge*, Manchester University Press.

LEGISLATORS AND INTERPRETERS

Zygmunt Bauman

... Apart from aesthetics, the areas most affected by the post-modern challenge are those philosophical discourses which are concerned with the issues of truth, certainty and relativism, and those which deal with the principles of societal organization. More often than not, these discourses generated legitimations for realities already structured by extant hierarchies of power; as long as such structures remained intact and unthreatened, however, there was little to distinguish between the articulation of legitimacy and legislating. Today, hierarchies are neither intact nor unthreatened. The tasks of legitimizing and legislating suddenly appear wide apart, once the reasons to assume the legislating power of legitimation have been progressively eroded. How can one argue the case for or against a form of life, for or against a version of truth, when one feels that one's argument cannot any more legislate, that there are powers behind the *plural* forms of life and plural versions of truth which would not be *made* inferior, and hence would not surrender to the argument of their inferiority? Suddenly, the two-centuries-old philosophical voyage to certainty and universal criteria of perfection and 'good life' seems to be a wasted effort. This does not necessarily mean that we do not like the terrains to which it has brought us; on the contrary, it is the refusal of others to admire them and to follow us there which makes us worry and prompts us to look for a new, stronger tune for the praise we still wish to sing. If we wish to defend the direction our journey took us, we need to redefine, retrospectively, its sense.

Ernest Gellner is arguably the staunchest and the most profound defender of the peculiar form of life born in the north-western tip of the European peninsula four centuries ago which has subordinated all other forms of life for the last two hundred years. His is perhaps the most convincing plea on its behalf:

> On balance, one option — a society with cognitive growth based on a roughly atomistic strategy — seems to us superior, for various reasons, which are assembled without elegance; this kind of society alone can keep alive the large numbers to which humanity has grown, and thereby avoid a really ferocious struggle for survival among us; it alone can keep us at the standard to which we are becoming accustomed; it, more than its predecessors, *probably* favours a liberal and tolerant social organization ... This type of society also has many unattractive traits, and its virtues are open to doubt. On balance, and with misgivings, we opt for it; but there is no question of an elegant, clear-cut choice. We are half pressurised by necessity (fear of famine, etc.), half-persuaded by a promise of liberal

Source: Bauman, Z. (1988) *Legislators and Interpreters*, Cambridge, Polity Press, pp.140–4.

affluence (which we do not fully trust). There it is: lacking better
reasons we will have to make do with these.
(1984, p.258)

This statement is modest — and, in a sense, apologetic. It is self-conscious
of its inadequacy in terms of the extant criteria of the elegance of philosophical proof. It justifies the *raison d'être* of the philosophical tradition,
which devoted its life and energy to exorcizing the ghost of pragmatic
relativism, in pragmatic terms — an ultimate irony, as it were. And the
argument it employs (again self-consciously, I am sure) is circular: this
system is better because it caters for the things which it taught us to like
better — like that 'standard to which we are becoming accustomed'. There
is nothing intrinsically wrong with such an argument. On the contrary, it
seems much more human and realistic than the philosophical elegance it
proposes to replace. That is, if we first agree to abandon philosophical
pretentions to universality.

Gellner's reasoning has a decisive advantage over many other arguments,
similar in their self-inflicted modesty, pragmatism and circularity. It is
honest about its own purpose, which is the defence of the world which
we, the intellectuals of the West, shaped by the two centuries of recent
Western history we collectively helped to shape, find to approximate
closer than any other world we know to the standards we set for a good
society. To phrase it differently, Gellner's argument makes explicit a case
for the kind of world which may provide (and has been providing, with
qualifications, for some time) a suitable setting for the Western intellectual
mode of life; and may also create a demand for the traditional (legislating)
role that Western intellectuals have learned to perform best. This makes
Gellner's argument particularly interesting; it demonstrates how difficult,
if not downright impossible, it is to argue the superiority of the Western
type of society in objective, absolute or universal terms. At its best, the
argument must be self-constrained, pragmatic and, indeed, unashamedly
circular.

Other reactions to the post-modern condition tend to be rather more confused. What they are outraged or horrified by, and what they wish to save
against all odds, is more often than not hidden behind new universal
philosophies of history or universal strategies for philosophy and/or
social science. Some, perhaps the least interesting ones, refuse to admit
realities which supply relativist arguments with somewhat different, and
arguably stronger, grounds than before, treat diagnoses of irreducible
pluralism of the world as a collective aberration, and continue to produce
'footnotes to Plato'. Other reactions, perhaps more numerous, probably
more exciting and certainly more vociferous, face the pluralism point
blank, accept its irreversibility and propose to reconsider the role a philosopher, or an intellectual in general, may learn to perform in such a hopelessly plural world with the same measure of respectability and profit that
the legislator's role once brought. Such propositions, however, are normally stated in a fashion which prevents rather than helps us to understand their purpose; unlike in Gellner's case, the proposals to abandon the

dream of the absolute are argued in absolutist terms. They are presented as new and improved versions of the old-style all-embracing theories of 'human nature', or the 'nature of social life', or both.

Whatever the structure of the argument, the reactions of the second category all point — overtly or implicitly — to a new role that intellectuals may usefully play, given their historically accumulated wisdom and skill: the role of interpreters. With pluralism irreversible, a world-scale consensus on world-views and values unlikely, and all extant *Weltanschauungen* [world views] firmly grounded in their respective cultural traditions (more correctly: their respective autonomous institutionalizations of power), communication across traditions becomes the major problem of our time. This problem does not seem temporary any more; one cannot hope that it will be solved 'in passing' by a sort of massive conversion guaranteed by the unstoppable march of Reason. Rather, the problem is likely to stay with us for a long, long time (unless, that is, its life expectation is drastically cut by the absence of an appropriate tonic). The problem, therefore, calls urgently for specialists in translation between cultural traditions. ...

A majority of the most influential recent developments in philosophy and social science point in the direction of such a specialism. To name only a few: the passage from the 'negative' to a 'positive' notion of ideology, which accepts that all knowledge is ultimately grounded in essentially irrational, arbitrarily chosen assumptions, related deterministically or randomly to partly enclosed traditions and historic experiences, and which replaces the old division between 'ideological' (wrong) knowledge and 'non-ideological' (true) knowledge with one between a knowledge system unaware of its localized character and one which employs such awareness in the service of rationalizing (that is, making communicatively effective) the exchange between knowledge systems; the rediscovery of hermeneutics and the enthusiasm with which philosophers and social scientists greeted Gadamer's *Truth and Method*, a sophisticated manifesto against methodical truth and true method, which attempts to redefine the task of philosophy or social science as one of interpretation, a search for meaning, making 'the other' comprehensible, making oneself understandable — and thus facilitating an exchange between forms of life — and opening up for communication words of meaning which otherwise would remain closed to each other; neo-pragmatism of Rorty's variety, which denigrates the ascendancy during the past three centuries of the Cartesian-Lockean-Kantian tradition as an effect of unfortunate historical accidents, wrong options and confusions, which declares a philosophical search for universal and unshakable foundations of truth as misdirected from the start, and which suggests that philosophers, instead, should focus their attention on continuing the civilized conversation of the West without the comforting, but misleading conviction of its universal validity.

None of these recent developments signals disenchantment with the kind of setting the West provided for the execution of the intellectual vocation (at least not in their mainstream manifestations). Appearances and shock effects notwithstanding, they are all in the end forms of defence of the

Western intellectual mode of life under the condition of distress caused by the progressive dissolution of certainty once grounded in the 'evident' superiority of Western society.

References

Gadamer, H.-G. (1975) *Truth and Method*, London, Sheed and Ward.

Gellner, E. (1984) 'Tractatus Sociologico-Philosophicus', in S.L. Brown (ed.) *Objectivity and Cultural Divergence*, Royal Institute of Philosophy, Lecture Series, 17.

READING E   THE CONSEQUENCES OF MODERNITY

Anthony Giddens

What does post-modernity ordinarily refer to? Apart from the general sense of living through a period of marked disparity from the past, the term usually means one or more of the following: that we have discovered that nothing can be known with any certainty, since all pre-existing 'foundations' of epistemology have been shown to be unreliable; that 'history' is devoid of teleology and consequently no version of 'progress' can plausibly be defended; and that a new social and political agenda has come into being with the increasing prominence of ecological concerns and perhaps of new social movements generally. Scarcely anyone today seems to identify post-modernity with what it was once widely accepted to mean — the replacement of capitalism by socialism. Pushing this transition away from centre stage, in fact, is one of the main factors that has prompted current discussions about the possible dissolution of modernity, given Marx's totalising view of history.

Let us first of all dismiss as unworthy of serious intellectual consideration the idea that no systematic knowledge of human action or trends of social development is possible. Were anyone to hold such a view (and if indeed it is not inchoate in the first place), they could scarcely write a book about it. The only possibility would be to repudiate intellectual activity altogether — even 'playful deconstruction', — in favour, say, of healthy physical exercise. Whatever the absence of foundationalism in epistemology implies, it is not this. For a more plausible starting point, we might look to the 'nihilism' of Nietzsche and Heidegger. In spite of the differences between the two philosophers, there is a view upon which they converge. Both link with modernity the idea that 'history' can be identified as a progressive appropriation of rational foundations of knowledge. According to them, this is expressed in the notion of 'overcoming': the formation of new understandings serves to identify what is of value, and what is not, in the cumulative stock of knowledge. Each finds it necessary to distance himself from the foundational claims of the Enlightenment yet cannot criticise these from the vantage point of superior or better-founded

Source: Giddens, A. (1990) *The Consequences of Modernity*, Cambridge, Polity Press, pp.46–53.

claims. They therefore abandon the notion of 'critical overcoming' so central to the Enlightenment critique of dogma.

Anyone who sees in this a basic transition from modernity to post-modernity, however, faces great difficulties. One of the main objections is obvious and well known. To speak of post-modernity as superseding modernity appears to invoke that very thing which is declared (now) to be impossible: giving some coherence to history and pinpointing our place in it. Moreover, if Nietzsche was the principal author disconnecting post-modernity from modernity, a phenomenon supposedly happening today, how is it possible that he saw all this almost a century ago? Why was Nietzsche able to make such a breakthrough without, as he freely said, doing anything more than uncovering the hidden presuppositions of the Enlightenment itself?

It is difficult to resist the conclusion that the break with foundationalism is a significant divide in philosophical thought, having its origins in the mid- to late nineteenth century. But it surely makes sense to see this as 'modernity coming to understand itself' rather than the overcoming of modernity as such. We can interpret this in terms of what I shall label *providential* outlooks. Enlightenment thought, and Western culture in general, emerged from a religious context which emphasised teleology and the achievement of God's grace. Divine providence had long been a guiding idea of Christian thought. Without these preceding orientations, the Enlightenment would scarcely have been possible in the first place. It is in no way surprising that the advocacy of unfettered reason only reshaped the ideas of the providential, rather than displacing it. One type of certainty (divine law) was replaced by another (the certainty of our senses, of empirical observation), and divine providence was replaced by providential progress. Moreover, the providential idea of reason coincided with the rise of European dominance over the rest of the world. The growth of European power provided, as it were, the material support for the assumption that the new outlook on the world was founded on a firm base which both provided security and offered emancipation from the dogma of tradition.

Yet the seeds of nihilism were there in Enlightenment thought from the beginning. If the sphere of reason is wholly unfettered, no knowledge can rest upon an unquestioned foundation, because even the most firmly held notions can only be regarded as valid 'in principle' or 'until further notice'. Otherwise they would relapse into dogma and become separate from the very sphere of reason which determines what validity is in the first place. Although most regarded the evidence of our senses as the most dependable information we can obtain, even the early Enlightenment thinkers were well aware that such 'evidence' is always in principle suspect. Sense data could never provide a wholly secure base for knowledge claims. Given the greater awareness today that sensory observation is permeated by theoretical categories, philosophical thought has in the main veered quite sharply away from empiricism. Moreover, since Nietzsche we are much more clearly aware of the circularity of reason, as well as the problematic relations between knowledge and power.

Rather than these developments taking us 'beyond modernity', they provide a fuller understanding of the reflexivity inherent in modernity itself. Modernity is not only unsettling because of the circularity of reason, but because the nature of that circularity is ultimately puzzling. How can we justify a commitment to reason in the name of reason? Paradoxically, it was the logical positivists who stumbled across this issue most directly, as a result of the very lengths to which they went to strip away all residues of tradition and dogma from rational thought. Modernity turns out to be enigmatic at its core, and there seems no way in which this enigma can be 'overcome'. We are left with questions where once there appeared to be answers ... A general awareness of the phenomenon filters into anxieties which press in on everyone.

Post-modernity has been associated not only with the end of foundationalism but with the 'end of history'. ... 'History' has no intrinsic form and no overall teleology. A plurality of histories can be written, and they cannot be anchored by reference to an Archimedean point (such as the idea that history has an evolutionary direction). ...

The break with providential views of history, the dissolution of foundationalism, together with the emergence of counterfactual future-oriented thought and the 'emptying out' of progress by continuous change, are so different from the core perspectives of the Enlightenment as to warrant the view that far-reaching transitions have occurred. Yet referring to these as post-modernity is a mistake which hampers an accurate understanding of their nature and implications. The disjunctions which have taken place should rather be seen as resulting from the self-clarification of modern thought, as the remnants of tradition and providential outlooks are cleared away. We have not moved beyond modernity but are living precisely through a phase of its radicalisation.

The gradual decline of European or Western global hegemony, the other side of which is the increasing expansion of modern institutions worldwide, is plainly one of the main influences involved here. The projected 'decline of the West', of course, has been a preoccupation among some authors since the latter part of the nineteenth century. As used in such a context, the phrase usually referred to a cyclical conception of historical change, in which modern civilisation is simply seen as one regionally located civilisation among others which have preceded it in other areas of the world. Civilisations have their periods of youth, maturity, and old age, and as they are replaced by others, the regional distribution of global power alters. But modernity is *not* just one civilisation among others, according to the discontinuist interpretation I have suggested above. The declining grip of the West over the rest of the world is not a result of the diminishing impact of the institutions which first arose there but, on the contrary, a result of their global spread. The economic, political, and military power which gave the West its primacy ... no longer so distinctly differentiates the Western countries from others elsewhere. We can interpret this process as one of *globalisation*, a term which must have a key position in the lexicon of the social sciences....

In terms of this analysis, it can easily be seen why the radicalising of modernity is so unsettling, and so significant. Its most conspicuous features — *the dissolution of evolutionism,* the *disappearance of historical teleology,* the recognition of *thoroughgoing, constitutive reflexivity,* together with the *evaporating of the privileged position of the West* — move us into a new and disturbing universe of experience. If the 'us' here still refers primarily to those living in the West itself — or, more accurately, the industrialised sectors of the world — it is something whose implications are felt everywhere.

READING F   FEMINIST EPISTEMOLOGY: AN IMPOSSIBLE PROJECT?

Margareta Hallberg

In this paper I shall be concerned with some of the problems confronting the feminist epistemological project. They may be formulated in many different ways, but there are at least three main tensions and oppositions that appear to be most influential and relevant to the present discussion. These are:

1   The tension between objectivism and relativism.

2   The problem with the social dimension in men's and women's thinking.

3   The opposition between different interpretations of the concept of 'difference'. ...

Objectivism and relativism

There are many more or less sophisticated definitions of these two terms, but I find that Richard Bernstein has given a valuable one in his book *Beyond Objectivism and Relativism* (1984, pp.4–5). He writes:

> By 'objectivism', I mean the basic conviction that there is or must be some permanent, ahistorical matrix or framework to which we can ultimately appeal in determining the nature of rationality, knowledge, truth, reality, goodness or rightness...

> In its strongest form, relativism is the basic conviction that when we turn to the examination of those concepts that philosophers have taken to be the most fundamental ... we are forced to recognize that in the final analysis all such concepts must be understood as relative to a specific conceptual scheme, theoretical framework, paradigm, form of life, society, or culture ...

Under objectivists Bernstein means to include not only the rationalists and empiricists, but also foundationalists and essentialists. Relativism, on

Source: Hallberg, M. (1989) 'Feminist epistemology : an impossible project?', *Radical Philosophy,* no.53, Autumn, pp.3–6.

the other hand, is defined as the dialectical antithesis of objectivism. It may be argued that this definition is too inclusive as far as objectivism is concerned, and that it misses some of the central aspects of relativism. ... For my purposes, however, this counterposition of two opposing trends has the advantage that it alerts us to some of the incompatible tendencies in feminist epistemologies.

The problem may briefly be described in the following way: If existing 'traditional' knowledge is considered false, and not only inadequate because of its one-sidedness, there must be possibilities for a true(r) knowledge. Also, there should be plausible and tenable ways of explaining why traditional knowledge is male-biased, while feminist knowledge is not. If both kinds of knowledge, the 'male' and the 'female' (or feminist), are considered biased, we are faced with a kind of relativism entailing that different views are equally (either) true (or false). Some feminist theorists tend to subscribe to this view, but I would not call it representative, at least not among feminist philosophers.

Unless one supposes that male-biased theories somehow misdescribe reality and misrepresent how things are, it is difficult to make sense of much of feminist science criticism. This assumption, however, tends to lead to some kind of objectivism: but objectivism is at the same time associated with a masculine epistemology, which feminism sets out to oppose. Thus we land in the difficult situation of having to defend a kind of 'feminist objectivism', while rejecting all other forms of objectivist claims. Consequently, feminist epistemologists need very strong and convincing arguments. They will have to answer some complicated questions about why women and/or feminists have correct versions of how things really are, and why they are the only ones who enjoy this privileged position. ...

Now, such a theory of knowledge is no doubt a non-relativist one, in as far as it does not support the view that there are many equally true conceptions of reality. Using Bernstein's definition, we can call it an objectivist view — one which holds on to a conviction concerning some kind of foundations for knowledge. The feminist version of objectivism is referred to as 'feminist standpoint epistemology'. It is founded on the claim that women have a cognitively privileged position in society, so that their knowledge is superior to men's knowledge. This privileged position is taken to be rooted in or generated by women's experiences, defined in a broad sense.

The contours of feminist epistemologies had hardly acquired a distinct identity, when they were challenged by postmodernist/anti-foundationalist thinking. Even though this postmodern trend is far from unitary and is wide-ranging in its opposition to modernity, some of its critical assumptions and insights are particularly significant when viewed from a feminist perspective. In brief, its critical position is really a radical one, because it challenges what lies at the root of the entire Enlightenment project, viz. the very idea of a foundation for knowledge.

Anti-foundationalism rejects all of the dichotomies on which Enlightenment epistemology rests, including subject/object, rational/irrational, reason/emotion, and language/reality. It also rejects the presuppositions involved in these dichotomies — the ideas of a coherent, unified self, a rationalist and individualist model of knowing and the possibilities of a metalanguage. The knowing 'subject' is taken to be always heterogeneous and socially constructed, so all kinds of essentialism are opposed.

What follows from these objections to the Enlightenment ideas is, among other things, that 'truth' is always plural and situated and that epistemology itself has to be questioned. All thought is biased and there exists no position from which a correct view, in an absolute sense, may be grounded. The term 'feminist epistemology' is itself misleading from an anti-foundationalist point of view. Postmodernist challenges, when taken seriously, undermine the feminist epistemological project, unless the idea of a new cognitively privileged position can be defended. In my reading of the feminist standpoint epistemology, the crucial issue of determining its plausibility is to what extent it is tenable to uphold women's experience as a legitimation of a grounding for knowledge. To examine that issue, I will now turn to the second of the above-mentioned tensions in feminist epistemology.

The problem with the social dimension in men's and women's thinking

Much of the feminist critique of traditional science and its philosophy presupposes that modern epistemology results from a male way of knowing, which of course in its turn assumes that there is a specific male form of thinking. The scientific revolution, for example, has been analyzed with respect to its so-called 'gender metaphors', where it is argued that the specific language used by the new scientists and the philosophers expresses a masculine way of thinking and reacting upon the world. Some feminists, such as Mary Daly ... or Dale Spender ... together with most of the French feminist deconstructivists, have asserted that theory as well as language is male-biased and completely permeated with masculinity. They are identifying Enlightenment rationalism as a distinctly male/masculine mode of thought. Closely related to this view is a concept of the essential female. Daly is but one example of feminists arguing for a return to a focus on femaleness. Most feminists involved in the epistemological turn seem to support this view in one way or another, and thus they believe that the fundamental dichotomies of Enlightenment thought are rooted in the male/female dichotomy. In my opinion, there are several problems with this view. First of all, it is far too inclusive — it gives no room to distinguish masculine aspects in thinking or in the products of thought, from aspects not genderized at all. It tends to see every idea (in, for example, philosophy or meta-theory) about everything as male-biased, as if the hegemony of dominant conceptions were complete. Patriarchy appears free of conflicts and contradictions, totally dominated by a unified masculinity. ...

Secondly, the assumptions cited rely too heavily on popular views of typical male and female behaviour, stereotyped versions of how we are supposed to act and think are reflected in these stances. Such views easily fall into mystifications about male rationality and female intuition, masculine clear thinking as opposed to feminine emotional thinking, without paying attention to the possibility of a dialectical interaction within the two sexes between the two principles — the masculine and the feminine. ...

The premise on which the argument rests, then, if a tenable one, postulates radically different experiences between men and women, and very similar and gender-specific experiences within the two sexes. The difficulty is, first of all, that it is problematic to define the communality in all women's and men's experiences. ...

The many difficulties of conceptualizing the meaning of the term 'experience', and the problems with defining both the categories male and female, have been recognized in recent feminist epistemological discussions. It has been admitted for instance that there are many women's experiences and that therefore it is possible to maintain that, epistemologically, lesbian women, black women, working-class women, Third World women and so forth, all have different and group-specific knowledge. A problem for a feminist epistemology based on experience, then, is that the recognition of differences seems to require that we postulate different groups of interests. 'Pluralism' may appear to solve problems within feminism, but this does not necessarily mean that the position of feminism is epistemologically strengthened vis-à-vis other theories. My main concern in this respect is where to draw the limit? Why not add even further categories, such as young women, old women, married or unmarried women, women with or without children, well-educated, professional women, and so on ... ? This multiplication of groups and specific interests I think shows that one somehow ends up in extreme subjectivism. On the other hand, if women are not thought of as having some epistemological communality, what is the point of trying to distinguish women's thinking from men's, since it does not add anything that is epistemologically interesting?

Given all this, how do we then ground a feminist epistemology? I do not think there is any feasible way of doing this. Taken to its extreme, the privileging of multiple experiences leads to a highly relativist view of knowledge and thus turns out to be a counter-argument that mitigates against the standpoint position. This is even more apparent in the third tension of a feminist theory, to which I now turn.

The opposition between different interpretations of the concept of 'difference'

As already suggested, the conceptualizing of differences has recently become more complicated in feminist discourse. Not long ago 'difference' was mainly related to differences between the two basic categories – men and women; these categories themselves were seen as relatively unproblematic. The new politics, however, taking into account the differences within these categories, is now challenging conventional feminist claims. It is clear that various qualifications have to be made if the concept of 'difference' is to be used in a meaningful way in the present context. I am certainly aware also of the difficulties of just transforming it to feminist thinking.

The term 'difference' stems from the 'poststructuralist' philosopher Jacques Derrida, and it is central to the discussion of many theorists today. In the contexts of feminist theory the term has emerged together with the oppositional trends that I have already outlined, flowing from the postmodernists and anti-foundationalists ... .

Most influential as far as feminist discourse is concerned is that the apprehension of difference within women is a project that cuts across the idea of a common feminist experience. One of the major achievements of the poststructuralist analysis of difference has been to criticize and deconstruct the 'unified subject', i.e. Enlightenment-man, present to him/herself, and capable of understanding other persons. ...

Now, when feminists make use of the poststructuralist conception of 'difference', they are in fact not just integrating the concept itself. What emerges is a new way of doing philosophy, which has as one of its basic tenets the rejection of a logic of identity. Many feminists seem to refer to multiple subjects that would be interpreted identically in an ideal situation. We find a gap, then, between the understanding of 'difference' as a term denoting many different realities, and looking at it as the mainstay for the anti-thesis to unified, present and limited entities. Only in the former case it is useful and valuable for defending the standpoint epistemology, taking the multiplicity of feminist experiences and 'realities' as a possible domain for grounding. 'Difference' in a poststructuralist sense, however, dissolves the unified subject wherever it is constructed; thus it radically undermines the possibility of defining any bases at all for the epistemological turn in feminist theory.

The problem concerning feminist uses of postmodern influences is further aggravated by the fact that, while there is no unique way in which one might conceptualize gender differences, at least not in any stable and interesting sense, at the same time women's oppression is not purely ideological or discursive. The postmodern turn to language itself as the determining factor, not only expressing but constructing consciousness, does not provide an adequate and sufficient account of power relations and dominating forces. There certainly are some important links between poststructuralism and feminism that need further elaboration, but they are not in favour of epistemology.

Conclusions

I have given a critical account of the attempts to construct a feminist epistemology, identifying three main tensions in feminist theorizing. It has been argued that none of the problems may be solved at the theoretical level. The tension between objectivism and relativism is inherent in the feminist standpoint epistemology and cannot be overcome. Either there is a feminist objectivist standpoint, grounded in a women's position in society, or there is no such standpoint. If it is recognized that there are many various, and sometimes necessarily contradictory, 'women's stand-points', there is no possible way of deciding which one is the objective one.

Furthermore, I have tried to demonstrate that 'experience' when used as a basis for knowledge is an extremely vague term. Experiences are always influenced by the contexts surrounding them, and therefore never coherent or identical for all women. Even if all women shared certain 'determining' experiences, it is by no means obvious that this would give rise to the same kind of knowledge.

I reject experience as a grounding for feminist epistemologies, and I oppose the proposals that men and women do have different ways to knowledge. I also reject the idea that philosophical and scientific concepts are totally genderized. Feminist philosophical challenges to science are in my view very important and valuable, in so far as they identify and contribute to a recognition of formerly ignored groups and problems; in the process feminists thus highlight new and important areas where research is needed. ...

Reference

Bernstein, R. (1984) *Beyond Objectivism and Relativism,* Oxford, Basil Blackwell.

ACKNOWLEDGEMENTS

Grateful acknowledgement is made to the following sources for permission to reproduce material in this book:

Chapter 1

Text

Callinicos, A. (1991) *The Revenge of History: Marxism and the East European Revolutions*, Basil Blackwell Ltd; Miller, D. (1990) *Market, State and Community: Theoretical Foundations of Market Socialism*, reproduced by permission of Oxford University Press; Giddens, A. (1990) *Socialism, Modernity and Utopianism*, Unpublished work, © Anthony Giddens 1990.

Illustrations

p.17: James Nachtwey/Magnum; *p.21:* G. Pinkhassov/Magnum; *pp.26 and 28:* Sue Cunningham; *p.33:* Tom Learmouth/Panos Pictures; *p.45:* Patrick Zachmann/Magnum.

Chapter 2

Text

Perlmutter, H.V. (1991) 'On the rocky road to the first global civilization', *Human Relations*, vol.44, no.9, September 1991, Plenum Publishing Corporation; Sklair, L. (1991) *Sociology of the Global System*, Harvester Wheatsheaf; Rosenau, James N. *Turbulence in World Politics: A Theory of Change and Continuity*. Copyright © 1990 by Princeton University Press. Reproduced by permission of Princeton University Press; Gilpin, R. (1981) *War and Change in World Politics*, Cambridge University Press.

Table

Table 1: Rosenau, James N. *Turbulence in World Politics: A Theory of Change and Continuity*. Copyright © 1990 Princeton University Press. Reproduced by permission of Princeton University Press.

Illustrations

p.62: Copyright Tom Van Sant/Geosphere Project Santa Monica/Science Photo Library; *p.68:* DALI, Salvador. *The persistence of memory*. 1931. Oil on canvas, 24.1 × 33cm. Collection, The Museum of Modern Art, New York. Given anonymously. Copyright DEMART PRO ARTE BV/ DACS 1992; *p.75:* Nick Robinson/Panos; *p.80:* Brana Radovic/Financial Times, 26th August 1981; *p.81:* Ron Giling/Panos; *p.89:* Albert Overbeek/Associated Press; *p.96:* George P. Widman/Associated Press.

Chapter 3

Text

Berger, P.L. (1987) *The Capitalist Revolution*, Gower; Lowe, P. and Flynn, A. (1989) 'Environmental politics and policy in the 1980s', in Moran, J. (ed.) *The Political Geography of Contemporary Britain*, Macmillan Education Ltd; Dobson, A. (1990) *Green Political Thought,* Unwin Hyman; Porritt , J. (1988) 'Greens and growth', *UK CEED Bulletin*, no.19, July–August 1988, UK Centre for Economic and Environmental Development; Pezzey, J. (1989) 'Greens and growth — a reply', *UK CEED Bulletin*, no.22, March–April 1989, UK Centre for Economic and Environmental Development.

Illustrations

p.123: Press Association/Martin Keene; *pp.127 and 128:* Greenpeace/Morgan; *p.134:* Greenpeace/Gremo; *p.138:* Tom Learmonth; *p.143:* Greenpeace/Greig.

Chapter 4

Text

Castells, M. (1989) *The Informational City*, Basil Blackwell Ltd; Gorz, A. (1989) *Critique of Economic Reason*, Verso; Murray, R. (1989) 'Fordism and post-Fordism', in Hall, S. and Jacques, M. (eds) *New Times*, Lawrence and Wishart, © Robin Murray.

Illustrations

p.182: Hoffmann/Greenpeace; *p.189:* Mike Abrahams/Network; *p.193:* R. Ian Lloyd/Hutchison Library; *p.199:* Paul Lowe/Network.

Chapter 5

Text

Hebdige, D. (1989) 'After the masses', in Hall, S. and Jacques, M. (eds) *New Times*, Lawrence and Wishart, © D. Hebdige; Harvey, D. (1989) *The Condition of Postmodernity*, Basil Blackwell Ltd.

Illustrations

p.223: Chris Woods/*Hackney Gazette*; *p.228:* BARBARA KRUGER 'Untitled' (Your body is a battleground) 112″ by 112″ photographic silkscreen/vinyl 1989. COURTESY MARY BOONE GALLERY, NEW YORK. Reproduced by permission of Barbara Kruger; *pp.233 and 245:* J. Allan Cash; *p.234:* Kathy Wilson; *p.243:* Griffin/London Features International.

Chapter 6

Text

Robins K. (1991) 'Traditions and translations: national culture in its global context', in Corner, J. and Harvey, S. (eds) *Enterprise and Heritage*, Routledge; Massey, D. (1991) 'A global sense of place', *Marxism Today*, June 1991; Parekh, B. (1989) 'Between holy text and moral void', *New Statesman and Society*, 23rd March 1989, The Observer Cover Stories.

Illustrations

p.276: Venice, The Academy; *p.294:* Henri Cartier-Bresson/Magnum; *p.300:* D.K. Hulcher/Panos; *p.303:* Gerald Foley/Panos; *p.306:* Börje Tobiasson/Panos; *pp.309 and 312:* Asadour Guzelian.

Chapter 7

Text

Lyotard, J.-F. (1984) *The Postmodern Condition*, Manchester University Press; Habermas, J. (1985) 'Modernity: an incomplete project', in Foster, H. (ed.) *Postmodern Culture*, Pluto Press; Dews, P. (1986) *Habermas: Autonomy and Solidarity*, Verso; Bauman, Z. (1988) *Legislators and Interpreters*, Basil Blackwell Ltd; Giddens, A. (1990) *The Consequences of Modernity*, Basil Blackwell Ltd; Hallberg, M. (1989) 'Feminist epistemology: an impossible project?' *Radical Philosophy*, no.53, Autumn.

INDEX